Marriage Can Be Forever—Pre
Walking a Path to a Spiritually-Based Marriage
~ A Workbook ~

WELCOME TO THE SECOND EDITION!
HERE'S WHAT'S NEW!

"You have done the seemingly impossible: to improve on an already superb work, and one which is, to say the least, long overdue." ~ Robert W. Horn, reviewer

ADDITIONS AND ENHANCEMENTS

The Second Edition of *Marriage Can Be Forever—Preparation Counts!* is in many ways **a new book** compared to the First Edition. It is enriched by:

- A **Foreword** from Marriage Therapist Dr. Paul Coleman
- **Training Developer**, Johanna Merritt Wu, Ph.D., as a new contributing author
- **New Chapters** about:

    Friendship ❤ Courtship ❤ Commitment ❤ Cohabitation ❤ Personality

- The **story of a couple** going through the marriage preparation process
- **Re-structuring** according to a **6-Step Marriage Preparation Process**
- **Revised and expanded content** throughout the entire book and **new chapter names**

NEW WORKSHEETS

There are **25 new worksheets** for your use as individuals, couples, and in workshops. (**Note:** The worksheets from the First Edition and those from the Second Edition are available as separate downloads from www.claricomm.com/publishing.)

EXPANDED ACCESSIBILITY

Marriage Can Be Forever—Preparation Counts! is based on the spiritual Teachings of the Bahá'í Faith. This edition, however, also uses examples and language for people of various faith paths, whether or not they are Bahá'ís or dating/marrying Bahá'ís.

"Keep up the fantastic work!!! We agree 100 percent that preparation does count!"
Whitney Gifford, 22, and Matin Katirai, 27—used the book; engaged 2003

What'zz the Buzz?

"This book is great!! A fabulous tool and resource. I unhesitatingly recommend it. The profound wisdom of sacred Writings, the accessible exercises, its sensible advice, all combine to provide the users with real tools for building strong relationships. But I must say that my favorite part of the book is the guidance to parents who need to know of their responsibilities in providing consent for marriage to their children. This wonderful law holds such promise for protecting family unity; this book helps to bring clarity and understanding to the parents' duty."
    ~ *Pat Cameron, M.Ed., Nancy Campbell Collegiate Institute - Vice Principal; Parent*

"Emerging data from the social sciences would suggest that it may be easier for a person to graduate from four years of medical school than to complete the first four years of marriage without significant violence, separation, or divorce. In the discouraging light of such facts, this workbook for creating strong, spiritually-based marriages by Susanne Alexander, Craig Farnsworth, and Johanna Merritt Wu could not have been written at a better time. It provides not only a set of practical tools for preparing for marriage and building strong families, but it also explores many of the psychological, philosophical and spiritual principles that animate healthy relationships in ways that are accessible to readers of diverse backgrounds and interests. It is indeed the most comprehensive and useful book in the area that I have yet seen."
    ~ *Michael L. Penn, Ph.D., Clinical Psychologist;*
      Associate Professor of Psychology, Franklin & Marshall College

"This book presents simple but thought-provoking and delightful perspectives on marriage preparation based on the Bahá'í Writings and personal experience."
    ~ *Abdu'l-Missagh Ghadirian, MD, Professor at McGill University*
    ~ *Marilyn Ghadirian, member of National Bahá'í Family Committee of Canada*
      Facilitators of workshops on marriage and family life

"We have been working our way through the book, with many long discussions about various things we have found. It has been a truly thought-provoking book for us."
    ~ *Maureen Jasulevich, married for 25 years*

"I am very impressed with the excellent work you have done, and I foresee many, many people benefiting from your efforts. It's a wonderful and much needed book."
    ~ *Harry J. Bury, Ph.D., Educator; Co-Author of College and Workplace Success Simplified*

"This book is extremely professionally done and very valuable. I think it would make an excellent manual/exercise for any couple contemplating marriage."
    ~ *Heather Nablo Cardin, Teacher and Parent*

Marriage Can Be Forever—Preparation Counts!

Walking a Path to a Spiritually-Based Marriage
~ A Workbook ~

> *From the sweet-scented streams of Thine eternity give me to drink, O my God.... From the crystal springs of Thy love suffer me to quaff, O my Glory.... Within the meadows of Thy nearness, before Thy presence, make me able to roam, O my Beloved.... To the melodies of the dove of Thy oneness suffer me to hearken, O Resplendent One...In the spirit of Thy love keep me steadfast..., and in the path of Thy good-pleasure set firm my steps, O my Maker!...*
>
> (Bahá'u'lláh: *Prayers and Meditations*, pp. 258-259)

Susanne M. Alexander and Craig A. Farnsworth
with Johanna Merritt Wu, Ph.D.

Marriage Can Be Forever—Preparation Counts!

© August 2003 by Susanne M. Alexander and Craig A. Farnsworth, Second Edition

International Standard Book Number/ISBN: 0-9726893-1-1

Library of Congress Control Number: 2003094432

Printed and bound in the United States of America by United Graphics, Inc. All international rights reserved. No part of this book other than reproducible pages described below, may be reproduced by any mechanical, photographic, or electronic process, or by any other means, in the form of a photographic or digital recording, nor may it be stored in a retrieval system, transmitted or otherwise copied for public or private use, including on the Internet, without the written permission of the publisher, except by a reviewer, who may quote brief passages in a review, and except where noted otherwise in the text.

ClariComm Publishing grants permission to copy ONLY the worksheets in this book for individual use and workshops/classes; however we prefer if you print them from the website: www.claricomm.com/publishing.

Thank you for respecting this copyright. Your integrity with this and respect for our work spreads positive spiritual energy throughout the world and makes us very happy.

This book is designed to provide helpful and educational information about marriage and marriage preparation. It is sold with the understanding that the publisher and the authors are not engaged in rendering legal, clinical, or other professional advice. No information, advice, or suggestions are intended to take the place of a therapist or professional. If expert assistance is required, the services of a competent professional should be sought. The authors and publisher shall have neither liability nor responsibility to any person or entity with respect to any loss or damage caused, or alleged to be caused, directly or indirectly by the information contained in this book.

Cover Design: Justice St Rain, Special Ideas, Inc., www.special-ideas.com, © 2003 Justice St Rain

Back Cover Author Photo: Steve Petti, *new image media*, www.newimagemedia.com, 216-514-1835

Illustrations: This book, including the front cover, is illustrated using royalty-free clip art and photos that are licensed for commercial use.

ClariComm Publishing
P.O. Box 23085
Cleveland, OH 44123
216-383-9943; www.ClariComm.com/publishing
Clear Communications and Bright Ideas

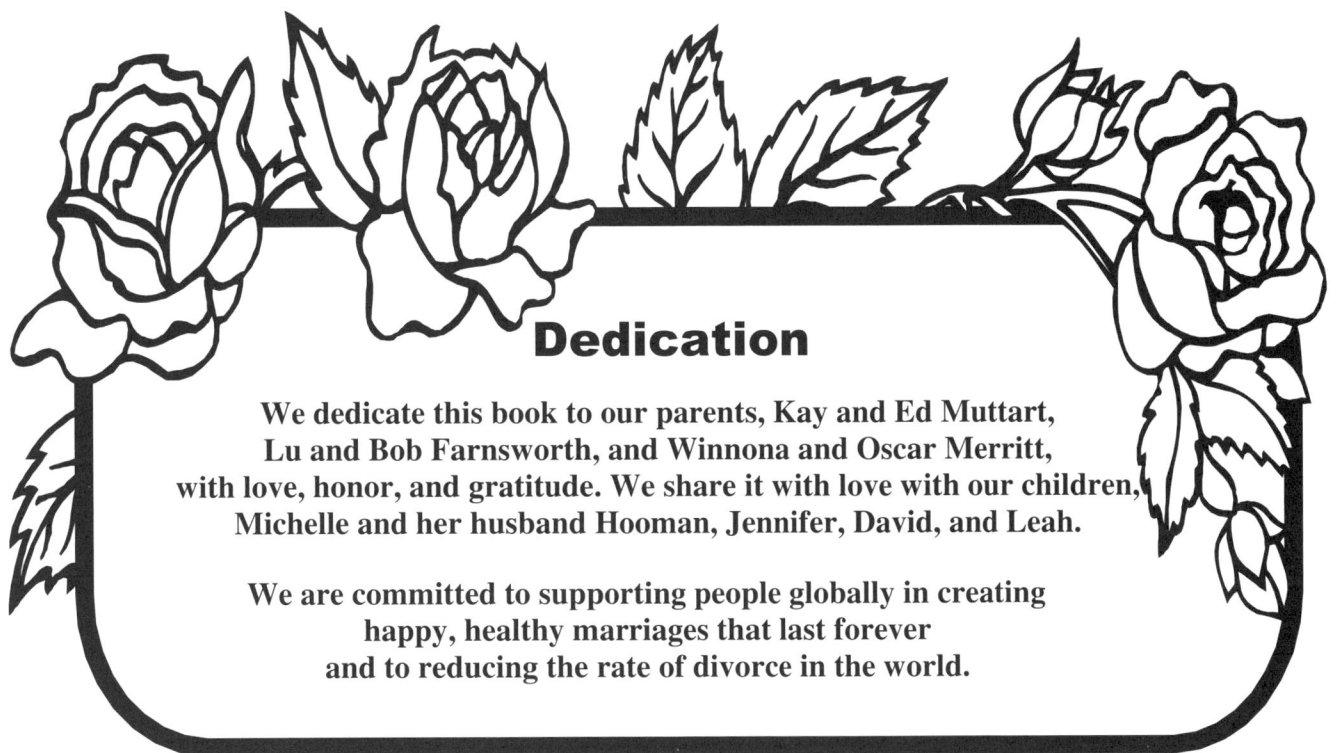

Dedication

We dedicate this book to our parents, Kay and Ed Muttart,
Lu and Bob Farnsworth, and Winnona and Oscar Merritt,
with love, honor, and gratitude. We share it with love with our children,
Michelle and her husband Hooman, Jennifer, David, and Leah.

We are committed to supporting people globally in creating
happy, healthy marriages that last forever
and to reducing the rate of divorce in the world.

Acknowledgements

This Second Edition has been greatly enhanced by the addition of Johanna Merritt Wu, Ph.D. as a collaborator. As an experienced developer of training courses and materials, she has worked tirelessly and prayerfully in developing new worksheets and ensuring that the text of the book is complete and clear. She has been extraordinarily generous in blending the work she had started for her own book into the First Edition. This has expanded and enhanced *Marriage Can Be Forever—Preparation Counts!* in ways that we hope will contribute to the lives of generations now and in the future.

Writing and editing a book is neither linear nor a process done during regular work hours. Susanne and Johanna wish to acknowledge the patience, support, and love that their husbands Craig Farnsworth and Steven Wu showed to them during their long hours working on this book. They also bless the friendship that has developed between them as they have worked together.

We are grateful to Paul Coleman, Psy.D., for his foreword and his acknowledgment of the importance of spiritually-based marriages.

Bahá'í Continental Board of Counsellors member Stephen Birkland kindly reviewed this edition, and Counsellor Abdu'l-Missagh Ghadirian, M.D., and his wife Marilyn Ghadirian, who serves on the National Bahá'í Family Committee of Canada, reviewed the first edition. We appreciate your time, keen and professional insights, and commitment to supporting our service.

Keyvan Geula, a marriage, family, and child counselor who leads marriage-preparation workshops, generously shared her materials and expertise with us. Sandra Bender, Ph.D., executive director of the Marriage Coalition in Cleveland, Ohio, assisted with the development of the chapter on cohabitation and provided referrals to many helpful resources.

After the first edition quickly sold out, we could not have accomplished a second edition so promptly without an extraordinary team of contributors, reviewers, editors, proofreaders, and those that offered material support. Some of you also helped out with the First Edition. You are each special to us:

Robert Ahdieh, Linda Ahdieh Grant, Tahereh Ahdieh, Dwight Allen, Jim Anderson, Valerie Anderson, Guitelle Baghdadi, Clark Benbow, Barbara Bonheur, Ronn Bonheur, Harry Bury, Gretchen Camacho, Pat Cameron, Jennifer Coates, John Cunningham, Leah Farnsworth, Alexis Fink, Tamaura Foley, Laura Hamill, Robert Horn, Kelly James-Enger, Nevin Jenkins, Frank Kelleher, Linda Kelleher, Sam Kelleher, Terah Kelleher, Peter Khan, Paula Larson, Louhelen Bahá'í School Marriage Weekend, Debra Major, Shoghi McClean, Karen McKye, Genevieve Merritt, Oscar Merritt, Winnona Merritt, Daved Muttart, Ed Muttart, Kay Muttart, Breda Nagle, Reggie Newkirk, Juliet Porch, Jamal Reimer, Research Department at the Bahá'í World Center, Sarah Sealy, Justice St Rain, Jeff Sinn, Michelle Tashakor, Homa Tavangar, Shahin Vafai, Tracey Wiley, Laquetia Williams, Steven Wu, Lynne Yancy (National Bahá'í Literature Review Office), and Melodie Yates.

We appreciate those who contributed testimonials, and thank you for your support:

Harry Bury, Pat Cameron, Heather Nablo Cardin, Liz (Gordon) Davis, Abdu'l-Missagh Ghadirian, Marilyn Ghadirian, Whitney Gifford, Robert Horn, Maureen Jasulevich, Matin Katirai, Reggie Newkirk, and Michael Penn.

We thank the many youth and adults who have participated in our workshops, and those who have taken time to give us valuable and generous personal insights and feedback.

Expert layout and design support came from Joyce Ashman and Linda Cenin. We couldn't have done it without you!

We appreciate having a lawyer with expertise in publishing who provides us great legal guidance. Thank you Sallie Randolph.

These acknowledgements from the First Edition still stand, as the Second Edition is built on its foundation:
- Barbara Whitbeck and Amelia Baxter, who invited us to do workshops, which started the development of the materials.
- David Bowers, who provided a wonderful essay for the Appendices.
- Author John Skeaff and his book, *Consent of Parents*, were very helpful resources.
- Spiritual Assembly of the Bahá'ís of Buncombe County, North Carolina.
- Carl and Terry Fravel, who got us started with developing questions.
- David Bowers, Cameron family, Kalyn Gibbens (author of *Marrying Smart*); Liz Gordon, Katie Greene, Michael Hughey, Heather Jensen, Dale Mitchell, Terri Mitchell, Judy Parsley, Naomi Parsley, Anne Marie Peacock, Bart Shull, Suzanne Sandusky, and Ban Twaddell, reviewed manuscript drafts, provided valuable feedback and editing suggestions, provided testimonials, researched, passed along helpful material, and did typesetting/layout.

We also appreciate all the people in our lives who support, nurture, and encourage our marriages to be strong and loving. This allows us to support and serve others.

Marriage Can Be Forever—Preparation Counts!

Marriage Can Be Forever—Preparation Counts!

Walking a Path to a Spiritually-Based Marriage
~ A Workbook ~

 ## Table of Contents: Steps on the Path

Foreword for the Second Edition by Marriage Therapist, Paul Coleman, Psy.D.

Introduction – What's It All About?: A [Not To Be Missed] Tour Through the Book

Step 1 Lay the Foundation: Before You Begin   Page Number

Chapter 1	Life Partners: Preparation and Marriage	2
Chapter 2	What's *Really* Important?: The Purpose of Life	8
Chapter 3	Let's Talk: Using the Tool of Consultation	12

Step 2 Get Yourself Ready: Starting Your Search

Chapter 4	You *Think* You Know: Deciphering Expectations	22
Chapter 5	Moving On: Learning from Relationships	30
Chapter 6	Your Bedrock: Assessing Character	38
Chapter 7	Knowing What You Want: A Great Marriage Partner	46
Chapter 8	I Like You: Friends Before Marriage	54

Step 3 Walk Carefully: Being a Couple

Chapter 9	An Initial Step: Do You Want to Date?	64
Chapter 10	Getting Serious: Courting the Special One	72
Chapter 11	Promising Forever: Making Commitments	80
Chapter 12	A Serious Sidestep: Living Together	90
Chapter 13	Know the Goal: A Strong, Eternal Marriage	96

Step 4 Explore Compatibility: Learning Together

Chapter 14	Can We Get Along?: The Value of Compatibility	102
Chapter 15	The Power of Attraction: Your Love for Each Other	112
Chapter 16	A Focus on God: Your Spiritual Life Together	118
Chapter 17	All In the Family: We'll Be Related	128

		Page Number
Chapter 18	On Partnership: Equality in Marriage	138
Chapter 19	Being Around You: Personality, Attitudes, and Behavior	146
Chapter 20	Of Minds and Hearts: Communicating with Each Other	156
Chapter 21	Doing It Better: Communication Skills	164
Chapter 22	An Abundance of Feelings: Expressing the Emotions	176
Chapter 23	A Personal Discussion: Chastity, Intimacy, and Sex	188
Chapter 24	Family Time: Children and Marriage	200
Chapter 25	On the Move: Service and Time Choices	210
Chapter 26	Money In, Money Out: Earning, Budgeting, and Spending	216
Chapter 27	Who Will Cook Tonight?: Your Future Home	228
Chapter 28	Rocks on the Path: Handling the Tough Stuff	236

Step 5 Come to Commitment: You and Your Parents

Chapter 29	What Do We Want?: A Vision of Marriage	246
Chapter 30	We Do or We Don't: To Marry or Not	252
Chapter 31	To Mom and Dad: Seeking Consent	258
Chapter 32	Now It's Up to You: Parents Considering Consent ****Chapter for Parents****	264
Chapter 33	When the Answer Is "No": Consent Denied	272

Step 6 Move Forward: Wedding and Marriage

Chapter 34	It's Almost Here: The Engagement Period	280
Chapter 35	The Big Day: Creating Your Marriage Ceremony	286
Chapter 36	An Adventure: The First Year Together	294
Chapter 37	It's Just the Beginning: Marriage Can Be Forever	300

Appendices

A	What's Your Character?: The Virtues Defined	304
B	The Spiritual Connection: Prayers for Marriage	309
C	*A Foundation for Well-Being's Fortress,* *An Essay on Marriage Preparation* by David Bowers	311
D	Spiritual Revelation: A Glimpse of the Bahá'í Faith	314
E	Our Gratitude for Use: Permissions	315
F	Behind the Scenes: About the Authors	316
G	Where Can I Get Copies?: Ordering Information	317

🌸 Worksheets 🌸

Note: New worksheets in the Second Edition are noted with an asterisk (*).

Page Number

3A	Consultation Skill Level*	19-20
4A	Identify Your Expectations	27
4B	A Vision of Your Marriage*	28-29
5A	Learning from Relationships	35
5B	Cleaning Up Previous Relationships*	36
5C	Developing Yourself as an Excellent Spouse*	37
6A	Assessing Virtues/Character Qualities	44
6B	Character Development Plan	45
7A	Describe Who You Are	52
7B	Describe Your Potential Marriage Partner	53
8A	Qualities of Friends*	61
8B	Widening Your Circle of Friends*	62
10A	Identify Activities to Learn About Each Other	78
10B	Setting Courtship Goals*	79
11A	Fears About Commitment*	87
11B	Log of Short-Term Commitments*	88
11C	History of Long-Term Commitments*	89
12A	The Topic of Cohabitation*	95
14A	What Do You Each Bring?	108
14B	Assessing Your Compatibility	109-111
15A	Married Couples and Love*	117
16A	A Faith Exploration for Couples*	125-127
17A	Parents' Marriage/Relationship Model*	134-135
17B	Learning from Parents*	136
18A	Applying the Equality of Women and Men in Marriage	144
19A	Assessing Personality, Attitudes, and Behavior*	152-155
21A	Understanding Communication Patterns*	172-174
21B	Communication Guidelines*	175
22A	Expressing Your Emotions*	184-185
22B	Your Partner's Emotions*	186
23A	Discussing Intimate Feelings and Sex*	196-199
26A	Preparing a Budget	225
26B	Calculating Net Worth	226
26C	Distinguishing Necessities and Luxuries*	227
27A	Experiences in Sharing Living Space*	235
29A	State the Intentions of Your Marriage	251
30A	Trends in Your Relationship*	257
35A	Planning the Marriage Ceremony	292
36A	Partnership – Your Goals for the Future*	299

DIG IN!

Marriage Can Be Forever—Preparation Counts!

Foreword for the Second Edition
by Marriage Therapist, Paul Coleman, Psy.D.

Marriage is a spiritual institution—most books and experts on marriage minimize or neglect that concept. Fortunately, *Marriage Can Be Forever—Preparation Counts!* is an exciting new book that reveals how one's spiritual focus is central to a living, breathing marriage and to the preparation leading up to that marriage.

I was immediately struck by an early chapter of the book that discussed "Your Purpose in Life." It doesn't mention happiness or success or fame or any other common goal. Simply put, our purpose in life is to know and love God, develop virtues that mirror Him, and to advance civilization. Simple yet profound. Marriage is a vessel by which we can hope to achieve such ends. Marriage is not an end in itself, and a happy marriage is not defined by how one feels on any given day. A happy marriage is a by-product of a life spent trying to fulfill one's sacred purpose.

But anyone with good intentions can get confused when it comes to selecting the right mate. *Are we really compatible? Do we agree enough on important issues? How can I tell if our backgrounds and family history are helping or hurting our relationship? What are our strengths and weaknesses?* The authors, Susanne Alexander and Craig Farnsworth, with Johanna Merritt Wu, take readers through each phase of a relationship in bloom and alert them to crucial questions and issues they need to consider. The book is laced with helpful worksheets, questionnaires, and informative lists—each designed to help the reader clarify concerns, issues, desires, and relationship goals. I have no doubt that any couple who takes the time to read this book and looks inward for an honest examination of who they are and what they want, will be richly prepared for all that married life has to offer.

Dr. Coleman is the author of:

- ❖ *The 30 Secrets of Happily Married Couples*
- ❖ *How to Say It for Couples: Communicating with Tenderness, Openness, and Honesty*
- ❖ *How to Say It to Your Kids: The Right Words to Solve Problems, Soothe Feelings, and Teach Values*

Introduction – What's It All About?: A [Not-To Be Missed] Tour Through the Book

In many ways, this book is an outflowing from our hearts to yours. It is an invitation to prepare for marriage with *both eyes open*, so that objectivity balances romance. We believe this will support you to choose a marriage partner wisely and increase the likelihood that you will create a lasting marriage.

We are heartsick over the pain we see in relationships and marriages that end in disharmony and divorce. This book's creation comes in part from that pain and from our confidence that there are spiritual and practical solutions to preventing broken relationships and the unhappiness that follows. **Marriage can be wonderful, strong, happy, and lasting, especially when couples thoroughly prepare themselves for it.**

You may be preparing yourself to be married—before you have someone in your life as a potential marriage partner. Later you will probably make the shift into joint preparation with someone else, which will include assessing his/her character and personality, in addition to your own. Alternatively, you may be picking this book up when you are already in a relationship or engaged, so you will study the quotes and perspectives, discuss the questions, and complete the worksheets and activities primarily as a couple. **Note:** We use the term "partner" throughout, to refer to each person in the couple.

You may be considering marriage for the first time; or you may have been married before and want to be more thorough in preparing for a new marriage. Some of you don't have children, while others may have children and will be creating blended families. ***We believe the contents of this book will assist you, whatever your age, background, faith path, culture, or experience level happen to be.*** We believe this book will help you give care and attention to ensuring that your relationship has a spiritual foundation and that you and your spouse are compatible. Our intent is for *Marriage Can Be Forever—Preparation Counts!* to be an active, practical tool that supports your preparation process and the creation of a friendship and eternal marriage bond.

Note: There are many subjects in this book and many of them quite complex, so it has not been possible to go into great depth in each chapter. We encourage you to study other materials about each of them. Beginning and maintaining relationships is an ongoing, active learning process and one source is unlikely to address all your questions and needs.

> Many people spend a great deal of time (and money) planning their *weddings*, something that lasts only a few hours. We believe that planning for your *marriage* is more crucial—it is intended to last forever. Marrying is one of life's major decisions, and it is a far-reaching and long-lasting decision. Marriage involves your heart, body, mind, and soul and when done well provides the stable base for families, communities, and our global society.

We wrote this book for people committed to religious and spiritual traditions who wish to have a **marriage that includes faith, with God at its heart**. We have chosen to contribute to this goal by weaving the gift of the spiritual guidance from the Bahá'í Faith throughout it. The Bahá'í Faith, the most recent among the world's religions (about 160 years old), offers useful insights on dating, courtship, marriage, and family life. We believe the perspectives from its Teachings will be valuable for you as you prepare for marriage, and you need not be a Bahá'í to find them applicable to your journey toward creating a spiritually-based marriage.

Also included in the book are the laws that apply to Bahá'ís who are involved in relationships and marrying. While only Bahá'ís are bound by these laws, people of any faith may find them useful. The law of parental consent for marriage, for instance, promotes family unity, something that people following any spiritual tradition are likely to appreciate. **Laws and spiritual practices from religious traditions** guide individuals and society to act in ways that benefit themselves and others. Many people feel a conflict between wanting to act as freely as they choose to and the requirement to follow laws. However, contrary to how many may have traditionally thought, just laws provide a structure that allows individuals to move more freely and to lead happier lives. Think about traffic signals, for instance. When there are stop signs and stoplights, traffic can move freely through intersections. Without these guidelines, vehicles are in gridlock at intersections, unable to proceed, and often involved in harmful accidents.

The Universal House of Justice, the international Bahá'í governing body, explains laws in this way:
> Just as there are laws governing our physical lives, requiring that we must supply our bodies with certain foods, maintain them within a certain range of temperatures, and so forth, if we wish to avoid physical disabilities, so also there are laws governing our spiritual lives. These laws are revealed to mankind in each age by the Manifestation of God [the Messengers for each religion], and obedience to them is of vital importance if each human being, and mankind in general, is to develop properly and harmoniously. Moreover, these various aspects are interdependent. If an individual violates the spiritual laws for his own development he will cause injury not only to himself but to the society in which he lives. Similarly, the condition of society has a direct effect on the individuals who must live within it.
>
> …Life in this world is a succession of tests and achievements, of falling short and of making new spiritual advances. Sometimes the course may seem very hard, but one can witness, again and again, that the soul who steadfastly obeys the law of Bahá'u'lláh, however hard it may seem, grows spiritually, while the one who compromises with the law for the sake of his own apparent happiness is seen to have been following a chimera: he does not attain the happiness he sought, he retards his spiritual advance and often brings new problems upon himself.
>
> (Universal House of Justice, *Messages 1963 to 1986*, p. 231)

It may assist people of other faiths to understand that Bahá'u'lláh, the Prophet-Founder of the Bahá'í Faith, teaches that there is only one God and that religious truth taught by Moses, Jesus, Buddha, Muhammad, and many others is all one whole. (See Appendix D for more information about the Bahá'í Faith.)

We were born and raised in North America, as were most contributors to this book, so in many ways, the book has this bias. We tried in this edition to be somewhat more inclusive, knowing that its readers are global, and the Teachings of the Bahá'í Faith are for all humanity. However, we know our effort is limited, and beg your patience and understanding—it will take ongoing input from culturally diverse participants to influence future editions.

Components of the Book

There are many ways to prepare for marriage, and this book provides one approach—it's not the only way. There is also **no timetable** associated with the process—you will follow the path that is best for you. It is likely you will use this book in a number of different ways—on your own, as a couple, or in a workshop setting. We have included enough options to meet most needs. **The details below will help you understand how to get the maximum value from each part of the book.**

Process Steps…The Path to a Spiritually-Based Marriage

The book's sections match each of the steps we suggest you take toward marriage preparation. Each section is then subdivided into chapters on related topics. Below are the steps you will follow.

Primary Steps in the Marriage Preparation Process

Step 1   Lay the Foundation: Before You Begin

Step 2   Get Yourself Ready: Starting Your Search

Step 3   Walk Carefully: Being a Couple

Step 4   Explore Compatibility: Learning Together

Step 5   Come to Commitment: You and Your Parents

Step 6   Move Forward: The Wedding and Marriage

Chapter Components and Tips for Successful Use

Poetry or Prose begin each chapter, and both the content and the varied design on each adds an arts element to your preparation process. The selections invite you into the topic of each chapter and provide you with material to meditate upon, read to each other, or discuss. Most of the poems are original creations of our own or close family or friends.

Focus Points clue you in to the key contents and chapter learning points. Workshop facilitators may also find this a helpful guide.

A Couple's Story is the fictional account of Lindsay and James, whose self-preparation, connecting as a couple, and then preparing for marriage threads throughout the book. This glimpse of their relationship will give you a view of one couple's journey and material for discussion. Their story won't match yours exactly but it may give you ideas.

Quotes for Guidance from the Bahá'í Writings have nine-pointed stars in front of them to designate the beginning of each quote. In each chapter, the quotes start with those of Bahá'u'lláh, the Founder of the Bahá'í Faith; and then includes, in order, quotes from 'Abdu'l-Bahá, His Son; Shoghi Effendi, his great-grandson; and the Universal House of Justice, the international governing body. Each of these has been or is the designated "head" of the Bahá'í Faith in succession over the last 160 years. The order of the quotes won't, therefore, match the order of the Focus Points. Some of you may prefer to read the quotes first; others may prefer to start reading the perspectives and then come back to read and understand the quotes.

Perspectives to Consider is our conversation with you. While the perspectives are based on the previous quotes, they also contain the wisdom and experience from our lives and the lives of many people who have contributed to this book.

Coaching is a sharing of collective wisdom and experience from people who wish to support you in being successful. The tips will give you thoughts to ponder and begin to incorporate in your life. Just as a coach on a sports team guides you with input on how to play the game, the coaching suggestions we've included are intended to be direct contributions to you and your future marriage. *Coaching is also a model for you to think about in your marriage—can you share and listen to different perceptions and influence each other in positive ways? Are you willing to be coached, to be influenced? Do you see how this will nurture your relationship?* **Note:** *This is not the same as criticism and complaining!*

Questions for Reflection and Discussion are included to provide you with the opportunity to talk to each other in depth about most issues that will affect your relationship. They will also give parents questions to ask a couple to assist them in being sure about their ability to create a successful marriage. Generally, the questions are addressed to "you," but they apply to both the man and the woman in a couple. You may have issues with someone asking you questions—you start out life asking many questions in your eagerness to discover the world, but over time, you may start to associate them with examinations in school or being in trouble with someone. Questions and answers are actually an opportunity for you to understand your thought processes and the emotions triggered during discussions.

Have the patience to use the questions as a tool to deeply listen to and understand yourself and each other. They are there to help you get to know each other as thoroughly as possible before being married. To be great communicators, use the questions as starting points for long, "soulful" conversations with each other. Remember the questions are not opportunities to argue and prove that your point of view is the "right" one; they are to provide a time to share and listen. *You may want to create a relationship journal, and answer the questions in writing as well, especially if you are completing this book as an individual while not in a relationship.* Make sure you create loving, quiet, and safe spaces for the discussions and journal writing. **Note:** Be prepared to answer any question yourself that you are willing to pose to someone else!

Activities are designed to prompt discussion, provide reflection and observation opportunities, create learning experiences, simulate some situations that are similar to marriage, and test compatibility. Activities using the arts are included, as they can help bring up thoughts and emotions that you weren't previously aware you had or give you practical perspectives on abstract concepts. While much of this book is about communicating with each other, it is vital that you be active and use your full observation powers to understand each other's character, personality, attitudes, and behavior.

Prayer and meditation are integral components for many of the activities and are essential tools in marriage preparation. Activities include worksheets and reflection questions. Remember to include reflection as a final stage for all activities so you understand what you have learned from participating in them. While there is some room throughout the book to write notes, you may also find it helpful to write in a journal as a way to process your thoughts, feelings, actions, behavior, relationship progression, and more. **Note:** Most worksheets may be printed from our website, www.claricomm.com/publishing. This will help you if you want more space to write, to work with a partner who doesn't have the book, or need extra copies for a workshop.

This caution sign, text boxes, **bolding**, *italics*, and ***bold-italics*** are used throughout the book to draw your attention to key points and information that is vital. Sidebars also contain useful information that did not fit in the flow of the perspectives.

We invite you to walk the marriage preparation path with practical feet. As you look through the book, you might be concerned that all this practicality will interfere with romance. We firmly believe that attraction, love, and romance are components of lasting marriages. We also believe that close friendship and compatibility are factors that contribute to ***lasting*** attraction, love, and romance. Creating a living, spiritual marriage is far more joyful and lasting than the brief rush that comes from "falling in love." So, think of this book as a guidebook filled with wisdom for the heart, body, mind, and soul so you are empowered to walk the path to creating a firm partnership with someone. The goal is to stay happily married *forever*.

A Note for Parents, Families, and Spiritual Assemblies/Religious Leaders

Parents, families, and religious communities can support couples as they prepare for marriage and adjust their lives to live as married partners. Throughout the book, you will see places where individuals and couples are encouraged to consult with you as they prepare to marry. We hope you see it as a joy and a responsibility to assist marriages to be covenants that last.

To support couples well, you may need to go through your own self-preparation and/or training process. *Your* commitment to marriage is part of what will support couples in *their* commitment to making marriage spiritual, happy, and a contribution to the well-being of their families and communities. **Note:** The Spiritual Assembly is an elected group of nine adults that guides and serves the Bahá'ís in its area. It is the officiating body for Bahá'í weddings when a couple marries. The graphic with this paragraph symbolizes the Spiritual Assembly throughout the book.

Interactive Process

We are committed to developing materials that support marriages and help reduce the divorce rate. Stories, feedback, and suggestions from you will ensure the usefulness of the materials, so we'd love to hear from you: ClariComm Publishing, P.O. Box 23085, Cleveland, OH 44123; www.claricomm.com (see also Appendix F).

May your marriage-preparation path be blessed!
Susanne, Craig, and Johanna

Step 1

Lay the Foundation: Before You Begin

Marriage Can Be Forever—Preparation Counts!

ABIDE VERILY

What does it mean
to join as husband, wife?
Two souls gathered
by God's Hands
uniting dreams
and thoughts
and touch
loving strongly
peaceful certainty
that joining is
forever blessed

Marriage changes things
no longer dating
or engaged
now entered in the
"fortress for well-being"*
where pearls of great price
must find a home
with dust and
scattered socks
where some days
doors might slam
and on others
"I love you" echoes
richly through the halls

Nurture the best
from each other
and on days when you
cannot be your best
then be patient and wait
tomorrow will be better

Though the fortress
God has built, not you,
you have the wondrous task
of lighting every hearth
with fires of warmth
and joyfulness
and softening the walls
with fragrant climbing
roses and throwing
windows open wide
to welcome in the sun
and filling it each day
with prayer so angels
guard and guide you

And then someday it
will be blessed again
as God smiles through
your lovely
children's laughter

~ Susanne Mariella Alexander

* Bahá'u'lláh: *Bahá'í Prayers*

CHAPTER 1 – Life Partners: Preparation and Marriage

WAIT! Did you remember to read the Introduction? Reading it first will help you walk the path through this book without stumbling.

Focus Points

- The importance of marriage preparation and compatibility
- Family and community involvement in the preparation process
- Marriage can be forever…and happy
- A union of two souls, hearts, minds, and bodies
- Marriage as a "fortress for well-being and salvation"

 A Couple's Story

In each chapter throughout the book you will have a glimpse into the lives of two people, Lindsay and James. You will read their unfolding story as they prepare themselves for marriage before they meet each other, build a friendship, date, enter into courtship, explore compatibility, and make a decision about marriage. These scenarios will give you a sense of the marriage preparation process, how you might use this book, and food for thought and discussion. Lindsay and James are both Bahá'ís in the story, but the development of their relationship, their challenges, and their choices have universal threads running through them that could apply to anyone of any faith. Here is an introduction to the characters:

Lindsay is a 22-year old college student majoring in civil engineering. She has a part-time job at the campus library cataloging and shelving books. She is friendly and outgoing and lives near the campus in a small apartment with a female roommate, Stacy, who is not a Bahá'í. Lindsay dated some in high school, with one serious boyfriend for about a year. In college, she has dated occasionally and had a brief relationship with someone whose marriage proposal she turned down. Lindsay became a Bahá'í at age 20, and she is the only Bahá'í in her family. She is still a virgin. Her parents divorced when she was 13. Her mother, Kerry, remarried when Lindsay was 16, and Lindsay interacted with her stepfather with a fair amount of animosity. They get along better now. Her father, Sam, dates but has not remarried. She is close to her younger brother, Jason, 20, who has struggled with alcohol and drug abuse.

James is 25 years old, easygoing and artistic. He is working fulltime as a graphic designer. He falls in love frequently, thinking each time that he has found "the one." James and his parents, Sondra and Marvin, have recently moved to the same town where Lindsay is going to college. His father had a heart attack a few months previously, so James is living in an apartment on their property to stay nearby. He and his parents are all members of the Bahá'í Faith, and he has no siblings. His parents have been married for 25 years. They have had a relatively stable marriage, although they separated for a few months when James was about 4 years old. James has struggled since that time with some concern about people leaving him—sometimes when James is dating, he breaks off the relationship when it starts to get serious, so the other person doesn't have a chance to leave him. James has been challenged in his dating relationships with the Bahá'í teachings about no sex before or outside marriage, and he has been sexually intimate with a couple of his girlfriends.

> **Quotes for Guidance**

✸ And when He [God] desired to manifest grace and beneficence to men, and to set the world in order, He revealed observances and created laws; among them He established the law of marriage, made it as a fortress for well-being and salvation, and enjoined it upon us in that which was sent down out of the heaven of sanctity in His Most Holy Book. He saith, great is His glory: "Enter into wedlock, O people, that ye may bring forth one who will make mention of Me amid My servants. This is My bidding unto you; hold fast to it as an assistance to yourselves."
(Bahá'u'lláh: *Bahá'í Prayers* (US 2002), p. 118)

 **Perspectives to Consider**

Welcome to the adventure and process of successfully **preparing yourself for marriage and choosing a compatible and eternal marriage partner**. You are becoming part of creating a culture shift away from the concept of "instant relationships" that just "magically happen." Many people jump into marriage with little forethought. Sometimes the result is an enduring relationship, but often it can fail when the couple marries and then discovers they don't know each other and aren't compatible. From a Bahá'í perspective, and that of many other faiths, marriage is intended to be an eternal, spiritual union between two people who love God, each other, and are attracted to each other. To support this goal, the couple must understand each other's character and be certain about their compatibility. It takes time to accomplish both of these, and this book will assist you in the process.

Another culture shift underway and encouraged in this book is an increase in **parents and communities actively supporting couples** as they prepare for marriage. Couples are encouraged to shift away from society's practice of isolating themselves while dating and spend more time with their families and involved in their communities and activities that support them in exploring compatibility. When a couple is seriously considering marrying, they are then "courting" each other. Courtship is currently a little-used term that is being revived and transformed. One of its essential characteristics today is spending time with parents. This allows the couple to get to know each other in a family setting, supports their commitment not to have sex before marriage, and assists the parents in knowing the character of the person their child wants to marry. Throughout the entire preparation process, communities are encouraged to support couples with workshops, courses, and study materials about marriage. They can also provide community activities where couples may have opportunities to understand each other's character and to test compatibility. (See Chapter 6 on character and Chapter 10 on courting.)

A unique feature in Bahá'í marriages is that after two individuals have chosen each other as partners (without parental interference), the marriage is conditional upon **consent of their parents**. While this is a requirement for Bahá'ís, it is also a model that people of other faiths may find beneficial—seeking parental approval is a way to bring blessings to a couple's marriage. Parental consent encourages family unity, harmony, and gratitude in the hearts of children toward their parents, who have given them life. When consent is given, the couple knows the parents have invited them into each other's families. If individuals and couples are well prepared for marriage, the consent process is more likely to be smooth, productive, and unifying.

Parents have often struggled with how to be effective in considering consent, and this book provides some support in raising it to a more meaningful level with practical tools. Parents will find it beneficial to prepare themselves for this significant responsibility through self-assessment and building the skills needed to evaluate with fairness and without prejudice the couple's readiness to unite in marriage. The questions for the couple throughout the book may be ones parents ask the couple, Chapters 6 and 19 about character and personality, and Chapters 31-33 about consent, will be particularly helpful.

By thoroughly using this book, you are choosing to be an **active and responsible participant** in preparing for marriage, seeking a partner, and determining compatibility with him/her. This is too important a decision to approach randomly or passively—God is more likely to guide you, and you are more likely to learn vital information, if you are in action. There is still a mystical, spiritual component to loving someone and joining your life with him or her. ***But choosing someone to be with forever is one of the biggest decisions of anyone's life.*** Careful preparation—a skill-building and spiritual process—is essential.

Your decision to marry has far-ranging effects on:

- You as an individual
- You as a couple
- Your extended families
- Your friends
- The children you have or who are nurtured within it

> If you spend time ensuring you know yourself and your partner, and do the best you can to ensure you will be compatible and balance each other, then you are more likely to be in a happy marriage that lasts...*forever*.

A new and wonderful creation results when a union between two entities occurs. **Marriage is a union of your souls, hearts, minds, and bodies**—you are not the same people after this union, and it creates energy and substance (and often children!). Creating this union is neither easy nor necessarily smooth and comfortable. There are many adjustments along the way. Your commitment to God, loving each other, praying together, and encouraging each other, can all sustain you through the adjustments. Marriage is the foundation for families, and families are the foundation for society, so more happy marriages and families are critically important for the future well-being of humanity.

Bahá'u'lláh, the Prophet-Founder of the Bahá'í Faith, describes marriage as "a fortress for well-being and salvation." He welcomes you as couples to enter into this fortress, establish and nurture your families within its protective walls, and keep humanity moving progressively forward. This image of a fortress is a metaphor that is used throughout the book. Bahá'u'lláh doesn't explain His use of the word "fortress," so try to understand it through developing your own images of it in relation to marriage. Below are some metaphors that may contribute to your perspectives on it.

Marriage—"A Fortress for Well-Being and Salvation"

- It's a place of permanence, safety, security, stability, and close relationships
- Love both provides part of the foundation for the fortress and lights the fire of warmth within its hearths
- Unity, harmony, and a common love for God between you as a couple and among your family members ensure that the walls of the fortress stay intact
- Maintaining marriage, like a fortress, is a commitment and responsibility
- Balance and compatibility between you as a couple will help to ensure that this unity and the fortress stay firmly established
- The security and grounding of the fortress gives you and your family the stability to reach out into the world to do God's will, to be of service to others, and for each person to reach his or her fullest potential
- The fortress is a place of respite, where you can rest and gain strength and support to continue to make a difference for others in the world

6   Chapter 1 - Life Partners: Preparation and Marriage

From the Bahá'í perspective and in most religious traditions, marriage is the place where a man and a woman live together, make love, serve others, have children, and are lifelong companions. Divorce, while permitted for Bahá'ís, is highly discouraged and considered a last resort after considerable efforts to reconcile. It is only permissible when a strong aversion exists between the individuals. Divorce is also discouraged or forbidden in many other faiths.

Using this book and considering the guidance it contains will help your assessment process and your overall preparation for a successful, rewarding, and happy marriage. Preparation starts with each person having a strong love for God. It includes the essential foundation of self-preparation—a process of developing your own character and achieving a level of maturity adequate to enter into full partnership with someone else. It also includes assessing the character and personality of the person you are considering marrying. And, perhaps most challenging of all, the process involves the ability to assess your mutual compatibility—something that will assist you to walk into a marriage with ***both eyes open***.

 **Coaching**

⇒ Be committed to the possibility that you can have a happy marriage, and resist the temptation to focus on divorce statistics as a reason not to be married.

 Questions for Reflection and Discussion

Note: Remember that "reflection" may include writing in a journal.

1. What are your opinions about the permanence of marriage?
2. What do you think are the contributing factors in creating a happy marriage?
3. What do you think about parents and community being involved in supporting your preparation process?
4. What are your perspectives on the "fortress for well-being and salvation"?
5. What do you think about the concept of two people, two souls uniting to form a marriage bond?
6. What are the things you have seen couples do or not do that you think have led to divorce?
7. What are the things you have seen other married couples do or not do that you think are important in making a marriage last?

 **Activities**

1. Pray, meditate, reflect, and write in your journal about how marriage is like a "fortress for well-being and salvation."

2. Look at this comic. How do you think marriage is like an "art"?

   _____

3. How do you think marriage is like a "science"?

   _____

"Marriage and relationships? ....That's under the Arts and Sciences."

Marriage Can Be Forever—Preparation Counts!

A Spiritual Nugget for Reflection and Discussion

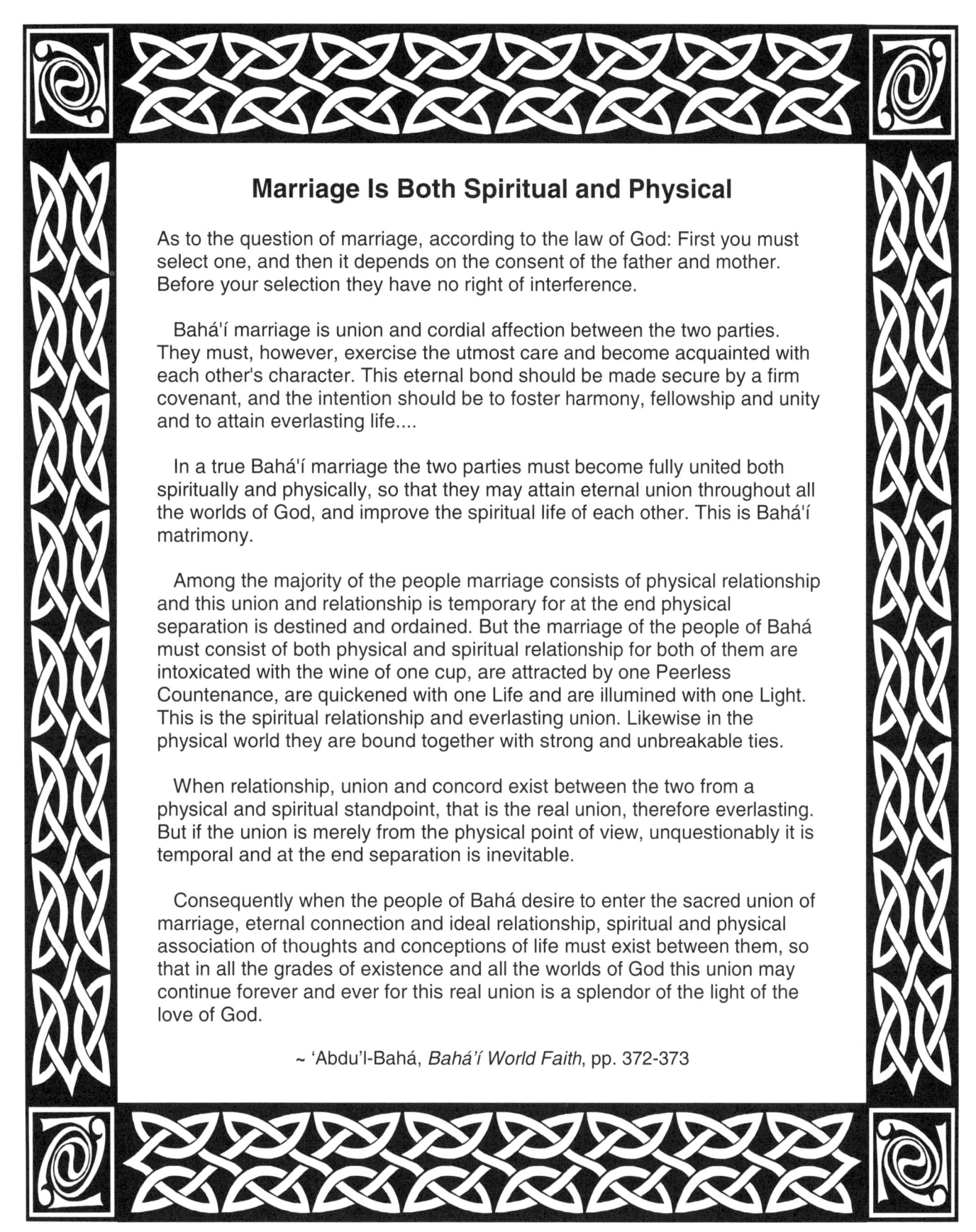

Marriage Is Both Spiritual and Physical

As to the question of marriage, according to the law of God: First you must select one, and then it depends on the consent of the father and mother. Before your selection they have no right of interference.

Bahá'í marriage is union and cordial affection between the two parties. They must, however, exercise the utmost care and become acquainted with each other's character. This eternal bond should be made secure by a firm covenant, and the intention should be to foster harmony, fellowship and unity and to attain everlasting life....

In a true Bahá'í marriage the two parties must become fully united both spiritually and physically, so that they may attain eternal union throughout all the worlds of God, and improve the spiritual life of each other. This is Bahá'í matrimony.

Among the majority of the people marriage consists of physical relationship and this union and relationship is temporary for at the end physical separation is destined and ordained. But the marriage of the people of Bahá must consist of both physical and spiritual relationship for both of them are intoxicated with the wine of one cup, are attracted by one Peerless Countenance, are quickened with one Life and are illumined with one Light. This is the spiritual relationship and everlasting union. Likewise in the physical world they are bound together with strong and unbreakable ties.

When relationship, union and concord exist between the two from a physical and spiritual standpoint, that is the real union, therefore everlasting. But if the union is merely from the physical point of view, unquestionably it is temporal and at the end separation is inevitable.

Consequently when the people of Bahá desire to enter the sacred union of marriage, eternal connection and ideal relationship, spiritual and physical association of thoughts and conceptions of life must exist between them, so that in all the grades of existence and all the worlds of God this union may continue forever and ever for this real union is a splendor of the light of the love of God.

~ 'Abdu'l-Bahá, *Bahá'í World Faith*, pp. 372-373

The Heart

Loud speaks the mind
Soft speaks the heart

When mind overpowers
The still voice from within
The existence is hollow
Where's the center? Where's the core?

The heart brings a guidance
That will seek for a balance
To bring one to contentment
A more vital being.

Of what speaks the heart?
The heart speaks of essence
Of reaching and growing
Of becoming one person.

The mind draws distinction
Sees one separate not connected
It draws more on externals
And keeps life more shallow

The world of the heart
Is a gentle yet stronger
Force from within
That will carry one home.

~ Craig A. Farnsworth

CHAPTER 2 – What's *Really* Important?: The Purpose of Life

Focus Points
- The blessing of God's love
- The individual and couple's responsibility to know and love God
- The role of marriage in carrying forward an ever-advancing civilization
- The value of developing virtues and the importance of practicing them

A Couple's Story

Lindsay (to herself): *Mmmm…it's so peaceful here by the lake. I've always loved God, although at times I've wondered where He was when Mom and Dad were arguing all the time. And praying was tough to do when I was fighting all the time with my boyfriend and stepfather. But, being here makes me feel close to God again. There's something different now that I'm a Bahá'í, too—praying every day is getting easier and so is reading the words of Bahá'u'lláh. I just feel more spiritually grounded. Of course, deciding on my career as a civil engineer has helped me to feel settled too. And it's fun that Stacy is willing to do a couple of spiritual things with me, like picking a virtue each week to focus on. She's a great roommate for me. I like seeing which of us can be the first one to come up with a way to practice honesty, assertiveness, or whatever we pick. I'm at such a good place in my life right now. If only I could find a guy that I could see as a husband.*

James (to himself): *Oh no, I forgot to pray again yesterday. And I'm late for work already today…well, it will just have to wait for later. Maybe before my date tonight. At least this new job is better than my last one, with some possibility for it to go somewhere. And it's not bad living in the apartment over the garage at Mom and Dad's, and this town is a much calmer place for them to be. I can keep an eye on him since his heart attack, but I have some privacy and independence, too. I wonder if they'd notice if I brought Selena back there tonight…probably. Oh well, I guess that helps to keep me out of trouble. Maybe I'd better listen to Mom and Dad's suggestion to meet with the Spiritual Assembly and see if they have anything to help me with what to do to find someone I'd like to spend my life with. All this dating is driving me nuts.* [The Spiritual Assembly is an elected group of nine adults that guides the Bahá'ís in its area.]

Quotes for Guidance

✸ Having created the world and all that liveth and moveth therein, He, through the direct operation of His unconstrained and sovereign Will, chose to confer upon man the unique distinction and capacity to know Him and to love Him—a capacity that must needs be regarded as the generating impulse and the primary purpose underlying the whole of creation.... Upon the inmost reality of each and every created thing He hath shed the light of one of His names, and made it a recipient of the glory of one of His attributes. Upon the reality of man, however, He hath focused the radiance of all of His names and attributes, and made it a mirror of His own Self. Alone of all created things man hath been singled out for so great a favor, so enduring a bounty.
(Bahá'u'lláh: *Gleanings from the Writings of Bahá'u'lláh*, p. 65)

Chapter 2 – What's *Really* Important?: The Purpose of Life

✸ Glory be to Thee, O God, for Thy manifestation of love to mankind!
   (Bahá'u'lláh: *Bahá'í Prayers* (UK), pp. 60-61)

✸ All men have been created to carry forward an ever-advancing civilization. The Almighty beareth Me witness: To act like the beasts of the field is unworthy of man. Those virtues that befit his dignity are forbearance, mercy, compassion and loving-kindness towards all the peoples and kindreds of the earth.
   (Bahá'u'lláh: *Gleanings from the Writings of Bahá'u'lláh*, p. 215)

 **Perspectives to Consider**

Ah, and you thought it was all just about romance! No, marriage is actually part of the greater context of who you are as a human being and your purpose in life.

~~ Your Purpose in Life ~~
- Knowing and loving God
- Advancing civilization
- Developing virtues that mirror the qualities of God

God's love for you and your **love for God** provide the foundation of all your acts and relationships. With this as a conscious basis for marriage, you will be more likely to choose a partner who also has this as the basis of his or her life. You're not likely to choose marriage as a frivolous, temporary act or be misled by a rush of romance into marriage without understanding its eternal nature and the importance of choosing a partner well.

Love can be seen in you and other people through your behavior and attitudes—it is perhaps most strongly visible in your interactions with other people. Sincerity, warmth, and courtesy are all signs that you are reflecting the love of God to others and recognizing the beauty that God has given each person. This love for God is also visible in your choice to pray and study spiritual teachings daily and also to turn to prayer during life's challenges.

 Bahá'u'lláh charges humanity with **carrying forward an ever-advancing civilization**, and marriage is a big part of that. At the foundation of the Bahá'í Faith, and of course marriage, is the concept of unity—one God, His religion is one and eternal, and mankind is one. Searching for and implementing what is best for the common good of all, carries the world forward.

One great purpose in your life is the **development of virtues**, the spiritual qualities such as truthfulness, kindness, faithfulness, and patience. Your love for God motivates you to fully develop these virtues, these positive spiritual habits. In turn, your positive character qualities contribute to the betterment of your life, marriage, family, and society as a whole. Therefore, the virtue development must be in progress before entering marriage, and it will continue to occur throughout your life and your marriage.

Although developing positive qualities may not be easy, it results when you focus on your areas for development or learn through challenging tests and difficulties that arise in life. One

> The unity and harmony of a married couple provide a firm foundation for all of society around the world, and the Bahá'í laws and the teachings of other faiths about marriage are designed to support and protect this foundation. This broader view can be helpful when the day-to-day effort of maintaining a marriage becomes difficult—successful marriage takes care, attention, and effort and the 100 percent commitment and involvement of both husband and wife.

of your roles as a couple is fostering the character development of each other (no, that *doesn't* mean designing challenges *for* each other!). Another is supporting each other by practicing the virtues during difficult periods.

 **Coaching**

⇒ The challenge with these purposes of life is that they are very broad and general. You will find it helpful to explore very specific applications of them in your life. Ask other people for examples, and observe the marriages of people in your life for behavior and attitudes that match or don't match with these purposes. In this way, you will begin to distinguish for yourself what is important for you to have in a marriage and what to avoid.

 Questions for Reflection and Discussion

1. What actions in your life demonstrate that you love God?
2. What does an "ever-advancing civilization" mean to you?
3. What actions are you taking or what actions might you take within marriage that advance civilization?
4. What virtues do you think are the most important for marriage? (**Note:** There are definitions of some virtues in Appendix A.)

 **Activities**

1. Often using the arts helps to bring up thoughts and emotions that you weren't previously aware of having. They can give you practical perspectives on abstract concepts, such as "carrying forward an ever-advancing civilization." Spend some time in prayer and meditation about this concept and then see what you discover through drawing a picture or making a collage of what marriage looks like to you as part of this concept. If you prefer, use the arts in some other way such as writing a poem, creating a song, or developing a dance. What new insights did you gain from this exercise? [**Note:** A collage is created by cutting out pictures and/or words from magazines and gluing them onto a large piece of paper or cardboard. In this case, you would look for things to cut out that illustrate "carrying forward an ever-advancing civilization."] Share your artwork or creation with someone and discuss your insights and feelings together.

2. Practice identifying virtues in yourself and other people by choosing a friend and spend time with him or her. After you have finished with your visit, pray and meditate about your positive qualities that came up during the visit and the positive qualities he/she demonstrated. Appendix A has suggestions of qualities.

My Positive Qualities: **My Friend's Positive Qualities:**

_____   _____

_____   _____

_____   _____

_____   _____

The Gift of Consultation

Consultation is one of the greatest bounties given to man. It is an art, a key which can unlock the mysteries of life and open the door to answers to the most perplexing questions—questions of intimate and personal concern, or questions of worldwide significance. It is a major tool for the coming-of-age of the human race, a fundamental element in the bringing into being of a new world civilization.

~ John E. Kolstoe,
Consultation, A Universal Lamp of Guidance, p. 5

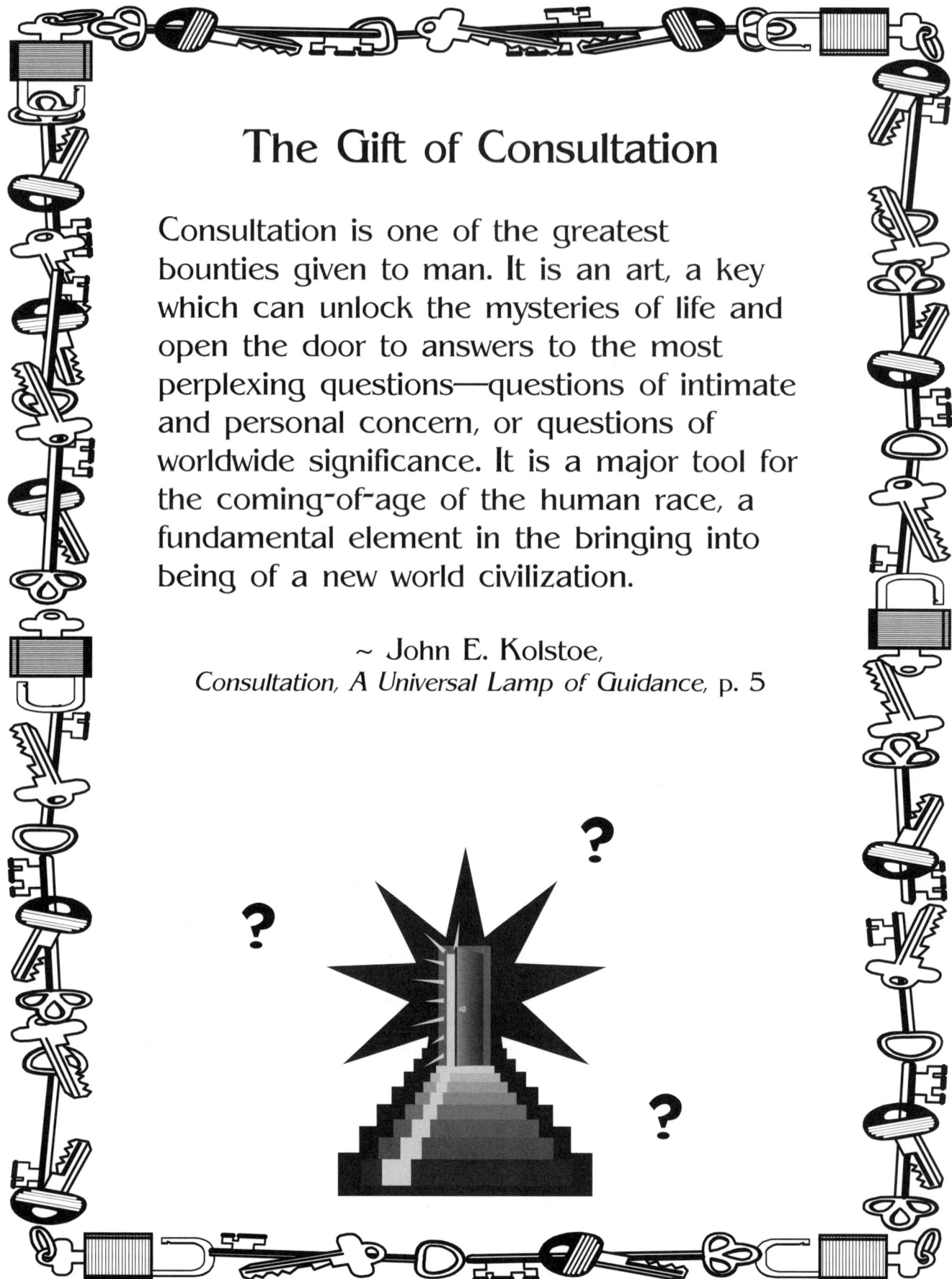

CHAPTER 3 – Let's Talk: Using the Tool of Consultation

Focus Points
- Definition of consultation
- Qualities for successful consultation
- Consultation as a couple
- Role of consultation in preparing for marriage

A Couple's Story

Lindsay (She and her roommate Stacy sit at their kitchen table talking about their relationships): "What's better than eating chocolate and drinking passion fruit tea when we are talking about guys?!" Lindsay says. Stacy responds with frustration, "I just wish I could find the right one for me."

"What about Rob?" asks Lindsay. "You've been dating him for a while. How do you know he's not 'the one?'"

"He just doesn't create any sparks, if you know what I mean," says Stacy.

"Yeah…that's why I've been taking a break from dating. But, I'm not giving up yet," says Lindsay. "Maybe I just need to put more effort into finding someone who will be a good partner for me."

James: "Thanks for agreeing to meet with me," James says to the Spiritual Assembly. "This is a little awkward, but here goes. I've dated many women but I'm not really finding someone I'd like to spend the rest of my life with, you know, get married to. My parents suggested I meet with you to see if there's any Bahá'í stuff that helps with relationships."

"You're welcome, and we're glad you've come to us," says Paola, on behalf of the group. "When you told us what you were coming to talk to us about, we did some quick research to see if there were any materials on dating and marriage preparation that we could give you. We've found a new book called *Marriage Can Be Forever—Preparation Counts!* that utilizes a process we think is worthwhile. If it is helpful for you, we might be able to recommend it to other singles in our area."

Paola hands this process to James along with a copy of the book:

Primary Steps in the Marriage Preparation Process
Step 1   Lay the Foundation: Before You Begin
Step 2   Get Yourself Ready: Starting Your Search
Step 3   Walk Carefully: Being a Couple
Step 4   Explore Compatibility: Learning Together
Step 5   Come to Commitment: You and Your Parents
Step 6   Move Forward: The Wedding and Marriage

Quotes for Guidance

✺ In all things it is necessary to consult...that consultation may be fully carried out among the friends, inasmuch as it is and will always be a cause of awareness and of awakening and a source of good and well-being.
(Bahá'u'lláh: *Compilation of Compilations, Vol. I*, p. 93)

✺ In this Cause consultation is of vital importance, but spiritual conference and not the mere voicing of personal views is intended.
('Abdu'l-Bahá: *Promulgation of Universal* Peace, p. 72)

✺ They must, when coming together, turn their faces to the Kingdom on high and ask aid from the Realm of Glory. They must then proceed with the utmost devotion, courtesy, dignity, care and moderation to express their views. They must in every matter search out the truth and not insist upon their own opinion, for stubbornness and persistence in one's views will lead ultimately to discord and wrangling and the truth will remain hidden.
('Abdu'l-Bahá: *Selections from the Writings of 'Abdu'l-Bahá*, p. 88)

✺ In order to find truth we must give up our prejudices, our own small trivial notions; an open receptive mind is essential. If our chalice is full of self, there is no room in it for the water of life. The fact that we imagine ourselves to be right and everybody else wrong is the greatest of all obstacles in the path towards unity, and unity is necessary if we would reach truth, for truth is one.
('Abdu'l-Bahá: *Paris Talks*, pp. 136-137)

✺ ...when a believer is uncertain about his affairs, or when he seeketh to pursue a project or trade, the friends should gather together and devise a solution for him. He, in his turn, should act accordingly. Likewise in larger issues, when a problem ariseth, or a difficulty occurreth, the wise should gather, consult, and devise a solution. They should then rely upon the one true God, and surrender to His Providence, in whatever way it may be revealed, for divine confirmations will undoubtedly assist.
('Abdu'l-Bahá: *Fire and Gold*, p. 270)

✺ [When asked about specific rules of conduct to govern the relationship between husbands and wives]...for example, the principle that the rights of each and all in the family unit must be upheld, and the advice that loving consultation should be the keynote, that all matters must be settled in harmony and love, and that there are times when the husband and the wife should defer to the wishes of the other. Exactly under what circumstances such deference should take place is a matter for each couple to determine. If, God forbid, they fail to agree, and their disagreement leads to estrangement, they should seek counsel from those they trust and in whose sincerity and sound judgment they have confidence, in order to preserve and strengthen their ties as a united family.
(Universal House of Justice: *Preserving Bahá'í Marriages*, pp. 5-6)

✺ Consultation has been ordained by Bahá'u'lláh as the means by which agreement is to be reached and a collective course of action defined. It is applicable to the marriage partners and within the family, and indeed in all areas where believers participate in mutual decision-making. It requires all participants to express their opinions with absolute freedom and without apprehension that they will be censured and/or their views belittled; these prerequisites for success are unattainable if the fear of violence or abuse are present.
(Universal House of Justice: An unpublished letter January 24, 1993, to an individual)

✺ The second principle is that of detachment in consultation. The members of an Assembly must learn to express their views frankly, calmly, without passion or rancor. They must also learn to listen to the opinions of their fellow members without taking offence or belittling the views of another. Bahá'í consultation is not an easy process. It requires love, kindliness, moral courage and humility.
(Universal House of Justice: *Lights of Guidance*, p. 180)

Perspectives to Consider

One thing that keeps things flowing smoothly in a relationship and within the marriage "fortress" is the practice of **consultation, a process of group decision making** without dictatorial authority. It can be formal or informal depending on the circumstances or people involved. It can be used for large decisions or small ones—the Bahá'í Writings advise using consultation under all circumstances, including within marriages and families. Consultation is also a key tool to use in marriage preparation for exploring subjects and making decisions.

You can use consultation to:

- Build consensus
- Solve problems
- Resolve conflicts
- Plan a course of action
- Probe for deeper meaning
- Discover the truth about a situation
- Take uncertainty and change it to certainty
- Deciding to marry or not
- Maintain unity while fully discussing issues
- Create unique decisions

There is wisdom in using consultation and group process to **make such a major decision as marrying someone** for all eternity. A teenager or single adult might turn to his or her Spiritual Assembly or spiritual leaders to consult with them about how to prepare for marriage. Throughout the process of building a friendship, dating, courting, exploring compatibility, and deciding to marry, a couple will use consultation extensively. A couple might also consult with a group of friends to seek input on their relationship. Individuals and couples can consult with their parents at any point in the process they choose to do so. And certainly consultation is likely to be part of effective parental consent, a law of Bahá'u'lláh's explored in depth in Chapters 31-33. Once a couple is married, consultation also becomes an essential part of the family relationship.

While there is some guidance about how to consult, there is great latitude with whom you consult and what methods to use—**use your creativity**! Consultation isn't just people sitting around a meeting table with someone taking notes (although that's certainly one way it is used). Ever consult while walking backward?! At the seashore? In the car? On a mountain?

Consultation can be used for collecting input and guidance and often leads to decisions being made. Below are basic steps that apply across most consultation scenarios.

Consultation Steps

- ❖ Pray to establish oneness and remain in a state of mindfulness.
- ❖ Identify and state the problem/issue so there is a common focal point.
- ❖ Gather the facts from all relevant sources.
- ❖ Identify and agree upon the spiritual principles that are relevant.
- ❖ Have a frank and loving discussion and apply the spiritual principles to the facts.
- ❖ Turn to God for guidance (pray and meditate).
- ❖ Make a decision based on the principles.
- ❖ Carry out the decision with wholehearted support, trusting in God.
- ❖ Evaluate the outcome.

When you are in a consultation situation, the thoughts or ideas expressed are no longer those of the person who expressed them; everyone can build on them, and the person who gave the input is free to change his or her mind. All those who were part of the consultation and those affected by the consultation must wholeheartedly act on the final decision in unity, even if a majority decision is reached rather than a unanimous one. If people choose to not follow the

> See Chapters 20 and 21 for further information about communication and consultation.

decision, then it becomes very difficult for anyone to know if it was correct or not, and it is difficult to quickly choose a new direction based on facts. It's like being in the middle of the lake in a boat with half the crew rowing one way and half rowing the other way—not much progress is made.

When you **consult as a couple** and there are only two of you, there obviously cannot be a majority decision. Therefore, even when it's difficult, you must come to a unified decision. This may require multiple consultation sessions on the same topic, especially if the matter is very important. At times, the outcome may include one person deferring to the other. When this happens, it will be especially wise to re-consult after a period of time to ensure you are on the best track. Be cautious that you don't "give in" and harbor resentment when you are deferring. Your attitude will be more positive if you accept that you are making a conscious decision to defer and accept the decision as "ours." The decision is then a mutual commitment you both can wholeheartedly support.

If you are **having difficulty consulting**, set up a time for daily communication, share your day with each other, what went well and what didn't, and raise concerns and issues that came up. Have patience with yourself and your partner—gradually your skill will increase.

As you are using **consultation during your marriage preparation process**, you will likely find it a challenge to learn how to talk about sensitive and close-to-your-heart topics. It will take practice over time to become more comfortable with this.

Some Phrases That Contribute to Effective Consultation

- That's a good idea
- I see what you mean
- That's an interesting way of looking at it
- We are looking at this issue from two different angles
- That's a unique perspective
- I'd like to reflect on that
- Let me see if I understand
- I think I need a bit more explanation
- Let's take a break and come back later
- Let's say a prayer and then talk about it
- What are the spiritual principles that affect this decision?
- Let's find some more facts
- I'm confused—could you please explain it again?
- Please help me to understand
- That was helpful to me

> Remember that consultation is a form of "spiritual conference" held in love, and not just airing your personal views. It is asking for God's guidance in the process.

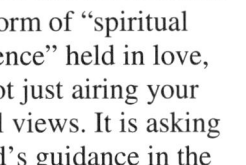

Some things that will be particularly helpful to increase your consultation comfort level are:
- Pray together
- Be very sensitive and careful about the words you use
- Be very aware of the potential effect of your words on the other
- Keep listening and resist the natural temptation to become defensive
- Check for understanding
- Pay attention to when you feel the need to request a pause and take a break

Is it easy to use consultation? No. It's a skill that everyone must learn and develop. Getting your ego out of the way, being frank, courteous, loving, and open-minded all at the same time takes practice. As does full participation and sharing thoughts and feelings frankly and lovingly. So, at times you will be happy with how it flows, and at times you won't. Don't give up on it though—persevere. It will be an invaluable skill for you to use throughout your life, including with a potential marriage partner and after marriage.

Note: There are five steps for making decisions in Chapter 30 on page 252.

⇒ Mixing the past with the present can confuse the current consultation and interfere with its effectiveness. Try to be aware when you are bringing incidents and emotions from the past into the discussion and straying from the current facts and feelings.

⇒ You may find it helpful to read *Consultation, A Universal Lamp of Guidance*, by John E. Kolstoe.

 Questions for Reflection and Discussion

1. How do you think that the important decisions in a marriage are best handled? (Examples: job changes, having children, buying a house, moving)
2. What experience have you had with consultation?
3. How do you feel when you are consulting?
4. What is the role of careful planning compared to allowing life "to just happen" and responding when it does? Which are you more comfortable with? Do you feel that is the most appropriate approach?
5. How can you improve your consultation skills?
6. When have you found consultation useful?

1. Pray, meditate, reflect, and write in your journal about your consultation skills and experiences.

2. Use Worksheet 3A to assess your consultation skills.

Marriage Can Be Forever—Preparation Counts!

3. Discuss the following:

**Who do you want to consult with
during the process of preparing for marriage?**

What do you want to request from them?

What are their responsibilities?

Date: _____

Worksheet 3A: Consultation Skill Level

DIRECTIONS: Review the quotes about consultation at the beginning of the chapter, pray, and then look over the list below. Each item addresses an aspect of your speaking and listening style. Often the way people speak and respond to others during consultation will affect the quality of the interactions and the ability of the group to reach a decision.

1. Look at each consultation item, consider the frequency with which you *currently* exhibit these behaviors, and circle the appropriate rating between 1 and 5. It will be helpful to ask someone who has recently consulted with you for his/her assessment of your style as well.

2. Go back through the list and put a checkmark (✓) on the line to the right of your rating for items where you need more *practice and skill development*.

3. At the bottom of the worksheet, note your goals and decide on a date to reassess your progress.

Note: Marriage Therapist Keyvan Geula contributed to this worksheet.

Worksheets may be printed from www.claricomm.com/publishing

Rarely	1	2	3	4	5	Usually

When you consult with others, how often do you: Rating   ✓

1. Stay focused and on the subject?   1 2 3 4 5 ___
2. Avoid dominating the consultation?   1 2 3 4 5 ___
3. Stay focused on the present and avoid bringing up the past?   1 2 3 4 5 ___
4. Carefully consider views already expressed before speaking?   1 2 3 4 5 ___
5. Graciously accept the others' views if you believe they are right?   1 2 3 4 5 ___
6. Share your views frankly but with courtesy, kindness, and goodwill?   1 2 3 4 5 ___
7. Express opinions as contributions, not "truth"?   1 2 3 4 5 ___
8. Consciously adjust your tone or body language to show you care?   1 2 3 4 5 ___
9. Suspend judgment to see if views of others make more sense to you?   1 2 3 4 5 ___
10. Willingly offer your opinion to be challenged in the interest of truth?   1 2 3 4 5 ___
11. Pause and ask for a break or prayer when you feel anger or frustration?   1 2 3 4 5 ___
12. Limit your talking so that you do not lose the attention of your listeners?   1 2 3 4 5 ___
13. Praise your listeners for their sound views and fairness?   1 2 3 4 5 ___
14. Patiently listen to others?   1 2 3 4 5 ___
15. Avoid talking *under* others (slower, softer, or too little) to control or shame them?   1 2 3 4 5 ___
16. Avoid talking *over* others (faster, louder, or constantly interrupting) to dominate them?   1 2 3 4 5 ___
17. Avoid taking offense if someone disagrees with you?   1 2 3 4 5 ___
18. Say, "Let me see if I understand you correctly" before responding?   1 2 3 4 5 ___
19. Avoid using remarks or gestures that ridicule or make fun of others?   1 2 3 4 5 ___
20. Ask for differing views and ideas to expand understanding and awareness?   1 2 3 4 5 ___
21. Say what you think instead of saying one thing but thinking and feeling something else?   1 2 3 4 5 ___

Rarely	1	2	3	4	5	Usually

When you consult with others, how often do you: Rating   ✓

22. Remember that being united and searching for truth is far more important than being right? 1 2 3 4 5 ___
23. Steer away from telling others what they should and should not think, feel, or want? 1 2 3 4 5 ___
24. Humbly ask for a summary of what you have said, to ensure accuracy? 1 2 3 4 5 ___
25. Briefly reflect, pause, and take a deep breath before you respond? 1 2 3 4 5 ___
26. Respect the personal space (closeness/distance) of others, and back up or move? 1 2 3 4 5 ___
27. Sincerely pause and ask if you are making sense? 1 2 3 4 5 ___
28. Reframe and rethink your initial thoughts out of consideration for others' feelings? 1 2 3 4 5 ___
29. Use appropriate humor to de-escalate a tense conversation? 1 2 3 4 5 ___
30. Use a kindly manner and voice to express concerns and grievances? 1 2 3 4 5 ___
31. Try to understand and respect others' points of view instead of complaining and criticizing them for disagreeing with you? 1 2 3 4 5 ___
32. Let go of your own thoughts and feelings in the interest of emerging ones? 1 2 3 4 5 ___
33. Avoid voicing your opinion as right and defending it with great passion? 1 2 3 4 5 ___
34. Avoid belittling others' thoughts or opinions? 1 2 3 4 5 ___
35. Apologize when you are in the wrong? 1 2 3 4 5 ___
36. Remember others' virtues and strengths and not their shortcomings? 1 2 3 4 5 ___
37. Put yourself in the other's situation and seek to understand his/her feelings? 1 2 3 4 5 ___
38. Share your feelings and take responsibility for them? 1 2 3 4 5 ___
39. Trust the consultation process as a channel for guidance? 1 2 3 4 5 ___
40. Fully support the decision in deeds and words? 1 2 3 4 5 ___

1. These are my goals for improving my consultation skills (especially where you circled numbers 1, 2, or 3):
   _____
   _____

2. Determine what situations you can get involved in to improve your consultation skills, and volunteer to get involved. Some examples might be serving on a committee, a non-profit board of directors, or on a team where you work. Perhaps there is a youth group activity that needs assistance, or a community neighborhood association. [**Note:** These groups may be unfamiliar with the concept of consultation, so you may actually have to introduce it to them.]
   a. _____
   b. _____
   c. _____

3. I will reassess my progress on this date: _____ (Mark it on your calendar.)

Step 2

Get Yourself Ready: Starting Your Search

Reaching

Reach up, reach in, and reach out
Reaching each and every day
Up to God in prayer
In to my true essence
Out to those nearby

Reach up, reach in, and reach out
Reaching up I tap a Power
That comes from nowhere else
Reaching in that Power connects
So strongly to myself
Reaching out the circle closes
And love begins to flow

Reach up, reach in, and reach out
Without reaching up
The well runs dry
Without reaching in
I live a lie
Without reaching out
I stop my growth

Reach up, reach in, and reach out
The reaching must be part of life
Over and over every day
Reach up, reach in, and reach out

~ Craig A. Farnsworth and Susanne Mariella Alexander

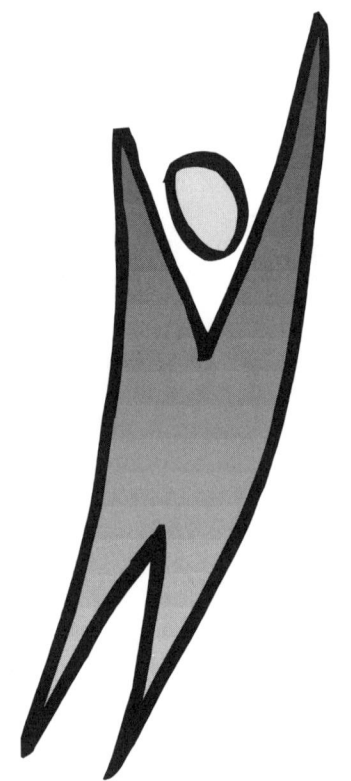

An Observation

I look into your eyes.
I see poetry and music written there for me.
I see many things that are not there.

~ Judy Parsley

CHAPTER 4 – You *Think* You Know: Deciphering Expectations

Focus Points
- Defining expectations
- Understanding your expectations of marriage
- Expectations in Western culture
- Realistic and unrealistic expectations

A Couple's Story

Lindsay: "You want backrubs every night from your husband?" says Lindsay to her friend Chandra. "It would be nice, but get real! How many guys do you think actually do stuff like that?"

"I don't care if it's realistic or not," says Chandra. "If he loves me he'll do anything I want him to."

"The most important thing to me is that my husband talks to me," says Lindsay. "I don't want to be with one of those guys that shuts you out and thinks that they're too cool to talk about their feelings. I want him to be like one of my closest friends. And a backrub or two wouldn't hurt!"

∞

James: "There's no way I want to be with a helpless female that expects me to do everything for her," James says to his friend Tony. "I don't mind doing stuff around the house, but I expect her to be able to hammer in a nail or take out the trash, if that's what needs to happen."

"Not me," Tony responds. "I know I'm old fashioned, but I want to be the man of the house, and I expect her to leave those things for me to do."

"I don't know, I think I want things to be a little more balanced," says James. "Me, I'm going for a partnership. And it wouldn't hurt if she's good looking, too!"

Quotes for Guidance

* Beautify your tongues, O people, with truthfulness, and adorn your souls with the ornament of honesty.
    (Bahá'u'lláh: *Gleanings from the Writings of Bahá'u'lláh*, p. 297)

* We cherish the hope that this people will henceforth shield themselves from vain hopes and idle fancies....
    (Bahá'u'lláh: *Gleanings from the Writings of Bahá'u'lláh*, pp. 69-70)

✹ Set your faces toward unity, and let the radiance of its light shine upon you. Gather ye together, and for the sake of God resolve to root out whatever is the source of contention amongst you.... Arise and, armed with the power of faith, shatter to pieces the gods of your vain imaginings, the sowers of dissension amongst you. Cleave unto that which draweth you together and uniteth you.
   (Bahá'u'lláh: *Gleanings from the Writings of Bahá'u'lláh*, pp. 217-218)

✹ O God! Refresh and gladden my spirit. Purify my heart. Illumine my powers. I lay all my affairs in Thy hand. Thou art my Guide and my Refuge. I will no longer be sorrowful and grieved; I will be a happy and joyful being. O God! I will no longer be full of anxiety, nor will I let trouble harass me. I will not dwell on the unpleasant things of life.
   O God! Thou art more friend to me than I am to myself. I dedicate myself to Thee, O Lord.
   ('Abdu'l-Bahá: *Bahá'í Prayers* (US 2002), p. 174-175)

✹ The first teaching of Bahá'u'lláh is the duty incumbent upon all to investigate reality. What does it mean to investigate reality? It means that man must forget all hearsay and examine truth himself, for he does not know whether statements he hears are in accordance with reality or not. Wherever he finds truth or reality, he must hold to it, forsaking, discarding all else; for outside of reality there is naught but superstition and imagination.
   ('Abdu'l-Bahá: *Promulgation of Universal Peace*, p. 62)

✹ He does not want the friends to be fearful, or to dwell upon the unpleasant possibilities of the future....
   (On behalf of Shoghi Effendi: *Lights of Guidance*, p. 299)

Perspectives to Consider

Merely mentioning the word "marriage" prompts most people to file swiftly through dozens of mental images and emotional experiences. Everyone has had the opportunity in life to **observe people who are married** and thinking about getting married. In some cases, the people are your parents. Beyond this close example, you may have watched marriages among other relatives, friends, and neighbors. Perhaps you were engaged or married before—maybe more than once. Sometimes you have observed or participated in positive relationships, and other times the relationships may not have gone well. You may have observed marriages that resulted in divorce, your own parents, or even you may have been divorced before.

In addition to your own observations, you have probably read books or magazines and watched movies that give you a variety of perspectives on what a relationship is "supposed" to look and be like. Many people have the impression that love and intimacy are instantaneous events rather than a process that develops over time. Phrases like "falling in love" and "love at first sight" often reflect momentary attraction and are not indicators that a relationship will last.

Relationships and marriages become stronger when you follow spiritual principles rather than make up your own rules or apply expectations based on the abundant images of passion and romance in magazines, music, books, and other media. In Western culture particularly there is often such an extreme of idealism and romanticism (and an emphasis on having amazing sex) on the one hand and extreme cynicism on the other hand. Couples have no hope of ever fulfilling the romanticized version and must struggle against the expectations of the cynical version.

Your observations and experiences color your perception of marriage and cause you to form **expectations of how things will or should be**. You may predict your own ability to be involved in a lasting and healthy marriage based upon them. The impressions gained from others' experiences might so greatly influence you that you are unwilling to consider being married yourself. Or, your expectations of marriage may include measuring up to other people's successes.

Marriage Can Be Forever—Preparation Counts!

The Bahá'í Writings offer a recreated model of ideal **marriage based on a strong spiritual foundation**, something that has traditionally been part of marriage and is now being renewed. This evolving model will be the building block for families and for a transformed, unified society. There is no promise in these Teachings that establishing and developing marriages and families is easy, and certainly, it is an ongoing, learning process. There are no quick-action pills to swallow or magic wands to wave to create instant happiness and trouble-free relationships.

You might expect to be taken care of, never be lonely, have all your problems solved and needs satisfied, or to always be happy. These expectations are not realistic in anyone's life and certainly not in marriage. Some of your needs will be met, especially for companionship, and you may be happy much of the time, but a marriage certificate is not a warranty that there will not be challenges in your relationship.

If you are thinking of marrying and you are past childbearing age, what are your expectations of marriage? In what ways are they different from when you were in your teens or twenties? You may have children from previous relationships and be considering grandchildren. You could be marrying someone simply for companionship, and children are not part of the picture at all. What are your expectations of handling health issues as you age?

Think about what you will set up in a marriage if you have **unrealistic expectations**. If your marriage partner can't live up to them, will you be happy? What if he or she doesn't know about your invisible standard and is frustrated by not being able to please you? Initially, neither of you may even realize the source of these frustrations.

What about **realistic expectations**? It *is* reasonable to expect your partner to be faithful to you, for instance. You might reasonably expect to live together after marriage (instead of in different cities or countries). You could expect to continue your education after marriage. Although all these expectations seem reasonable, they will only happen if you and your partner agree on them. It is this agreement that moves the expectation from being unstated (even unknown) into being a mutual commitment and then into reality.

Coaching

⇒ You may find it helpful to ask a Spiritual Assembly representative, clergyperson, or other respected person to facilitate and assist you individually or as a couple with explorations and discussions about expectations.

⇒ Once you have identified a potential marriage partner, it is wise for the two of you to have very frank and honest discussions about the expectations you each have about marriage generally and about marriage to each other specifically. If you clarify these beforehand, you can avoid many potentially disunifying conflicts. Often couples are able to assist one another in dismantling and even eliminating long-held idealistic or unreasonable ideas about marriage, allowing them to go forward less inhibited by past impressions and experiences. These discussions allow you to agree which expectations are reasonable and make a mutual commitment to fulfill them with action.

Chapter 4 – You *Think* You Know: Deciphering Expectations

? Questions for Reflection and Discussion

Note: While these questions below will be useful for consultation with a partner at some point in time, they are intended to be for self-reflection at this stage, perhaps by writing in a journal.

1. What behaviors do you believe are appropriate when a couple is alone but never appropriate in public?
2. What are your beliefs about husbands and wives praying or not praying together?
3. What spiritual activities do you think are good ones for couples to participate in?
4. Do you have expectations about special events like birthdays or anniversaries? (Examples: receiving flowers, giving cards, having parties)
5. Is it important or not important to have a well-developed career before marriage?
6. Do you expect your spouse to greet you at the door when you walk in?
7. What expectations do you have about sexual experiences between wives and husbands?
8. What are your expectations about food and mealtimes? Specific foods or food preparation? Eating together? Are meals to be ready at the same times every day?
9. How much time alone and how much time together would you want to spend when you are both free?
10. What expectations do you have about having children? Having grandchildren?
11. What are your beliefs about your spouse crying when he or she is upset?
12. Are there things that are unwise to share with your dating or courting partner? Things you think are best kept from your partner once you are engaged? From your spouse?
13. What are your expectations about tests and difficulties arising during marriage and how they might be handled?
14. How much income do you expect to have after marriage? Will you generate this together, or will just one of you?
15. What physical needs do you expect your spouse to meet for you?
16. What spiritual needs do you expect your spouse to meet for you?
17. What emotional support and friendship do you expect your spouse to provide you compared to other people? How would you adapt if you and your spouse felt differently about this?
18. What needs do you expect to have met by others or resources outside your marriage?
19. What are your expectations about arguments or disagreements and how to resolve them?

Activities

1. Pray, meditate, reflect, and write in your journal about your expectations of marriage.

2. Use Worksheet 4A to give careful thought to your wide range of expectations about marriage.

3. Complete Worksheet 4B as an exercise envisioning your ideal marriage, and try to understand what is realistic and what is not.

Date: _____

Worksheet 4A: Identify Your Expectations

DIRECTIONS: The purpose of this worksheet is to help you identify the spiritual, emotional, physical, and mental expectations you have of marriage, whether the expectations are realistic, and why you expect them to happen. First, mentally picture the most significant marriages you have been in or observed.
- Do you have beliefs that wives or husbands should generally or always behave a certain way?
- Think about such areas as: money, diet, cleanliness, orderliness, responsibilities and relationships with Bahá'í/religious service, community/civic service, children, sex, celebrations, vacations, in-laws, education, exercise, location, property, arguments, decision-making, friends, handling tests and difficulties, drugs/alcohol, sports or recreation, work demands, career paths, sharing household responsibilities, lifestyle, conversation, dress, behavior, attitudes, etc.

Next, write down your expectations on the worksheet. After you have filled in as many possibilities as you can think of, set aside the sheet for a while, perhaps overnight or for a few days (set a specific date in your calendar to re-look at the worksheet). Turn back to it and re-ask yourself honestly whether your expectations are realistic for your own marriage (or for others').

Note: If you are already in a relationship, try to distance yourself mentally from your current situation so you are not tempted to change your list based on him or her

Worksheets may be printed from www.claricomm.com/publishing

What are your expectations of marriage and of your future spouse?	Realistic?		Reason
	Yes	No	
Example: Husbands and wives agree on everything		✓	People have different opinions
Example: I should always receive expensive presents on wedding anniversaries		✓	Not financially responsible
Example: Major financial decisions should be made through consultation	✓		Follows spiritual principle

1. How realistic or desirable is it that what you listed above would occur this way in your own marriage? Think about and write about why or why not:

_____

_____

Date: _____

Worksheet 4B: A Vision of Your Marriage

DIRECTIONS: This is an exercise to help you envision what a marriage for you might include. It may also assist you with distinguishing what might be realistic and what might be ideal but unattainable. As you dream and hope about marriage, you start to create a picture in your mind and heart of what marriage can be like for you. While your vision may be somewhat unrealistic at this stage, this exercise will help you start to understand the importance marriage has to you and the positive facets that you'll be able to help create.

Worksheets may be printed from www.claricomm.com/publishing

1. What do you see in other people's marriages that you dislike or that you admire?

Qualities of the Worst Marriages	**Qualities of the Best Marriages**
_____	_____

2. Which are the most important positive qualities you want to see in *your* marriage?

   _____   _____

3. What else describes the perfect, successful marriage for you? Be as specific as possible.

   _____

Marriage Can Be Forever—Preparation Counts!

4. What are the potentially unrealistic aspects of this ideal?
   a. _____
   b. _____
   c. _____
   d. _____

5. What parts of your ideal do you realistically think are attainable?

   _____
   _____
   _____
   _____

6. Based on your study of books about marriage and the quotes in this book, what are four actions you could take that could assist you in preparing to achieve a realistically wonderful marriage? (Examples: praying, planning a service project, babysitting for an afternoon)
   a. _____
   b. _____
   c. _____
   d. _____

> A person who is truly in love is like a lamp that is lit and gives off a lovely light. He or she is different from a person who is not in love. Such a person may still be a very good lamp but will not give off light or warmth. Many of us look for and are attracted by the shape of the lamp rather than its light, although we are looking for warmth and light.
>
> ~ Mehri Sefidvash, *Coral and Pearls*, p. 83

To Be Conscious

To be conscious
    Is to feel
    Is to see
    Is to be present in the moment

To be conscious
    Is true life
    Not sleepwalking
    Through the hallways

To be conscious
    Is to hear
    Is to speak
    From the depths of my soul

To be conscious
    Is the key
    To unlock the floodgates
    To enter into true life.

To be conscious
    Is to be present
    And honor the presence
    In each soul all about.

To be conscious
    Will give strength
    To build the future
    Out of this moment.

To be conscious
    Is my goal
    Is my hope
    Is my desire.

For without this I am trapped as a prisoner of my thoughts.

~ Craig Farnsworth

CHAPTER 5 – Moving On: Learning from Relationships

Focus Points
- Assessing relationships in your life
- Assessing yourself before, during, and after a close relationship ends
- Closure on emotions from previous relationships
- Identifying any lessons learned
- Fear of failure
- Determining your motives for wanting to be married
- Reassessing and resetting your goals

A Couple's Story

Lindsay (Talking with Stacy; following dates with a fellow student and becoming upset at things he does):

"What happened?" asks Stacy.

"Everything he did reminded me of some other guy I've dated," says Lindsay. "And one thing he did kept reminding me of my stepfather. And it wasn't even that he was a bad guy or anything. I just kept feeling upset when I was with him."

"You have major guy issues, Lindsay," says Stacy. "How are you ever going to get married when you get upset every time you date? I wonder if the campus counselor can help you?"

"I saw a counselor for a while in high school," says Lindsay, "but you're right, I think I need a bit more help to get past being hurt."

∞

James (to his friend, Tony after he breaks a date with someone he'd gone out with a few times):

"Man, she was a great girl," says Tony. "What are you doing?!"

"I'm sure she was thinking about breaking up with me anyway," says James. "No way am *I* getting rejected."

"You are messed up in the head," says Tony. "How are you going to get married someday if you walk out whenever things get serious? You'd better get over it."

James pauses and then concludes. "I guess if I meet someone really special, I'm going to have to, aren't I?"

Quotes for Guidance

✸ He hath known God who hath known himself.
   (Bahá'u'lláh: *Gleanings from the Writings of Bahá'u'lláh*, p. 178)

✹ O SON OF BEING! Bring thyself to account each day ere thou art summoned to a reckoning; for death, unheralded, shall come upon thee and thou shalt be called to give account for thy deeds.
   (Bahá'u'lláh: *Hidden Words*, Arabic No. 31)

✹ No man shall attain the shores of the ocean of true understanding except he be detached from all that is in heaven and on earth.
   (Bahá'u'lláh: *Kitáb-i-Íqán*, p. 3)

✹ The first teaching of Bahá'u'lláh is the duty incumbent upon all to investigate reality. What does it mean to investigate reality? It means that man must forget all hearsay and examine truth himself, for he does not know whether statements he hears are in accordance with reality or not. Wherever he finds truth or reality, he must hold to it, forsaking, discarding all else; for outside of reality there is naught but superstition and imagination.
   ('Abdu'l-Bahá: *Promulgation of Universal Peace*, p. 62)

Perspectives to Consider

Each relationship that you have builds on every other relationship. Generally, your mother/father is the first person you interact with of the opposite sex. As you go through childhood, each friendship, sibling relationship, and teacher brings a variety of lessons learned. These lessons provide the background for the "romantic" relationships you enter later. (See Chapter 17 about family relationships.)

Some people marry the first person with whom they have a close relationship, but most people have a number of experiences and relationships with people of the opposite sex before choosing to marry. Each of these is an opportunity for learning and growing. You will find it valuable to spend time assessing and understanding what worked well and what didn't in the relationships and what drew you into them.

As you **assess your past relationships**, look carefully at any problem you may have encountered. There may be a lesson you didn't recognize at the time, but your assessment now will give you clarity. Did you discover an area where greater character development is necessary? Did you learn that you have a number of mature strengths?

How were your interactions with the other person? Were you compatible in some areas but not in others? Had you made good judgments about his or her character? It will be good to identify what to repeat or not repeat in a future relationship or marriage.

Relationships are usually difficult to end, especially with honesty, tactfulness, and courage. Alternatively, a relationship may have ended because of something out of your control, such as death. **At the end of relationships**, you may be filled with a variety of emotions—sadness, happiness, anger, despair, the need for escape, and so on. All these emotions must be processed, accepted, and understood before you can effectively begin another relationship. At this initial stage, you might have insights about why the relationship failed or ended. ***Some insights, however, might only be possible with the passing of time and the calming of your emotions.*** Unresolved emotions have a tendency to resurface in subsequent relationships and cause confusion and negative reactions in a new partner. An increased understanding of your emotions will give you a greater ability to maintain unity in any future relationship.

When the relationship that has ended was long-term or very emotional, such as a marriage, you may need to have **professional counseling** to resolve lingering issues. Counselors can provide a safe and confidential place to express your feelings. They can often give perspectives on the relationship because they are not emotionally involved. Be cautious, however, that the counselor is familiar with the Bahá'í spiritual principles or the principles of your faith. For instance, some counselors have suggested a sexual affair to get over a previous relationship, which would be against most religious teachings. Your Spiritual Assembly or clergyperson may keep a list of trustworthy and knowledgeable counselors. You may also wish to meet with them for **spiritual counseling**.

Based on experiences in past relationships, you may have a **fear that you will fail at a future relationship**. This projection of the past into your present and future reduces your ability to have healthy relationships. Each person can choose to deal powerfully with this issue and refuse to base current choices on past difficulties, especially if you have taken steps to resolve the issues that caused the difficulties. It is possible for most people to create a marriage that shows a positive example to others, benefits the family, and serves the greater community.

When you are ready for a relationship again, this may be a good time to complete the worksheets in Chapter 7. What goals do you want to set so that you are actively involved in finding someone? Where do you want to go? Who do you want to assist you with preparing yourself and finding someone? How much time do you want to search for him/her? This is a good time to examine your motives for wanting to be married. Some may not be wise. Consider the list below.

Unwise Marriage Motivators

Many unhealthy reasons can draw a person into a relationship, setting up unhappiness down the road. Some of the signs to watch out for are:

- Pressure from friends, family, or your biological clock
- Feeling lonely and desperate
- Needing financial security
- Desiring sex, without solidifying the relationship first
- Thinking that anything would be better than being alone
- Needing to be distracted from stress at school, home, or work
- Wanting someone else to "fix" you or take care of you so you don't have to do your own personal development work
- Wanting to "fix" someone else
- Fear of hurting the other person if you break up or that they may do something drastic if you do
- Wanting to run away from problems of any kind
- Trying to compensate for your own inner emptiness
- Guilt that you aren't giving your parents a son-in-law or daughter-in-law and grandchildren
- Wanting a caretaker for you as you age

(See also Chapter 14 on compatibility.)

Coaching

⇒ Look to see if you were misled during the relationship into thinking that the person was the only possible one for you and there was some reason you were "meant to be" together. Sometimes going too far into this state of mind can blind you to things that are not working well in the relationship or to where there are true incompatibilities.

⇒ Review how well you were able to assess the character, personality, attitudes, and behavior of the person and see what you might do differently to understand these traits better. (See Chapters 6 and 19.)

⇒ Take time to pray, reflect, and evaluate previous relationships. Ensure that you have forgiven yourself and other people for what has happened. Take action if an apology or making amends is needed and appropriate. Seek professional or spiritual counseling if you require assistance in this area.

Questions for Reflection and Discussion

1. How has your relationship with your mother influenced your views of marriage relationships? Your relationship with your father? With your friends?
2. What is your history of romantic relationships? How many have there been? Short-term? Long-term?
3. How have you handled breakups or endings of previous relationships (including previous marriages)? What were the challenges and outcomes learned from the experiences?
4. What issues from previous relationships are unresolved and might be carried forward to your next relationship/marriage? What are your plans to resolve them?
5. What effort, beliefs, attitudes, actions, and so on are needed to make a relationship and marriage work? What is most important? What is most destructive?
6. Did you start to take each other for granted and quit nurturing your relationship? How might you prevent this from happening another time?
7. If your previous partner died, how have you/are you handling the grieving process?
8. How will you relate to other men and women outside of marriage?
9. Do you understand the reasons that your parents or friends have gone through breakups or divorces? How might those outcomes have been avoided if it were you? What are your fears about divorce?
10. What is your understanding of how to prevent divorce from happening?
11. Are there things from previous relationships that you will definitely share with a spouse? Things you will keep private?
12. What is your experience with choosing partners that are right for you? Wrong for you in some important way? Do your partners consistently have major problems they are dealing with, such as alcoholism, abuse, etc.?
13. Have you stayed friends with someone after a romantic relationship broke up? How have subsequent partners viewed this relationship? Is jealousy an issue?
14. What are your fears about being in a relationship?
15. What could you do to build your confidence about being in a successful marriage?
16. If you are currently in a new relationship, do you know about each other's previous relationships? Do you need to be? Do you want to be?

Activities

1. Pray, meditate, reflect, and write in your journal about all the relationships you have had in your life.

2. Use Worksheet 5A to record what you have learned from each major relationship you have had in your life.

3. Use Worksheet 5B to assess any unfinished business, lingering issues, incomplete communications, and so on with any of these relationships. Take any necessary actions to resolve them.

4. Use Worksheet 5C to assist you in identifying your strengths and development needs as a potential spouse.

Date: _____

Worksheet 5A: Learning from Relationships

DIRECTIONS: First, list all your significant relationships from the past and present in the worksheet below, including family members, close friendships, and romantic/marital relationships. Next, in the column by each relationship, identify what lessons you have learned, including what you have learned about yourself that might relate to marriage and family life. Examples of this might include:
- ⇒ Mother: How important it is to be listened to and accepted regardless of the circumstances.
- ⇒ Jessica (friend): How harmful it is to tell a lie.

Think about both positive and negative experiences – both of which lead to learning.
What would you want to repeat? What would you not want to repeat? You may find it helpful to do this worksheet with someone else. Finally, for further insight, seek input from someone else who had the opportunity to observe the relationship you list.

Worksheets may be printed from www.claricomm.com/publishing

Relationship	What I Learned

Marriage Can Be Forever—Preparation Counts!

Date: _____

Worksheet 5B: Cleaning Up Previous Relationships

DIRECTIONS: Having assessed your previous relationships, you may have identified some unfinished business, lingering issues, incomplete communications, and so on in some of these relationships. This worksheet will give you an opportunity to clarify whatever needs to be handled to free you in moving forward with confidence. *Be aware that there are some circumstances where it might be unwise, damaging, or unsafe to be in direct communication with someone from your past. If you have any concerns of this nature, please consult a professional or trusted advisor before taking action.* **Remember, too, that you can always pray and write in a journal to assist you with emotionally resolving the relationship.**

Worksheets may be printed from www.claricomm.com/publishing

1. Which relationships you raise feelings of regret, anger, resentment, or unresolved attachment?

   _____
   _____
   _____

2. What will you do to resolve these feelings? (Examples: pray, forgive, communicate)

   _____
   _____

3. Are there any relationships where you may choose to be in communication to say something that was left unsaid, to ask for forgiveness, apologize, or clear up a misunderstanding, and so on? Which ones? [**Note:** Remember to avoid potentially destructive interactions; consult others if you are unsure.]

   _____
   _____
   _____

4. What, if anything, is in the way of you handling these communications? What support do you need?

   _____
   _____
   _____

5. Once you have taken action, note the outcome below:

   _____
   _____
   _____

6. How do you feel now? What else you need to do?

   _____
   _____
   _____

Marriage Can Be Forever—Preparation Counts!

Date: _____

Worksheet 5C: Developing Yourself as an Excellent Spouse

DIRECTIONS: Complete the following questions to identify your strengths and development needs as a potential spouse.

Worksheets may be printed from www.claricomm.com/publishing

1. List three things you have done very well in current or past relationships, such as with someone you dated, a previous spouse, family members, or close friends.

    a. _____
    b. _____
    c. _____

2. List three qualities you would like to develop to be a better future spouse.

    a. _____
    b. _____
    c. _____

3. Talk to other people that you respect and who know you well. What do they think are your strengths as a potential spouse?

    a. _____
    b. _____
    c. _____

4. What improvements do they think you could make?

    a. _____
    b. _____
    c. _____

Reflection:

1. How does your self-perception differ from or match that of others' about you?
   _____
   _____

2. Where would you like to concentrate your efforts for further growth?
   _____
   _____

3. What are some goals to accomplish this growth?
   _____
   _____

4. By when will you assess your progress? Date: _____ (Mark it in your calendar.)

Marriage Can Be Forever—Preparation Counts!

prayerfulness reverence flexibility integrity

(border words, left side, top to bottom): confidence, helpfulness, excellence, honesty, thankfulness

(border words, right side, top to bottom): faithfulness, courtesy, justice, honor, service, gentleness

Speak the Language of the Virtues

Language has great influence to empower or discourage. Self-esteem is built when shaming, blaming language is replaced by acknowledging each other for the virtues we see or calling each other to the virtues that are needed. If you fill a home, a school, or a workplace with words such as lazy, stupid, and bad, that is the behavior which follows, but if you use words such as courage, helpfulness, and flexibility, you are empowering those behaviors, whether in a child, an employee, or a friend.

~ Linda Kavelin-Popov, *The Family Virtues Guide*, p. 19

creativity tolerance courage determination

CHAPTER 6 – Your Bedrock: Assessing Character

Focus Points
- Defining character
- Self-knowledge and self-preparation
- Perceiving your partner's character
- Difference between character and faith
- Aspects of character
- Self-justification, denial, and blind spots

A Couple's Story

Lindsay: Lindsay rushes through the college hallways with her engineering term paper in her hand. Unfortunately the paper is a day late. "Here's the paper," she says to her professor. "I, uh, had a family emergency come up. I'm sorry it's late."

The professor looks at her, clearly doubting her excuse, but he accepts the paper. That evening, Lindsay's conscience is troubling her. Lying is not something she is comfortable with or usually does. She just doesn't want to get a poor grade on the paper. By the next morning, however, she decides she doesn't want this on her conscience and that she has made a choice that doesn't respect either herself or the professor. She heads across campus to find him.

"I'm sorry, Professor Jacobs, I need to tell you that I wasn't exactly truthful when I handed in my paper. There was no family emergency. I just didn't get it done on time. I'm willing to accept a lower grade for handing it in late."

⁂

James (*to himself*): *Man, this character inventory in this marriage preparation book is tough. I'm glad there are definitions in the back. Let's see if I can think of some examples…Marianna thought I was generous with gifts. I'm starting to hang out with Tony and I helped him change his tire the other day, so I can check off "helpfulness." Shamara thought I was courteous to her Mom when I met her… And I know I'm responsible—I've done a good job caring for Dad since his heart attack. But I could sure do some work on orderliness—my apartment would probably drive anyone crazy, and I haven't been involved in much community service lately. Prayerfulness could use a boost, too. Better set some goals, I guess….*

Quotes for Guidance

✺ …man should know his own self and recognize that which leadeth unto loftiness or lowliness, glory or abasement, wealth or poverty.
   (Bahá'u'lláh: *Tablets of Bahá'u'lláh*, p. 35)

Chapter 6 – Your Bedrock: Assessing Character

❋ Let there be naught in your demeanor of which sound and upright minds would disapprove, and make not yourselves the playthings of the ignorant. Well is it with him who hath adorned himself with the vesture of seemly conduct and a praiseworthy character. He is assuredly reckoned with those who aid their Lord through distinctive and outstanding deeds.
(Bahá'u'lláh: *Kitáb-i-Aqdas*, p. 77)

❋ Bahá'í marriage is the commitment of the two parties one to the other, and their mutual attachment of mind and heart. Each must, however, exercise the utmost care to become thoroughly acquainted with the character of the other, that the binding covenant between them may be a tie that will endure forever. Their purpose must be this: to become loving companions and comrades and at one with each other for time and eternity....
('Abdu'l-Bahá: *Selections from the Writings of 'Abdu'l-Bahá*, p. 118)

❋ God has given man the eye of investigation by which he may see and recognize truth.... Man is not intended to see through the eyes of another, hear through another's ears nor comprehend with another's brain. Each human creature has individual endowment, power and responsibility in the creative plan of God. Therefore, depend upon your own reason and judgment and adhere to the outcome of your own investigation….
('Abdu'l-Bahá: *Promulgation of Universal Peace*, p. 293)

❋ In order to achieve this cordial unity one of the first essentials insisted on by Bahá'u'lláh and 'Abdu'l-Bahá is that we resist the natural tendency to let our attention dwell on the faults and failings of others rather than on our own. Each of us is responsible for one life only, and that is our own. Each of us is immeasurably far from being "perfect as our heavenly father is perfect" and the task of perfecting our own life and character is one that requires all our attention, our will-power and energy.
(Shoghi Effendi: *Living the Life*, pp. 3-4)

❋ There is a difference between character and faith; it is often very hard to accept this fact and put up with it, but the fact remains that a person may believe in and love [the Bahá'í Faith]—even to being ready to die for it—and yet not have a good personal character, or possess traits at variance with the teachings. We should try to change, to let the Power of God help recreate us and make us true Bahá'ís in deed as well as in belief. But sometimes the process is slow, sometimes it never happens because the individual does not try hard enough.
(Shoghi Effendi: *Unfolding Destiny*, p. 440)

❋ A couple should study each other's character and spend time getting to know each other before they decide to marry, and when they do marry it should be with the intention of establishing an eternal bond.
(On behalf of the Universal House of Justice: *Lights of Guidance*, p. 380)

Perspectives to Consider

The first task as you think about your future marriage is to use reflection, prayer, and meditation to **look completely and honestly** at yourself. This will assist you with understanding your character strengths and weaknesses. Character qualities, such as honesty, friendliness, and helpfulness are visible as actions that affect other people. How will your character affect a marriage partner?

Character is your moral or ethical strength, and it is tested and developed over time. No one would expect someone to be perfect when they get married...or would they?! Indeed, people may have that expectation. You might even find that *you* have that expectation if you pause and honestly evaluate your hopes for a partner. While it is unrealistic to expect perfection from others, or yourself, it is wise to consider being at a certain stage in development before attempting eternal partnership and parenthood. And, since most of your character is formed early in life, an honest assessment of it now will give you a good idea of your readiness for marriage.

Character and personality are somewhat linked with each other. Character can be considered a part of your personality, which is the total sum of your character, behavioral, temperamental, emotional, and mental traits. For this workbook, however, they have been separated into character qualities here in Step 2, using some of the virtues as a guide to assessing character; and personality, attitudes, and behavior are part of Step 4 on compatibility (See Chapter 19).

Ideally, you will do your character assessment before you have a potential partner in your life, although it is valuable at any juncture and is likely to be an ongoing part of your life. The earlier in your life you do the self-assessment, the more time you will have to identify your strengths and build on them, as well as identify your weaknesses, and concentrate on building them into strengths. Self-honesty is often very difficult. It's easy for you to make excuses for why you are the way you are or why you do the things you do. But addressing character issues and honestly accepting how you are or how you behave opens up the possibility for you to grow and change in new and positive directions. [**Note:** It is actually a very wise spiritual practice to do a behavior check every day to ensure your character is developing on a positive track.]

Part of character self-assessment is the ability to take **responsibility for yourself, your actions, and the outcome**. Being responsible includes understanding the nature and condition of your character. You cannot effectively address any character development issues unless you can see, understand, and accept your character the way it truly is. *A signal that you (or a partner) are unable or unwilling to take responsibility for your character is a pattern of blaming other people or circumstances for the outcomes of your own choices.*

One of the best ways to see the status of your own character development is to assess how well you understand specific aspects of **character virtues** and how often you practice them. Are you truthful, or do you lie regularly? Are you loyal to friends, or do you backbite about them every chance you get? Are you compassionate with your parents when they are having a difficult day, or are you rude to them and withhold assistance or support? Do you (or did you) do your schoolwork yourself, or do/did you cheat? Do you have the courage to try new things, or do you get scared and keep doing the same old things? Do you respect yourself and others, and are you loving to yourself and others as divine creations? In other words, when you look at yourself, how well are you showing virtuous behavior? When friends and family look at you, what do they see? Consider asking them for input. (**Note:** Definitions of many virtues are in Appendix A.)

Some virtues might be ones that you think are very important in a marriage. You will complete Worksheet 6A to help you look at them and see whether you are practicing them or not. If you aren't practicing these virtues, what can you do to further develop them? How will you be able to tell if you have improved? Are you happy, serving, and loving toward everyone, or only toward potential partners or others you want to impress?

Once you have a potential partner in your life, you begin the process of **assessing his or her character and behavior** to the best of your ability. This requires many high-quality interactions over time and the development of trust and intimacy—it's not something that can be done instantly. Often character assessments are very difficult, because people have a tendency to hide their negative qualities and only show their positive ones to others, especially "romantic" others. Before making a commitment to be married, however, you each must have a clear view of the other's virtues, strengths, and weaknesses, and how these show up in daily behavior. Showing your true selves is the ideal, even if it leads to less than perfect interactions as you assess compatibility. *Premarital* behavior and problems often become *marital* behavior and problems.

> One way to tell if you know the character of someone in your life is if you are asked to describe him/her to someone. If your friend says, "Tell me all about him!" or asks you about her, and all you can come up with is, "Oh, he is so nice," or "She is wonderful!" spend time concentrating on this area.
>
> Another warning sign could be if you can only describe the person in relation to you. For instance, when asked to tell what the person is like, you might say, "He's so good *to me*" or "She's always doing things *for me*." You must be skilled enough at assessing another person to be able to say he/she is generous, friendly, stubborn, and courageous, ***not just what their behavior is toward you.***

Marriage Can Be Forever—Preparation Counts!

From the beginning of a relationship, you will start to observe spiritual character qualities during your interactions. Honor and respect are part of the foundation of any relationship, and you can experience them at the moment you first meet someone. As you get to know each other, is there compassion for previous experiences? Are faithfulness and loyalty between you valued? Do you show trust and trustworthiness? Are you able to be prayerful together?

The more you do things together, the clearer you will be about whether the qualities of balance, mutuality, and equality are present in your relationship. The old model of male dominance is losing its viability. The new model of give and take, joint decision-making, full expression by both parties, and partnership is developing and taking flight. Can you use this new model of equality?

Just as it is often difficult to completely assess your own character and behavior due to **self-justification, blind spots, and lack of awareness**, it can be difficult to lift the veils that block your vision when assessing the character of someone else. Passion, romance, self-delusion, lack of regular contact, and many more things can get in the way. Being successful takes great patience, observation, reflection, prayer, and perseverance. Remember that you are also simply using your best judgment and stating your *perceptions* of their qualities—only God can completely know who we are.

You may resist this assessment process out of reluctance to being critical or judgmental. This is not about condemning yourself or someone else, but rather honestly understanding each other's character development. While your partner does not have to be "perfect," if there are character traits that will be a constant source of friction and disunity, it is better to know this before deciding to marry, and to consult about it in depth before you choose to marry.

> **Resistance to character assessment** might also arise because of concern that in-depth assessment of each other will interfere with or destroy "true love." In fact, love often grows stronger through a greater understanding of your partner's positive qualities and an appreciation of his or her wholeness, which includes some negatives. Mutual investigation of character is a consultative process that leads to insights, something that will bring you closer. Society teaches you more about how to look for specific standards of physical beauty rather than the beauty of character that ensures long-lasting happiness. This often bears no resemblance to the messages you receive in popular movies, music, or books. Physical attractiveness does not prevent divorce.

Spending time in activities together based on mutual interests can help in this character assessment. It's important to do a wide variety of activities together and to include rendering **service to others**. This calls on you to use the qualities of love, patience, compassion, helpfulness, kindness, and other important virtues in ways that other activities, like going to the movies, usually doesn't.

Character assessment is vital in determining whether to proceed with a potential marriage relationship or not. If either of you has a serious concern about some aspects of the other's behavior, you are wise to think carefully about marrying, and parents will want to carefully consider whether it is wise to give consent to the marriage (see Chapters 31 and 32). While it is painful to end a close relationship, it is always easier to do it before the commitment of marriage has taken place.

Coaching

⇒ The more specific you are about developing your character, and the more you persevere in your goals, the greater the chance of success. It can often be a good growth exercise to choose a specific virtue and focus on it for a day or a week. This will make you very conscious of opportunities to practice it.

⇒ Often you may have difficulty gaining a clear view of yourself—both your positive strengths and areas for growth. You may find it helpful to pray, meditate, and consult with a trusted and close friend or relative and ask him or her to assist you with this assessment.

⇒ Your character qualities may be well developed, or they may be uncut gems just waiting to be shaped and polished.

⇒ When each of you has individually completed his or her character assessment (Worksheet 6A), you will partially get to know each other's character through comparing your worksheets.

❓ Questions for Reflection and Discussion

Self-Assessment

1. What areas do you generally consider your strengths and your weaknesses?
2. What will be your strongest and weakest areas as a spouse?
3. What is your attitude toward yourself? Positive? Negative? Success? Failure? Person of worth? No good?
4. What do you feel are the important character qualities in a person that indicate he or she is mature enough and is spiritually prepared for marriage?
5. What character qualities in you or the other person are warning signs that either of you aren't ready for marriage?
6. What will enable you to be an enjoyable partner and parent?

After You Have a Potential Partner

1. Are you generally a good judge of character? If so, how do you know? How could you improve your skill in this area if this is not a strength?
2. Are you ever perceived as being overly judgmental or having unrealistically high standards? How might this affect the character assessment of another person?
3. What virtues are strongly developed in his/her character?
4. What are his/her negative qualities?
5. Are there any character weaknesses that you see?
6. Ask yourself specific questions for each of the virtues listed in Worksheet 6A. An example for the virtue of "determination" is:
   - Does he/she finish projects once they start or does he/she procrastinate or perpetually leave them only partly done? How do you respond to that?

Activities

1. Pray, meditate, reflect, and write in your journal about your character qualities.

2. Use Worksheet 6A as an aid in assessing your character. **Note:** If there are others who would live with you after marriage, such as a child or parent, you may wish to assess them as well.

3. Use Worksheet 6B (or your journal) to assist you with a character development plan for marriage.

4. When you have a special person in your life, go back to Worksheet 6A to assess his or her character.

Marriage Can Be Forever—Preparation Counts!

44   Chapter 6 – Your Bedrock: Assessing Character

Date: _____

Worksheet 6A: Assessing Virtues/Character Qualities

DIRECTIONS: The specific ways you and your partner act may suggest a strength or weakness in a character quality (see Appendix A for some definitions). Take time to assess both your own strengths and areas of growth and those of your potential partner. The chart below is one way of assessing character. ***Don't rush through this.***
- Place a checkmark (✓) in the strength or weakness columns next to each virtue/character quality. Note in the "Issues?" column if there are development issues. See Worksheet 6B to create a personal development plan.
- After finding a potential marriage partner, return to this worksheet and complete the columns below about him/her. Note if there are any maturity or compatibility issues.

Worksheets may be printed from www.claricomm.com/publishing

The list of the virtues below is taken from The Virtues Project, Inc., and definitions of them are contained in Appendix A for your reference. Virtues definitions are excerpted from the Virtues Cards with permission of The Virtues Project, Inc., www.virtuesproject.com. They are based on *The Family Virtues Guide* by Linda Kavelin-Popov.

Quality	Strength		Weakness		Issues?
	He	She	He	She	
Assertiveness					
Caring					
Cleanliness					
Commitment					
Compassion					
Confidence					
Courage					
Courtesy					
Creativity					
Detachment					
Determination					
Enthusiasm					
Excellence					
Faithfulness					
Flexibility					
Forgiveness					
Friendliness					
Generosity					
Gentleness					
Helpfulness					
Honesty					
Honor					
Idealism					
Integrity					
Joyfulness					
Justice					
Kindness					

Quality	Strength		Weakness		Issues?
	He	She	He	She	
Love					
Loyalty					
Mercy					
Moderation					
Modesty					
Obedience					
Orderliness					
Patience					
Peacefulness					
Prayerfulness					
Purposefulness					
Reliability					
Respect					
Responsibility					
Reverence					
Self-Discipline					
Service					
Steadfastness					
Tact					
Thankfulness					
Tolerance					
Trust					
Trustworthiness					
Truthfulness					
Unity					
Other:					
Other:					

1. How do you feel about doing this character assessment? On yourself? On another person?
   _____

2. What can you do to feel more comfortable about it?
   _____

Marriage Can Be Forever—Preparation Counts!

Date: _____

Worksheet 6B: Character Development Plan

DIRECTIONS: This worksheet assists you to set a character development plan in preparation for marriage.
- Generally, you will choose from the virtues that need development, but you may simply choose ones you feel are vital to a successful marriage.
- Select a target date for achieving the goals, so you will be more likely to stay focused on action and take time to assess your progress.
- When you are ready to assess your progress, you might talk to others, look over your journal notes, examine your behavior, or pray and meditate.
- Note: Mark the reassessment dates in your calendar.

Worksheets may be printed from www.claricomm.com/publishing

Virtue/Character Quality I want to further develop before marriage:	
How will I know I've improved?	
Actions to take:	**By when?**
Signed:	**Date:**

Virtue/Character Quality I want to further develop before marriage:	
How will I know I've improved?	
Actions to take:	**By when?**
Signed:	**Date:**

Marriage Can Be Forever—Preparation Counts!

The Valley of Knowledge

There was once a lover who had sighed for long years in separation from his beloved, and wasted in the fire of remoteness. From the rule of love, his heart was empty of patience, and his body weary of his spirit; he reckoned life without her as a mockery, and time consumed him away. How many a day he found no rest in longing for her; how many a night the pain of her kept him from sleep; his body was worn to a sigh, his heart's wound had turned him to a cry of sorrow. He had given a thousand lives for one taste of the cup of her presence, but it availed him not. The doctors knew no cure for him, and companions avoided his company; yea, physicians have no medicine for one sick of love, unless the favor of the beloved one deliver him.

At last, the tree of his longing yielded the fruit of despair, and the fire of his hope fell to ashes. Then one night he could live no more, and he went out of his house and made for the marketplace. On a sudden, a watchman followed after him. He broke into a run, with the watchman following; then other watchmen came together, and barred every passage to the weary one. And the wretched one cried from his heart, and ran here and there, and moaned to himself: "Surely this watchman is Izra'il, my angel of death, following so fast upon me; or he is a tyrant of men, seeking to harm me." His feet carried him on, the one bleeding with the arrow of love, and his heart lamented. Then he came to a garden wall, and with untold pain he scaled it, for it proved very high; and forgetting his life, he threw himself down to the garden.

And there he beheld his beloved with a lamp in her hand, searching for a ring she had lost. When the heart-surrendered lover looked on his ravishing love, he drew a great breath and raised up his hands in prayer, crying: "O God! Give Thou glory to the watchman, and riches and long life. For the watchman was Gabriel, guiding this poor one; or he was Israfil, bringing life to this wretched one!"

Indeed, his words were true, for he had found many a secret justice in this seeming tyranny of the watchman, and seen how many a mercy lay hid behind the veil. Out of wrath, the guard had led him who was athirst in love's desert to the sea of his loved one, and lit up the dark night of absence with the light of reunion. He had driven one who was afar, into the garden of nearness, had guided an ailing soul to the heart's physician.

Now if the lover could have looked ahead, he would have blessed the watchman at the start, and prayed on his behalf, and he would have seen that tyranny as justice; but since the end was veiled to him, he moaned and made his plaint in the beginning. Yet those who journey in the garden land of knowledge, because they see the end in the beginning, see peace in war and friendliness in anger.

~ Bahá'u'lláh, *Seven Valleys and Four Valleys*, pp. 13-15

CHAPTER 7 – Knowing What You Want: A Great Marriage Partner

Focus Points

- Identifying what you bring to a marriage relationship
- Choosing what to look for in a marriage partner
- The quality of perseverance
- No such thing as only one potential marriage partner or "soul mate"
- Prayer as a tool
- Sharing what you are looking for with others

A Couple's Story

Lindsay (*To herself, while sitting at her kitchen table*)**:** *I'm glad I've been working with the counselor at the college. I'm starting to feel better about being in a relationship and maybe even getting married. I think it makes sense for me to write down some things that would be important to me in a husband. Divorcing like my parents did is not an option—way too much pain. Maybe if I write down what I'm like and then write down traits he has to have, it will help me recognize someone for me to be with. Not like Richard, who proposed to me on our fourth date! We had so little in common. Let's see, I'm an extrovert, so it's important to me that the guy is comfortable being social. Since I'm into the theater, it would be great if he loved theater, too. And he'd better be able to be a great father—I want to be with someone who's good with kids.*

∞

James (*To himself, while lounging on his couch with the marriage preparation book and worksheets*)**:** *I never thought about writing down what's important about me as a marriage partner and what is important for me in someone else. It's probably a good idea to do it. I just thought I'd keep dating a bunch of girls and eventually I'd figure out who I was supposed to be with. I guess that way I could have ended up with a really bad match or spent a long time looking. My parents have been together a long time, but it seems rare these days for marriages to last, and they did have some troubles early on, so I'm glad I'm being more careful now about this process. Hmm…I'm on the go a lot, so it wouldn't work for me to be married to someone who just likes to stay home. I like girls who are smart and know what's going on in the world so we can have great conversations about all kinds of topics. I'd like a travel companion too…someone who wouldn't mind packing up and taking off to other countries.*

Quotes for Guidance

✸ The diversity in the human family should be the cause of love and harmony, as it is in music where many different notes blend together in the making of a perfect chord. If you meet those of a different race and color from yourself, do not mistrust them, and withdraw yourself into your shell of conventionality, but rather be glad and show them kindness.
   ('Abdu'l-Bahá: *The Advent of Divine Justice*, p. 38; *Lights of Guidance*, p. 528)

✸ Love is the cause of unfoldment to a searching mind, of the secrets deposited in the universe by the Infinite!
   ('Abdu'l-Bahá: *Tablets of 'Abdu'l-Bahá, Vol. 3*, p. 526)

✸ Persevere in your efforts, let not obstacles damp your zeal and determination and rest assured that the Power of God which is reinforcing your efforts will in the end triumph and enable you to fulfill your cherished desire.
   (Shoghi Effendi: *Arohanui: Letters to New Zealand*, p. 25)

✸ There is no teaching in the Bahá'í Faith that 'soul mates' exist. What is meant is that marriage should lead to a profound friendship of spirit, which will endure in the next world, where there is no sex, and no giving and taking in marriage; just the way we should establish with our parents, our children, our brothers and sisters and friends a deep spiritual bond which will be ever-lasting, and not merely physical bonds of human relationship.
   (On behalf of Shoghi Effendi: *Lights of Guidance*, p. 206)

Perspectives to Consider

It's very difficult for someone to establish and sustain a committed relationship or marriage when they are always wondering whether they made a mistake, and the person actually destined for them is still wandering around. Maybe he's in China. Maybe there was a wrong turn a few streets back, and she's sitting in a different restaurant. It's a recipe for starting marriage without full commitment and with one foot in divorce court. Remember, as well, that you are responsible for your own happiness. Part of the reason the "soul mate" myth is so popular, is because people are walking around believing that if they just find this one special person, they will be happy. Happiness is a spiritual force within you, and happy couples result from nurturing a relationship over time.

Are There Soul Mates?

Sorry to disappoint your expectations, but there is no such thing as **"the one"**—that one "right" person for you. Nor is there any such thing as a "perfect match" or a "match made in heaven" or something that "just happens" as you may believe. Often these expectations of such a "magical" connection result in people never marrying or never being satisfied and happy once they do marry. With such a feeling of "fate" being in charge, you may not recognize your personal responsibility to be fully involved in preparing for marriage and choosing your partner. Or you may marry and undermine your marriage by continuing to look for "the one."

The term "soul mate" implies that the partners are rising above physical attraction, and there is a deep and mystical bond between them. The problem with this concept is not the desire for a deep and mystical bond, but the belief that **soul mates** are found or stumbled upon. *There is better evidence that a soul-mate relationship is created rather than found.*

If soul mates were "found," wouldn't we see a much lower divorce rate? When a couple thinks they have found their soul mate before having an opportunity to share life experiences, the relationship is probably based on complementary emotional needs. They may be two survivors of previous bad marriages or troubled childhoods, or maybe just two lonely people who are overwhelmingly delighted to discover that the other accepts them. They may also have a real chemistry—but without true character and personality compatibility, this will likely fizzle and die. (See Chapters 6 and 19.)

Marriages are strongest when set on a **foundation of friendship and compatibility**. In spiritual terms, developing a soul mate connection will follow naturally when people are with someone they are friends with, love deeply, and can live and raise children with peacefully. The possibilities of finding *this* kind of relationship are far more realistic than the idea of there being only one person that matches up.

Marriage Can Be Forever—Preparation Counts!

This does not mean that you won't ask for **God's guidance and assistance** in the process—prayer always helps. And some of the best prayers can be asking His assistance in being ready for marriage, being a good partner, and for your potential future spouse. However, He also requires you to be in action in order to guide you. And, yes, there is a special connection and spiritual bond of love that forms between people who intend to marry—this is not a business transaction after all. How could a marriage last through all its joys and challenges without that bond of love for each other? The point, though, is to use your minds to investigate reality and compatibility, not just focus on the "passion-filled festival of the heart" as one person describes romance. (See Appendix C for full essay.)

With the freedom of knowing that there are many potential mates for you out of the billions in the world, you can relax and be friends with people. Gone is the hyper-vigilance of having to make sure you don't miss seeing your "only intended partner." Your focus can be on ensuring you are a good match by developing your character and friendships with people and exploring your compatibility with them. You may then more easily identify someone who will be a full partner with you in creating a long-lasting marriage that contributes to each of you, your families, your communities, and the world at large.

Individually, or before you are in a relationship, it will help you to be clear about what makes you a **unique person**. You will explore these things in Worksheet 7A so that you know who you are as a marriage partner. As a second step, you will use Worksheet 7B to clarify what you want in a partner by writing down exactly what you are looking for. It is better to do both of these activities before you are in a relationship if possible. Otherwise, you may be tempted to edit the lists to match up with your current "love interest" and lose sight of what is most important to you. Is this someone who can be a true spiritual partner for you? Is this someone who can support your personal goals? Can you create mutual life visions and goals.

Here is a list to start you thinking about the wide array of things that make you or a potential partner unique. ***This is a partial list and in no priority order; it is simply to get you started thinking.*** Everyone's list will be different, because each list will be based on individual needs, preferences, values, and personality. Create a list that reflects what is important *to* you. **Note:** It is unwise to be too specific about physical attributes in a partner, unless it is something truly non-negotiable. Think carefully about what is spiritual, mental, and emotional in addition to physical.

Examples About You or Your Potential Partner

- Consultative decision maker
- Effective listener
- Organized housekeeping habits and skills
- Responsible with money
- Appreciation of nature, plants, and animals
- Sense of humor
- A model for children
- Sense of adventure, risk-taker
- Musician
- Non-smoker, no drugs, and no alcohol
- Positive attitude toward work
- Positive attitude toward service
- Attractive physically/sexually
- Sexually chaste
- Mature in handling tests and difficulties
- Able to pray and study spiritual books alone and with others

- Willing to have children
- A strong sense of purpose
- Playful and a sense of fun
- Need for high level of social activity
- Comfortable hosting others in home
- Vegetarian
- Willing to develop spiritual qualities
- Understanding of Hispanic culture
- Need for high physical activity: exercise, dancing
- Medium level of daily energy
- Able to discuss difficult issues
- Loyal to friends
- Willing to live in another country
- Willing to foster positive qualities in others
- Able to easily express love
- Able to share thoughts and feelings easily
- Able to express emotions maturely

- Positive relationships with family members
- Need for regular quiet time/alone time
- Generous with money, regularly buying presents
- Committed to completing bachelor's degree
- Good parent qualities
- Early riser, even on weekends
- Appreciation of art and artistic/creative talents
- TV sports watcher
- Tennis player
- Financially responsible
- Responsible about school and work assignments
- Courteous and loving toward parents
- Trustworthy; keeps commitments
- Able to live with my bad habits

Speaking of **bad habits**...the above list is mostly things that seem rather positive. Here's a place where it's important to be honest, because your own bad habits can certainly be friction points in a relationship. So, include some of them on your description list too.

Bad Habit Examples:

- Leave dirty clothes in a pile and never do laundry
- Rarely open the mail
- Get busy and forget to pray
- Miss due dates for school projects
- Late for meetings and/or meals
- Ignore children

Be aware that you might have some **internal barriers** in place that may interfere with this part of the marriage preparation process or being in a close relationship. *If you are seriously struggling with any of these, seek professional or spiritual counseling.* They may include:

- Fear of commitment (see Chapter 11)
- Fear of intimacy or sharing who you are with someone else (see Chapter 23)
- Fear of rejection

This is not the time to be in denial or unrealistic; it is the time to be thorough and detailed. *If you don't know who you are or what you are looking for, then anyone will do, and you will likely end up in a string of relationships that are unhappy.* And you'll keep wondering why.

Coaching

⇒ Clarity about what you bring to a marriage and what you are looking for in a marriage partner will contribute to your compatibility discussions (Step 4). You can often like and love someone and appreciate being with him/her, but if your key goals and needs are not met, a marriage could be an unhappy mistake.

⇒ Share what you are looking for in a partner with others. Someone else may spot a person who matches you before you do.

⇒ Pause to pray, reflect, and listen for answers. Request that God help guide you to someone who can be a good partner for you and for whom you can be a good partner. And take a look at who is already in your life—is there someone you have overlooked as a possibility?

⇒ If you set goals, you are more likely to accomplish them. Consider setting a date by when you want to be married. You may not make it by that date, but it will make you conscious of taking the necessary steps to accomplish the goal. If you don't make the goal, evaluate whether you were in action or not (such as doing effective character and personality assessments); change or reset the goal if indicated; and practice perseverance.

❓ Questions for Reflection and Discussion

1. When you look for someone with whom to share your life, what are the most important things?
2. How can you stay focused on what you are looking for in someone and not get sidetracked by a passionate response to someone who doesn't match up in key areas?
3. After you spend time with someone and you realize that he or she doesn't match your list, what do you do with the relationship?
4. What if you are tempted to edit the most important things on your list to fit someone in your life?
5. How do you feel about sharing who you are with someone else? Can you handle being vulnerable?
6. Do you fear you will lose your identity in a relationship? In what way?
7. How do you feel about sharing your mental, emotional, physical, and spiritual needs with someone else?

Activities

1. Create a quiet, meditative space for yourself. Pray and spend a few minutes envisioning yourself married:
   a. What are you like in this relationship?
   b. What is he/she like?
   c. What are you doing together?

   What does your vision look like? Describe it below, write a poem, or draw/paint pictures to illustrate it.

   _____
   _____
   _____

   Find a friend and role-play part of the vision. What would you now like to change about it?

   _____

2. Use Worksheet 7A to be very specific in describing who you are and what you would bring as a unique individual into a marriage.

3. Use Worksheet 7B to identify what you are looking for in a potential marriage partner.

Marriage Can Be Forever—Preparation Counts!

Chapter 7 – Knowing What You Want: A Great Marriage Partner

Date: _____

Worksheet 7A: Describe Who You Are

DIRECTIONS: Describe who you are and what you bring as a unique individual into a marriage. Use the examples in this chapter and ahead in Step 4 on compatibility to trigger your thinking. Consider the possibilities below. **Note:** It is best to de-emphasize physical things, unless something is critical for or about you.

- qualities
- spiritual practices
- needs
- likes
- dislikes
- habits
- goals
- commitments
- dreams
- fears
- attitudes
- assets
- desires
- appearance
- behaviors
- cultural customs
- family history
- hopes
- beliefs
- education
- hobbies

Worksheets may be printed from www.claricomm.com/publishing

What Do You Bring To A Marriage?	

Marriage Can Be Forever—Preparation Counts!

Date: _____

Worksheet 7B: Describe Your Potential Marriage Partner

DIRECTIONS: The purpose of this worksheet is to describe the person you think you would like to marry. No two people are exactly alike, and differences often add variety and opportunities for growth in a relationship. However, it's important to assess your likes, dislikes, habits, goals, strengths, areas for growth, commitments, dreams, fears, hopes, and the details of your everyday life (see 7A for a list).

- Where is compatibility critical? **Mark those as "non-negotiable." Note:** Be very specific and very realistic. Consider a maximum of 7-10 non-negotiable items. If you are identifying more than 10, consider how realistic your expectations may be. Is there anything you want to change on the list?
- Where is it important but you can make some adjustment to accommodate the needs of your partner? **Mark those as "flexible."**
- Where is it less important? **Mark these as "nice, but not essential."**

Use the examples in this chapter and in the chapters in Step 4 on compatibility to trigger your thinking. (You will compare your list with your potential partner's list in Worksheet 14B.)

Worksheets may be printed from www.claricomm.com/publishing

Description	Non-Negotiable	Flexible	Nice, But Not Essential

After completing the worksheet, Identify at least one person you trust and discuss your list and any concerns that have arisen. Is there anything you now want to change on your list?

Marriage Can Be Forever—Preparation Counts!

FRIENDSHIP

Your friend is your needs answered.
He is your field which you sow with love and reap with thanksgiving.
And he is your board and your fireside.
For you come to him with your hunger, and you seek him for peace.
When your friend speaks his mind you fear not the "nay" in your own mind,
nor do you withhold the "ay."
And when he is silent your heart ceases not to listen to his heart;
For without words, in friendship, all thought, all desires,
   all expectations are born and shared, with joy that is unacclaimed.
When you part from your friend, you grieve not;
For that which you love most in him may be clearer in his absence,
   as the mountain to the climber is clearer from the plain.
And let there be no purpose in friendship save the deepening of the spirit.
For love that seeks aught but the disclosure of its own mystery is not love
   but a net cast forth: and only the unprofitable is caught.
And let your best be for your friend.
If he must know the ebb of your tide, let him know its flood also.
For what is your friend that you should seek him with hours to kill?
Seek him always with hours to live.
For it is his to fill your need, but not your emptiness.
And in the sweetness of friendship let there be laughter, and sharing of
   pleasures.
For in the dew of little things the heart finds its morning and is refreshed.

~ Kahlil Gibran, The Prophet

CHAPTER 8 – I Like You: Friends Before Marriage

Focus Points
- What is friending/friendship
- The qualities and gifts of friendship and being friendly
- The importance of friendship as a basis for marriage
- Friendship skills that contribute to marriage
- Widening your circle of friends and potential spouses
- Challenges of meeting new people

A Couple's Story

Lindsay (Lounging on the couch in her apartment, Lindsay calls her long-time friend, Chuck):

"Hey there, Chuck. This is Lindsay."

"Hi, Lindsay, great to hear from you," says Chuck. "How did your last exam go? You were stressing out about it so much last week."

"It turned out okay," says Lindsay. "Thanks for helping me calm down about it—you're a good friend."

"Ah…anytime!" he responds.

"Hey, speaking of friends," says Lindsay, "Stacy and I were talking last night about staying friends with someone after you date them. She's thinking about breaking up with Rob. She likes him, but wants to stop dating him."

"That would be a tough thing to do," says Chuck. "You and I both decided not to date each other, so we didn't go through that. Maybe they could agree to spend a few months apart and then try the friendship thing? Frankly, he may *never* agree to try friendship—and it may not be as easy as Stacy hopes…."

∞

James (With his former girlfriend, Marianna, sitting over coffee at a local restaurant):

"It's great to have you here for a visit," says James. "I miss talking with you. How is the Bahá'í community back home doing?" They chat about people they both know.

Marianna and James dated for a few months and then decided to stay friends. They realize now that their choice to not have sex while they were dating has made it easier to remain friends.

"Hey, I have a great book from my new Assembly on marriage preparation. Since you and Carlos are getting serious, you might want to get a copy. Take a look at this…," says James.

Quotes for Guidance

✺ Do not be content with showing friendship in words alone, let your heart burn with loving kindness for all who may cross your path.
   ('Abdu'l-Bahá: *Paris Talks*, p. 15)

✺ …man and woman should truly be friends, and should be in sympathy with one another. Their understanding should have a basis in reality and not be based upon passion and desire… .
   ('Abdu'l-Bahá: *Sexuality, Relationships and Spiritual Growth*, p. 121)

✺ In this glorious [Bahá'í] Cause the life of a married couple should resemble the life of the angels in heaven—a life full of joy and spiritual delight, a life of unity and concord, a friendship both mental and physical.
   ('Abdu'l-Bahá: *Compilation of Compilations, Vol. I*, p. 397)

✺ The love of God has brought us together, and this is the best of means and motive. Every other bond of friendship is limited in effectiveness, but fellowship based upon the love of God is unlimited, everlasting, divine and radiant.
   ('Abdu'l-Bahá: *Promulgation of Universal Peace*, p. 442)

✺ Enkindle with all your might in every meeting the light of the love of God, gladden and cheer every heart with the utmost loving-kindness, show forth your love to the strangers just as you show forth to your relations.
   ('Abdu'l-Bahá: *Tablets of 'Abdu'l-Bahá Vol. 3*, p. 503)

✺ You must love your friend better than yourself; yes, be willing to sacrifice yourself.
   ('Abdu'l-Bahá: *Promulgation of Universal Peace*, p. 218)

✺ …marriage should lead to a profound friendship of spirit… .
   (Shoghi Effendi: *Compilation of Compilations, Vol. II*, p. 452)

Perspectives to Consider

Casual friend. Good friend. Best friend. Girlfriend. Boyfriend. Hanging out with friends. Friends night out. Just a friend. Special friend. Long-time friend. "Friend" is a word that wanders through our speech with great regularity. It may be helpful to understand more deeply the **connection between being friends and searching for and finding a marriage partner.**

Friendship is a deep connection between two people. Usually, but not always, friends are unrelated to each other. The two people can be the same gender or not. There can be any span of age difference between the two, although more commonly friends are similar in age. Usually there are many people in their lives they are friendly with, but generally, only a few that they are very close to. At one point, you may be very involved with a friend, and then circumstances change and you drift apart.

Reaching out and being a friend requires you to be courageous and willing to be vulnerable. At times, you may choose to be alone rather than risk someone close to you hurting you. Over time, however, you will start to realize that there is usually far greater pain in constant loneliness than in occasionally being hurt.

When you think about the great relationships in your life, what are the **special qualities of those friendships**? Think about whether you would like most of them in a spouse. Some of them might be:

- Honesty and sharing
- Spontaneous fun and laughter
- Support and empathy during difficulties
- Loving, spiritual connection
- Encouragement
- Acceptance
- Common life experiences and memories
- Enjoyment of doing the same things
- Opportunities to learn together
- Disagree constructively
- Service to others together
- Reconnect easily even when apart for years
- Motivational nudging (the person helps gets you going forward when you need a push)

Friends are gifts in your life, because they are a constant thread of love and warmth through your heart. They hug you when you are down and when you are excited. They are only a phone call, email, or touch away. Friendships take effort and care to maintain so that hurt feelings, jealousy, or neglect don't cause them to fade away. There are also many friendships that have such strong spiritual and emotional connections, they last through tests, challenges, geographical distances, and long separations. ***Be wary of people who set up exclusive friendships*** and behave as if being with other people is a waste of time—true friendliness is an open and inclusive quality.

Friendship is particularly important as the foundation of a marriage relationship. Ideally, you will be closer to your spouse than to any other human being. If you start your relationship with a friendship that has provided you with mutual support and understanding, the foundation of your marriage is likely to be stronger. You will already have had the practice of confiding in each other, seeing each other through difficulties, sharing your joys, and turning to each other for fun and relaxation. Marriage is very much about companionship and is in many ways one long conversation with a close friend, so choose someone with whom you love to talk and spend time.

Learning to do the **process of "friending"** well is a foundational skill for your marriage preparation process, which includes seeking out, establishing, and nurturing friendships. Through interactions with your friends, you can learn:

> ### "Friending" Defined
>
> One of the best indicators of success and a strong foundation for a future marriage is to begin with deep friendship with someone. Another indicator of success is both you and your partner having a few dear friendships that enhance rather than threaten your relationship with each other.
>
> "Friending" is the wonderful process of finding someone who you feel very comfortable being with and exploring each other's lives. With friendship, you like and respect each other, confide your deepest thoughts and fears to each other, enjoy each other's company, support each other during difficulties, and encourage each other to fulfill dreams and goals. Ask a potential marriage partner how he or she defines friendship. Some might define it as someone to confide in, while others might simply say a friend is someone to go out and have fun with in a variety of activities.

- What is helpful
- What is hurtful
- How to communicate effectively
- How to share
- Respect for boundaries and limits
- What triggers strong emotions
- When to tease and when to be serious
- How to keep confidences
- How to trust and be trustworthy
- How to be honest and truthful
- When a relationship is constructive
- When a relationship is harmful or damaging
- How to communicate without speaking negatively of others

Maintaining a friendship is not easy—it takes commitment, time, attention, and love. Being a steadfast friend requires patience and the ability to understand, forgive, and get past unpleasantness or disagreements. These things are also true for marriage.

When you feel you are ready to start dating and looking for a potential spouse, you will likely discover that you have to look beyond your immediate friends and **widen the circle of those you know to include new people.** Of course, this doesn't mean that you will only maintain a friendship with someone if they have the potential to be a marriage partner. It does mean, though, that you have to be responsible for creating a variety of relationships in your life and be aware of their partner-potential.

Think broadly about the types of people you can meet, without letting prejudices or assumptions interfere with your approach. Where and how can you look for new acquaintances? Would they have potential to be friends? Is it likely that some you meet in this way may be good possibilities for becoming your spouse? How many friends do you want to have? What feels comfortable to you? There are many possibilities for widening your circle, and some are in the list below to think about.

CAUTION — WATCH YOUR STEP
Get involved in activities that you have a genuine interest in. Otherwise, you might give an inaccurate impression to a new acquaintance that you are interested in what they are doing, and it will probably lead ultimately to your own frustration. When your interest fades, there may be a negative effect on your relationship.

Meeting New People

Possible Things to Do
- Ask your friends who they know and might be willing to introduce you to
- Enroll in school, college, university, or community education classes
- Take arts-related classes or volunteer at art museums, concert halls, or theaters
- Participate in poetry centers or writing retreats
- Tutor students at an after-school or weekend program, or facilitate a Bahá'í or other religious/spiritual study circle
- Attend conferences or workshops
- Participate in Bahá'í or other religious weekend or summer school sessions
- Coordinate a community service project
- Join a committee addressing a civic or social issue
- Volunteer your time for activities of all kinds

Possible Places to Consider
- Religious centers and gatherings
- Workplaces
- Sports activities or events
- Hobby-related groups
- Fitness or health club facilities
- Friends' family picnics
- Neighborhood associations
- College or civic clubs
- Social or activity areas where you live

Possible Things to Try
- An Internet listserve
- Established dating services
- Personal ads
- Internet chatrooms
- Internet matchmaking services
 (**Note:** Completing the services' personal profiles can provide insights about yourself.)

CAUTION — WATCH YOUR STEP
The Internet or personal ads can often be effective, especially if they are spiritually-based services, but they can also make it easy to present a **false image**, which results in a bad relationship experience. Some commonsense guidelines are wise and helpful to follow: Don't give out your phone number or address, and guard your personal information from people you don't really know. Be a little skeptical, as people can pretend to be someone else in online chatrooms and ads. This way you get to know a false image, not who the person really is. The Internet also makes it easy for some to carry on multiple relationships at one time. Avoid and don't respond to communications that are abusive, violent, lewd, crude, or that in any way make you feel

uncomfortable. If you do meet someone in person that you have encountered through the Internet, make sure others know the details about it, and meet the person in a safe, public place or group setting.

Our culture has created an atmosphere that communicates it is unwise to be friendly to others. At times, this is a good caution for your own safety and protection, but the unfriendliness is often excessive. **Being friendly is a positive spiritual practice, and this quality will allow you to meet many people.** You may develop close and meaningful relationships with only a few, however, and those who are potential marriage partners are even fewer. Friendship activity will give you experience in identifying what you are looking for in a mate, assessing someone's character and personality, and determining his/her compatibility with you, all activities that are part of the preparation process. Over time, you will develop the ability to tell early on in a relationship whether it is one you want to keep. If you have serious doubts about the person's potential as a friend or potential marriage partner, it is best to stop investing time in sustaining the connection between you.

A friendship you have with someone may start to show **possibility as a romantic relationship**. The transition from one to the other may feel emotional and a bit risky. Spend some time praying and meditating about having a friendship with someone that might change to a friendship-based romantic relationship.

Think about what makes the relationships different. Do your expectations change? For instance, if a friend doesn't call you for a few days, you may not get upset. However, if someone you consider a boyfriend or girlfriend doesn't contact you, you will likely be upset or concerned. When you are in a transitional relationship, have an honest and sincere dialogue with each other to understand the changes you are experiencing and your expectations. Communicating your feelings will be important.

Alternatively, you may have a romantic relationship with someone that **will work better as a friendship only**. You may need time apart to give you a bit of emotional distance and assess what you envision as your future relationship. (**Note:** Previous physical intimacy between you can complicate the ease of remaining friends.) Choosing to be friends and having other relationships may be a very healthy circumstance for you, but be aware that it may prompt discomfort or jealousy in a new partner. You may have to make adjustments in the amount of time you spend with the former partner if there is disunity caused between you and your new partner. Or you may see the new person's issues as inappropriate. Will you discuss it with them and resolve it? Or, will you choose to stop seeing him/her?

> **Maintaining Self-Respect**
>
> Every encounter in every setting has the potential for positive or negative outcomes, partially depending on your ability to be honest with and about yourself. Large conferences, especially those with many people your own age, can provide you the opportunity to meet many people, but they can also tempt you into trying to be someone you aren't. Remember: You aren't participating in an impersonal "meat market" of mate hunting where you are required to wear a false mask and present an unrealistic picture of yourself. If you start a relationship with someone on this basis, it will likely falter as you start to present your "real self."
>
> When the events are national or international, your initial attraction to someone might be difficult to sustain effectively and respectfully, and it may simply die a geographically challenged death.

Coaching

⇒ Be open-minded as you look for new friends. You may be tempted to look for someone "just like you," but your best mate might not fit that profile. Look broadly before you narrow down prospects for marriage.

⇒ The old adage of "if you want a friend, be a friend" has great validity. The better friend you are willing to be, the more likely you will have good friends that last.

Marriage Can Be Forever—Preparation Counts!

⇒ Sometimes when you have invested a lot of time and energy into a friendship, you may be tempted to ignore the signs that the friendship is not one that supports you, or it is unwise or unhealthy for you. However, if you don't detach from it, you will sap energy that is best directed elsewhere. Use prayer, wisdom, and consultation with trusted others to do what is best for your mental, emotional, and spiritual well-being.

❓ Questions for Reflection and Discussion

1. What do you consider the most important qualities you have that make you a good friend?
2. What qualities do you look for in your friends?
3. Who are the people in your life that you consider good friends?
4. What do you value about the friendships you have?
5. What do you see as the benefits of friendships?
6. What have you done to maintain those friendships?
7. What efforts have you made to establish new friendships?
8. When have you felt a friend violated your trust? How did you feel about this? How did you handle it?
9. What are your favorite activities to do with friends?
10. What are the signs that you would be wise to end a friendship?
11. What has happened when you have ended friendships?
12. Have you had a friendship that became a romantic relationship? How did that turn out?
13. Have you had a romantic relationship that went back into being a friendship? How has that turned out?
14. Is there a friend currently in your life who has the potential to be a future marriage partner? What would you have to do to shift your relationship in that direction? Are you willing to do this?
15. Is there space to continue friendships after marriage? With both sexes?

Activities

1. Pray, meditate, reflect, and write in your journal about the qualities you value in a good friend.

2. Identify a person of the opposite sex you would like to get to know better. Select an activity that you would enjoy doing and that would support developing a deeper friendship and invite him/her to participate in it with you. After the activity, consciously identify what new information you learned about him/her and yourself. Does the person have potential as a future spouse for you?
   _____
   _____

3. Select a friend who has been difficult to communicate with at times. Spend time with him/her with the focus of developing a new and improved pattern of communication. How did it go? How might the ability to communicate with this person relate to communication with a marriage partner?
   _____
   _____

4. Use Worksheet 8A to identify the positive qualities of two close friends, one male and one female.

5. Share the lists of positive qualities with your friends.

6. Use Worksheet 8B to help you identify what you can do to widen your circle of friends and potential spouses.

Date: _____

Worksheet 8A: Qualities of Friends

DIRECTIONS: This worksheet is to help you appreciate your friends and better understand the qualities you would also like to see in a spouse.
- In the spaces below, list the things you like about two of your *non-romantic* friends, one male and one female.
- If you need assistance, look at the character qualities listed in Chapter 6 or the personality, attitude, and behavior list in Chapter 19.
- Share these lists with your friends and note their responses.
- Then note in the last question the qualities your friends have that you would like to see in your spouse.

Worksheets may be printed from www.claricomm.com/publishing

1. Male Friend's Name: _____

   The qualities I appreciate about him are:

   _____   _____
   _____   _____
   _____   _____
   _____   _____

2. Female Friend's Name: _____

   The qualities I appreciate about her are:

   _____   _____
   _____   _____
   _____   _____
   _____   _____

3. What has identifying these qualities taught you?

   _____
   _____
   _____
   _____

4. When you shared the lists with your friends, how did they respond? How do you feel about their response?

   _____
   _____
   _____
   _____

5. The qualities that these friends have that I would like to see in a spouse are:

   _____   _____
   _____   _____
   _____   _____

Marriage Can Be Forever—Preparation Counts!

Date: _____

Worksheet 8B: Widening Your Circle of Friends

DIRECTIONS: Complete this worksheet to help you understand how you are currently spending your time and whether you are doing the things that will widen your circle of friends and potential marriage partners. This will also help you determine what you could be doing instead.

Worksheets may be printed from www.claricomm.com/publishing

What are the top 5 activities/ways you spend your time in any given week?

Activity	**Percentage of Time Per Week**
_____	_____
_____	_____
_____	_____
_____	_____
_____	_____

Total percentage of week accounted for =   approx. 100%

1. How do these activities contribute to you meeting new people?
   _____
   _____

2. Do these activities help you meet people who would be potential partners for you?
   _____
   _____

3. What are a few new activities you would like to become involved in and by when? (Mark the dates in your calendar.)

   _____ Date:_____
   _____ Date:_____
   _____ Date:_____
   _____ Date:_____

4. How can these activities assist you to find a person who could be a potential partner?
   _____
   _____

5. After you have participated in the activities, note below your assessment of them. Do you want to continue being with them? Why or why not?
   _____
   _____
   _____

Marriage Can Be Forever—Preparation Counts!

Step 3

Walk Carefully: Being a Couple

Marriage Can Be Forever—Preparation Counts!

BEST GIFT

laughter bubbles up
and bursts as
over up around
we visit land
of funny and absurd

gift of laughter
lingers later chuckles
unexpected laugh
remembers triggers
once again
connects explodes

then ever after
little words
and mention slip
between the ordinary
and a smile
touches fills
the spirit
heart
and soul

Susanne Mariella Alexander

CHAPTER 9 – An Initial Step: Do You Want to Date?

> **Focus Points**
> - The concept of dating
> - The benefits and challenges of dating
> - Different gender and cultural approaches
> - Appropriate dating behavior and maintaining chastity/abstinence
> - Dating activities

A Couple's Story

James is working many overtime hours at his new job and hasn't yet joined his new Bahá'í community's study circle. Since the Spiritual Assembly advised that he get out and meet new people, he decides that the study circle is a great place to start the process. The room is filled with about 10 people when he arrives, and he is quickly introduced.

"Hi," James says to Lindsay.

"Great to meet you," she replies. "I'd heard there was a new family in the community." At the end of an evening sitting next to each other, both realize they like each other and say they hope to see each other the next week at another meeting.

James and Lindsay see each other at meetings a few times, and are finding that they laugh a lot together, think the same way about many things, and get along with each other very well. There is a growing and obvious spark of attraction between them. James is wondering whether to initiate their going out together beyond the study circle. He normally wouldn't hesitate about asking someone out on a date, but this time he is a little nervous. *Lindsay seems really special,* thinks James. *I don't want her to say "no" and then be uncomfortable around me.*

"Uh, James," begins Lindsay tentatively the next time she sees him. "There's a great music group playing at the coffee house on the town square on Saturday. I wonder if you'd like to meet me there?"

"That would be great," responds James, with an inner sigh of relief…a chance to get to know her better.

Quotes for Guidance

✹ Ye were created to show love one to another.…
   (Bahá'u'lláh: *Tablets of Bahá'u'lláh*, p. 138)

✹ In the teachings there is nothing against dancing, but the friends should remember that the standard of Bahá'u'lláh is modesty and chastity. The atmosphere of modern dance halls, where so much smoking and

drinking and promiscuity goes on, is very bad, but decent dances are not harmful in themselves. There is certainly no harm in classical dancing or learning dancing in school. There is also no harm in taking part in dramas. Likewise in cinema acting. The harmful thing, nowadays, is not the art itself but the unfortunate corruption which often surrounds these arts. As Bahá'ís we need avoid none of the arts, but acts and the atmosphere that sometimes go with these professions we should avoid.
<small>(Shoghi Effendi: *Dawn of a New Day*, p. 153)</small>

✽ ...there is nothing in the Bahá'í Writings which relates specifically to the so-called dating practices prevalent in some parts of the world, where two unmarried people of the opposite sex participate together in a social activity. In general, Bahá'ís who are planning to involve themselves in this form of behavior should become well aware of the Bahá'í Teachings on chastity and, with these in mind, should scrupulously avoid any actions which would arouse passions which might well tempt them to violate these Teachings. In deciding which acts are permissible in the light of these considerations, the youth should use their own judgment, giving due consideration to the advice of their parents, taking account of the prevailing customs of the society in which they live, and prayerfully following the guidance of their conscience. It is the sacred duty of parents to instill in their children the exalted Bahá'í standard of moral conduct, and the importance of adherence to this standard cannot be over-emphasized as a basis for true happiness and for successful marriage.
<small>(On behalf of the Universal House of Justice: An unpublished letter February 5, 1992, to an individual)</small>

✽ As you know, in the *Advent of Divine Justice* [Shoghi Effendi] has stated the principles of Bahá'í conduct which apply and he has condemned easy familiarity and frivolous conduct. Certainly the practice of indiscriminate kissing and embracing involving unrelated people of opposite sexes is not desirable and is discouraged. Particularly in these days when restraints are being abolished one by one, the Bahá'ís should make great efforts to uphold, in their personal lives and in their relationships to each other, the standards of conduct set forth in the teachings. The following extract from a letter written by the Universal House of Justice outlines the responsibility of the individual in determining how the Bahá'í standards apply to daily life, and the means by which this is accomplished:

> It is neither possible nor desirable for the Universal House of Justice to set forth a set of rules covering every situation. Rather is it the task of the individual believer to determine, according to his own prayerful understanding of the Writings, precisely what his course of conduct should be in relation to situations which he encounters in his daily life. If he is to fulfill his true mission in life as a follower of the Blessed Perfection, he will pattern his life according to the Teachings. The believer cannot attain this objective merely by living according to a set of rigid regulations. When his life is oriented toward service to Bahá'u'lláh, and when every conscious act is performed within this frame of reference, he will not fail to achieve the true purpose of his life.
>
> Therefore, every believer must continually study the sacred Writings and the instructions of [Shoghi Effendi], striving always to attain a new and better understanding of their import to him and to his society. He should pray fervently for Divine Guidance, wisdom and strength to do what is pleasing to God, and to serve Him at all times and to the best of his ability.
>
> It is not surprising that serious-minded Bahá'í youth growing up in a bewildering moral environment are asking for specific guidance on the matter of proper conduct in friendship between boys and girls, men and women. It is also not surprising that their parents and other adult advisors are themselves sometimes confused on the issues that arise as they find old standards are changing and new patterns of behavior are developing in society which are unsettling, possibly even frightening to them. The primary protection for the friends in these matters, both young and old alike, is to continue to deepen, truly deepen, in the Teachings so that their behavior more readily conforms to the high standards of the Faith....

<small>(On behalf of the Universal House of Justice: An unpublished letter February 5, 1992, to an individual)</small>

✽ [In] "The Advent of Divine Justice" [Shoghi Effendi] is describing the requirements not only of chastity, but of "a chaste and holy life"—both the adjectives are important. One of the signs of a decadent society, a sign which is very evident in the world today, is an almost frenetic devotion to pleasure and diversion, an insatiable thirst for amusement, a fanatical devotion to games and sport, a reluctance to treat any matter seriously, and a scornful, derisory attitude towards virtue and solid worth. Abandonment of "a frivolous conduct" does not imply that a Bahá'í must be sour-faced or perpetually solemn. Humor, happiness, joy are characteristics of a true Bahá'í life. Frivolity palls and eventually leads to boredom and emptiness, but true happiness and joy and humor that are parts of a balanced life that includes serious thought, compassion and humble servitude to God, are characteristics that enrich life and add to its radiance.

Shoghi Effendi's choice of words was always significant, and each one is important in understanding his guidance. In this particular passage, he does not forbid "trivial" pleasures, but he does warn against "excessive attachment" to them and indicates that they can often be "misdirected." One is reminded of 'Abdu'l-Bahá's caution that we should not let a pastime become a waste of time.

(On behalf of the Universal House of Justice: *Compilation of Compilations, Vol. I*, p. 53)

Perspectives to Consider

A date is an opportunity to meet or be with someone, which allows you to get to know them better. ***Be aware that many character qualities and personality traits in someone only become obvious when they are interacting with other people besides just you.*** You will usually choose to date someone that you like and want to develop a friendship with—a better choice than going out with someone to gain popularity, as a favor to someone who wants to double-date, or because it's what your friends are doing. (Double-dating is two couples going out together.)

The concept of dating, where a couple goes out in a social setting, has primarily evolved in the last 100 years in the West, supported in part by the easy availability of cars as well as by changing moral standards. Dating has become the accepted choice for recreation, companionship, fun, and selecting a mate. It tends to be self-supervised, with little or no parental or family involvement. There is a lot of **pressure to date** in Western culture, which results in some feeling desperate or panicky if they aren't dating. Alternatively, they may compromise and keep dating someone who isn't compatible just to fit in with peers.

Before considering going on a formal date with someone alone, you can get to know them better in these ways:

- On the telephone
- E-mails or instant messages
- In activities with a group

At the beginning, keep your focus on continuing to develop your friendship with the person you are dating. This is an opportunity to **practice your relationship and communication skills** so you are more prepared for a close relationship in marriage.

Use Wisdom

Unfortunately, dates can turn from being fun occasions into activity that is unwise, unhealthy, or even unsafe. Wisdom, caution, staying in group or family settings, and going slowly can all help to protect you.

Dates can result in sexual and physical violence, or abstinence is abandoned. The outcome has unexpected and unwanted consequences, such as pregnancy and/or the guilt that can weigh down your heart and soul.

Sexual activity can often be tempting when there are special occasions such as a high school dance night, Valentine's Day, birthdays, and so on, when emotions are high, and it may seem like a way to celebrate. What structures do you need in place to support your chastity/abstinence in these circumstances?

People often enter into or are coerced into sexual relations without being sufficiently familiar with the other person involved. Parents and communities can support abstinence for both genders by providing social opportunities where couples are not isolated from other people.

Many religions and cultures have guidelines and concerns about dating and may regard it as immoral. Often it's not forbidden, but there are cautions about the process, as some dating activities can lead a couple into physical intimacy prematurely.

Be aware of **gender differences** with dating. There can be potential for miscommunication and upset at the transition time from friendship into dating and from dating into courting. Sometimes the man may wait for the woman to define for them that they do, in fact, have a serious relationship. On the other hand, the woman may wait for the man to take the lead. Communication has its risks, as neither of you may want to appear to be rushing the other, but no communication could produce a far worse result. So, talk about what you think and how you feel. This can be touchy and sensitive, so make sure you are receptive to the other's feelings, trying to be non-threatening and courteous, while honest. This can offer you as a couple some of your earliest opportunities to use the tool of consultation (see Chapter 3).

Dating can give you opportunities to observe and learn about each other through some of the following:

- Interactions with sales clerks or waiters
- Interactions with people of other genders and cultures
- The level of courtesy shown to others
- How he/she acts in a crowd
- How money is handled
- How communication initiates and flows
- How you handle maintaining chastity/abstinence
- What are favorite activities

Pay attention and **assess your observations**—what do you like and what don't you care for in your dating partner. Should you go forward with a relationship with this person or stop dating him/her? Remember as you date to compare the person to your list of what you desire in a marriage partner (Worksheet 7B). If you don't see what you are looking for in this person, do you really want to continue dating him/her?

One way to meet people is agreeing to let a friend or relative set up a **"blind date."** When someone knows you and another person and arranges for the two of you to meet socially, it's called a blind date, because neither of you know what the other looks like. This may create an awkward first meeting, but sometimes it can work. It is wise to have the meeting happen in a public place, and for you to have a way to leave and get yourself home if the meeting is excessively uncomfortable. You may also want to consider double-dating.

Being attracted to someone you deeply care for may have a strong physical component associated with it. For Bahá'ís and anyone who values abstinence, one dating challenge is maintaining **premarital chastity**. This includes avoiding the kinds of touching and kissing that risk your commitment to this standard. Dating and courting are evolving concepts, so consult together about how to watch *the balance* between dating and courting for an excessive length of time before marriage, and on the other hand, taking enough time to ensure you know each other thoroughly.

You may find that it supports your commitment to chastity and to getting to know each other socially if you choose to spend time together with other people. This may be with friends or families (see Chapter 10 on courting). Your spiritual values will support you in establishing boundaries and clearly communicating these boundaries to a dating partner. If the limits are clear to both of you, they will help prevent mutual desire from pushing you toward greater intimacy, or a "giving in" for fear of offending the other or losing the relationship.

Maintaining Chastity and Abstinence

Isolating yourselves from other people can be a warning sign that you are forgetting to tend to other relationships in your lives and possibly setting yourselves up to engage in sexual activity outside of marriage. Which of these might assist you?

- ❏ Meet in venues that are public
- ❏ Go out with a group of people
- ❏ Use appropriate body language
- ❏ Maintain appropriate physical boundaries
- ❏ Dress in a manner that is not tempting
- ❏ Keep conversations appropriate, respectful, and limited
- ❏ Do activities with others
- ❏ Do not spend extended time alone together

You as a couple can choose to be a participant in the evolutionary process of *creating new dating behavior that increasingly reflects spiritual guidance*. As you study, reflect on, and discuss how you choose to behave as a couple, you will find new and creative ways to be together, get to know each other, and at the same time, follow spiritual principles. Below is a sampling of activities that you may wish to try both together and with friends and family. Determine what works best for you…and see what other ideas you can generate. These activities may also be ones you choose to do as a courting couple, when you have made a commitment to seriously consider a future marriage (see Chapter 10 about courting).

Activity Ideas to Do As a Couple or with Friends/Family

Share Time
Nature walks
Art museum
Shopping
Amusement park
Walk on the beach
Meditation class
Pet walking/care
Library
Praying
Hanging out with friends
Dancing
Bookstore
Spend time with family
Go to a concert

Serve/Work
Visit seniors
Plan a conference
Teach a children's class
Start a business
Care for children
Handle Taxes/finances
Volunteer; join a committee
Plan a devotional
Facilitate a study class

Be Creative
Building or decorating projects
Art projects
Cooking
Write a book
Plant a garden

Enjoy Sports/Adventure
Cooperative games
Karaoke
Cross-country skiing
Travel (separate rooms; stay with friends)
Volleyball
Camping (group activity)
Yoga class
Cave mining, spelunking
Hiking/outdoor activities
Canoeing/rafting
Mountain climbing
Tennis
Biking
Walking
Exercising
Rollerblading
Bowling
Swimming

Coaching

⇒ Everyone's ideas of dating will vary, and practices will evolve over time as spiritual principles are applied to the process. Contribute to this evolution by coming up with creative new ways to date, socialize, and learn about each other's character, personality, attitudes, and behavior.

⇒ A strong sense of self-respect mixed with self-confidence will guide you to make wise and healthy decisions during the dating process (and are great qualities for happiness in marriage, too).

⇒ Meditate, pray, and consult with trusted others to help guide you in choosing your companions and actions.

? Questions for Reflection and Discussion

1. What is your view of dating? Is it something you want to take part in? Why or why not?
2. What are your parents' views of dating? What is your view of their attitudes?
3. What are the dating practices in your culture?
4. If you have dated in the past, what have the relationships been like?
5. What is your commitment to chastity and abstinence? What might challenge you in keeping a commitment to them?
6. What can you do to protect your commitment to chastity and abstinence? What might support you?
7. What are your boundaries relating to intimacy and touch? Is one of you pushing for greater intimacy more than the other is comfortable with having? Do you know and respect each other's boundaries?
8. How much contact and interaction do you want with each other's families?
9. What do your family members say about your relationship?
10. How much interaction do you want with each other's friends?
11. What do your friends say about your relationship? How valid are their opinions?
12. What are the pros and cons of arranging to meet someone you want to get to know better at a Bahá'í or other religious conference or activity?
13. How might dating someone in your religious community cause unity or disunity?
14. Dating often involves driving places—what is your driving behavior like? Seatbelts? Speed? Accidents? Tickets? Response to other drivers? To a traffic officer?
15. What do you do with your time in the car? Argue? Consult? Listen to music? Sit silently or awkwardly?
16. How are you handling disagreements between you? Peacefully? Listening to each other? Fighting?

Do you want to date?

What type of dating partner do *you* want to be?

Hiding things or communicating?

Activities

1. Pray, meditate, reflect, and write in your journal about dating and the reasons you want to date or not date.

2. Together, create a collage of possible dating activities. Take a piece of poster paper and cut and glue onto it magazine photos and words that suggest things a couple might do together or with a group such as friends or family. See if you can come up with some new and interesting things to do. What have you agreed on as some of the dating activities you will do? What won't you do?
   _____
   _____
   _____

3. Meet with your parents and discuss the viewpoints and beliefs you each have about dating. What are the concerns that have been raised? What is your response?
   _____
   _____
   _____
   _____
   _____

4. If you are over 35 and looking for someone to marry, is there any difference in how you approach dating now than when you were younger? What if you are over 50? 60? 70? 80? Married before or never married?
   _____
   _____
   _____

5. Study the cartoon below. What would be the warning flags for you to stop dating someone?
   _____
   _____
   _____

"I'm sorry, Max, but bells didn't go off when I first met you. They were more like police sirens, as a matter of fact."

Love Letters

Letters are chances for the soul to speak, a mood captured in the fibers of the paper, a world in an envelope which will not exist until it is opened.

Love letters make love stay visible. You can rub it, smell it, touch it, share it, and sleep with it under your pillow.

Write a love letter on a bed sheet with magic markers—sleep under it.

Write a love letter on the sidewalk with purple chalk—really big.

Write a love letter in the sand and leave it to wash away.

~ SARK, *Inspiration Sandwich*, pp. 19-20

CHAPTER 10 – Getting Serious: Courting the Special One

Focus Points
- Building a new model of courtship
- Family involvement in courtship
- Courtship and compatibility activities
- Warning signals during courtship

A Couple's Story

Lindsay and James get to know each other for a couple of months. They continue to go to the study circle together, James helps Lindsay out with building the set for her college theater play, they discover a mutual love of music and attend most of the concerts in the area, and they help with a city park cleanup. They have recently expressed their love to each other and feel they are ready to see each other exclusively. James buys a copy of the marriage preparation book and gives it to Lindsay as a present. The couple has talked about what they are looking for in a marriage partner and are quite serious about each other.

James hasn't met Lindsay's parents yet, as they live out of town. However, Lindsay meets James' parents, Sondra and Marvin, at community meetings, and as the parents see the two becoming close, they invite the couple over for dinner. James loves his parents, but he is a bit concerned they'll chase Lindsay away by asking her too many questions too soon about herself and her family. He also doesn't want her to think that he is pressuring her to move forward too fast. They pray and consult about it until they feel some resolution and assurance and then go on to the dinner.

Lindsay greets Sondra and Marvin. "Thanks for inviting me to dinner," she says.

After dinner, the four sit and talk while enjoying dessert and coffee. "Lindsay and I have agreed that we are getting serious about each other," says James. "We hope you'll be supportive of us."

"I really want to learn from you both," says Lindsay. "You guys have been married a long time. This is hard to say, but with Mom and Dad divorced…it scares me sometimes that I won't be able to maintain a long-term relationship. When I get married, I want to stay married. I want to know how you do it."

"Yeah, we want a lasting relationship," says James. He grins at his parents and says, "Now just because Lindsay and I are serious, Mom and Dad, that doesn't mean we want you grilling us with endless questions. But we do want your help getting to know each other and making sure it would be good for us to go forward."

Sondra and Marvin look at each other and smile back at the couple. "We do want to support what you are doing…being careful is a good idea," Sondra says. "But as far as questions go, I love to ask them, so we'll just see how it goes." She laughs and says, "Just stop me if I start sounding like one of Lindsay's professors giving a test!"

Chapter 10 – Getting Serious: Courting the Special One

Quotes for Guidance

❋ ...they [a courting couple] must show forth the utmost attention and become informed of one another's character and the firm covenant made between each other must become an eternal binding, and their intentions must be everlasting affinity, friendship, unity and life.
   ('Abdu'l-Bahá: *Tablets of 'Abdu'l-Bahá, Vol. 2*, p. 325)

The following is a letter written by the Universal House of Justice in response to an inquiry from a father about his sons:

❋ As you know, courtship practices differ greatly from one culture to another, and it is not yet known what pattern of courtship will emerge in the future when society has been more influenced by Bahá'í Teachings. However, there is no indication that it will resemble the practices extant in existing cultures.... In this interim period, the friends are encouraged to make great efforts to live in conformity with the Teachings and to gradually forge a new pattern of behavior, more in keeping with the spirit of Bahá'u'lláh's Revelation. In this context, we offer the following comments.
   Although a Bahá'í may, if he chooses, seek his parents' advice on the choice of a partner, and although Bahá'í parents may give such advice if asked, it is clear from the Teachings that parents do not have the right to interfere in their children's actual choice of a prospective partner until approached for their consent to marry. Therefore, when discussing the issue of courtship with your sons, it would be best to discuss it on the level of principle without reference to individuals.
   In the context of the society in which your family now lives, a society in which materialism, self-centeredness and failing marriages are all too common, your sons may well feel that it is wise to have a long period of courtship in which the prospective partners spend much time together and become thoroughly acquainted with each other's character, background and family. This practice does not in itself contradict Bahá'í law and, as it is not unacceptable in ... [country name removed], it appears to be a viable option. As you are aware, Bahá'u'lláh ordained that Bahá'í engagement should not exceed 95 days, and, although this law has not yet been applied universally, it highlights the desirability of marrying quickly once the decision to marry has been firmly taken and parental consent obtained. However, in a relationship in which such a decision has not been taken and in which the law of chastity is strictly observed, there is no objection, in principle, to a prolonged friendship in which the two individuals entertain the possibility of marrying each other at some time in the future.
   You have mentioned that your sons like to invite their girlfriends to spend a lot of time with the family and that you are not entirely happy with this situation. Each family member has rights which should be respected, and if you wish to have some time in your home without the presence of non-family members, the other members of your family should take this seriously into consideration. However, we hasten to point out to you that the situation which you describe, in which your sons wish their friends to be involved with your family, is much more in line with the Teachings than the common pattern in Western countries in which many youth virtually exclude their parents from interacting with their peers, sometimes distancing themselves from their families in order to have the freedom to engage in frivolous and even unchaste behavior....
   (Universal House of Justice: An unpublished letter August 28, 1994, to an individual)

Perspectives to Consider

Once you are past the initial meeting phase, and you've decided you have an interest in each other, you will usually choose to do more activities together in order to get to know each other better. If you feel a strong attraction toward each other and a solid friendship is forming, you may choose to focus on a **committed, exclusive relationship**. You may be starting to talk about marriage and are certain that you want to consider this seriously.

The term that may be most appropriate for you at this stage, however, is **"courting,"** which might be considered dating taken to the next level. It has the specific intention of moving you toward marriage, without cohabiting or premarital sexual relations. Courting used to be common, but today, at least in the Western part of the world, it is a term and practice that is rarely used. It is appropriate to reactivate it now because it is in line with the spiritual principles that lead a couple toward a strong marriage, such as encouraging family unity. Courtship is an excellent prelude to the parental consent process, which is required for Bahá'ís (see Chapters 31-33). ***This would be a good time to share with parents the law of consent, which will give them time to learn about it and understand the importance of their role.***

Courtship today must be in an altered state with fewer ceremonies, rules, and obligations, and with less of the former practice that involved families overseeing all aspects of the relationship. It supports thoroughly understanding each other's character and allows time for the couple to get to know each other well (see Chapters 6 and 19 on character and personality). It does not include the concept of "blind love," where the relationship is exclusively based on physical attraction and not at all on establishing a long-term and firm foundation. (And yes, physical attraction is appropriate for a couple considering marriage.)

Courtship appears to be less self-centered than the more common dating model, which usually has you isolated from your families. Courting **includes parents and family**, who may guide you through and support your marriage preparation process. While parents are not to interfere in your selection of a partner, spending time with your families will give you opportunities to build family unity and give your parents an opportunity to get to know the character and personality of your courting partner. Parents often know you best and have a good idea what kind of person would make you happy. Remember that parents also have a responsibility to learn about your prospective mate's character as part of the parental consent process. This family time should include ensuring each of you has one-on-one time with each others' parents. This will also give you the opportunity to see how the other behaves and responds in family settings.

Courtship is a time for enjoying being together and provides opportunities to observe and understand each other's **character, personality, attitudes, and behavior** (see Chapters 6 and 19). For this reason, you will want to participate in activities that support this process. It won't help you to become sure of each other as lifetime partners if you only do activities that allow your true self to hide—or use activities to hide your emotions. Get to know each other very well—unpleasant surprises after the wedding can create disunity and heartache.

Courtship activities will vary from couple to couple. Movie watching for one couple might be a way to hide their thoughts and emotions from each other and avoid communication. For another couple who are deeply immersed in the arts, a movie might provide an opportunity for an in-depth and lively discussion. (Chapter 9 on dating has some activity ideas.)

When involved in a courtship, you will grow in your knowledge of the other person. As you do this, pay attention to **things that concern you,** and do not brush them aside or deny that they are important. Some, you may find, can be prayed about, consulted about, and resolved; others may cause you to stop being in a close relationship. Below are some warning signals indicating there is an issue that requires particular attention. **Note:** You may need to seek counseling for any serious concerns.

Chapter 10 – Getting Serious: Courting the Special One

Warning Signals During Courtship

- Major character flaws (Examples: habitual lying, laziness, chronic disrespect toward you or others)
- A Bahá'í or someone of any other religion refuses to participate in meetings, doesn't pray, questions the validity of scripture, or picks and chooses parts of the religion he or she likes and rejects the rest
- Incompatibility of basic values about faith, career, finances, and raising children
- Mutual attraction seems to be fading
- Constant complaining and behaving like a victim; carrying around excessive emotional baggage.
- Extreme jealousy, possessiveness, or controlling tendencies
- Argumentative; frequent fights and/or violent tendencies; frequent anger and bad temper
- Constant criticism
- Substance abuse or addictions (Watch for slowed responses, slurred speech, glassy eyes, extreme mood swings, unexpected absences, failure to keep dates, or financial problems)
- Being "co-dependent" with someone, especially one who is abusing substances or addicted—getting deeply involved in their problems and trying to fix them; losing your identity in someone else's problems
- Mental, emotional, or physical abuse
- Eating disorders; unusual eating habits; sudden or frequent weight gains and losses
- Excessive time spent with others such as friends and family and leaving the other alone; the relationship is rarely a priority
- Excessive flirting with and teasing other people
- Determination to change the other (Watch for: constantly and often publicly criticizing, judging, scrutinizing, and correcting)
- Constantly changing to please the other
- Lack of communication; boredom; disinterest; little to talk about
- Trouble holding a job; expects others to pay bills

(Marriage Therapist Keyvan Geula contributed to this list.)

Note: The list above points out the warning signals for you. The chapters ahead in Step 4 that address compatibility will be a powerful resource and tool for you as you go through courtship and will provide you with many of the *positive relationship signals*. The discussions and activities you will do regarding compatibility will support you in deciding whether to marry or not.

Coaching

⇒ You may find it helpful to participate in conferences, workshops, summer schools, and other Bahá'í or religious events as a significant part of your courting process.

⇒ Include many types of service to each other and to others in your time spent together. Service is one of the best ways to gain insights about someone's character and personality.

⇒ Continually be open with your courting partner and don't give mixed emotional and physical messages. The way you conduct yourself in a serious investigative relationship carries over into the marital relationship. Think about how betrayed you would feel if you discovered something very important about your partner after the wedding. Think about the anxiety you would feel when hiding something from the other—how might he or she respond upon discovering it later? Those moments of discovering secrets are painful and can seriously disrupt a marriage, even at times destroy it if the matter is serious enough. You can prevent this now.

Marriage Can Be Forever—Preparation Counts!

Questions for Reflection and Discussion

1. What does courtship mean to you?
2. What activities do you want to include in your courtship? What ones do you want to avoid?
3. How much family involvement is important to you in the courtship process? How will you set this up? What will you do together?
4. What involvement from your friends and religious community will support you during courtship? Who will you ask? How will you ask them for support?
5. What do you see as important activities for you during this stage?
6. What warning signals, if any, are you seeing in your relationship? What positive signs are there?
7. What structures and agreements will support you in maintaining abstinence and avoiding premarital sex?
8. Determine when you may be close to breaking your agreement to abstain from premarital sex? What specifically could you do to address it at that time? What about before it gets to that point?
9. What communications and actions from your parents might seem like inappropriate interference in your relationship? Have you communicated your views to your parents? Are you able to come to a consultative agreement on boundaries?

Activities

1. Pray, meditate, reflect, and write in your journal about your views and vision of courtship.

2. Use Worksheet 10A to identify some specific activities to assist you in understanding each other's character, personality, and behavior. Complete as many identified activities as possible.

3. What did you learn from these activities?

    _____
    _____
    _____

    Which activities did you particularly enjoy? What about them did you enjoy?

    _____
    _____
    _____

    Which activities do you want to do again?

    _____
    _____
    _____

4. Use Worksheet 10B to set goals for your courtship.

Chapter 10 – Getting Serious: Courting the Special One

Date: _____

Worksheet 10A: Identify Activities to Learn About Each Other

DIRECTIONS: Complete this worksheet on your own or together. It will support you in assessing your partner's character, personality, and behavior if you make conscious choices about your activities. See how well you get along as companions and if you can be effective in what you are trying to accomplish together. Over time you will want to see if you can maintain unity and harmony between you in a wide variety of circumstances, including under stress.

Worksheets may be printed from www.claricomm.com/publishing

What activities support you in learning about your partner?	What do you want to learn from this activity?	Is this an activity you would enjoy doing?
Example: Cleaning an elderly friend's home	**Example:** To see if he/she has a positive attitude about service to others	✓

Marriage Can Be Forever—Preparation Counts!

Date: _____

Worksheet 10B: Setting Courtship Goals

DIRECTIONS: Complete this worksheet separately or together. The period of your courtship, which precedes consent and engagement, will be primarily a time to explore compatibility. You may get to know your parents better during this period as well. Below, identify the key goals you want to accomplish during this courtship time.

Worksheets may be printed from www.claricomm.com/publishing

1. What do you most want to learn about your partner that will tell you if he/she will be a good spouse for you?
   _____
   _____
   _____
   _____
   _____

2. What do you want to make sure to do with him/her during courtship?
   _____
   _____
   _____

3. How often do you plan to be with your parents? With his/her parents? Separately? Together?
   _____
   _____
   _____

4. In what ways will being with your parents together support you in preparing for marriage?
   _____
   _____
   _____

5. What guidelines for communication and behavior will support you in courtship?
   _____
   _____
   _____

6. How long do you see courtship lasting?
   _____
   _____
   _____

7. What else is important to you at this time?
   _____
   _____
   _____

Marriage Can Be Forever—Preparation Counts!

COMMITMENT

Until one is committed there is hesitancy, the chance to draw back, always ineffectiveness. Concerning all acts of initiative (and creation), there is one elementary truth, the ignorance of which kills countless ideas and splendid plans: that the moment one definitely commits oneself, then Providence moves too. All sorts of things occur to help one that would never otherwise have occurred. A whole stream of events issues from the decision, raising in one's favor all manner of unforeseen incidents and meetings and material assistance, which no man could have dreamt would have come his way.

I have learned a deep respect for one of Goethe's couplets:

"Whatever you can do, or dream you can, begin it.
Boldness has genius, power, and magic in it."

~ W. H. Murray, *The Scottish Himalayan Expedition*

The moment you believe you can do something, power seems to stream into you; the moment you believe you cannot do it, you have lost more than half the battle, you seem to be drained of the force necessary to do it.

~ Rúhíyyih Rabbani, *Prescription for Living*, p. 39

CHAPTER 11 – Promising Forever: Making Commitments

Focus Points

- Defining commitment and fear of commitment
- Commitment to yourself and others
- Understanding how you handle commitments
- Marital commitment as part of God's Covenant
- Warning signs of lack of commitment
- Value of commitment

A Couple's Story

"I really want to make sure we are very close friends first before we commit ourselves to anything," says Lindsay. "And you've had a lot of girlfriends and have had sex with a couple of them. I want to be sure you can really commit to being loyal and faithful just to me."

"I know I've wandered around some," says James. "But I don't want that anymore. And I was never unfaithful or disloyal when I was in a relationship. I really do want to get married."

"Let's just take this a step at a time and see how it turns out," says Lindsay. "We don't have to rush." She pauses, and hesitates. "And James…I…uhh…really need you to be tested for HIV/AIDS to be sure you're okay too."

"Ah, you're right. That's a good idea. What else can I do to help you trust me?" asks James.

Quotes for Guidance

✺ …say not that which thou doest not.
  (Bahá'u'lláh: *Hidden Words*, Arabic No. 29)

✺ He should not…promise that which he doth not fulfill.
  (Bahá'u'lláh: *Gleanings from the Writings of Bahá'u'lláh*, p. 266)

✺ Bahá'í marriage is the commitment of the two parties one to the other, and their mutual attachment of mind and heart. Each must, however, exercise the utmost care to become thoroughly acquainted with the character of the other, that the binding covenant between them may be a tie that will endure forever. Their purpose must be this: to become loving companions and comrades and at one with each other for time and eternity....
  ('Abdu'l-Bahá: *Selections from the Writings of 'Abdu'l-Bahá*, p. 118)

✺ There is no doubt about it that the believers in America, probably unconsciously influenced by the extremely lax morals prevalent and the flippant attitude towards divorce which seems to be increasingly prevailing, do not take divorce seriously enough and do not seem to grasp the fact that although Bahá'u'lláh has permitted it, He has only permitted it as a last resort and strongly condemns it.

The presence of children, as a factor in divorce, cannot be ignored, for surely it places an even greater weight of moral responsibility on the [husband] and wife in considering such a step. Divorce under such circumstances no longer just concerns them and their desires and feelings but also concerns the children's entire future and their own attitude towards marriage.
(Shoghi Effendi: *Compilation of Compilations, Vol. II*, p. 242)

❋ In all matters, great or small, word must be the complement of deed, and deed the companion of word: each must supplement, support and reinforce the other.
(Shoghi Effendi: *Compilation of Compilations, Vol. II*, p. 346)

❋ It is an important principle of the [Bahá'í] Faith that one must not promise what one is not going to fulfill.
(On behalf of the Universal House of Justice: *Lights of Guidance*, p. 335)

Perspectives to Consider

Are you **afraid to make a commitment**? Some people think making a commitment is something horrible to be avoided. And commitment to marriage certainly seems absent when couples live together. It is a complex concept, but one that is vital for a healthy marriage. As you explore this, you may be surprised how good you actually are at making and keeping commitments.

When you **make and keep promises** that are based on clearly thinking through their implications and your ability to fulfill them, you are making commitments. You make a pledge inside yourself to do something, state the commitment out loud to someone else, and then act in agreement with your words.

If you look back over your life, you will see that one type of commitment you make regularly is a **commitment to yourself**. These commitments, when kept, increase your self-respect and well-being. A commitment to yourself might include a decision to pray regularly, eat healthy food, read a good book, take a class, exercise, meditate, and much more. Take a moment to reflect on your history of keeping—and breaking—commitments to yourself.

You have also had considerable practice in making and keeping **commitment to other people**. From the time you were small, you've had opportunities to promise something and successfully keep the promise. In your family, friendships, schools, workplaces, and community, over and over again, you have said you would do something and then did your best to complete the task. You valued and kept your word and experienced the benefits that resulted. You also learned along the way that breaking your promises resulted in negative consequences. These consequences then trained you and reinforced for you the importance of keeping promises.

Keeping promises has prepared you for making increasingly significant commitments. When you were little, you may have promised to return a toy or book, clean your room, do your homework, walk the dog, or bake a cake. As a teenager or young adult, there is/was the opportunity to be successful at longer-term commitments. For example, enrolling in college, signing a contract for a job, enlisting in the Peace Corps, or taking out a loan on a car all involve agreeing to do something for an extended period of time. These agreements include the understanding that there will be a mutual exchange. Each party involved in the agreement gives and gets something, whether it is money, education, or service. You will take the commitment skills you have learned over the years and apply them during dating and courting.

Marriage Can Be Forever—Preparation Counts!

In spiritual terms, a promise or commitment is often referred to as **a covenant**. God has made a Covenant with mankind to always provide us with spiritual guidance through inspired Teachers, Prophets, and Messengers. Within that larger framework, there are other spiritual covenants. One includes the promise from those Messengers to give us what we need to live our spiritual lives—things like the Golden Rule. Another spiritual covenant is between a couple and God to establish a marriage and family.

What a courting couple does is **investigate each other's character**, and when they are sure that it is possible and wise, create a "binding covenant" and a "most sacred and binding tie" between them to stay married for all eternity. It is a commitment to love forever. This is not a commitment to make lightly or without careful preparation, but neither is it an impossible one to make. It takes prayer, meditation, consultation, friendship, and family involvement and support. Look carefully at your doubts, hesitations, and fears and decide what has validity, and what doesn't.

As you are courting, you will have many opportunities to **observe how your partner keeps commitments**, both to you and to other people. When you make a date to be together, is it kept? Does he/she arrive on the right date and at the agreed time? Are promises kept? When he/she has agreed to do something for another person, is there follow-through and completion?

Commitment within a marriage has many facets. Some are listed below.

Commitment in Marriage

- Deep caring about someone else and his/her welfare
- Loyalty
- Faithfulness to each other; not being involved in romantic or sexual relationships with others
- Trust
- Perseverance; staying power; not giving up when there are difficult times
- Striving for unity
- Avoiding conflict and contention; praying and consulting instead
- Forgiveness and acceptance of faults
- Being encouraging and loving in words and actions
- Sharing from your heart, mind, and soul
- Maintaining mutual interests and goals, while giving each other the space to have separate ones

So, what if you marry without carefully thinking about the commitment involved? Marriage is not just the wedding party or the romance. It includes being willing to use prayer, consultation, and love to see you through the tough stuff, loving each other even when you behave badly. It means handling a myriad of endless practical details—taking out the garbage, diapering the baby, returning books to the library, and paying the bills. But, ideally, the upside is you get to do all these with your best friend.

Marriage Can Be Forever—Preparation Counts!

The consequences of taking a marriage commitment lightly are significant. **Divorce and family breakups** are devastating. So think about the **warning signs** below.

- Do you habitually make promises half-heartedly or without intending to follow through and keep them?
- What words do you use when you commit to be somewhere or do something? When you make date and time commitments, do you keep them?
- Do you make promises under pressure without committing your heart to them?
- Do you enter into relationships where you don't have much in common with the person beyond physical/sexual attraction?
- Are you unable to talk to each other as friends? Do you always turn to other people to meet your communication needs?
- Is there a lot of talk about doing things that does not result in action?
- Do you have frequent misunderstandings with people about whether they have committed to do something with you or not? Or them with you?
- How do you handle broken commitments? When you cannot keep a commitment, do you avoid being in communication with the people affected?

Any of these behavior patterns are indications you may have trouble keeping the commitment that is required for marriage. But if you have a history of being able to faithfully and consistently keep your promises, commitment to marriage is possible.

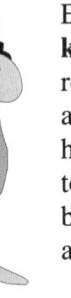

Evaluate your observations and experiences with the commitments **other people in your life have kept or not kept** and understand how that has shaped your attitude. If your parents, other relatives, or close friends have gone through divorces, you may be skeptical about your own ability to keep a commitment. If you have been on the receiving end of many broken promises, how has that affected your faith in others? You may find it difficult to trust others and impossible to trust the person who has repeatedly broken his/her word. If you are suspicious of everyone because of the actions of one, however, it will negatively affect your ability to develop friendships and a close relationship with a potential spouse.

Think about the positive outcomes of making commitments and keeping them. They can balance out the fears and concerns you might have about commitment generally and to a marriage partner.

The Value of Keeping Commitments

- People trust you
- You experience a feeling of satisfaction
- You are relaxed and happy instead of feeling guilty and uncomfortable about letting others down
- You are able to be truthful about what you are doing
- You are free to pursue personal development and support the well-being of your family members
- The bond of love between you and others is maintained
- You can focus on deepening your friendship with your partner
- You can be in harmony with God
- Your communication with others is usually more open and effective
- You are happier
- You are more likely to work through and resolve a problem with someone rather than run away or be destructive toward your relationship

Coaching

⇒ Take time to understand the reasons behind any resistance you feel about commitment.

⇒ Look at commitment as something that frees you to be with a close companion who will create a family with you, instead of something that restricts you.

⇒ Both of you must come to marriage with the realization that it is not a circumstance where you each give about 50 percent and hope you meet halfway and it adds up to a whole marriage. You must each give the relationship 100 percent; both of you must give it a high level of attention and sustained effort. Laziness about addressing personal and joint relationship issues will likely lead you to divorce.

⇒ Restate your commitments from time to time as an affirmation to yourself and the other person.

Questions for Reflection and Discussion

1. How do you define commitment?
2. What aspects of commitment do you see as spiritual? Mental? Emotional? Physical?
3. Are any of these aspects more important to you than others?
4. What is your history of keeping promises? Of making commitments? How do you feel about this history?
5. What has been your experience of keeping promises made to each other?
6. How do you handle it when you break a promise? When someone else does?
7. What things have you done to cover up for breaking a promise?
8. What scares you about commitment?
9. What do you love about commitment?
10. In what ways, if any, are commitments to a romantic partner different than commitments to other people?

Activities

1. Pray, meditate, reflect, and write in your journal about any fears you have about commitment and marriage.

2. Use Worksheet 11A to examine your fears about marriage.

3. Finish the worksheet and then write in your journal or discuss with a friend or each other about whether your fears are realistic or not.

_____
_____
_____
_____

4. Use Worksheet 11B to keep a log for a week of all the times you make and keep short-term commitments.

Marriage Can Be Forever—Preparation Counts!

5. Use Worksheet 11C to examine your history of long-term commitments (more than 1 year).

6. Make a list of the major goals and activities in your life you are committed to:
   _____
   _____
   _____
   _____
   _____
   _____

7. How important is it to you that your partner be committed to these same things?
   _____
   _____

8. What are your commitments in your courting relationship?
   _____
   _____
   _____
   _____
   _____

9. Do you think your commitments will shift with marriage? What might your new commitments be?
   _____
   _____
   _____
   _____
   _____

Date: _____

Worksheet 11A: Fears About Commitment

DIRECTIONS: Fear can stop you from making a commitment to marry someone. Complete the sheet below to help you understand your fears. Use the questions below to get you started, but recognize that other issues are likely to be relevant to you as well. Each raises a point about something that may leave you with a fear that will stop you from being committed to someone.

Worksheets may be printed from www.claricomm.com/publishing

a. What if I change (you will)?
b. What if he/she changes (he/she will)?
c. What if we have sexual problems?
d. What if I get bored?
e. What if I'm not "good enough"?
f. Can I be a good parent?
g. Can I handle the responsibilities of family finances?
h. What if he/she falls out of love with me?
i. What if I become attracted to someone else?
j. What if one of us gets sick and can't earn an income?
k. What if he/she changes physically?
l. What if we just can't agree about vital matters?

1. If I marry, I am afraid the following things *might happen*:
   _____
   _____

2. How likely is it that these things will happen?
   _____

3. These are the things I could do to prevent them from happening:
   _____
   _____

4. If I marry, I am afraid the following things *might not* happen:
   _____
   _____

5. These are the things I could do to have them happen:
   _____
   _____

6. These are the benefits to me if I commit to marriage:
   _____
   _____

7. These are the benefits to others if I commit to marriage:
   _____
   _____

8. These are the disadvantages to me if I commit to marriage:
   _____
   _____

9. These are the disadvantages to others if I commit to marriage:
   _____
   _____

10. This is what I'm willing to do to address my concerns: (Examples: counseling, training, reassurance from your partner; often, regularly, weekly)
    _____

Marriage Can Be Forever—Preparation Counts!

Date: _____

Worksheet 11B: Log of Short-Term Commitments

DIRECTIONS: Use the table below to record your commitments over the span of a few days or a week.
- Record the short-term commitments you make, such as a medical appointment, and the promises you make, such as agreeing to meet a friend for coffee or a game of basketball.
- Note whether you kept the commitment or not.
- Examine what got in the way if you didn't keep the agreement and what assisted you to keep it, if you did.

Worksheets may be printed from www.claricomm.com/publishing

Commitment/Promise Made	Kept?	What Prevented You?	What Assisted You?

1. What excuses and reasons do you habitually use for not keeping commitments?

    ___ I didn't have time
    ___ It wasn't important anyway
    ___ They weren't really expecting me
    ___ I'm a busy person
    ___ Something came up
    ___ Others: _____

2. Do you communicate with the people you have made commitments to and re-negotiate the commitment instead of just missing it? ___ Yes ___ No
   Why or why not?
   _____

3. What would assist you to keep commitments?
   _____

4. What would assist you to communicate with the other person when a commitment cannot be kept?
   _____

5. Journal or discuss how you feel about breaking and keeping commitments. What commitments and promises are you going to keep during the next week? How do *you* feel when others break commitments to you?
   _____
   _____
   _____

Marriage Can Be Forever—Preparation Counts!

Date: _____

Worksheet 11C: History of Long-Term Commitments

DIRECTIONS: Use this worksheet to examine your history of long-term commitments (more than 1 year). Identify what you have learned from them and the obstacles you have overcome in keeping them. Is your list something to celebrate?

Worksheets may be printed from www.claricomm.com/publishing

1. What long-term commitments have you made?
   - ___ Installment loan
   - ___ College degree
   - ___ Marriage
   - ___ Parenting/Childcare
   - ___ To a religion
   - ___ Developing a creative skill: _____
   - ___ Career/Job
   - ___ Others: _____

2. What have you learned from making these commitments?
   - ___ Responsibility
   - ___ Self-respect
   - ___ Confidence
   - ___ The value of keeping promises
   - ___ Managing details
   - ___ The benefits to other people
   - ___ Others: _____

3. What difficulties have you overcome to keep these commitments?
   - ___ Work layoff
   - ___ Finding a new job
   - ___ Divorce
   - ___ Prejudice
   - ___ Objections from others: _____
   - ___ Doing what felt more fun in the short-term
   - ___ Studying when friends were having fun
   - ___ Others: _____

4. How do you feel about your partner's history of being able to make and keep long-term commitments?
   _____
   _____
   _____

Marriage Can Be Forever—Preparation Counts!

MARRIAGE, NOT COHABITATION

In marriage,...there must be a conviction, a commitment from the start that the relationship is good, that it will get better, and that it is for keeps. The try and see attitude has no place in marriage. Because that, in itself, will undermine the determination and the commitment to make it the very best and lasting relationship possible. Marriage should not be entered into with the idea of 'til divorce us do part.

This is one reason why cohabitation, trial marriages, and other forms of pre-marriage intimacy are bad ideas to begin with. They have a large element of hesitancy, trepidation, and leaving an escape hatch. Marriage is a total commitment and that is the only way that it is going to be successful. The only two alternative thoughts in marriage have to be: it will either succeed or it will succeed! This commitment together with the willingness to do the work in an atmosphere of equality, respect, and love make for a successful marriage.

~ Khalil A. Khavari and Sue Williston Khavari
Together Forever, p. 12

CHAPTER 12 – A Serious Sidestep: Living Together

> **Focus Points**
> - Marriage as a spiritual institution
> - The benefits of marriage
> - The challenge of high standards: morality and chastity
> - The consequences of choosing cohabitation
> - The difficult transition from living together to marriage

A Couple's Story

"We're together all the time now," says James. "What difference would it make if we live together and get to know each other better under the same roof?"

"It's just not right, James," says Lindsay. "My parents might be okay with it, but how could we face your parents—there's no way they'd approve with it being against the Bahá'í Teachings. Besides which, I'm afraid it wouldn't really get our marriage off to a good start. Everything I've read says living together without a commitment can just lead to divorce when you marry later."

James pauses for reflection. "I know you're right, and I want to follow the Bahá'í Teachings," says James. "I don't want to get my parents upset either. It's just that I love you so much, and it's hard being apart."

They take a break and James goes for a walk and prays. He's calmer when he returns. "I guess I'll just have to be patient while we get to know each other better and are really sure."

Quotes for Guidance

✸ When, therefore, the people of Bahá undertake to marry, the union must be a true relationship, a spiritual coming together as well as a physical one, so that throughout every phase of life, and in all the worlds of God, their union will endure; for this real oneness is a gleaming out of the love of God.
   ('Abdu'l-Bahá: *Selections from the Writings of 'Abdu'l-Bahá*, p. 117)

✸ …man's supreme honor and real happiness lie in self-respect, in high resolves and noble purposes, in integrity and moral quality, in immaculacy of mind.
   ('Abdu'l-Bahá: *Secret of Divine Civilization*, p. 19)

✸ As regards flagrantly immoral relationships, such as a man living with a mistress, this should be brought to his attention in a loving manner, and he should be urged to either marry the woman if he is free to do so, or to give up this conduct, so detrimental to the [Bahá'í] Faith and to his own spiritual progress.
   (On behalf of Shoghi Effendi: *Lights of Guidance*, p. 382)

- ✱ Concerning the positive aspects of chastity the Universal House of Justice states that the Bahá'í Faith recognizes the value of the sex impulse and holds that the institution of marriage has been established as the channel of its rightful expression. Bahá'ís do not believe that the sex impulse should be suppressed but that it should be regulated and controlled.

    Chastity in no way implies withdrawal from human relationships. It liberates people from the tyranny of the ubiquity of sex. A person who is in control of his sexual impulses is enabled to have profound and enduring friendships with many people, both men and women, without ever sullying that unique and priceless bond that should unite [husband] and wife.
    (On behalf of the Universal House of Justice: *Compilation of Compilations, Vol. I*, p. 50)

- ✱ The Bahá'í Teachings do not contemplate any form of "trial marriage." A couple should study each other's character and spend time getting to know each other before they decide to marry, and when they do marry it should be with the intention of establishing an eternal bond. They should realize, moreover, that the primary purpose of marriage is the procreation of children.
    (On behalf of the Universal House of Justice: *Lights of Guidance*, p. 380)

- ✱ As to chastity, this is one of the most challenging concepts to get across in this very permissive age, but Bahá'ís must make the utmost effort to uphold Bahá'í standards, no matter how difficult they may seem at first. Such efforts will be made easier if the youth will understand that the laws and standards of the Faith are meant to free them from untold spiritual and moral difficulties in the same way that a proper appreciation of the laws of nature enables one to live in harmony with the forces of the planet.
    (On behalf of the Universal House of Justice: *Lights of Guidance*, pp. 362-363)

Perspectives to Consider

Faced with the high divorce statistics and the unhappiness of friends and relatives you may have seen go through divorces, you may **ponder whether living together first** to ensure compatibility is a sensible choice. On the surface, this may sound logical; however, it is essentially *an illusion*. The "fortress" of marriage is a place of protection that is more likely to ensure your happiness and well-being.

Marriage as a spiritual institution includes the concepts of commitment and partnership and includes the blessings of God. A "trial marriage" cannot have these essential characteristics, so how could it really give you a true picture of what is involved in being married?

The spiritual standard of **sexual chastity and purity** is difficult for many people to achieve. This is especially so in a society where you are surrounded by images in the media and the example of others that demonstrate a totally different standard. Making a choice that will support your happiness and well-being requires prayer, meditation, support of friends, effort, vigilance, a strong sense of self-respect, and inner discipline.

It is common for cohabiting couples to believe they will have a greater chance of success in marriage if they live together first. If they decide to marry, they find it difficult to transition from being together without a firm commitment to being together in marriage. The **divorce rate is no better** for couples that live together first without commitment and then later marry than it is in the general population.

Over the last two decades, especially in the West, many couples have chosen to live together instead of marrying. As social scientists study this trend, they are increasingly finding evidence that marrying is the choice that best leads to strong, healthy relationships. Below are some benefits they are starting to identify as being associated with marriage.

Marriage Can Be Forever—Preparation Counts!

Benefits of Being Married Instead of Cohabiting

- A higher level of commitment; greater confidence in the longevity of the relationship
- Better communication and problem-solving
- Less conflict and violence
- Families and community members offer their wisdom, support, and experience in greater abundance
- Relationships are more settled, and parents are more likely to include the couple in family events or trips and offer emotional support during difficulties
- There is greater family unity
- Children are born into or live in a more stable household and relationship; their health, well-being, and achievement are higher
- Tendency to be more productive in the workforce and have higher incomes
- Greater physical and mental health and happiness; a tendency to live longer
- Families tend to share their financial resources with them, including financing education
- A higher level of satisfaction, including greater sexual satisfaction; greater motivation within marriage to please a partner rather than looking for sexual satisfaction from multiple partners
- More faithfulness; less likelihood of an affair; faithfulness contributes to protecting partners from sexually transmitted diseases

(Some of these benefits draw on "Why Marriage Matters," published by the Institute for American Values.)

In a spiritual context, when cohabitation is forbidden, as it is in the Bahá'í Faith, living together causes a variety of **disruptions**. Your religious community cannot openly show support for your relationship as it can when you are married. You, as individuals and as a couple, are also in the position of feeling hypocritical if you participate in activities while pretending to be not living together. Or you may be asked by religious leaders to restrict your community activities. In either case, the result is spiritual estrangement. This is not a healthy condition within which to grow as an individual or a nurturing environment for a relationship.

If you have been living together and then you wish to **transition to being married**, it is still wise to take time to assess yourselves and prepare for the change in your circumstances and relationship. It is not an easy process to go from living in an uncommitted relationship to marriage, a relationship that requires loyalty and faithfulness to your spouse. You may have maintained totally separate finances and made your financial decisions independently of the wishes of the other person. Marriage includes consultation with each other on most things, even if you maintain or establish separate lines of credit or bank accounts.

In living together, couples may have developed the habit of turning to friends when needing to talk about and resolve difficulties instead of handling them together, and this may be a difficult pattern to change. If you are living together, you always have in the back of your mind that you can easily leave if it doesn't work out. With marriage, leaving and divorce are last resorts to be pursued only in extreme circumstances. Many couples decide with each other early in their relationships that divorce will never be a proposed solution to any problem that comes up between them, which allows them to focus their energy on resolving the issues instead.

Coaching

⇒ If you are considering cohabitation, seek input and guidance from your family and people you trust in your religious community.

⇒ If you are at the point of deciding to live together, consider taking a physical and emotional break from each other and establish some distance to gain perspective on your choices and their consequences.

⇒ Where parents have clearly said to their children they should not have sex before marriage and should not live with someone without marriage, there is greater likelihood that they will choose a positive path.

Questions for Reflection and Discussion

1. Why are you considering living together instead of marrying?
2. What are your beliefs about sexual chastity and abstinence?
3. What are your expectations about living together?
4. What do your family members think of this choice between you? Your parents? Siblings? Grandparents? Children?
5. How might your choice affect your relationships with your family members?
6. What does your religious community think of this as a choice?
7. What are the potential consequences of choosing to live together?
8. What do you think the effect of those consequences on you might be?
9. What are your future plans about marriage?
10. What would your household rules and boundaries be if you moved in together?
11. How would you manage finances?
12. How would you handle birth control and the possibility of children?
13. If you already have children, what would be the effect on them from your living together without marriage?

Activities

1. Pray, meditate, reflect, and write in your journal your feelings about cohabitation and marriage.

2. Complete Worksheet 12A then share and discuss the answers with trusted advisors.

Date: _____

Worksheet 12A: The Topic of Cohabitation

DIRECTIONS: Complete this worksheet separately, and then discuss it with each other and with trusted advisors. (Example: parents, close friends, spiritual counselor)

Worksheets may be printed from www.claricomm.com/publishing

1. What are your beliefs about a couple living together without being married?
   _____
   _____

2. What are your parents' (or important others') beliefs about a couple living together without being married?
   _____
   _____

3. Living together would have the following pros and cons:

PROS	CONS

3. How would living together now affect your relationship three years from now?
   _____
   _____

4. How might cohabiting affect your thoughts and beliefs about marriage? What motivates you to be willing to live with someone but not be willing to marry them? Is that okay with you?
   _____
   _____

5. What would support you in choosing to not live together without being married?
   _____
   _____

Marriage Can Be Forever—Preparation Counts!

Thoughts on Love, Sex, Intimacy, and Marriage

When we unite love with sex in its proper place, which is a home, we have an abiding fountain of happiness and strength from which to draw. Sex can strengthen love, love can sublimate sex into a spiritual communion, a joy for the soul as well as the body.

Marriage must be viewed in its correct relation to the individual and to the community at large. You will never get the most out of anything unless you understand its proper function. Marriage should be looked forward to, primarily, for the lifelong comradeship it provides. It is likely that your life partner is going to outlast all your other intimate relationships. Your parents will most probably die before you do, your children will grow up and make lives for themselves, your brothers and sisters and friends will have their own intimate relationships in life which will perforce have to take first place. But your partner, your wife or husband, will be there with you always. Joys and sorrows will have to be shared, the home, the children, the income, to a great extent your interests and diversions, will be a common holding. Before you marry you have to realize this, you have to ponder whether you two can go through all that together satisfactorily.

Do not expect too much of marriage, or too little, water cannot rise above its own level. Your union cannot produce more than you two contribute to it. If you are full of imperfections, intolerant, impatient, exacting, dictatorial, suspicious, short-tempered, selfish, do not imagine that these characteristics are going to make your marriage happy or that by changing your partner a new union will be more successful! Marriage, like all our other relationships in life, is a process which, among other things, serves to grind the sharp edges off us. The grinding often hurts, the adjustment to another person's character is difficult at first, that is why love is needed here more than in any other relationship. Love, being essentially a divine force, binds; it leaps like a spark the gaps between people's thoughts and conflicting desires, between perhaps widely different temperaments. It heals the wounds we all inflict on each other whether inadvertently or in moments of rage, jealousy or spite. To the influence of love in marriage is gradually added another powerful catalyst: habit. The common home, the daily association produces a common framework, and habit, one of the most powerful forces in life, begins to knit husband and wife together. It acts as a wonderful stabilizer; if love is allowed to fail, habit itself may be strong enough to preserve the union.

~ Rúhíyyih Rabbani, *Prescription for Living*, pp. 69-70

CHAPTER 13 – Know the Goal: A Strong, Eternal Marriage

Focus Points
- Purpose of marriage
- Marriage has a spiritual foundation and is eternal
- The Will of God
- Marriage is also a physical union
- Sanctity of marriage; Condemnation of divorce

A Couple's Story

Lindsay and James decide to go visit her mother, Kerry. They want to use part of their time with her to better understand the lessons from Lindsay's parents' mistakes and how they can avoid them. This visit is the first time that Kerry realizes with some discomfort that Lindsay's new boyfriend is a different race than she is. Kerry gets along with him well, however, so she doesn't speak up about her concerns.

After showing Kerry their marriage preparation book and explaining to her mother that they are quite serious about each other, Lindsay broaches a delicate subject. "Mom, can you tell us some of why your marriage to Dad didn't work out?" asks Lindsay. "James and I want to understand the pitfalls so we can really believe that it's possible for a marriage between us to last."

"Well, Lindsay, there were a number of challenges that all just added together and led us to divorce," says Kerry. "And it's taken me lots of counseling sessions since to sort them all out. As you know, I was pregnant with you when we got married, so we realized we'd had sex way too soon—we didn't know each other well enough. We got some marriage counseling for a while, and that helped a lot. We had fun together with you and your brother when you were little. But then things got difficult again and we mostly stopped talking to each other about anything that mattered. Your father kept changing jobs constantly or having long stretches of being unemployed, and that was stressful for both of us. Our parents had also never approved of our relationship, so we did not have their support. Finally, we realized we couldn't go on."

"I really admire the way you two are carefully getting to know each other first," Kerry continued. "By the time we've done all this studying and talking together, we'll all be a lot more sure about whether your marriage is a good idea or not."

Quotes for Guidance

✺ Wherever there is a Bahá'í family, those concerned should by all means do all they can to preserve it, because divorce is strongly condemned in the Teachings, whereas harmony, unity and love are held up as the highest ideals in human relationships.
   (On behalf of Shoghi Effendi: *Compilation of Compilations*, Vol. 1, p. 244)

Marriage Can Be Forever—Preparation Counts!

✺ There is nothing more beautiful than to have young Bahá'ís marry and found truly Bahá'í homes, the type Bahá'u'lláh wishes them to be.
   (On behalf of Shoghi Effendi: *Family Life*, p. 399; *Lights of Guidance*, p. 221)

✺ He realizes your desire to get married is quite a natural one, and he will pray that God will assist you to find a suitable companion with whom you can be truly happy and united in the service of the [Bahá'í] Faith. Bahá'u'lláh has urged marriage upon all people as the natural and rightful way of life. He has also, however, placed strong emphasis on its spiritual nature, which, while in no way precluding a normal physical life, is the most essential aspect of marriage. That two people should live their lives in love and harmony is of far greater importance than that they should be consumed with passion for each other. The one is a great rock of strength on which to lean in time of need; the other a purely temporary thing which may at any time die out.
   (On behalf of Shoghi Effendi: *Lights of Guidance*, p. 380)

✺ They should realize, moreover, that the primary purpose of marriage is the procreation of children. A couple who are physically incapable of having children may, of course, marry, since the procreation of children is not the only purpose of marriage. However, it would be contrary to the spirit of the Teachings for a couple to decide voluntarily never to have any children."
   (On behalf of the Universal House of Justice: *Lights of Guidance*, p. 380)

✺ Bahá'ís should be profoundly aware of the sanctity of marriage and should strive to make their marriages an eternal bond of unity and harmony. This requires effort and sacrifice and wisdom and self-abnegation.
   (On behalf of the Universal House of Justice: *Lights of Guidance*, p. 391)

Perspectives to Consider

One partner for all eternity—not that any of us can really visualize eternity—is an amazing concept to consider. And this partner is someone that you choose to have in your life, not someone who is there without you choosing, such as a sibling. However, eternity happens step-by-step. Successful marriage requires creating and recreating love and caring on a daily basis on the road to eternity. It means creating partnership in every sense of the word. It also means adjusting to a myriad of spiritual and physical changes, all of which require practicing the virtues of flexibility and respect as well as communicating boundaries and needs.

For your marriage to be eternal, obviously it must have a **spiritual foundation**. If you will be having a Bahá'í wedding (a requirement for Bahá'ís), the marriage vow from Bahá'u'lláh is, **"We will, all, verily, abide by the Will of God."** This is a declaration of a new spiritual relationship. If you look at marriage as a triangle, God is at the top point with the couple at the corners along the base. As you receive God's love and both draw closer to God and His Will, you will be drawn closer together. Also as you have common goals and make progress together toward them, the closeness will grow. One way that some couples resolve disagreements is to ask what would best serve God. Vows that you write yourself or that are part of another faith tradition may also stress the importance of God in your relationship.

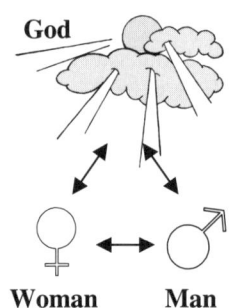

The Bahá'í vow is identical for both of you. You both state it and agree to apply it fully to your lives if you have a Bahá'í wedding [**Note:** You do not have to be a Bahá'í to have a ceremony with this vow. Anyone can have a Bahá'í wedding ceremony if they are willing to follow the Bahá'í marriage laws.]. In the couple's commitment to live by God's Will, it implies all of the commitments that come with marriage and which may be familiar from wedding ceremonies of other faiths. These vows are the promises to love, honor, and cherish each other; to care for each other regardless of material health or wealth; and to share with and be of service to one another.

Marriage Can Be Forever—Preparation Counts!

Part of the challenge is determining what God's Will is in any particular circumstance. As with individuals, couples will find their answers through:

- Prayer
- Meditation
- Observation
- Consultation

- Setting goals
- Action
- Feedback
- Evaluation of their actions

One key spiritual principle established with the Bahá'í wedding vow is the importance of both of you being willing to put God first and abide by His Will instead of by the imposed will of each other. It is important that you gain a mutual understanding of what this means, but also recognize that this understanding will grow and mature with time and experience.

Marriage will have a **ripple effect on all the relationships** you have with other people. You will have new family members to connect with and care about. Some friendships you had will become shared. Other relationships will fade away. Others will see you as a couple, different from before. You will be different as individuals as well. Then, when you have children, you create other eternal bonds with them. In fact, all these changes are part of what sometimes confronts people and scares them away from marriage—or draws them to it.

Also on the road to eternity, a married couple must go through **living together physically**. It's not an easy thing to go from having your own private space (unless you were in a college dorm or living with your sister, brother, or friend) to sharing it with another person. It's also an adjustment to share possessions and furniture, but over time, it all generally falls into place.

Yet, ***often what couples find most irritating are the little things***—someone leaving the cap off the toothpaste or the toilet seat up, projects left half done, or things out of place. It's wise to know each other well enough to identify and then talk about these habits or idiosyncrasies you each have before you share space together. You can also consult on the best manner and timing to communicate about these issues to minimize any upset over them. You have choices for how to handle what irritates you. Deciding that something just isn't going to bother you is an option—although a difficult one! And you may decide there are too many irritating things about each other for you to live peacefully in the same home. An alternative, though, is each individual *voluntarily* deciding to change, or both of you practicing the virtue of tolerance.

People marry at many **different ages and have endless variations in their circumstances**—fortresses don't come in just one design! When you are young enough to have children, your marriage will evolve around your growing family. If you have been married before, children born through other relationships will affect your marriage. Widowhood or divorce might have you looking for a partner after your children have been raised and moved out. Marriage partnerships have many values besides just raising children. Friendship, establishing a new eternal bond with someone, intimacy and sex, and the ability to serve others together are certainly among these.

Paired with committing to maintain a strong marriage is the agreement to regard divorce as an option to be considered only under extreme conditions. Marriage is a daily act of prayer, commitment, and faith. Above all, it requires a deep spiritual commitment to always rely on God and to turn to Him for guidance through prayer and meditation.

Coaching

⇒ Getting along with each other requires developing your virtues both separately and together. One way to do this both in courtship and in marriage is to choose a virtue to focus on for a day or a week. You can then compare stories with each other about the opportunities you had to practice it. (See Appendix A for some virtue definitions.)

⇒ Going into a marriage not mentioning an issue and just hoping that someone or something will change, including yourself, then getting upset and resentful when it doesn't, is a recipe for constant marital friction.

⇒ It can also be frustrating and ultimately damaging to a marriage if you go into it "in love with the potential" you see in another person—a potential that may or may not ever be fulfilled.

⇒ Often people go into marriage looking for physical, emotional, financial, or even spiritual security that they didn't have growing up. If your primary motive for marriage is to "fix" the past, the marriage may fail in the future. (See Chapter 5 about learning from relationships.)

? Questions for Reflection and Discussion

1. What are your thoughts about the temporary or eternal nature of marriage?
2. What is your level of confidence in being able to sustain a marriage for all eternity?
3. What factors strengthen or weaken that confidence?
4. How do you relate to the Bahá'í wedding vow, "We will, all, verily, abide by the Will of God"?
5. What attitudes, behaviors, and actions might show that you are following this vow?
6. Is there any other wedding vow that will apply to you? How do you feel about what it says? Does it ask you to promise something you object to or would have difficulty fulfilling?
7. What does a spiritual bond between two people look like?
8. What else might create a strong bond between you? What habits/practices could help keep you together?
9. What relationships with others in your life might change with marriage? How does that make you feel?
10. What are the little things that irritate you in households? What do you do that might irritate the other?
11. What are your attitudes toward and feelings about divorce?
12. What are your spiritual beliefs about divorce?
13. Under what circumstances do you think divorce is the best option, if ever?
14. If one or both of you have been divorced, what key thing do you feel you need to know about the experiences from the previous relationships?

Activities

1. Pray, meditate, reflect, and write in your journal about eternity, the eternal nature of marriage, and divorce.

2. Write a poem, free verse, song, or journal entry (or some other artistic expression) about your dreams and wishes of what marriage could be for you. Share what you created with each other, and explore any discoveries you made while writing.

3. Meet with a married couple and discuss what has contributed to their marriage being strong and lasting. What questions do you want to ask them? (Look throughout this workbook for ideas.)

_____

_____

What key things did you learn from the discussion?

_____

Step 4

Explore Compatibility: Learning Together

Marriage Can Be Forever—Preparation Counts!

Out of the fusion of two souls a third subtle entity is born. Though invisible and intangible on earth it is the composite soul of true lovers. The progress of one mysteriously influences the other, they become the tutors of each other's soul. Distance or death, being physical forces, cannot cause its disintegration.

~ Rosemary Sala

The Bahá'í World, Volume 7, p. 763

CHAPTER 14 – Can We Get Along?: The Value of Compatibility

Focus Points

- Recognizing compatibility
- The vital role of truthfulness and honesty
- Compatibility brings harmony
- The importance of observation and communication
- Studying marriage
- Examining your motives
- Qualities of successful couples

A Couple's Story

"I used to think I had to find a woman who was exactly like me," says James. "No wonder my last girlfriend drove me crazy—we were way too much alike!" Lindsay sits with him at a table. They both have their lists in front of them of what they bring to a relationship and what is important to them in a partner, and they are comparing them.

"Look," says Lindsay, "it's good that we both like to socialize with people. Since we both like being with people, that should help us do community service together. But I wonder if it's a concern that you really like to play tennis and I don't know how?"

"Nah," says James. "Either I'll teach you or I'll find other partners. That's a flexible thing for me."

"Here's a tough one though," says Lindsay. "You want to travel the world, and I want to have kids while I'm still young. How do we work that out?"

"Well, once you have your civil engineering degree, we could travel to other countries for a couple of years and then settle down," suggests James. "There's bound to be a need for your skills in other countries doing development projects. Or, we could just do trips. Let's keep talking this one through for a while. The solution isn't clear yet, but I'm sure it will be if we keep consulting and take it seriously."

"Yeah, who knows?" responds Lindsay. "I might like traveling so much the kids will just come with us!"

Quotes for Guidance

✵ Deal ye one with another with the utmost love and harmony, with friendliness and fellowship.
(Bahá'u'lláh: *Gleanings from the Writings of Bahá'u'lláh*, p. 288)

✵ The first [teaching of Bahá'u'lláh] is the independent investigation of truth....
('Abdu'l-Bahá: *Selections from the Writings of 'Abdu'l-Bahá*, p. 248)

Marriage Can Be Forever—Preparation Counts!

- ❋ In short, whatsoever thing is arranged in harmony and with love and purity of motive, its result is light, and should the least trace of estrangement prevail the result shall be darkness upon darkness….
  ('Abdu'l-Bahá: *Selections from the Writings of 'Abdu'l-Bahá*, p. 88)

- ❋ It is incumbent on you to have union and harmony. It is incumbent upon you to have affinity and accord, so that ye may become united in body and soul....
  ('Abdu'l-Bahá: *Tablets of 'Abdu'l-Bahá Vol.1*, p. 2)

- ❋ The love between husband and wife should not be purely physical, nay, rather it must be spiritual and heavenly. These two souls should be considered as one soul. How difficult it would be to divide a single soul! Nay, great would be the difficulty!... The foundation of the Kingdom of God is based upon harmony and love, oneness, relationship and union, not upon differences, especially between husband and wife. If one of these two becomes the cause of divorce, that one will unquestionably fall into great difficulties, will become the victim of formidable calamities and experience deep remorse.
  ('Abdu'l-Bahá: *Lights of Guidance*, p. 393)

Perspectives to Consider

Here is an interesting and challenging part of your marriage preparation—establishing together whether you are **compatible or not**. And be cautious, because *being compatible doesn't necessarily mean that you are both the same, nor is any couple 100 percent compatible. Often, compatible means you are different in many ways that balance and complement each other, just as different notes ♪ or musical instruments can be harmonious when played at one time.* You may also be incompatible in some ways that can be addressed with flexibility and patience rather than stopping your relationship from going forward. Consult together about where there is harmony, potential conflicts or concerns, mutual interests and unique differences that could provide or affect the foundation of a marriage between you.

Your discussion must be broad ranging, covering the major areas that will affect you as a couple. Some are listed below.

Major Topics to Discuss
(Each of these topics is covered in depth in this section on compatibility.)

- Love
- Your spiritual life
- Your families
- Partnership and equality
- Personality, attitudes, and behavior
- Communication
- Emotions
- Chastity, intimacy, and sex
- Children
- Service and time choices
- Money
- Setting up a household
- Tests and difficulties

CAUTION — WATCH YOUR STEP This consultation process requires a high level of **mutual commitment and honesty**. Stay open-minded and don't begin assuming you are compatible and therefore miss important incompatibilities. Some people tend to single-mindedly pursue a goal (like marrying a particular person) and be very determined to achieve it. This kind of focus could stop you from seeing warning signs about the relationship. Each couple must thoroughly explore these areas of your relationship:

- Spiritual
- Emotional
- Intellectual
- Physical

Marriage Can Be Forever—Preparation Counts!

You may feel very vulnerable in the process of determining compatibility, and it may seem risky. But the reward will be great. *Some preliminary relationship research a few decades ago proposed the theory that people who are totally opposites attract each other, and that in spite of major differences between them, a couple could have a successful marriage. While this theory has persisted as a myth, research now shows a strong correlation between compatibility and the ability of a couple to sustain a marriage.* How could you be true companions if you had little in common?

You can learn a lot about each other and your feelings and attitudes toward marriage and family by **reading books about marriage together**. It can be a warning sign when one of you wants to study and discuss issues together, and the other does not. Studying together and/or with your parents, another couple, representatives of a Spiritual Assembly, or a clergyperson will help you to understand the spiritual principles that best guide marriage and family life. Many Bahá'í schools or other facilities also offer sessions on this topic. Understanding these principles will often see you through difficult times as you build a marriage and family.

Examine Your Motives For Getting Married

Part of the compatibility exploration process also includes an honest examination of your motives. You might reconsider marriage if you:

- Are focused on having someone to cook or clean for you

- Are looking at the person as a source of income

- Are moving ahead just so you can have sex

- Believe things that are problems in you, the other person, and the relationship will magically resolve with marriage

- Are more excited about your future in-laws than your marriage partner

- Want to be involved in a couples lifestyle more than you want to be with the person you would share it with

- Think you should get married because all of your friends are

- Want parenthood more than marriage (especially if your potential partner already has children)

- Are looking at the other person more as a parent to your child(ren) rather than seeing him/her as a partner for you

(See also Chapter 5 about learning from relationships.)

When you spend a lot of time together, you can often assume you have thoroughly shared and discussed key experiences, wants, needs, and goals from your lives. On the other hand, there may be things that you are deliberately withholding out of fear of disrupting your relationship. It is vital that you deal with this fear and share your concerns with each other—with support or counseling if necessary. Revealing now what you are keeping to yourself may disrupt your current relationship, but waiting until marriage is likely to cause far greater damage. Think about the trust between you that would be negatively affected and difficult to rebuild. By sharing, you will ensure that this will not cause misunderstanding later on down your path together.

While there are **compatibility issues** that don't arise until you actually live with your spouse, with careful forethought, most can be identified and talked about ahead of time. Together, you can determine where your needs match, what is flexible, and what is non-negotiable. Full, frank, and truthful consultation is vital. Don't hold back information—it could set up a disunifying conflict later on.

You don't exist in isolation, and seeing how **each of you behaves in social situations** will give you valuable information about compatibility. Do you both like large groups, or do you prefer solitude or small groups? Can you relax socially with other people, or do you always check to see how your partner is doing and then act accordingly? Do you have similar social needs? Feedback from friends and relatives who spend time with you regularly is invaluable in the exploration process. While in the final analysis, a friend's opinion cannot outweigh your own, listening to any comments or concerns he or she has may provide insights. The friend's feedback may be biased for any number of reasons (jealousy, concern about losing you), or he/she may have genuine insights based on knowing you very well.

CAUTION — WATCH YOUR STEP: *There is balance to maintain at this stage of the process. It is vital that you keep an open mind and both eyes open, that you fully explore issues. Don't jump to any premature conclusions OR compromise on something that is very important to you, just to "keep the peace."*

At this stage in your relationship, you may be looking through **"rose-colored glasses"** at each other instead of looking clearly at behavior or attitudes that might be troublesome later on. You may be fooled into believing in "fate," that you are "meant to be together" in spite of *serious evidence to the contrary*. On the other hand, you may have a tendency to give up on a relationship at the first sign of trouble, especially if you are repeating patterns from the past. You might also hesitate if you have expectations of having the relationship be "perfect," and these aren't being met (Are they realistic?). Couples can have differences of opinion and still love each other. How serious are the disagreements? What you might examine is whether you can disagree with kindness and without the differences becoming destructive?

Some Qualities of Compatible Couples

- They pray together regularly
- Each person is able to function independently and maturely
- They love each other as well as themselves
- They are happy and harmonious together
- They enjoy being alone as well as together
- They have some common goals
- They know themselves and each other
- They express their feelings, ideas, and wishes
- Decisions are made through consultation
- They are united in service to each other and to others
- They are fulfilling their purpose in life (See Chapter 2)
- They are comfortable/established in their work or occupations (or working toward this goal)

Coaching

⇒ Look carefully at how you each handle discussions about compatibility. Don't ignore concerns or uneasy feelings—listen to your heart and respect your intuition. Being "in love" might prompt you to convince yourself that the other person will change or that things will be different later, but this will not necessarily be the case. *Counting on* either of you changing is probably a dangerous way to enter a life-long commitment.

⇒ Re-visit the chapters in Steps 1, 2, and 3 together to ensure you have covered the discussion points from them.

⇒ The next few chapters look at some areas of compatibility in more depth. At this stage, identify whether there are any warning signs or areas that you need to explore more deeply. You can then focus on those areas.

Marriage Can Be Forever—Preparation Counts!

Questions for Reflection and Discussion

1. How do you define compatibility? How will you know if you are observing it?
2. In which areas are you different, but you balance each other?
3. In which areas are you the same, and this may cause conflicts in your relationship?
4. In which areas are you confident that you are compatible?
5. What is it like to be in social situations with each other?
6. Are there any important things about yourself that you haven't yet shared? When will be a good time?
7. Why do you want to be married?
8. How do you feel about living with each other's faults forever? [**Note:** We all change, but counting on a partner changing can lead to unhappiness and separation.]
9. What do you believe are the qualities of a successful marriage?
10. What do you believe about the concept that "opposites attract?" If you are very different, what are your thoughts about your ability to have a strong marriage?
11. When you examine the differences between you, and how they might affect you as a dating/courting or married couple, which are the ones that are a concern? Are any of these an issue?:
    a. Age
    b. Socio-economic status
    c. Race or culture
    d. Religion
    e. Others? In what ways are they issues?

Activities

1. Pray, meditate, reflect, and write in your journal about what you might be like in a marriage and as a wife or husband.

2. Together review Worksheet 7A, "Describe Who You Are," and complete Worksheet 14A with what you both bring to a marriage.

3. Complete Worksheet 14B using your Worksheet 7B, "Describe Your Potential Marriage Partner" from Chapter 7 that you both previously completed. Use the worksheet to prompt discussion about your compatibility as a couple.

4. List below the reasons you want to be married and discuss them with your partner.

_____
_____
_____
_____
_____
_____
_____

Date: _____

Worksheet 14A: What Do You Each Bring?

DIRECTIONS: The purpose of this worksheet is to understand what you each would contribute to a marriage. Some of what each other brings will seem positive and compatible and some of it won't.

- Using the copies you each completed of Worksheet 7A "Describe Who You Are" from Chapter 7, complete the first column of this worksheet with what you listed as individually bringing to a potential marriage.
- Then, the female should examine the list of *"What He Brings"* indicating
    o Whether each item is something you agree exists
    o Whether you appreciate it or not
    o Any comments
- Then the male should do the same thing with *"What She Brings."*
- Discuss your findings and conclusions.

Worksheets may be printed from www.claricomm.com/publishing

Hers:

What He Brings	Appreciate Yes? No?	Comment

His:

What She Brings	Appreciate Yes? No?	Comment

Marriage Can Be Forever—Preparation Counts!

Date: _____

Worksheet 14B: Assessing Your Compatibility

DIRECTIONS: No two people are exactly alike, and differences often add variety and opportunities for growth and development in a relationship. However, it's important to assess your likes, dislikes, habits, goals, activities, commitments, dreams, fears, hopes, and the details of your everyday life. Where is compatibility critical? Where is it unimportant? Are any of these warning signals of potential disunity? **Note:** This is the time for frank and open discussion. Hiding important information may cause problems later in your relationship.

You will both need your completed Worksheet 7B, "Describe Your Potential Marriage Partner" from Chapter 7.
- List all your "non-negotiable," "flexible," and "nice, but not essential" items from both of your lists, marking which is "his" or "hers."
- When the lists are complete, begin discussing each item. This process could take a few hours, a few weeks, or even a few months. **Don't set an arbitrary or unreasonable time frame.**
- After discussing each item, make a note in the "Result of Discussion" column.
  - Did either of you shift from "non-negotiable" to "flexible" with new insights from the discussion?
  - Did the incompatibility remain after discussion?
  - How serious is it? Is there anything specific you can do to address it?

Worksheets may be printed from www.claricomm.com/publishing

Non-Negotiable Items

His or Hers?	Non-Negotiable Items	Compatible? Yes	Compatible? No	Result of Discussion

Marriage Can Be Forever—Preparation Counts!

Flexible Items

His or Hers?	Flexible Items	Compatible? Yes	Compatible? No	Result of Discussion

Nice, But Not Essential Items

His or Hers?	Nice, But Not Essential Items	Compatible? Yes	No	Result of Discussion

Know thou of a certainty that Love is the secret of God's holy Dispensation, the manifestation of the All Merciful, the fountain of spiritual outpourings. Love is heaven's kindly light, the Holy Spirit's eternal breath that vivifieth the human soul. Love is the cause of God's revelation unto man, the vital bond inherent, in accordance with the divine creation, in the realities of things. Love is the one means that ensureth true felicity both in this world and the next. Love is the light that guideth in darkness, the living link that uniteth God with man, that assureth the progress of every illumined soul. Love is the most great law that ruleth this mighty and heavenly cycle, the unique power that bindeth together the divers elements of this material world, the supreme magnetic force that directeth the movements of the spheres in the celestial realms. Love revealeth with unfailing and limitless power the mysteries latent in the universe. Love is the spirit of life unto the adorned body of mankind, the establisher of true civilization in this mortal world, and the shedder of imperishable glory upon every high-aiming race and nation.

~ `Abdu'l-Bahá, *Selections from the Writings of `Abdu'l-Bahá*, p. 27

Contrary to popular opinion, love is rarely a thunderbolt out of the sky. It is, rather, a hundred thousand million tiny raindrops that fill us up and sweep us out to the ocean. It is the result of small, repeating positive interactions. It is knowledge born of consistent contact. It is a flame that must be fed tiny twigs before being given sturdy sticks or large logs.

~ Justice St Rain, *Falling into Grace*, p. 112

CHAPTER 15 – The Power of Attraction: Your Love for Each Other

> **Focus Points**
> - Defining love
> - Love in marriage
> - Romance and passion
> - The boundaries and value of love

A Couple's Story

"I know you love me," says James. "And you've told me so. But it seems to be difficult for you to express it to me. What's going on?"

"Hmm…I never really thought about it before," says Lindsay. "I guess I didn't hear it much around my house. And so many friends I have are crazy in love one week, saying 'I love you' constantly, and then totally turned off by the guy the next week."

James listens, pauses, and says, "I think I get where you're coming from, Lindsay. And the way I see it, you act out your love more than you talk about it, which is really the most important thing. I see you taking care of your roommate's cat, babysitting so Janice can go to meetings, buying me a book as a surprise gift the other day, stuff like that." James pauses again. "It's just that it would mean a lot to me to hear you say 'I love you' more often."

"It may be hard at first, but I guess it would be good for me to learn to do it more easily," responds Lindsay. "You'll help?"

Quotes for Guidance

✸ What a power is love! It is the most wonderful, the greatest of all living powers.

Love gives life to the lifeless. Love lights a flame in the heart that is cold. Love brings hope to the hopeless and gladdens the hearts of the sorrowful.

In the world of existence there is indeed no greater power than the power of love. When the heart of man is aglow with the flame of love, he is ready to sacrifice all—even his life. In the Gospel it is said God is love.

There are four kinds of love. The first is the love that flows from God to man; it consists of the inexhaustible graces, the Divine effulgence and heavenly illumination. Through this love the world of being receives life. Through this love man is endowed with physical existence, until, through the breath of the Holy Spirit—this same love—he receives eternal life and becomes the image of the Living God. This love is the origin of all the love in the world of creation.

The second is the love that flows from man to God. This is faith, attraction to the Divine, enkindlement, progress, entrance into the Kingdom of God, receiving the Bounties of God, illumination with the lights of the

Kingdom. This love is the origin of all philanthropy; this love causes the hearts of men to reflect the rays of the Sun of Reality.

The third is the love of God towards the Self or Identity of God. This is the transfiguration of His Beauty, the reflection of Himself in the mirror of His Creation. This is the reality of love, the Ancient Love, the Eternal Love. Through one ray of this Love all other love exists.

The fourth is the love of man for man. The love which exists between the hearts of believers is prompted by the ideal of the unity of spirits. This love is attained through the knowledge of God, so that men see the Divine Love reflected in the heart. Each sees in the other the Beauty of God reflected in the soul, and finding this point of similarity, they are attracted to one another in love. This love will make all men the waves of one sea, this love will make them all the stars of one heaven and the fruits of one tree. This love will bring the realization of true accord, the foundation of real unity.

But the love which sometimes exists between friends is not (true) love, because it is subject to transmutation; this is merely fascination. As the breeze blows, the slender trees yield. If the wind is in the East the tree leans to the West, and if the wind turns to the West the tree leans to the East. This kind of love is originated by the accidental conditions of life. This is not love, it is merely acquaintanceship; it is subject to change.

Today you will see two souls apparently in close friendship; tomorrow all this may be changed.

Yesterday they were ready to die for one another, today they shun one another's society! This is not love; it is the yielding of the hearts to the accidents of life. When that which has caused this 'love' to exist passes, the love passes also; this is not in reality love.
('Abdu'l-Bahá: *Paris Talks*, pp. 179-181)

* O ye beloved of the Lord! The Kingdom of God is founded upon equity and justice, and also upon mercy, compassion, and kindness to every living soul. Strive ye then with all your heart to treat compassionately all humankind — except for those who have some selfish, private motive, or some disease of the soul. Kindness cannot be shown the tyrant, the deceiver, or the thief, because, far from awakening them to the error of their ways, it maketh them to continue in their perversity as before. No matter how much kindliness ye may expend upon the liar, he will but lie the more, for he believeth you to be deceived, while ye understand him but too well, and only remain silent out of your extreme compassion.
('Abdu'l-Bahá: *Selections from the Writings of 'Abdu'l-Bahá*, p. 158)

Perspectives to Consider

Love is a powerful force of attraction between you and God and between you and other people. Love for each other, grounded in your mutual love for God, is the emotionally electrical force that keeps you together as a couple despite daily annoyances and major difficulties, it lights your faces as you look at each other, it sustains you through marriage, it grows as your family expands, and it generates joy and happiness in your union. With love, you put the other person's well-being first. A happy marriage without love is virtually impossible. Love pulls you away from being self-centered and keeps you connected to your spouse.

Early in a relationship, it can be easy for you to feel so "in love" (or "in lust") that nothing else matters. The attraction may be **based on a relatively flimsy foundation**—anything from the way someone looks or prays, to how he or she focuses on school or work. The gift that time and interactive exposure to one another brings is the ability to truly develop a friendship and fully explore whether you can be compatible in marriage. Often the "in love" magic cannot sustain itself. Sometimes it was just a brief need for drama, excitement, and adventure. Sometimes, however, the initial attraction deepens and sustains itself, and mutual love becomes the foundation for an eternal relationship.

Love is not just a noun; it is also **an action word**. Loving behavior is demonstrated through many of the virtues—the caring you show toward each other, courtesy of your interactions, acceptance of each other, forgiveness of hurts without harboring resentments, and being of service in your relationship and future household.

Love is clearly present when you trust, are honest, and share your hearts with each other. It is demonstrated in your excitement about each other's successes and your comfort during failures and difficulties. It is a warmth, a fire, a heat that will hopefully never cool.

Strong, long-lasting marriages often have a quality of **sustained love, energy, and passion** that are visible in the couple to the people around them. This passion shows up as a deep interest in all things related to what your partner is doing. It manifests itself in the projects you do together and the service you offer to others. It is demonstrated by a desire to be together in all ways. It is also a daily choice—to love your partner as a conscious act.

How Deep Is Your Love?

Examine together what boundaries you have with love, and if your boundaries are different, how might that affect you in a marriage. Whom do you value loving? For instance, some people believe that they should only love their immediate family members. Others believe they should only love people who are the same race as they are or who come from the same country. Some believe that they should love only people of the same religion, and all others are enemies. In the Bahá'í Faith, the guidance is to be kind and loving to all mankind, regardless of faith, race, gender, and so on. The only *caution*, as noted in the quote earlier in the chapter, is that when you interact with loving-kindness with a liar or thief, it makes them continue to behave poorly.

So, if one of you loves just a few types of people, and the other loves a broader range of people, does that make a difference to you? To your families? Would it make a difference if there were a disagreement between you about something? Would any difference in values in this area make a difference in your ability to pray for each other or someone else? Is love a unifying force between you?

Coaching

⇒ Look at how much of your relationship is imaginary—composed of your dreams—rather than reality.

⇒ Try to separate your physical attraction from your feelings of love, and become clear about the love's strength or weakness.

Questions for Reflection and Discussion

1. How do you define love in marriage and what does it look like between individuals who are married?
2. What has your family taught you about love?
3. Who do you believe is acceptable to love beyond your spouse? In what way?
4. How will you know if you are in love or in lust?
5. How will you know if you are only in love with the idea or dramatic feel of being in love?
6. What are the qualities you love about each other?
7. What actions of each of you demonstrate love is present? How often do you observe them happening?
8. Are you loving and respectful to yourself? Why or why not? How does this affect your relationships?
9. How do you speak about or to each other when the two of you are alone? When someone else is present?

10. Are you able to praise and encourage the other consistently? Examples? Are your words ever critical and destructive? Examples?
11. Do actions that start out feeling loving ever escalate into hitting, slapping, or other violent behavior? How do you respond?
12. Is either of you ever violent toward the other and then compensate by attempting to be very loving? How do you respond?
13. Are you still feeling strong feelings of attraction or love toward someone else/others? Who? How is this an issue?
14. Do you flirt with people other than your partner? Has your partner seen this? Is this an issue?
15. How would you handle feelings of love that could develop with someone other than your spouse?

Activities

1. Pray, meditate, reflect, and write in your journal about what love looks like to you in marriage.

2. Compose a poem, song, or some other creative means that expresses your love for the other and share with him/her. Carefully observe your partner's response. Did he/she understand your message of love?

3. Identify and carry out a special loving service to each other. What did you choose to do?
   _____

   How did the other respond? Was this the response you wanted or expected? What would you have preferred?
   _____
   _____
   _____

4. Use Worksheet 15A to guide you through interviews with married couples about love.

5. Discuss the following and its implications for marriage:

A LIFELONG SHARING

Love cannot remain by itself—it has no meaning.
Love has to be put into action and that action is service.
Whatever form we are,
able or disabled,
rich or poor,
it is not how much we do,
but how much love we put
in the doing;
a lifelong sharing
of love with others.

Mother Teresa

Date: _____

Worksheet 15A: Married Couples and Love

DIRECTIONS: Use this sheet to guide you through interviews with married couples. Your goal is to increase your understanding of love and marriage as well as the actions you might be able to take to sustain the love between you as a couple over time.

Worksheets may be printed from www.claricomm.com/publishing

1. Meet with a couple that has been married for less than 3 years. Ask them how they specifically realized they had a sustainable love between them before they got married.

   _____
   _____
   _____

2. How do they still know they love each other? What do they do to show love to each other? What did you observe that told you they love each other?

   _____
   _____
   _____

3. Meet with a couple who is a good role model and who has been married for a long time, preferably at least 15 to 25 years. What have they done so that their love has lasted over time?

   _____
   _____
   _____

4. How has their love changed? How do they still show love to each other? What loving acts did you observe?

   _____
   _____
   _____

5. What difficulties in loving have these couples experienced and how have they overcome them?

   _____
   _____
   _____

6. Go for an agreed period of time (a week or two) without contact of any kind with each other. What positive and negative emotions did you feel? Were there any changes in either of your emotions?

   _____
   _____
   _____

Marriage Can Be Forever—Preparation Counts!

On Marriage

Then Almitra spoke again and said, "And what of Marriage, master?"
And he answered saying:
You were born together, and together you shall be forevermore.
You shall be together when white wings of death scatter your days.
Aye, you shall be together even in the silent memory of God.
But let there be spaces in your togetherness,
And let the winds of the heavens dance between you.
Love one another but make not a bond of love:
Let it rather be a moving sea between the shores of your souls.
Fill each other's cup but drink not from one cup.
Give one another of your bread but eat not from the same loaf.
Sing and dance together and be joyous, but let each one of you be alone,
Even as the strings of a lute are alone though they quiver with the same music.
Give your hearts, but not into each other's keeping.
For only the hand of Life can contain your hearts.
And stand together, yet not too near together:
For the pillars of the temple stand apart,
And the oak tree and the cypress grow not in each other's shadow.

~ Kahlil Gibran, *The Prophet*

One of the qualities of the soul is its deep-felt desire to *belong*, to belong to somebody—ultimately, of course, to God. We are not islands and it is definitely not good for a person to be alone. By nurturing our spiritual bonds, we feel we belong to one another and can face any storm.

~ Mehri Sefidvash, *Coral and Pearls*, p. 57

CHAPTER 16 – A Focus on God: Your Spiritual Life Together

> **Focus Points**
> - Marriage as a spiritual entity; being "as one soul"
> - The oneness of religions; Bahá'í and interfaith marriage
> - The importance of spiritual harmony in the home
> - The relationship you each have with God
> - Developing mutual spiritual habits and practices
> - Praying and serving together
> - Freedom to believe and follow your beliefs

A Couple's Story

Lindsay is traveling to visit her father, Sam, during a college break, and she and James are apart for the first time since they started dating. They talk each day on the phone.

"So, how was your day at work?" Lindsay asks James.

"I spent most of the day working with a new client. I'm really excited about this account—it will be the first time since I've been here that I've had the responsibility of doing all the graphics for a project."

"Cool!" she says. "I know you've been hoping to get more responsibility. I've had a good day with my Dad, too. He introduced me to Nora, the woman he's dating. She seems okay. I wish you were here with me though—just to hang out—and to pray with me…it's never completely comfortable being here."

"There's no rule that says we can't pray over the phone," James teases her.

Lindsay agrees, and they decide any time they are apart, they will still pray together.

Quotes for Guidance

* Recite ye the verses of God every morn and eventide. Whoso faileth to recite them hath not been faithful to the Covenant of God and His Testament….
    (Bahá'u'lláh: *Kitáb-i-Aqdas*, p. 73)

* Bahá'u'lláh promulgated the fundamental oneness of religion. He taught that reality is one and not multiple, that it underlies all divine precepts and that the foundations of the religions are, therefore, the same. Certain forms and imitations have gradually arisen. As these vary, they cause differences among religionists. If we set aside these imitations and seek the fundamental reality underlying our beliefs, we reach a basis of agreement because it is one and not multiple.
    ('Abdu'l-Bahá: *Promulgation of Universal Peace*, p. 175)

Marriage Can Be Forever—Preparation Counts!

- The true marriage of Bahá'ís is this, that husband and wife should be united both physically and spiritually, that they may ever improve the spiritual life of each other, and may enjoy everlasting unity throughout all the worlds of God.
    ('Abdu'l-Bahá: *Selections from the Writings of 'Abdu'l-Bahá*, p. 118)

- Marriage, among the mass of the people, is a physical bond, and this union can only be temporary, since it is foredoomed to a physical separation at the close. Among the people of Bahá, however, marriage must be a union of the body and of the spirit as well, for here both husband and wife are aglow with the same wine, both are enamored of the same matchless Face, both live and move through the same spirit, both are illumined by the same glory. This connection between them is a spiritual one, hence it is a bond that will abide forever. Likewise do they enjoy strong and lasting ties in the physical world as well, for if the marriage is based both on the spirit and the body, that union is a true one, hence it will endure. If, however, the bond is physical and nothing more, it is sure to be only temporary, and must inexorably end in separation. When, therefore, the people of Bahá undertake to marry, the union must be a true relationship, a spiritual coming together as well as a physical one, so that throughout every phase of life, and in all the worlds of God, their union will endure; for this real oneness is a gleaming out of the love of God.
    ('Abdu'l-Bahá: *Selections from the Writings of 'Abdu'l-Bahá*, p. 117)

- Remembrance of God is like the rain and dew which bestow freshness and grace on flowers and hyacinths, revive them and cause them to acquire fragrance, redolence and renewed charm.
    ('Abdu'l-Bahá: *Prayer, Meditation, and the Devotional Attitude*, p. 232)

- Chant the Words of God and, pondering over their meaning, transform them into actions!
    ('Abdu'l-Bahá: *The Importance of Prayer, Meditation, and the Devotional Attitude*, p. 233)

- Know thou, verily, it is becoming in a weak one to supplicate to the Strong One, and it behooveth a seeker of bounty to beseech the Glorious Bountiful One. When one supplicates to his Lord, turns to Him and seeks bounty from His Ocean, this supplication brings light to his heart, illumination to his sight, life to his soul and exaltation to his being.... By these attractions one's ability and capacity increase. When the vessel is enlarged the water increases, and when the thirst grows the bounty of the cloud becomes agreeable to the taste of man.
    ('Abdu'l-Bahá: *The Importance of Prayer, Meditation, and the Devotional Attitude*, p. 235)

- ...wed Thou in the heaven of Thy mercy these two birds of the nest of Thy love, and make them the means of attracting perpetual grace; that from the union of these two seas of love a wave of tenderness may surge and cast the pearls of pure and goodly issue on the shore of life. "He hath let loose the two seas, that they meet each other: Between them is a barrier which they overpass not. Which then of the bounties of your Lord will ye deny? From each He bringeth up greater and lesser pearls."
    O Thou kind Lord! Make Thou this marriage to bring forth coral and pearls. Thou art verily the All-Powerful, the Most Great, the Ever-Forgiving.
    ('Abdu'l-Bahá: *Bahá'í Prayers* (US 2002), pp. 119-120)

- It seems to him that just as you leave your husband free to believe or not to believe in whatever pleases him, he should accord you the same rudimentary privilege. Surely the right to worship God in the way one believes to be right is the greatest fundamental freedom in the world? On the other hand no one should force one's own convictions on another and if Mr. ... objects to your Bahá'í affiliation you should carry on your activities not secretly, but not in such a way as to force him to be constantly conscious of them. In other words, you should, for his sake, sometimes forgo the pleasure of attending a Feast or meeting if there is something he wants you to do with him.
    (On behalf of Shoghi Effendi: *Lights of Guidance*, p. 224)

Marriage Can Be Forever—Preparation Counts!

Perspectives to Consider

Marriage is a spiritual institution, **created by God**, and the spiritual life you create within that framework is very important to the happiness and longevity of your marriage. While spiritual compatibility is unlikely to sustain your relationship if it is your only area in common, it is nevertheless a vital component.

At the heart of living a spiritual life is the love you feel toward God (or whatever name you are familiar with for a Supreme Being). When you **both love God**, you become closer together as you worship Him and follow His guidance. The degree to which you carry out individual spiritual practices like daily prayer and doing service for others, the more you will draw close to God and each other. In marriage, your souls become as close as is possible for two human beings to do.

No matter how close the couple draws toward each other, however, so that they are even **"as one soul,"** they remain in essence **two separate souls** with individual relationships with God. At the core, this relationship with God must be inviolable. Spiritual steadfastness often ebbs and flows over the course of your life. If one of you in a marriage shifts and pulls away from God or your chosen faith path, the other must continue to be steadfast without interference from the other. This is a test to a marriage, as any shift in one of you affects the other. You will want, however, to assist your partner in a loving way to draw close to God or faith again. The more you support each other's spiritual strength, the stronger your marriage is likely to be.

In marriage, you would probably continue to use the **spiritual practices** you have developed as an individual, like praying at certain times of the day, reading spiritual books, spending time in meditation, and so on. However, you will also develop new spiritual practices together. As you look at your compatibility, talk to each other about and practice some blending of your spiritual lives. This could include praying together daily (even on the phone, if you happen to be apart), something that supports lasting marriages. You might attend a study circle together or some kind of activity that has you studying spiritual books together. Some people find that they cannot pray together—it is such an intense personal experience, that it's not possible to do it with another person. If praying with your spouse is important and comfortable to one of you and not to the other, you may consider that you are not compatible in this aspect of your lives. For you, how important is praying together in a marriage?

Part of your spiritual life together in marriage will involve **being of service** to the people in your household and to others. There are endless choices, and here are some examples: cleaning out the kitchen cupboards, planting a garden, organizing a food donation drive, serving on a planning committee, and so on. Some people can work on projects harmoniously, and some find that they can only do it by themselves or with people they aren't related to. This will be something for you to attempt and find what is successful for you and what isn't. Some couples choose to avoid working on the same things together. Other couples find that this is an important part of marriage and a strong source of joy. Those couples would not want to marry unless there was the probability of serving peacefully and productively together.

Sometimes you may fall into the trap of making assumptions just because **both of you are members of the same faith**. Regardless, ensure that you discuss with each other your level of religious community participation, sharing your faith with others, giving donations, and praying together. What if one of you is appointed or elected to serve in a position of responsibility, and it takes you from the other and your children at times? How would you handle this?

If you are of **different faiths or one of you is of no faith**, your discussion must include the implications of this on your marriage and your ability to maintain harmony in your family and home. Interfaith couples often find it more challenging to keep their marriages together than couples who have the same faith. It will help if you focus on the points of belief where you agree, rather than your points of disagreement. Explore the implications for your relationship of similar and different beliefs and daily spiritual practices, such as prayer.

Some people are comfortable participating in the services of another's faith, some not, and some faiths restrict attendance at various meetings to believers, so consult about what your involvement would be in each other's chosen faith. Your discussion will include the crucial area of raising children and agreeing on how you would handle their spiritual upbringing. Profound difficulties can arise in a marriage if you have differences in beliefs and on how to raise your children spiritually. There may also be potential disharmony between spouses over the amount of time you spend in service to your faith community and the donations you make to support it. Discuss these points thoroughly.

Whether you are of the same faith or of different ones, as you explore the area of spiritual compatibility, focus on this question: How would you sustain a spiritual life together? Be honest, thorough, and thoughtful, as the implications of this question are far-reaching.

Coaching

⇒ Sharing your favorite prayers or quotes together can build a spiritual bond.

⇒ If you meet each other during an intense spiritual experience such as a youth trip, teaching trip, pilgrimage, or serving at the national or global administrative offices of your religion, you may feel strong spiritual attraction to each other. The intensity of this bond may be a great foundation for a relationship, but it is not a complete picture. Be together in other circumstances to see how you behave and interact on a regular daily and ongoing basis.

⇒ Do a regular activity or service to build your spiritual understanding and experience with a mutual spiritual life.

Questions for Reflection and Discussion

Questions for All

1. Do you believe in God? What does this mean to you?
2. What does following God's will mean to you? How would you know if you are following it?
3. What do you observe in your partner that demonstrates he/she has a strong faith in God?
4. What do you believe about the oneness of all religions?
5. Are you following different faiths? What are the implications of this?
6. Do either of you feel pressure to convert the other to your faith? Why or why not? Do either of you feel the desire to convert to the other's faith? Why? Do you sincerely believe in it?
7. What are your views on having spirituality and faith as part of daily life?
8. Do you pray daily? If not, how often? Why or why not daily?
9. How do you feel about praying together? In a group? As a family?
10. Do you meditate? What methods do you use? In what ways do they improve your spiritual life?
11. Do you fast? When? How might this affect your meals and time together?
12. What things might you do in a marriage to draw closer to God?

Marriage Can Be Forever—Preparation Counts!

13. What do you think of the concept of improving the spiritual life of your spouse? What things might you do to improve the spiritual life of each other?
14. What is possible for you to share about your spiritual struggles with ego and humility?
15. What spiritual practices will you use in making decisions?
16. What are your attitudes toward the other's spiritual life? How do you view his/her commitment to his/her faith? To involvement and service to his/her faith community? To teaching others about his/her faith?
17. Have you had any time when you felt estranged from God or your faith? Why? How did you resolve this? Or did you? How do you feel about it now? How does your partner feel about it?
18. Are there any teachings of your own religious faith you struggle with or have issues with understanding or accepting?
19. Do you think that there might be situations where you feel you have to choose between something best for your marriage and something best for the Bahá'í Faith/your religion? What could you imagine in this scenario, and how would you deal with it? How can you minimize this type of dilemma?
20. What if either or both of you were persecuted for your beliefs—how would you handle it? What would be difficult? Would your faith be a refuge or a place to run from? What if your children were persecuted?
21. What does spirituality look like to you? What does family spirituality look like to you?

Points to Explore Primarily If You Are Both Bahá'ís

1. What is your commitment to the Bahá'í Faith? How do you feel about accepting and encouraging your partner's involvement in serving it?
2. Are there any of the Bahá'í laws that you are seriously struggling to obey? If this were to happen after marriage, would you share this with your spouse? Would you be able to request and receive assistance from him/her?
3. What activities have you done to get to know each other outside of a spiritual setting? Do you need to do more? What will you do?
4. Is there a mutual interest in pioneering to an area that needs Bahá'ís or in travel teaching?
5. Have you been on a Bahá'í pilgrimage? What are your plans to go?
6. How familiar are you with the Bahá'í Writings? Do you plan to study them and learn together?
7. Do you read the Bahá'í Writings at least twice daily, morning and evening? How does this assist you?
8. What is your relationship with and attitude toward the institutions of the Bahá'í Faith such as Spiritual Assemblies, Regional Bahá'í Councils, the Universal House of Justice, or the Continental Board of Counsellors and their Auxiliary Board members?
9. Are you willing to serve on these institutions if you are elected or appointed to them? How might this service affect your marriage, both positively and as a potential struggle?

Activities

1. Pray, meditate, reflect, and write in your journal about what a spiritually-based marriage would be like.

2. There are many activities you can do to strengthen your spiritual life together. Choose at least two from the list below and try them out *together* for a few weeks. Each could take place in a variety of ways, so be creative and do what works best for you. Carefully observe how you interact with each other while doing them.

    a. Memorize a spiritual quote or prayer once a week for a month.
    b. Experiment with using a new form of meditation.
    c. Attend a Bahá'í school or other religious course.
    d. Plan the devotions for a meeting.
    e. Co-facilitate a study circle.
    f. Travel to share your beliefs with others.
    g. Carry out a community service project.
    h. Attend devotional meetings from each other's faith.

3. Assess the experience:

    a. How did you choose what to do?
    _____

    b. What did you learn from the experience? What did you notice about your compatibility?
    _____
    _____

    c. What would you do again?
    _____
    _____

    d. What would you not do again?
    _____
    _____

    e. What concerns, if any, arose from doing these activities?
    _____
    _____

    f. What would you like to do together next?
    _____
    _____

    g. What did these experiences tell you about what your spiritual life might be like after marriage?
    _____
    _____

4. Complete Worksheet 16A to explore faith issues together.

Marriage Can Be Forever—Preparation Counts!

Date: _____

Worksheet 16A: A Faith Exploration for Couples

DIRECTIONS: This worksheet is primarily for couples who are of different faiths, and it will help you to determine if you can be compatible and unified in your marriage. *However, many of the questions may be useful for you even if you are of the same faith.* When a couple has different faiths, sometimes maintaining unity in a family and sustaining a marriage are a challenge.
- It is best if each of you separately complete the answers below.
- Then, come together and discuss your responses.
- Consult and reach the necessary decisions for you to be confident that religion will be a source of unity and harmony in your home.

Note: Do not blind yourselves to how vital these questions are. They can help you prevent future pain if you are both honest with yourselves and each other now.

Worksheets may be printed from www.claricomm.com/publishing

1. What are the beliefs and practices that you have in common?
   _____
   _____

2. What are your differences and similarities in beliefs? Are any differences an issue?
   _____
   _____

3. Do you have a spiritual practice of some kind other than practicing a formal religion? What form would that take in your marriage?
   _____
   _____

4. What are your differences and similarities in spiritual practices like prayer, fasting, worship services, sharing beliefs with others, and so on? Are any differences an issue?
   _____
   _____

5. What are your differences and similarities in the practical aspects of spiritual life such as funerals, use of alcohol, food restrictions, and so on? Are any differences an issue?
   _____
   _____

6. How freely would you be able to practice your own faith's beliefs? What restrictions would there be?
   _____
   _____

7. What do you strongly disagree with in the other's beliefs? Which of these beliefs would affect your marriage?
   _____
   _____

Marriage Can Be Forever—Preparation Counts!

8. Are you an atheist (don't believe in God) or agnostic (someone who is unsure whether to believe in God or not)? How would that affect your marriage?

9. To what extent do you plan to share in the practices of each other's faith?

10. Do either of you feel coercion to convert to the other's faith? From each other? From family? From friends?

11. Do either of you feel desire to convert to the other's faith? Do you believe in it? Are there other reasons?

12. How would you feel about not being able to share the same faith?

13. What would be the religious education and values that you draw on to raise current and future children? How do you expect to feel if your children choose to follow your spouse's beliefs rather than yours?

14. How would you address any differences you may have with laws that affect your children? (Examples: sex, drinking alcohol, drug use, homosexual acts, backbiting, consent for marriage)

15. How would you respond if someone persecuted your spouse and/or children for their beliefs?

16. How would you handle religious donations? Would you have to split your income to handle religious donations separately?

17. How would you handle religious donations made in a will or through a trust fund? How would you decide the amount?

18. How would you handle service and involvement in your religious communities?

19. How would you feel about your spouse sharing his/her beliefs with others? In your presence? In your home?

20. Would you attend one another's religious events or services? Which ones?

21. Would you attend one another's religious conferences, summer schools, or holy day events? If not, would you encourage your spouse to attend his or hers? Where would the children go?

22. How would you feel if an event or place of worship is for believers only and you cannot attend with your spouse? How will he/she feel?

23. How would your families likely react to your religious differences? Would this cause a problem for you?

24. Would you be able to pray together? Regularly? With your children?

25. Are there any other issues to discuss with each other?

Family Relationships

After a couple (marries) the relationships they form with their respective in-laws may well determine the health and harmony of their own marriage. All good relationships depend on good communication and this is particularly true of the relationship we have with our in-laws. It is worth spending time developing good communications with our in-laws and giving our relationship with them much attention. Each partner must develop respect for the parents and family members of his spouse. Such mutual respect for parents and relatives, of course, should not go beyond certain limits, such as accepting interference in the way we as a couple live our lives.

~ Mehri Sefidvash, *Coral and Pearls*, pp. 70-71

CHAPTER 17 – All In the Family: We'll Be Related

Focus Points

- Family relationships
- Unity in the family
- Extended family
- Marrying someone like one of your parents
- Family from previous relationships
- Past family patterns; repeating history

A Couple's Story

Lindsay's father, Sam, comes to town to visit her. He and James meet for coffee one evening by themselves. They chat for a few minutes about general subjects and then shift to talking about Lindsay.

"So, James, I understand you and Lindsay are pretty serious about each other," says Sam.

"Yes, sir," says James. "She's very special to me."

"And to me," says Sam. "And I think you know she and I have had our difficulties. It was hard on her, me leaving her mother when I did," says Sam. "She was 13 and just starting to be interested in boys and them in her. She really felt I abandoned her. I stayed in the same city as her and her brother, but for a couple of years, I was angry, bitter, and just stayed away from the kids. It was a lousy time, and I've apologized to Lindsay, but I don't think she's quite forgiven me."

"We've been talking some and praying about that," says James. "I think she's making some progress. In the three years since she's been here at school, she's finally inviting you to visit. That's a good sign, don't you think?"

Quotes for Guidance

✺ When you love a member of your family or a compatriot, let it be with a ray of the Infinite Love! Let it be in God, and for God! Wherever you find the attributes of God love that person, whether he be of your family or of another.
   ('Abdu'l-Bahá: *Paris Talks*, p. 38)

✺ He will pray for your husband and son and your daughter-in-law, that, through drawing near to Bahá'u'lláh, they may be united and uplifted into a happier and more harmonious atmosphere, for the Bahá'í Cause can heal friction if people will let it and make the effort themselves as well.
   (On behalf of Shoghi Effendi: *Compilation of Compilations*, Vol. I, p. 243)

✺ Regarding your other question concerning the strained relationship between you and your mother-in-law and what you can do to alleviate the situation, we feel you should, with the help and consultation of your husband,

persevere in your efforts to achieve unity in the family. From your description of the unfriendly attitude your mother-in-law displays toward you it is clear that you will not have an easy task. However, the important thing is that you, as a Bahá'í, are aware of 'Abdu'l-Bahá's admonition to concentrate on an individual's good qualities and that this approach to your mother-in-law can strengthen you in your resolve to achieve unity. And furthermore, perseverance in prayer will give you the strength to continue your efforts.
(Universal House of Justice: *Lights of Guidance*, p. 221)

✸ ...the aim of the Bahá'ís should be to foster family unity.
(On behalf of the Universal House of Justice: *Developing Distinctive Bahá'í Communities*, 6.11)

Perspectives to Consider

You each had relationships with your families long before you met each other, and there are many emotional complexities among them. **When you marry each other, you marry each other's families** as well, so understanding the relationship dynamics will help you build family unity and understand each other. Observing how your partner interacts with his or her parents will help you to understand his/her character. How your parents interact with each other will give your partner clues about how you may interact with each other. How you interact with your parents and siblings might also indicate what you might be like as a parent.

Then there's the mysterious thing that can happen in relationships—you **"turn into" each other's father and mother**. Often you choose each other (sometimes unconsciously) because they remind you of one of your parents. Sometimes this isn't an issue, and your marriage can be successful; sometimes it's disastrous. What if you greet your intended spouse in a little girl voice like you did your Daddy? What if your spouse is as domineering as your mother was? What if you become overly dependent on your spouse and put him or her in a parental role?

You might also be thinking about avoiding marrying someone that reminds you of your parents. Determined to marry someone whom you hope will be more affectionate than your father, you might unconsciously choose someone just as withdrawn. It will help if you are clear about the things that your parents did that you don't want to repeat. Evaluate your own approaches and preferences and where they come from. [A book that may assist you in understanding this is *Getting the Love You Want* by Harville Hendrix.]

CAUTION WATCH YOUR STEP — ***Patterns are very difficult to break, so be aware that there is a risk.*** If your partner grew up in an abusive home, for instance, he or she may have a tendency to be abusive toward you or your children. It will be particularly wise in this circumstance to spend time together interacting with and looking after children before you marry. This will help you identify potential problems.

Sometimes you might assume that what went on in your home growing up is the same as what everyone does, whereas **family patterns are often unique**. This assumption can be a setup for conflict later with your spouse. *What do you mean you aren't going to pick up after me? My Dad always waited on my Mom.* There might be patterns that you unconsciously expect will happen in your marriage and roles that you expect your spouse to fill. Who drove the car when the family went out? Who set limits on spending? Who bailed family members out of trouble? (See Chapter 4 about expectations.)

Of course, family relationships continue after marriage, and they will sometimes be wonderful and sometimes drive you crazy. Unity in the family is important, however, so agree on how to handle the **relationships and interactions**. Which relationships concern you? Here are some questions to discuss:

- Will you regularly visit and phone your in-laws?
- Do you believe that in-laws are just the same as blood relatives, and the relationships should be just as close? What if that doesn't happen?

Marriage Can Be Forever—Preparation Counts!

- What about when there's something a family member does that bothers you—how will you handle that?
- Will you be resentful if a family member receives a lot of attention from your spouse?
  - What if he's doing repairs at his mother's house every weekend?
  - What if she's talking on the phone with her sister for hours every week?

With family love and unity as your focus, you will **look for the positive qualities** in each family member and look for opportunities to build close, loving relationships wherever possible. Part of your relationship is **what you would call each other's parents**. Some of you may choose to call your in-laws "Mom" and "Dad." Some may be more comfortable with first names. Others may be formal and use "Mr." and "Mrs." The decision should be a mutual one between you, however, not a unilateral one. What if your mother-in-law prefers "Mom," and you aren't comfortable with it? How will you resolve this? Can you be flexible? Why is it an issue?

If you have been married previously, you will have relationships with the **family of your former spouse**. You may have developed friendships with family members that you want to maintain. If you had children, then you will likely have contact with the children's grandparents, aunts, uncles, and cousins (as well as the children's parent, of course). You and your partner will have to consult on and agree about the level of contact you and your children would have with your former family and arrangements that would not cause disunity in your new family. What issues arose in the *previous* marriage and family, and how might these affect your *new* marriage and family?

Become conscious whether there were problems in your parent's marriage or in your previous marriage, and *you are going into a new relationship determined to fix old unhappiness.* Put your focus on creating current happiness, not on dragging the past forward into the present.

Coaching

⇒ Spend time with your potential future in-laws, with and without your partner, so you gain a more complete perspective on family interactions. If you have children, include them at times, too.

⇒ Be clear about your extended family's attitudes and beliefs about religion. Investigate whether there is risk of disunity on spiritual issues both with you as a couple and with your present or future children.

Questions for Reflection and Discussion

Note: There are complex issues raised in these questions for you to consider carefully over time. Reflect on the questions individually and write in a journal. Then discuss your perspectives together. Look carefully at where your family backgrounds are different and similar and how these factors might affect your marriage. Observe each other as you interact with family members.

Family History and Description

1. What is the composition of your family? Parents? Stepparents? Siblings? Foster parents or siblings? Adopted?
2. Were your parents married? How would you describe their happiness or unhappiness about being together?
3. How do you describe your childhood experience generally? Did you have parents or parent substitutes?
4. Are the extended families from different faiths? Are there issues that would require acceptance, education, and support?

5. How were your relationships with your parents when you were growing up? When you were a teenager? How are your relationships now?
6. How were your relationships with your siblings when you were growing up? When you were a teenager? How are they now? What are the similarities and differences between these relationships and the ones you would like to have among your children?
7. Is there any divorce in your family? How has this affected you?
8. How did your parents raise you? (Examples: Country or city? Strict or loose discipline? Religious or not?) What are your thoughts and feelings about how they raised you?
9. How did your parents handle problems? How were they able to resolve conflicts?
10. Was one of your parents dominant over the other? How has that affected you and your view of partnership in marriage?
11. What was the atmosphere in your family home? What is it like there now? Loving? Peaceful? Argumentative? Embarrassing? Affectionate? Critical? Happy? Sad? What would you want to duplicate in your married home? How would you want it to be different?
12. Were your parents faithful to each other? How did this affect you?
13. What is your parents' education level? Siblings? What value did your family place on education? Are you similar or different in this value? How might this affect raising children together?
14. What was the family's economic level? How did this affect you?
15. What are your histories and traditions of personal or family celebrations? Birthdays? Anniversaries? Graduations? Valentine's Day? Ethnic holidays? Religious Holy Days? Do you agree with what is important to each other about celebrating these? What will be important for you as a couple to attend? What are your expectations about gift giving? Do you expect greeting cards on special occasions? What activities are important to you on special occasions? (Examples: going out to dinner, a party, a family outing)
16. How have you responded when your partner has given you a gift or card?
17. How were decisions made in your family? Were you encouraged to think independently and taught how to make decisions? Do you think you learned these skills?
18. Were you taught to express or suppress emotions? By which parent/person? How has this affected your ability to express emotions now? Does your partner agree that this is how you express them?
19. How were conflicts and disagreements handled in your home? How did you feel about this? What conflict resolution skills have you learned from your family?
20. How did your family handle privacy and sharing space? How would you handle them in your home together?

The Family and You as a Couple

1. How is your partner like his/her mother and father, and how does he/she differ? How is he/she like your mother and father? What are the implications for a marriage between you?
2. How are you like and unlike your own mother and father? How will this affect your marriage?
3. What kind of relationships do you plan to have with extended family on both sides?
4. What are your expectations about the role of the particular members of your extended family in your marriage? What do they have the right to advise you on? When will you turn to them, together or separately, for advice, comfort, or assistance? How obligated would you feel to follow their wishes?
5. Are there inter-racial or inter-cultural differences, prejudices, likes, or dislikes that could be a source of conflict and disrupt unity? What are the positive aspects of the differences?
6. Who in your family are of the same religion as you are? How is your relationship with them?
7. Under what conditions would you be willing to live with your parents? Live near them?
8. How would you feel about the responsibility of caring for aging parents? How might you manage it?
9. If you come from different cities or countries, how would you feel about moving to where your partner lives? For how long would you be willing to live there? What if you had children—would you want them living there? Would they be willing/able to?
10. Are there any issues of class or status?
11. Are you observing any destructive or dysfunctional patterns in family behavior? What is your response?
12. Are you comfortable with the thought of having each other's families as relatives?

If You Were Previously Married

1. What were the communication patterns in the relationship?
2. What was constructive in the relationship that you would bring into a new marriage?
3. What was destructive that you want to leave behind? How will you do this?
4. Were there any issues with your in-laws? Were they resolved? How?
5. Will you be maintaining a relationship with family from the previous marriage? Why or why not? How will this affect your new spouse?

Activities

1. Pray, meditate, reflect, and write in your journal about what a truly unified extended family would act like.

2. On a large sheet of paper, "map" your family relationships. Put a circle in the middle of the page with your name in it. Put other circles around you, one for each family member. Put each person's name in one of the circles and draw lines between their circles and yours. Draw additional lines between the ones related to each other. Note next to each circle the quality of your relationship with the person. Share your map with your partner.

   What new information have you learned about your family? Your partner's family?
   _____
   _____

   What do you like about his/her family?
   _____
   _____

   What concerns do you have after observing his/her family interactions?
   _____
   _____

3. Use Worksheets 17A and 17B to assess your parental role model(s) as you were growing up and how they have affected your attitudes and expectations for your own marriage.

4. Plan a social activity with your potential in-laws with the goal of finding out new things about them and them finding out new things about you. What new information did you learn? What did they learn?
   You: _____
   They: _____

5. Make a list of positive qualities you have observed in your potential in-laws.

   Name: _____ Qualities: _____
   Name: _____ Qualities: _____
   Name: _____ Qualities: _____
   Name: _____ Qualities: _____
   Name: _____ Qualities: _____

134   Chapter 17 – All In the Family: We'll Be Related

Date: _____

Worksheet 17A: Parents' Marriage/Relationship Model

DIRECTIONS: The purpose of this worksheet is to help you understand the primary parental model you observed growing up and its quality. You will use this to help you understand the effect of the model on you and your future marriage and family relationships.
- Complete the assessment below about your parents.
    - If your parents never married or they divorced and/or re-married, please complete this for the most significant parental model(s) you saw and experienced growing up. The model could apply to your parents, stepparents, your parent's partner, grandparents, foster parents, or others.
    - This may be either a positive or a negative model of parenthood.
- Circle the number next to each item that best matches view of your parent, using the scale below.
- Add the scores for your mother and then for your father. If the cumulative score of either of your parents is under 37, there may be some issues to understand better and examine.
    - Look at the lower scoring items, as well as the overall picture of the survey results, to consider where you perceive that they struggled in their relationship.
- Additionally if you rated either parent with scores of 1 or 2 on any item, examine the item carefully. Consider how it may affect the skills you were able to develop in that area as a child, and therefore as an effective future marriage partner and parent.

Worksheets may be printed from www.claricomm.com/publishing

Very Negative Example	1	2	3	4	5	Very Positive Example
←						→

Mother (or Mother Figure):

To what degree did you perceive the following were positive or negative examples and models for you?

1. Your mother's interactions with your father/father figure	1	2	3	4	5
2. Her commitment to the relationship	1	2	3	4	5
3. How she disciplined children	1	2	3	4	5
4. Her use of touch and sexual behavior	1	2	3	4	5
5. Her communication skills with your father	1	2	3	4	5
6. Her communication skills with children	1	2	3	4	5
7. Her communication skills with others	1	2	3	4	5
8. How she resolved conflict with your father	1	2	3	4	5
9. How she resolved conflict with children	1	2	3	4	5
10. How she resolved conflict with others	1	2	3	4	5
11. Her use of humor	1	2	3	4	5
12. Her attitude of playfulness and fun	1	2	3	4	5
13. How she spoke to and with others	1	2	3	4	5

Subtotals ___ ___ ___ ___ ___

Total of all columns _____

Marriage Can Be Forever—Preparation Counts!

Very Negative Example	1	2	3	4	5	Very Positive Example
	←				→	

Father (or Father Figure):

To what degree did you perceive the following were positive or negative examples and models for you?

1. Your father's interactions with your mother/mother figure   1   2   3   4   5
2. His commitment to the relationship   1   2   3   4   5
3. How he disciplined children   1   2   3   4   5
4. His use of touch and sexual behavior   1   2   3   4   5
5. His communication skills with your mother   1   2   3   4   5
6. His communication skills with children   1   2   3   4   5
7. His communication skills with others   1   2   3   4   5
8. How he resolved conflict with your mother   1   2   3   4   5
9. How he resolved conflict with children   1   2   3   4   5
10. How he resolved conflict with others   1   2   3   4   5
11. His use of humor   1   2   3   4   5
12. His attitude of playfulness and fun   1   2   3   4   5
13. How he spoke to and with others   1   2   3   4   5

Subtotals ___ ___ ___ ___ ___

Total of all columns _____

1. What skills have you learned from your parents' positive actions and example?
   _____
   _____

2. How can you utilize these positive assets in your future marriage and family?
   _____
   _____

3. What patterns exist in their model that may negatively affect your actions and attitudes in marriage and raising children?
   _____
   _____

4. How can you learn from these potentially destructive patterns to create your marriage and family differently?
   _____
   _____

Marriage Can Be Forever—Preparation Counts!

Date: _____

Worksheet 17B: Learning from Parents

DIRECTIONS: Complete the questions below separately and then discuss the answers with each other. If you did not witness your parents' relationship, answer the questions according to the primary marriage or relationship that you grew up witnessing. If you grew up with more than one parental-type relationship, answer the items below for each of them.

Worksheets may be printed from www.claricomm.com/publishing

1. What attributes/characteristics would you use to describe your parents' relationship?

    a. _____   c. _____
    b. _____   d. _____

2. What have you learned from them that you would like to repeat in your marriage?

    a. _____   c. _____
    b. _____   d. _____

3. What have you learned from them that you would *not* like to repeat in your marriage?

    a. _____   c. _____
    b. _____   d. _____

4. What negative aspects of your parents' relationship are you imitating?

    a. _____   c. _____
    b. _____   d. _____

5. What positive aspects of your parents' relationship are you imitating?

    a. _____   c. _____
    b. _____   d. _____

6. What other aspects of their relationship do you want to adopt?

    _____
    _____
    _____

7. What have you observed about your partner's interactions with his/her parents? Are the interactions similar to or different from the interactions between you and your parents? How do you want to address any differences or similarities?

    _____
    _____
    _____

Marriage Can Be Forever—Preparation Counts!

Spiritual Nuggets for Reflection and Discussion

What does "family" look like to you?

If love and agreement are manifest in a single family, that family will advance, become illumined and spiritual…..
~ 'Abdu'l-Bahá: *Promulgation of Universal Peace,* p. 144-145

When you love a member of your family or a compatriot, let it be with a ray of the Infinite Love! Let it be in God, and for God! Wherever you find the attributes of God love that person….
~ 'Abdu'l-Bahá: *Paris Talks*, p. 38)

According to the teachings of Bahá'u'lláh the family, being a human unit, must be educated according to the rules of sanctity. All the virtues must be taught the family. The integrity of the family bond must be constantly considered…. The injury of one shall be considered the injury of all; the comfort of each, the comfort of all; the honor of one, the honor of all.
~ `Abdu'l-Bahá: *Promulgation of Universal Peace*, p. 168

Chapter 18 – On Partnership: Equality in Marriage

Who knows what women can be when they are finally free to become themselves? Who knows what women's intelligence will contribute when it can be nourished without denying love? Who knows of the possibilities of love when men and women share not only children, home, and garden, not only the fulfillment of their biological roles, but the responsibilities and passions of the work that creates the human future. It has barely begun, the search of women for themselves.

~ Betty Friedan, *The Feminine Mystique*

In a society where the rights and potential of women are constrained, no man can be truly free. He may have power, but he will not have freedom.

~ Mary Robinson, President of Ireland

One of the things about equality is not just that you be treated equally to a man, but that you treat yourself equally to the way you treat a man.

~ Marlo Thomas

To me equality is the important thing. I don't want preferences, I don't want to be preferred as a woman. But I want it acknowledged that I am a human being who has the capacity to do what I have to do, and it doesn't matter whether I was born a man or woman. The work will be done that way.

~ Mary Eugenia Charles, Prime Minister, Commonwealth of Dominica

'Tis woman's strongest vindication for speaking that *the world needs to hear her voice*. It would be subversive of every human interest that the cry of one-half the human family be stifled...The world has had to limp along with the wobbling gait and one-sided hesitancy of a man with one eye. Suddenly the bandage is removed from the other eye and the whole body is filled with light. It sees a circle where before it saw a segment. The darkened eye restored, every member rejoices with it.

~ Anna Julia Cooper,
In Celebration of Women, A Selection of Words and Paintings by Helen Exley

CHAPTER 18 – On Partnership: Equality in Marriage

> **Focus Points**
> - Equal partners
> - Types of equality
> - Physical force and domination
> - Respect for women
> - Balance, power, and control
> - Roles and responsibilities
> - Acting as examples for children

A Couple's Story

Lindsay and James decide to do some community service together at a new Literacy Center in town, knowing that it will allow them to get to know each other in a new way. Because Lindsay works at her school library, she knows she can get used books from them to donate as well. Today, Lindsay and James are part of the team setting up the center for its grand opening. They arrive at the center prepared to work. They meet Pradha, the executive director, to get their assignments.

"Hello James, hello Lindsay," says Pradha. "I'm glad you're here. Lindsay, I'd like you to be in the kitchen setting up the food. James, I want you in charge of organizing and running the registration and donation table."

James and Lindsay look at each other for a moment and then back at him. They both are instantly sure that they've been assigned jobs along traditional lines and that the jobs do not fit them very well.

"We're glad to be here Pradha, and we are willing to do whatever needs to be done. But, James is much better in the kitchen than I am," says Lindsay.

"And Lindsay is much better at organizing things and handling the money," says James. "I think we'd better switch."

Quotes for Guidance

✹ And among the teachings of Bahá'u'lláh is the equality of women and men. The world of humanity has two wings—one is women and the other men. Not until both wings are equally developed can the bird fly. Should one wing remain weak, flight is impossible. Not until the world of women becomes equal to the world of men in the acquisition of virtues and perfections, can success and prosperity be attained as they ought to be.
   ('Abdu'l-Bahá: *Selections from the Writings of 'Abdu'l-Bahá*, p. 302)

✹ The world in the past has been ruled by force, and man has dominated over woman by reason of his more forceful and aggressive qualities both of body and mind. But the balance is already shifting—force is losing

its weight and mental alertness, intuition, and the spiritual qualities of love and service, in which woman is strong, are gaining ascendancy. Hence the new age will be an age less masculine, and more permeated with the feminine ideals—or, to speak more exactly, will be an age in which the masculine and feminine elements of civilization will be more evenly balanced.
('Abdu'l-Bahá: *Lights of Guidance*, p. 616)

✻ Woman's lack of progress and proficiency has been due to her need of equal education and opportunity. Had she been allowed this equality, there is no doubt she would be the counterpart of man in ability and capacity. The happiness of mankind will be realized when women and men coordinate and advance equally, for each is the complement and helpmeet of the other.
('Abdu'l-Bahá: *Promulgation of Universal Peace*, p. 182)

✻ …when perfect equality shall be established between men and women, peace may be realized for the simple reason that womankind in general will never favor warfare. Women will not be willing to allow those whom they have so tenderly cared for to go to the battlefield. When they shall have a vote, they will oppose any cause of warfare.
('Abdu'l-Bahá: *Promulgation of Universal Peace*, p. 167)

Perspectives to Consider

Society is shifting in its view of equality, and increasingly, couples are recognizing that they must approach marriage as **equal partners**. However, equality is a word that is easy to say and sometimes hard to put in practice. It will challenge you determining how to put it into action in every aspect of your relationship—attempting to behave in a spirit of equality with each other can often be confusing. Your efforts to incorporate it into your lives will affect the dynamics of your marriage—your treatment of each other, your roles, your decision-making, and much more.

The image of a bird that requires two wings to fly effectively is a helpful one for you to study. It's a model that demonstrates you have your separateness, and you are also dependent upon each other as partners to get off the ground. It is within the context of equality that you as a couple will make decisions about many facets of your life together:

- Your own education/careers and the education of your children
- The sharing of labor within your household
- Money management
- The priorities each of you gives to community service
- The respect, honor, and courtesy of your own interactions

Society has long-held traditional values about male dominance and superiority. What will you do to guard against this creeping into your relationship? Your focus on equality will guide your choices, attitudes, and actions. One of the most obvious aspects of equality is the **balance of power as defined by the rights and responsibilities** of each person, which ensures that neither of you is unfairly dominant over the other, and decisions are made through joint consultation. Focus on declaring true partnership by sharing, not dictating. You may easily see where equality is applicable in society in general, but on a personal level, there are many nuances. It can include such things as jointly deciding who sleeps on what side of the bed after marriage or whether your male and female children play with dolls or trucks or both. It includes the tone of speech you use when you speak to each other, the words you choose to use, and how you treat each other's possessions. It includes how you make decisions and who initiates action on family matters, intimacy, or problems.

Open communication on the issue of equality and all the areas it affects will support you learning about it in greater depth as your relationship and marriage progress. **Guard against making assumptions** or automatically doing what you or your parents did in other family situations. An openness and willingness to learn about gender roles and differences will affect every aspect of your marriage. This includes a willingness to reverse certain "traditional" roles. Women can build shelves; men can wash dishes or do the laundry.

Role reversal has its limits, however. For instance, in addressing instructions to Bahá'ís, Bahá'u'lláh lays special emphasis on the importance of the mother's role in the early education of children. When you make decisions about who will do what in your household and in your family, carefully determine what is best for you in light of the applicable spiritual principles (see Chapter 24 about children).

Equality respects the **value of each other** as human beings and the capacity you each have to think, love, and be of service to others. It doesn't mean that you do the exact same things. In fact, physically, men and women are obviously different. Often men have stronger muscles; only women are capable of carrying and giving birth to babies.

Your **interactions with others** also reflect the principle of equality, especially how you speak of your partner to others and how you act toward him/her in public. It can also show up in how you support the development of equality in other's attitudes and behavior and the degree to which you show the example of equality to your children. In the greater society, the degree to which you as a couple champion the principle of equality has a direct bearing on the establishment of peace in the world.

Achieving equality is not easy; it is a culture change in progress. Many character qualities or virtues can assist you with applying a greater level of equality in all your interactions, and particularly into marriage. At the end of this chapter is a list of some of them for you to consider and practice. (See Appendix A for more definitions.)

Note: The difference in how women and men approach issues, communicate, share emotions, and much more is a very complex subject. Social scientists are discovering new information regularly, and an exploration of this topic is beyond the scope of this book. Learning about each other, however, might include studying and discussing information about male/female relationships.

Coaching

⇒ It is easy to become oversensitive to the issue of equality and verbally react or become defensive and upset when you perceive someone has behaved toward you in an unequal way. Take a deep breath, reflect, and re-examine the situation together in the light of the applicable spiritual principles. Remember you are both learning.

⇒ One way to explore and understand how the principle of equality might be demonstrated in a marriage is to observe and understand the relationship each of your parents and your potential in-laws has or had with each other. Parents are the first teachers of attitudes and behavior toward someone of the opposite sex.

⇒ You may also explore whether you have attitudes formed from experiences in previous sibling, friend, and romantic relationships.

⇒ The tasks you would each perform in your home would shift and adjust depending on your family's needs, your service commitments, and your work schedules. Equality isn't divided up according to who does what, but rather according to whose skills apply to the need and who has the time. Ask yourselves at the end of each day, "Was today a partnership?" or "Were we equitable today?" and "What will we do differently tomorrow?"

Chapter 18 – On Partnership: Equality in Marriage

? Questions for Reflection and Discussion

1. What are your interpretations of the equality of women and men?
2. What practical ways do you see this principle applying to marriage? Would it apply in your marriage?
3. What do you think are the differences between men and women in things such as strength, endurance, attitudes, emotional life, capabilities, assertiveness, intuition, instincts, and sexuality?
4. What roles do you expect your partner to play, and what tasks do you expect him or her to do?
5. Who would usually cook dinner after both of you have had a long and tiring day (either with career or with taking care of the children and home)?
6. How would you teach equality to your children? To other couples?
7. How would you communicate if you felt things were inequitable? How would you encourage change?
8. What skills are you willing to learn that would balance the equality in your marriage? How will you learn them?
9. What is your level of commitment to the principle of equality in marriage? What does that commitment look like to you in practical application?
10. What might demonstrate that things are equitable or inequitable in your relationship?
11. What tone do you use to speak to each other when you are happy with each other? What about when you are unhappy with something the other has done?
12. How do you speak of each other when you are away from each other?
13. When have you observed your partner demonstrating the principle of equality? What did he/she specifically do?
14. What actions of your partner tell you that the principle of equality is important to him/her?

Activities

1. Pray, meditate, reflect, and write in your journal about your perceptions of equality between husbands and wives.

2. Make a collage of women and men doing non-traditional tasks. To make a collage, you cut out pictures and words from a magazine and glue them onto a large sheet of paper or cardboard.

   a. What are your thoughts and feelings about what the people are doing?
   _____

   b. Do you have any observations about equality as you look at the pictures?
   _____
   _____

   c. What expectations about how you and your partner might behave in a marriage have now come up?
   _____
   _____

   d. Did you have any trouble finding activities of men or women doing non-traditional activities? What do you notice about the pictures in popular magazines?
   _____
   _____

3. Together complete Worksheet 18A that lists household tasks and other responsibilities.

4. When you have completed the worksheet, reflect and then discuss any expectations or assumptions you might have that would indicate gender bias. Was there anything you found surprising? Upsetting? Did you gain a common understanding?
_____
_____
_____

5. Seek out someone who can teach you skills you don't already have. (Examples: prepare a meal, do the laundry, change the oil in a vehicle) I will learn this task: _____ by this date: _____. (Mark it on your calendar.) **Note:** It's a good idea to experiment with trying out and learning new tasks on a regular basis.

6. Early on in her marriage, a woman chose to use humor and creativity to share a message about household inequality with her husband through writing the following poem in his voice. Discuss the poem and how you might communicate with your spouse about a situation if either of you felt it was unequal.

Ode to a Housewife

Somebody has to do it
so it might as well be you
'cause wiping up the apple juice
and scraping off the poo
isn't my idea of a
cool thing to do.
So if you want fulfillment
and recognition too
quit talking of the drudgery
and always looking blue
'cause somebody's got to do it
and it might as well be you.

Just wait—twenty years from now
we'll bid those kids adieu
and we'll enjoy our holidays
and go—just me and you.

'Course, when I have my coronary
or maybe go googoo
after all these years of practice
you will know just what to do.
'Cause somebody has to do it
and it might as well be you.

But in the meantime, honey,
try to take the broader view.
Maybe say some extra prayers
or go buy something new.
And sweetheart, please remember
I simply love your great beef stew!
I don't know how you manage
to cope here in this zoo.
I wouldn't want to do it,
So it might as well be you!

~ Blair Maxwell

Date: _____

Worksheet 18A: Applying the Equality of Women and Men in Marriage

DIRECTIONS: Together put a checkmark (✓) in the columns next to each task to indicate whether the wife or husband should/will do the responsibilities listed below, whether they should be shared, or whether someone else should do them. There are no right or wrong answers, simply examine your assumptions about the activities and ideas of husbands and wives. Indicate any concerns in the Notes column.

If you are completing this as an individual, look at your expectations of who should do the tasks. If you are a couple completing it, you may want to complete this separately and then compare answers. Discuss whether your answers demonstrate the principles of balance and equality.

Worksheets may be printed from www.claricomm.com/publishing

Who should or will primarily do the following:	Husband	Wife	Shared	Another Person	Notes
Prepare the reading for a spiritual meeting					
Fix the car					
Do the laundry; ironing					
Change your baby's diapers					
Handle bedtime responsibilities with children (tucking them in, reading to them, getting glasses of water, etc.)					
Shop for groceries					
Shop for clothes (for husband, wife, children)					
Make phone calls that are difficult or to strangers, such as a plumber or creditors					
Cook meals					
Wash and dry dishes; load and empty dishwasher					
Clean toilets and bathrooms					
Clean the rest of the house					
Pick up things that have been left lying around					
Initiate sexual activity					
Earn money					
Balance the checkbook and pay the bills					
Drive when you are both in the car					
Discipline children					
Repair the house					
Mow the lawn					
Plant or weed the garden					
Buy furniture					
Maintain the social calendar					
Initiate discussion on difficult issues					
Prepare for guests					
Other:					
Other:					

Marriage Can Be Forever—Preparation Counts!

SOME VIRTUES REQUIRED TO ACHIEVE THE EQUALITY OF WOMEN AND MEN

ASSERTIVENESS	Be positive and confident you can treat women and men equally
CARING	Give love and attention to people and things that matter to you
COMPASSION	Understand and care about someone who has made a mistake
COURAGE	Be brave in the face of fear
DETERMINATION	Focus and stick to a task until it is done
FLEXIBILITY	Be open to the need for change
FORGIVENESS	Overlook the mistakes of others
GENEROSITY	Share something meaningful to you, without thought of reward
HUMILITY	Are willing to serve others and know they are as important as you are
JUSTICE	Be fair and see with your own eyes
LOVE	Care and want to be near and share with someone
MODERATION	Achieve balance
PATIENCE	Accept things you cannot control
RESPECT	Honor and care about the rights of others
RESPONSIBILITY	Be dependable
SERVICE	Look for ways to help rather than being asked
TACT	Share the truth so that it helps rather than hurts the other person.
TOLERANCE	Accept things that you wish were different
TRUST	Have faith and rely on and believe in someone

These Virtues definitions are excerpted from the Virtues Cards with permission of The Virtues Project, Inc., www.virtuesproject.com. They are based on *The Family Virtues Guide* by Linda Kavelin-Popov. The Virtues Project, Inc. holds the copyright, and no duplication is permitted without its permission.

Behavior in Relationships

We learn from science that adaptability is the basis of survival. Those who are unwilling to adapt and change their behavior or consider compromise a sign of weakness do not understand that there is a world of difference between giving way to another person because we are forced to do so, or because we are threatened, and giving way because we want to, or out of affection. Indeed, such flexibility, far from being a weakness, is a sign of great strength of mind. Between people who love each other, giving is very important. What we think we are losing in power, control or self-affirmation, we are in fact recovering in maturity, wisdom and serenity....

Nearly all of us have had the experience of a situation in which there was a lot of tension or people's nerves were frayed and a shared laugh was enough to make the atmosphere warm and joyful again. All too often we underestimate the importance of a smile, an embrace, a kind word, a sincere compliment or the giving of one's attention. It is precisely the small things that can change difficult moments into special ones.

~ Mehri Sefidvash, *Coral and Pearls*, pp. 10-12

A trap we all fall into is to hurt the most those we love the most—we fail to respect them. We continue to correct what we consider to be their mistakes, we criticize their decisions, we try to change their attitudes and we argue about matters of form. Of course, there is nothing wrong in expecting the best from those we love, but to try to improve our partner by continually making negative comments about him or criticizing him is certainly not the best way to help him better himself or to show him respect....

Respect means wanting the other person to grow and develop into what he is and can be. Respect automatically excludes exploitation and selfish expectations. To have respect for a person we love means having the desire that he should grow and develop according to his own wishes and his own capabilities, and not just because this is useful for us.

~ Mehri Sefidvash, *Coral and Pearls*, p. 26

When the attraction between two people takes the form of an unhealthy emotional dependence, it is very difficult, if not impossible, for each person to get to know the true character of the other. Such an attachment blinds us and encourages us to keep the relationship alive, while we ignore all the signs that tell us that our behavior, and that of our partner, is immature and irresponsible.

~ Mehri Sefidvash, *Coral and Pearls*, p. 37

CHAPTER 19 – Being Around You: Personality, Attitudes, and Behavior

> **Focus Points**
> - Examining personality, attitudes, and behavior
> - Personality traits set early in life
> - Personality compatibility
> - Care in judging a trait as negative or positive
> - Looking at traits through a spiritual filter
> - Your personality as a couple

A Couple's Story

James and Lindsay hear about a neighborhood project to replace the playground equipment in a park. They contact the leader of the planning committee and volunteer to help. They attend a planning meeting one evening and discover that Lindsay is very comfortable sitting in the meeting working through the details. James is very restless, however, a bit bored, and has trouble making it through the evening. In talking about it later, James and Lindsay decide it's better for them if Lindsay serves on the committee and James helps with the on-site installation. Soon, the day comes for all volunteers to help with the installation of the new equipment.

"What a great day for this," says James. "Perfect weather." He turns to Lindsay, who has become assistant project manager and grins at her. "So, 'boss-lady,' where shall I start?"

Lindsay smiles back at him affectionately. "Smart aleck! Well, actually we have it all worked out carefully who should do what. Here's the first thing that you are assigned to." She gives him the directions, and he starts working with the other volunteers.

"Hey, everyone, wait a minute," James calls out, part way through the day. "There's something not quite right about how these two pieces look together. Let's stand back and see if we should shift one of them sideways."

The group takes a break and considers James' suggestion. "I agree with James," says Lindsay. "I'm glad he spoke up. He has a good eye for how things flow together. Let's move it."

Quotes for Guidance

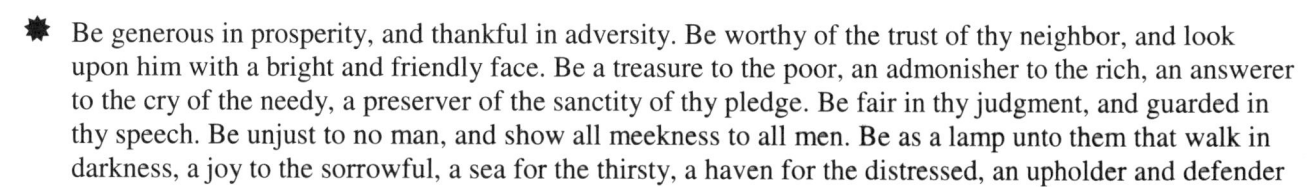

✸ Be generous in prosperity, and thankful in adversity. Be worthy of the trust of thy neighbor, and look upon him with a bright and friendly face. Be a treasure to the poor, an admonisher to the rich, an answerer to the cry of the needy, a preserver of the sanctity of thy pledge. Be fair in thy judgment, and guarded in thy speech. Be unjust to no man, and show all meekness to all men. Be as a lamp unto them that walk in darkness, a joy to the sorrowful, a sea for the thirsty, a haven for the distressed, an upholder and defender

of the victim of oppression. Let integrity and uprightness distinguish all thine acts. Be a home for the stranger, a balm to the suffering, a tower of strength for the fugitive. Be eyes to the blind, and a guiding light unto the feet of the erring. Be an ornament to the countenance of truth, a crown to the brow of fidelity, a pillar of the temple of righteousness, a breath of life to the body of mankind, an ensign of the hosts of justice, a luminary above the horizon of virtue, a dew to the soil of the human heart, an ark on the ocean of knowledge, a sun in the heaven of bounty, a gem on the diadem of wisdom, a shining light in the firmament of thy generation, a fruit upon the tree of humility. We pray God to protect thee from the heat of jealousy and the cold of hatred. He verily is nigh, ready to answer.
(Bahá'u'lláh: *Epistle to the Son of the Wolf*, pp. 93-94)

* Do not busy yourselves in your own concerns; let your thoughts be fixed upon that which will rehabilitate the fortunes of mankind and sanctify the hearts and souls of men. This can best be achieved through pure and holy deeds, through a virtuous life and a goodly behavior.
  (Bahá'u'lláh: *Gleanings from the Writings of Bahá'u'lláh*, pp. 93-94)

* I hope that, with a divine strength and a godlike personality, with a heavenly guidance, with a divine attraction and with a spiritual zeal, thou wilt educate the people.
  ('Abdu'l-Bahá: *Tablets of 'Abdu'l-Bahá, Vol. 2*, p. 341)

* …their attitude toward all men is that of goodwill and loving-kindness….
  ('Abdu'l-Bahá: *Promulgation of Universal Peace*, p. 402)

* A chaste and holy life must be made the controlling principle in the behavior and conduct of all Bahá'ís, both in their social relations with the members of their own community, and in their contact with the world at large.
  (Shoghi Effendi: *Advent of Divine Justice*, p. 29)

* How staunch was her faith, how calm her demeanor, how forgiving her attitude, how severe her trials….
  [Bahíyyih Khánum; Bahá'u'lláh's daughter]
  (Shoghi Effendi: *Bahá'í Administration*, p. 189)

* The Teachings of Bahá'u'lláh are so great, and deal with so many aspects of both the inner life of man and his communal life, that it takes years to really plumb them to the depths. He has brought spiritual food for the soul of the individual, to help each one to find himself and become a finer and better developed personality; and also He has brought the laws and principles needed to enable all men to live in harmony together in a great, united world. The Guardian hopes you, together with..., will do all in your power to help the believers to understand both aspects of the teachings, and to develop both as individuals and as a community, an ever higher, finer way of life.
  (On behalf of Shoghi Effendi: *Lights of Guidance*, p. 570)

Perspectives to Consider

Whenever you **describe another person**, the words are usually about his or her personality, attitudes, and behavior—he's serious, she's fun, she's analytical, he's easygoing. Personality traits are often more easily spotted and visible than character traits, which take more time to discover and have a more internal quality to them. It doesn't take quite as long to see that someone has a great sense of humor or likes to be in charge as it does to understand if someone has the character qualities of truthfulness or courage.

Character and personality are somewhat linked with each other, however. Character can be considered a part of your personality, which is the total sum of your character, behavioral, temperamental, emotional, and mental traits. For this workbook, however, personality, attitudes, and behavior are part of Step 4 on compatibility and located here in this chapter. The character qualities are in Chapter 6 of Step 2, as part of searching for a prospective mate.

As with the character assessment in Chapter 6, it makes sense to start with yourself. Your own personality may not be something that you've thought about, or you may know yourself fairly well. In any case, it will help you to be clear on your strongest points and begin to understand how those traits might interact with similar or different traits of another person.

Your personality traits and those of a potential partner are likely to be fairly set by the time you are thinking about marriage preparation. While it is possible to modify your personality to some extent, personality traits tend to **form early in life and essentially stay constant** or become more pronounced. *Although many aspects of your relationship will* **change**, *don't enter a relationship assuming yours or someone else's personality will significantly change.* You must spend time testing your perceptions of just how compatible your personalities are. You will be living together in a "fortress for well-being," and the way your personalities blend and interact together will directly affect the quality of your marriage. Companionship is one of the greatest joys of marriage, and personality compatibility is part of achieving it.

Your personality and attitudes (and your diet/health) affect how you behave and **interact with others**. They will often control the quality of the relationships you have with others. Do you have a superior attitude that annoys people? Are you a peacemaker when people around you start to argue? Are you organized and is your organizational tendency moderate, or does it spread compulsively throughout all you do? Understanding all of these kinds of interactions will help you and a potential marriage partner determine your compatibility.

Determining compatibility is an interesting puzzle when it comes to personality, attitudes, and behavior. And, since no one is an exact or perfect match, it includes determining which traits and characteristics of another person are a large problem for you, which are annoying but tolerable, and which ones are different from your own but complementary. If you both like to be in charge and run things, you may be so competitive that you fight frequently, or you may just both work hard toward goals together. If one of you is cheerful in the morning and the other grumpy until noon, you might have difficulty living together, or simply agree to avoid being sociable in the morning.

It can be difficult to judge whether a personality trait, attitude, or behavior is **positive or negative**. Often a trait can be one or the other depending on the circumstances and people involved. Being forgetful might seem like a negative trait, but if the person is good at forgetting others' faults, well, that might be a good thing. Being a loner might seem like a negative thing to an extrovert, but may be a positive thing for an introvert.

It is good to put a **spiritual lens** up to your eyes as you look to understand someone, as there are personality qualities that could interfere with the spirituality of your future home. For instance, if you value working and earning a living to support your family as a spiritual principle, and you perceive that your partner has the personality trait of "laziness," this might be an issue. If it's important to you to have times when there is an atmosphere of prayer and reverence in your life, and your partner tends to be consistently loud and talkative, this could be a concern.

Your choices for how you spend your time closely relate to your personality. Think about what your personality is like and what you choose to do, such as in these examples:

- Watch TV or movies
- Talk during mealtimes
- Have people in your home for socializing
- Listen to music all day

- Work long hours
- Sleep in late
- Talk on the phone all night
- Play sports

Marriage Can Be Forever—Preparation Counts!

All of these and many more could be points of compatibility, or they may be issues in a marriage relationship between you (See Chapter 25 about time choices).

There's an interesting phenomenon related to personality. When a couple has been together for a while, they often have a **"couple personality"** that is a blend of their individual traits. Others may describe you as a lively couple, a happy couple, an argumentative couple, or a playful couple. This description can be an indicator of compatibility or incompatibility, so invite others to describe you together.

Coaching

⇒ Personality traits can be positive under some circumstances and negative under others. Be cautious before you label something as a negative trait. Be equally cautious about explaining away a negative trait, either in yourself or in another.

⇒ Find opportunities to be in many different circumstances together so that you experience the full range of your own and your partner's personality, attitudes, and behavior. Activities done together will begin to show your level of compatibility.

Questions for Reflection and Discussion

1. What is your attitude toward yourself? Positive? Negative? Success? Failure? Person of worth? No good?
2. What is your general attitude toward other people? When do you make exceptions to this?
3. What do you feel are important personality qualities to look for in a person that indicate he/she is mature enough and spiritually prepared for marriage? Do you observe these in your partner?
4. What personality traits would be warning signs that either of you would have difficulty in being a fully participating marriage partner? Are you observing any of these traits?
5. What will prepare you to be an enjoyable partner and parent? Are you doing this preparation?
6. What do you like about your own personality?
7. What would you like to change about your personality? What do you find annoying about yourself?
8. What do you like about his/her personality?
9. What do you find annoying about him/her? How will you deal with that?
10. Are you prepared for him/her to stay the same throughout your marriage? (**Note:** The desire to change others can be a major trap.) What do you wish was different? Do you anticipate that the annoying things will probably go away? Is this realistic?
11. Is there any personality trait that could cause a problem in your marriage? When have you observed it?
12. Is there any attitude that concerns you? When have you observed it?
13. What times has your own behavior been a concern to you?
14. What times has your partner's behavior been a concern to you?
15. Are your personality types compatible? Introvert/extrovert (depends on whether you re-charge your energy by being alone or with other people)? Analytical or creative? Laid back or driving action to make things happen? Do you seem to balance each other?
16. Is he/she a risk-taker? What kind of risk (ranges from changing jobs to sky diving)? What is the outcome when he/she takes a risk? Are you comfortable with the risks each other takes?
17. Is he/she domineering or controlling? Or just a natural leader?
18. Is he/she emotionally expressive or withdrawn?
19. Is he/she a "snoozer" in the morning? Morning person? Night person? Light sleeper? Stays up all night?

20. Is he/she dependent on you? Does it feel excessive? In what ways do you effectively function independently of each other?
21. How well does he/she listen? Do you feel listened to?
22. Is he/she physically affectionate? Does he/she snuggle or regularly seek to be touched in an affectionate way? Are you comfortable or uncomfortable with this? What are your needs in this area?
23. How attached is he/she to music? Is it playing all the time? Rarely? What kind of music?
24. How attached is he/she to the television? Is it on all the time? Rarely? What kind of shows?
25. How attached is he/she to playing video games? How often does he/she play them?
26. How attached is he/she to spending time on the Internet? What is his/her purpose for being online? How many hours a day does this occur?
27. Do you call each other personal nicknames or endearments like "honey," "baby," or "sweetheart"? Are you comfortable with the names used?
28. Draw on your powers of observation, and ask yourself specific questions for *each* of the qualities listed in Worksheet 19A. This is an example of questions that go with the quality of "organized":
    - Does he/she need to have everything orderly and well organized? Is this tendency rigid, obsessive, or compulsive? Is there a tendency toward perfectionism? Is it balanced?

Activities

1. Pray, meditate, reflect, and write in your journal about the importance of personality assessment and compatibility as part of preparing for marriage.

2. Identify two activities that you feel will support you in observing and understanding each other's personality, attitudes, and behavior. You might consider being involved in some kind of group project that will use your skills and abilities in a natural way. It's important that the activities you pick have other people involved, so you aren't just interacting with each other. What do you want to do?

    a. _____
    b. _____

3. Use Worksheet 19A to assess your personality, attitudes, and behavior and those of your partner. **Note:** If there are others who would be living with you after marriage, such as a child or parent, you may wish to include them in your assessment as well.

4. Consider taking personality tests such as Myers-Briggs or using personal inventories such as 4th-step inventories used by 12-step groups. Some personality tests are specifically designed for couples. Remember these are not "right" and "wrong" assessments, but simply designed to help you understand yourself and how your personality might fit with or complement each other. Information on Myers-Briggs can be found at: www.discoveryourpersonality.com .

5. Meditate on the quote below and its relationship to personality assessment. Discuss it with your partner.

> "As I interpret the Course [of Miracles], 'our deepest fear is not that we are inadequate. Our deepest fear is that we are powerful beyond measure. It is our light, not our darkness, that most frightens us.' We ask ourselves, Who am I to be brilliant, gorgeous, talented, fabulous? Actually, who are you *not* to be? You are a child of God. Your playing small doesn't serve the world. There's nothing enlightened about shrinking so that other people won't feel insecure around you. We are all meant to shine, as children do. We were born to make manifest the glory of God that is within us. It's not just in some of us; it's in everyone. And as we let our own light shine, we unconsciously give other people permission to do the same. As we're liberated from our own fear, our presence automatically liberates others."
> ~ Marianne Williamson, *A Return to Love*, pp. 190-191

Date: _____

Worksheet 19A: Assessing Personality, Attitudes, and Behavior

DIRECTIONS: This worksheet is to help you observe and understand yourself and your partner.
- Pray and meditate to achieve clarity about your personality traits, attitudes, and behaviors.
- Complete the worksheet separately and then discuss the results together.
- Place a checkmark (✓) next to each word or phrase that applies to you.
- After you each complete the worksheets, identify together your similarities and differences, and then whether there are any compatibilities or incompatibilities starting to be clear.
- Note any concerns that arise by placing a checkmark (✓) or by writing comments in "Issues?/Notes."

Worksheets may be printed from www.claricomm.com/publishing

Traits	He	She	Issues? Notes
Accepting			
Active listener			
Adaptable			
Adventurous			
Affectionate			
Agreeable			
Aggressive			
Alienating			
Amiable			
Analytical			
Angers easily			
Animated			
Anxious			
Antagonistic			
Argumentative			
Asks (vs. Tells)			
Balanced			
Bashful			
Behaved			
Bold			
Boring			
Bossy			
Bouncy			
Brassy			
Calm			
Casual			
Cautious			
Centered			
Changeable			
Cheerful			
Clear			
Competent			
Competitive			
Complaining			

Traits	He	She	Issues? Notes
Complimentary			
Compromising			
Confronting			
Consistent			
Consultative			
Contented			
Controlled			
Controlling			
Convincing			
Cooperative			
Crafty			
Creative			
Critical			
Cross-examining			
Cultured			
Cute			
Daring			
Decisive			
Decides quickly			
Decides slowly			
Deep			
Delightful			
Demonstrative			
Depressed			
Detailed			
Devotional			
Diplomatic			
Disciplined			
Disorganized			
Disruptive			
Dominating			
Domineering			
Doubtful			
Drives self			

Marriage Can Be Forever—Preparation Counts!

Traits	He	She	Issues? Notes
Drives others			
Dry Humor			
Eccentric			
Efficient			
Embarrassing			
Emotional			
Encouraging			
Energetic			
Empathetic			
Ethical			
Expressive-emotions			
Expressive-verbal			
Extravert			
Fact-oriented			
Fair-minded			
Family-focused			
Fearful			
Foolish			
Forceful			
Forgetful			
Formal			
Forgiving			
Fragile			
Frank			
Friendly			
Free-flowing			
Frustrated			
Frustrating			
Fun-loving			
Funny			
Fussy			
Generous			
Genuine			
Giving			
Haphazard			
Happy			
Hard-to-please			
Hardworking			
Headstrong			
Helpful			
Hesitant			
High integrity			
Hopeful			
Hopeless			

Traits	He	She	Issues? Notes
Hostile			
Impatient			
Impulsive			
Inadequate			
Inconsistent			
In-charge			
Inclusive			
Indecisive			
Independent			
Indifferent			
Ingratiating			
Inoffensive			
Inquiring			
Insecure			
Inspiring			
Intellectual			
Intense			
Interrupts			
Intimidating			
Intolerant			
Introvert			
Investigative			
Involved			
Irresponsible			
Irreverent attitude			
Jealous			
Laid-back			
Lazy			
Leader			
Legalistic			
Life of the party			
Listener			
Lively			
Loner			
Loud			
Manipulative			
Mediator			
Meditative			
Messy			
Mixes easily			
Moderate			
Moody			
Motivating			
Mover			

Marriage Can Be Forever—Preparation Counts!

Traits	He	She	Issues? Notes
Moves quickly			
Moves slowly			
Musical			
Naïve			
Needy			
Negative attitude			
Nervy			
Nonchalant			
Obliging			
Oblivious			
Open			
Opinionated			
Optimistic			
Organized			
Outspoken			
Over-sensitive			
Overwhelming			
Passionate			
Passive			
Patronizing			
Peaceful			
Peacemaker			
Perceptive			
Perfectionist			
Permissive			
Persistent			
Persuasive			
Pessimistic			
Philosophical			
Plain			
Planner			
Playful			
Pleasant			
Popular			
Positive attitude			
Prayerful			
Predictable			
Pressuring			
Productive			
Promoter			
Proud			
Punctual			
Purposeful			
Quick-thinking			

Traits	He	She	Issues? Notes
Rash			
Rational			
Refreshing			
Realistic			
Reckless			
Relaxed			
Reliable			
Reluctant			
Repetitious			
Resentful			
Reserved			
Resistant			
Resourceful			
Responsive			
Restless			
Results-oriented			
Reticent			
Revengeful			
Reverent attitude			
Risk-taking			
Safe			
Satisfied			
Scary			
Scatterbrained			
Scheduled			
Self-confident			
Self-indulgent			
Selfless			
Self-reliant			
Self-sacrificing			
Sensitive			
Serious			
Sheltering			
Short-tempered			
Show-off			
Shy			
Sincere			
Skeptical			
Slick			
Sluggish			
Sneaky			
Sociable			
Spacey			
Speaks loudly			

Traits	He	She	Issues? Notes		Traits	He	She	Issues? Notes
Speaks softly					Thinks slowly			
Spirited					Time Conscious			
Spiritual					Timid			
Spontaneous					Too sensitive			
Steadfast					Trivializing			
Stressed					Trusting			
Strong					Trustworthy			
Strong-willed					Unaffectionate			
Structured					Undisciplined			
Stubborn					Unenthusiastic			
Stuck-up					Unforgiving			
Submissive					Unfriendly			
Subtle					Unity-building			
Superior					Unity-destroying			
Supportive					Uninvolved			
Sure					Unpopular			
Suspicious					Unpredictable			
Sympathetic					Unreliable			
Tactful					Unstructured			
Tactless					Unsympathetic			
Talkative					Violating			
Talks quickly					Violent			
Talks slowly					Wants credit			
Task-oriented					Welcoming			
Teacher					Whining			
Tells (vs. Asks)					Withdrawn			
Tenacious					Witty			
Tentative					Workaholic			
Thoughtful					Works with hands			
Thinks quickly					Worrier			

1. Identify a few traits that appear to be very compatible:
   _____ _____ _____
   _____ _____ _____

2. Identify a few traits that have the least compatibility:
   _____ _____ _____
   _____ _____ _____

3. What are your concerns?
   _____
   _____

4. Can they be addressed? If so, how? If not, why not? And how does all this affect the relationship?
   _____
   _____

Communicating is giving of ourselves, which is all that we are. *Communication* is the link necessary to integrate two persons with separate identities into a marriage. The kinds of communication that nourish a marriage are listening with understanding, appreciating and affirming your partner, making requests for what you want, making and keeping promises, and expressing your feelings. These communications will increase intimacy and develop a partnership that will bring out the best in each person.

~ Sandra Gray Bender, Ph.D., *Recreating Marriage with the Same Old Spouse*, p. 87

The Rose That Binds Us

Roses are red...
Well, sometimes they're yellow
But then what becomes of my rhyming scheme?
'Cause "fellow" simply won't wax sentimental.
Oh really, ending a line with "sentimental"
    My love for you is elemental?
Roses are...white
And violets are...violet.
    I married you because you're the best guy-I-met.
Best leave the violets, the roses, the poesy
Thank the Lord that my love's
More sublime than my poetry.

~ Judy Parsley

CHAPTER 20 – Of Minds and Hearts: Communicating With Each Other

Focus Points
- Verbal and non-verbal communication
- Re-visiting consultation
- Character qualities to use in communication
- Cultural and gender influences
- Listening effectively

A Couple's Story

Lindsay and James are getting out of the car at the park where they are going to have a picnic with some friends.

"James, please be sure to…"

"Yeah, Lindsay, I'll lock the car when everything's out." He knows she's security conscious.

She looks at him with frustration. "What I started to say was 'Please be sure to get the bottle of sunscreen out from under your seat.' The bottle slid underneath it. It really makes me upset when you assume what I'm going to say instead of listening to me," Lindsay says.

"You're right," James says. "I'm sorry. Sometimes I just want to act like I'm on your wavelength. I'm afraid if I can't figure out what you're going to say that there's something not right between us."

Lindsay smiles at him. "Nah, nobody's a mind reader. I just need you to allow me to say what I need to, and you'll get it just fine. Otherwise, interrupting just slows things down and makes me upset. Let's go eat…but please grab the sunscreen first!"

Quotes for Guidance

✹ Consort with all men, O people of Bahá, in a spirit of friendliness and fellowship. If ye be aware of a certain truth, if ye possess a jewel, of which others are deprived, share it with them in a language of utmost kindliness and good-will. If it be accepted, if it fulfill its purpose, your object is attained. If any one should refuse it, leave him unto himself, and beseech God to guide him. Beware lest ye deal unkindly with him. A kindly tongue is the lodestone of the hearts of men. It is the bread of the spirit, it clotheth the words with meaning, it is the fountain of the light of wisdom and understanding....
(Bahá'u'lláh: *Gleanings from the Writings of Bahá'u'lláh*, p. 289)

✹ Settle all things, both great and small, by consultation. Without prior consultation, take no important step in your own personal affairs. Concern yourselves with one another. Help along one another's projects and plans. Grieve over one another. Let none in the whole country go in need. Befriend one another until ye become as a single body, one and all.
('Abdu'l-Bahá: *Lights of Guidance*, p. 179)

Chapter 20 – Of Minds and Hearts: Communicating with Each Other

✺ Be in perfect unity…. Love the creatures for the sake of God and not for themselves. You will never become angry or impatient if you love them for the sake of God. Humanity is not perfect. There are imperfections in every human being, and you will always become unhappy if you look toward the people themselves. But if you look toward God, you will love them and be kind to them, for the world of God is the world of perfection and complete mercy.
('Abdu'l-Bahá: *Promulgation of Universal Peace*, p. 93)

✺ They must in every matter search out the truth and not insist upon their own opinion, for stubbornness and persistence in one's views will lead ultimately to discord and wrangling and the truth will remain hidden.
(Shoghi Effendi: *Bahá'í Administration*, p. 22)

✺ In any group, however loving the consultation, there are nevertheless points on which, from time to time, agreement cannot be reached. In a Spiritual Assembly this dilemma is resolved by a majority vote. There can, however, be no majority where only two parties are involved, as in the case of a husband and wife. There are, therefore, times when a wife should defer to her husband, and times when a husband should defer to his wife, but neither should ever unjustly dominate the other. In short, the relationship between husband and wife should be as held forth in the prayer revealed by 'Abdu'l-Bahá which is often read at Bahá'í weddings: 'Verily they are married in obedience to Thy command. Cause them to become the signs of harmony and unity until the end of time.'
(Shoghi Effendi: *Lights of Guidance*, pp. 226-227)

👓 Perspectives to Consider

Communication is vital, exasperating, challenging, wonderful, scary, clear, messy, risky, intimate, and a long list more. Verbal and non-verbal communication connects every aspect of your friendship and partner relationship, and they have emotional, mental, physical, and spiritual components to them. Your mutual communication may leave you feeling satisfied and happy or frustrated and miserable, depending on your compatibility, maturity, and skill level. Communication in marriage will affect your ability to live together peacefully, reach wise decisions, teach your children to communicate well, influence each other's growth and development, prevent misunderstandings, be intimate, and on and on. It can strengthen a relationship immeasurably when it goes well and can quickly become destructive when it doesn't.

Don't Clam Up!

In a family, you will communicate about everything and interact with each other on every imaginable topic, including, how to organize your home so it supports everyone's needs, having children, what to wear, or what kind of food to buy and how much to spend on it. Sometimes these will be general discussions; other times you will fully utilize the tool of consultation (see Chapter 3). It is one of the most significant ways you will communicate with each other. You will use it to explore your thoughts, feelings, and goals, and the more skill you develop in consulting, the smoother your communications and decision making will be. Remember that making decisions as a twosome is different from group consultation, because there is no such thing as a majority vote. This challenges you to reach mutual agreement wherever possible. If it has been a while since you assessed your consultation skills, it may be time to revisit Worksheet 3A. Where do you still need to focus for skill development?

Consultation is one way that your communication has a spiritual component. This includes beginning with prayer and seeking God's guidance in your decisions. Praying together by itself is also a form of communication. You agree on what you are praying for/about, read or say prayers out loud with each other, and build a spiritual connection between you through the prayers. Positive spiritual qualities of character also apply to communication. This includes being *kind and courteous* in your interactions, *courageous* in speaking up when difficult issues must be raised, *assertive* in addressing small problems so that they don't become big ones, *patient* when listening, and much more.

Effective communication takes time and is **built on trust**. The degree to which you trust each other affects your ability to risk being vulnerable and share important things about yourself. Getting to know and trust someone is essential to intimate and safe communication about personal issues. What can you do to increase your trust in each other? How will you know when it is safe to share something? What does breaking trust look like to you? How can you re-build it when it's been broken? Do you want to re-build it?

When the trust is well-established, and you are getting to know your partner and are seriously considering marriage, it feels joyful to share what's in your heart, soul, and mind. There can be a real spark of connection between you and a feeling of communicating **"on the same wavelength."** You may experience knowing what is on your partner's mind before he or she speaks or be able to finish each other's sentences. You may be very aware of each other's moods and emotions. While being on the same wavelength can be great when it works well, *don't place excessive importance on it*. Some people will never have the ability to sense emotions and thoughts in another person clearly, and this is not a requirement for marriage. It would simply require that your verbal communication skills are very good.

A component of verbal communication that may not be intuitively obvious is **effective listening**. When someone *truly* listens to you, it enhances trust and harmony in your communications, and you feel respected, validated, and appreciated. Allow your partner to communicate fully without interruption, listen with your heart as well as your mind, and check to make sure you have fully understood what the other is saying before you respond. Listening with your heart means listening with love, with

---

Consulting About the Big Issues?

In many cases, it will be wise to set aside judgment about whether something is big or small when it comes to consultation and decision-making. Even small things can become big, for example, if they are left to build up inside, if one of you minimizes the issue, if it relates indirectly to another "bigger" issue, or if you bypass consultation. As is natural, at any given time, you will probably have different perceptions of what is big or small.

Because you can't be certain of your partner's perspective, the qualities of tact and wisdom are crucial for in-depth consultations of all kinds. Larger, deeper issues may involve many emotions that will require expression and sensitive responses. Additional **pauses or breaks** may assist you if your emotions are escalating during the discussion and leading you to say things you will later regret. Agree ahead of time to call for a "time out" if needed. If you can maintain a spiritual attitude and remember that preserving the quality of your relationship is very important, you will likely communicate in a loving way and be happier and more satisfied with the outcome of the consultation.

Many topics might qualify as "big" ones for you, depending on how they will affect your future and your relationship. These might include whether to marry or not, purchasing or selling a home, when to/whether to have or adopt children, and so on. Consultations on more intense subjects usually **take more time**. You may be able to share with each other and resolve a matter in a short session; alternatively, it may take several sessions over a period of a days, weeks, or months.

The physical setup for more serious and in-depth consultations can also be very important. You may need to be away from your usual environment and set up space where you can be focused and undisturbed.

While **praying for guidance** at the beginning of a consultation is always important, it becomes even more necessary when you are facing decisions that have a serious or long-term effect. It may be wise to pause repeatedly during the consultation for prayer as well.

When a matter is very serious, it is also wise to agree to **wait for a while after making the decision** and then re-visit it to confirm whether it is still the right choice.

Marriage Can Be Forever—Preparation Counts!

caring, and with compassion. When people feel heard, it boosts their self-confidence, and they are likely to feel more loving toward you—and to improve their own listening skills.

Communication, especially in a close relationship, can be **emotionally hazardous at times**. Misunderstandings may happen, you may unintentionally hurt your partner's feelings, or you could accidentally (or intentionally) use words that make the other upset. All this could make you wonder occasionally whether it's easier to just stay silent... In the long run, though, it's more productive to keep patiently developing your sensitivity and communications skills. (See Chapter 21)

There may also be **cultural or gender-related influences** that affect your communication patterns. Some cultures teach that it is important *not* to be honest or direct in communication, if there is any chance that it will upset the listener. Other cultures train people to share loudly and often with each other, assuming everyone should be thick-skinned enough to take it. Some families and cultures teach male children not to express themselves but to stay quiet and let females do the communicating; others teach male dominance and that females should be demure and silent. Studying—and getting exposure to—each other's cultures as well as reading books about gender differences in communication may support you in understanding your compatibility in this area.

Ways to Know You are Mature and Compatible in Communication Styles

You may be wondering how to tell if you are each mature and skilled in communicating and whether you are **compatible in your ability to communicate.** Here are some ways you could assess that:

- You are self-aware and raise issues promptly and appropriately, rather than letting them fester and grow
- You have regular communications and consultations that are unified and productive
- Your consultations usually flow smoothly, and you reach decisions you are both comfortable with at the end, leading to unified action.
- As you carry out the decisions and see their wisdom, you are confident that the decision was sound because you shared all relevant thoughts, facts, and opinions during the consultation process.
- You have developed communication skills that are healthy and constructive (see Chapter 21)
- There is a flow of openness between you about your hopes, dreams, emotions, thoughts, and experiences
- You can laugh together—especially over tense issues
- Over time and with lots of practice, you will likely develop the ability to express profound love and respect toward one other consistently.

When it comes to **non-verbal communication**, you will need to hone your observational skills to see, hear, and understand messages your partner is giving *without* speaking. This type of communication includes a glance, a stare, a frown, a smile, a loving look, a hand gesture, and much more. Your tone of voice is also a powerful non-verbal cue beyond the words that you say. Non-verbal signals can enrich communication and help express your personality. They can also communicate strong meaning along with your words, sometimes appropriately and helpfully, sometimes not. Be conscious of the impact of gestures or intonations that emphasize your points—do they make your message too strong? If you smile while you are telling a story, do your words have greater meaning for the people who are hearing it? If you frown when talking, does that expression overwhelm the meaning of anything you might say?

When communication works well, it weaves the fabric that binds you closely together, and you begin to know—and appreciate—each other more than any other person. Rather than un-raveling the relationship via poor communication and hurtful interactions, you create a beautiful tapestry that can warm, protect, and comfort you as you sit together in front of the fireplace of your marriage "fortress."

Coaching

⇒ While being in a close relationship with someone gives you greater sensitivity to each other's thoughts and emotions, and sometimes you can guess what the other is thinking, it can be unwise to make assumptions about what the other person thinks or feels. Neither is it wise to expect your partner to read *your* mind. It is a **romantic myth** that couples should always be able to "read each other's minds" and know what the other means, thinks, and needs. In fact, assuming that you do know can often feel to your partner like an *invalidation* of his/her feelings and thoughts. Clear communication lessens the possibility of misunderstandings.

⇒ Remember the analogy that marriage is like one long conversation with your partner, your companion for life—choose someone with whom you enjoy communicating!

⇒ If you rearrange the letters of **LISTEN** they form the word **SILENT**. The Chinese written characters for "listen" include the concepts of listening with the ears, mind, eyes, and heart.

⇒ If you are having difficulty communicating or consulting, set up a regular, daily time to share with each other how you think your communication flowed that day, what went well and what didn't. Remember to share your successes, as well as the difficulties. This daily analysis will help your skills gradually improve.

⇒ Sometimes when communication feels like a struggle, you may start questioning your relationship. While there may valid concerns worth examining, you should not immediately ask whether there is something wrong with your relationship or whether your partner loves you based on a single instance or miscommunication. If you have to repeat something you've already said, if one of you won't let something drop and pursues it single-mindedly, or if one of you is distracted by a concern, it doesn't mean that your relationship is at risk necessarily.

Questions for Reflection and Discussion

1. How do you prefer to communicate with your partner on important topics? How about on daily matters? In-person conversation? E-mail? Instant messaging? Written notes? A hug? Others? All of these?
2. Does one of you prefer one approach and the other something different? (Example: one doesn't enjoy long talks on the phone, one *must* be looking someone in the eye to have a serious conversation, one finds it easier to write a letter or email to the other first before having a difficult conversation?)
3. Do you prefer to carry a cell phone and be available all the time? Would you rather not be that available?
4. How do you feel about the amount of communication between the two of you? Would you prefer more or less?
5. Do you notice a difference in your communication if you pray together first?
6. What might be an indication that you need to have an in-depth consultation?
7. Can you effectively solve difficulties through consultation? Examples?
8. Do you patiently listen to each other?
9. What character virtues do you regularly use in your communications? (See Appendix A)
10. How well do you listen to your partner? How well does he/she listen to you?
11. Do you feel each of you is able to concentrate on listening to the other without your attention wandering?
12. Does either of you ever use a tone of voice that bothers the other? What can you do to remind yourself to avoid using it?
13. What may indicate that one of your parents or others taught you to avoid direct communication in resolving issues?

14. Does the amount of communication your partner has with others seem excessive or annoying to you? How do you deal with this?
15. With whom is it appropriate or inappropriate to talk about your relationship? Are there topics that should be confidential and not shared? Finances? Feelings? Sex and intimacy? Other matters? What would you expect of your spouse in this matter?
16. How do you talk about each other and your relationship in front of others? How do they feel and respond when you do?

Activities

1. Pray, meditate, reflect, and write in your journal about the importance of communication between you and your partner in marriage. You also may wish to reflect on the current state of your communication.

2. Have an in-depth consultation(s) with each other about all of the topics below that are relevant to you. The object is to have a *meaningful* consultation so you both understand each other's views on the issue, and you are also able to assess your ability to consult. Choose another topic than the ones listed, if necessary. This consultation may take awhile, so remember that you may want to pray first, and then identify an appropriate, time and place without distractions.

    - Whether to finish college before getting married or not
    - How to show affection
    - Geographical distance from each other and/or family before and after marriage
    - Where to live after marriage
    - How you would handle moving to another location (Examples: employment, religious service, college enrollment, being near parents)
    - How you would handle sibling rivalry among your children or conflicts among half- or stepchildren
    - Whether you would be willing to loan money to others and under what circumstances

3. Discuss together how the communication on the above subjects flowed and how you felt about it:

    a. Were you able to listen completely?
    b. Did you each feel heard?
    c. How did each of you listen in a manner that was helpful?
    d. Did either of you interact in a manner that was *not* helpful?
    e. What are some verbal and non-verbal listening skills you'd like to alter in yourself and/or in your partner?
    f. Did either of you withhold information?
    g. Was it difficult to be honest with your partner about your thoughts and feelings?
    h. Were you sensitive to each other's feelings?
    i. Were you able to reach consensus peacefully? Are you both ready and committed to abide by the decisions you came to?
    j. What might you do differently another time?

4. List below the character qualities that you believe can contribute to effective communication in your relationship (see Appendix A for suggestions). Do you each demonstrate these?

_____   _____   _____

_____   _____   _____

5. Say a few of the following phrases to each other in a variety of different tones of voice and with varied expressions on your face. Watch your partner's reaction to these different non-verbal cues. Discuss which ones you like and which ones you would prefer *not* to have as part of your communication with each other.

    a. Sit down
    b. Yes, dear
    c. Come with me
    d. Let the dog out
    e. Pass the salt
    f. Will you call me
    g. Why did you do that
    h. Can you hear me
    i. All right, I'll do it

6. What did you discover during this exercise about communication?

    _____
    _____
    _____

7. If you identify that you/your families have different cultural backgrounds, study books on the cultures involved and identify activities that will further your understanding. This might include watching movies, attending a family reunion, visiting a cultural museum, and so on. What did you do? What did you learn from the experiences that would make a difference to you in a marriage?

    _____
    _____

8. Visit a library or bookstore to get a couple of current books that address gender differences in communication. Read through and discuss the key points together with the goal of identifying what applies to your relationship. **Note:** It is clear that men and women (and all individuals!) have differences in how they communicate. However, as you study the differences, remember the goal is unity, and don't focus so much on stereotypical or side-taking models of communication that stress your differences and don't assist you to bridge them. What did you learn new that will be useful in your communications with each other?

    _____
    _____
    _____

Marriage Can Be Forever—Preparation Counts!

If we have a relationship based on love, we can be open and honest with our partner without fear of being judged and knowing that support will be extended to us. We are sure that our partner is our best friend and will, whatever happens, always help us. Where there is love in our relationship, we can allow ourselves certain liberties: the liberty to get angry now and again, or even to lose control without fearing that a permanent scar will be left; the liberty to be imperfect; the liberty to make a fool of ourselves without losing the respect of our partner; the liberty to change and to grow and also to make mistakes without fearing that we will be abandoned at our moment of greatest need or that we may be subjected to a barrage of recriminations and judgments, the worst of which is undoubtedly "I told you so!"

We need support particularly when the worst side of our character is exposed to our partner. It is just at this time that the acceptance and affection of our partner become the mainstays of our life. To preserve our personal dignity, we all need to feel the warmth and approval of someone we love and respect.

~ Mehri Sefidvash, *Coral and Pearls*, pp. 41-42

When giving support and encouragement, it is essential to accept and love the other person, not only for what he is but also for what he could become—to love his potential. This is not the same thing as trying to change him in some way. We must support and encourage our partner without trying to alter his life. Love in this sense is then conceived as an interest in the life and growth of those to whom we are attached. If this interest is lacking, then there is no love.

Love is contagious. Loving is a force that produces love and, as a result, a joy for living. It is certainly true, of course, that in the process of growth we may sometimes feel lost or go through periods when we don't feel up to the task before us. It is then that the encouragement and support provided by a loving partner can see us through.

~ Mehri Sefidvash, *Coral and Pearls*, pp. 44-45

CHAPTER 21 – Doing It Better: Communication Skills

> **Focus Points**
> - Key communication skills
> - Risks of communication; importance of truthfulness and honesty
> - Handling issues peacefully
> - Poor communication habits
> - Problem-solving
> - Avoiding contempt, faultfinding, backbiting, or criticism
> - Using encouragement and praise
> - Communicating with humor

A Couple's Story

Lindsay calls James on his cellphone at his office. "James, did you remember to pick up the cake for your Mom's birthday party this weekend?" She is careful to sound loving, although she is a bit concerned and impatient he may have forgotten.

"Yes, Lindsay," he says with a bit of annoyance. "I said I would."

"You're mad that I called to remind you, aren't you?" she responds. "I guess I should have trusted you'd remember."

"A bit, but that's okay," says James. "I know you want the party to go well—and I can be forgetful sometimes. I'll call your cellphone when I'm leaving work so we can meet at the party supply store."

"Thanks, honey," says Lindsay. "The call will help me get there. I've got a project to start this afternoon."

Quotes for Guidance

✸ He must never seek to exalt himself above any one, must wash away from the tablet of his heart every trace of pride and vainglory, must cling unto patience and resignation, observe silence and refrain from idle talk. For the tongue is a smoldering fire, and excess of speech a deadly poison. Material fire consumeth the body, whereas the fire of the tongue devoureth both heart and soul. The force of the former lasteth but for a time, whilst the effects of the latter endureth a century. That seeker should, also, regard backbiting as grievous error, and keep himself aloof from its dominion, inasmuch as backbiting quencheth the light of the heart, and extinguisheth the life of the soul.
(Bahá'u'lláh: *Gleanings from the Writings of Bahá'u'lláh*, pp. 264-265)

Marriage Can Be Forever—Preparation Counts!

- If any soul speak ill of an absent one, the only result will clearly be this: he will dampen the zeal of the friends and tend to make them indifferent. For backbiting is divisive…. If any individual should speak ill of one who is absent, it is incumbent on his hearers, in a spiritual and friendly manner, to stop him, and say in effect: would this detraction serve any useful purpose? Would it please [Bahá'u'lláh], contribute to the lasting honor of the friends, promote the…[Bahá'í] Faith, support the Covenant [of Bahá'u'lláh], or be of any possible benefit to any soul? No, never! On the contrary, it would make the dust to settle so thickly on the heart that the ears would hear no more, and the eyes would no longer behold the light of truth.

  If, however, a person setteth about speaking well of another, opening his lips to praise another, he will touch an answering chord in his hearers and they will be stirred up by the breathings of God. Their hearts and souls will rejoice….
  ('Abdu'l-Bahá: *Selections from the Writings of 'Abdu'l-Bahá*, pp. 230-231)

- Consider that the worst of qualities and most odious of attributes, which is the foundation of all evil, is lying. No worse or more blameworthy quality than this can be imagined to exist; it is the destroyer of all human perfections and the cause of innumerable vices.
  ('Abdu'l-Bahá: *Some Answered Questions*, p. 215)

- O ye beloved of the Lord! In this sacred Dispensation, conflict and contention are in no wise permitted. Every aggressor deprives himself of God's grace.
  ('Abdu'l-Bahá: *Will and Testament*, p. 13)

- Never speak disparagingly of others, but praise without distinction…. Let not your heart be offended with anyone. If some one commits an error and wrong toward you, you must instantly forgive him. Do not complain of others. Refrain from reprimanding them, and if you wish to give admonition or advice, let it be offered in such a way that it will not burden the bearer. Turn all your thoughts toward bringing joy to hearts. Beware! Beware! lest ye offend any heart. Assist the world of humanity as much as possible. Be the source of consolation to every sad one, assist every weak one, be helpful to every indigent one, care for every sick one, be the cause of glorification to every lowly one, and shelter those who are overshadowed by fear…. In brief, let each one of you be as a lamp shining forth with the light of the virtues of the world of humanity. Be trustworthy, sincere, affectionate and replete with chastity. Be illumined, be spiritual, be divine, be glorious, be quickened of God, be a Bahá'í.
  ('Abdu'l-Bahá: *Promulgation of Universal Peace*, p. 453)

- We can never exert the influence over others which we can exert over ourselves. If we are better, if we show love, patience, and understanding of the weaknesses of others; if we seek to never criticize but rather encourage, others will do likewise….
  (Shoghi Effendi: *Lights of Guidance*, p. 83)

- The use of force by the physically strong against the weak, as a means of imposing one's will and fulfilling one's desires, is a flagrant transgression of the Bahá'í Teachings. There can be no justification for anyone compelling another, through the use of force or through the threat of violence, to do that to which the other person is not inclined.
  (Universal House of Justice: *Developing Distinctive Bahá'í Communities*, 15.26)

Perspectives to Consider

Effective communication requires **extensive skills** that will develop over your lifetime. Together you will practice and refine them through the closeness of your evolving relationship both before and after marriage. A number of **vitally important spiritual principles** will guide you in communicating with each other (and with others).

Consider the spiritual principles below.

- Being honest; not lying
- Resolving issues peacefully, without conflict or contention
- Not backbiting
- Refraining from complaining and criticizing
- Giving sincere encouragement and praise
- Bringing joy to other's hearts

Even when you know the spiritual principles, it can be difficult to follow them, as the standards are very high. It can feel as if there are both **risks and rewards** related to communicating, and it takes perseverance, effort, and self-honesty to follow the principles consistently. For instance, when you want to know someone else fully and have him or her know you, you might abandon the principle of honesty and slip into being fearful and hiding information or playing games that distort your past or aspects of yourself. You may even resort to lying about things to cover up uncomfortable aspects of your personality or life. However, this would result in a weak marriage, one based on dishonesty and distrust.

On the other hand, courtship gives you many opportunities to practice the positive spiritual principle of giving **sincere encouragement and praise**. Using this principle in your communications with each other builds love, affinity, and confidence in each other and in your relationship. The more you practice it, the more you and your relationship will blossom.

Each of you has learned and practiced **many ways to communicate**, adopting and adapting what you have observed from parents or friends. Some of these practices probably follow spiritual principles and are healthy and constructive, while some may not be. Identifying any negative patterns you have allows you to focus on eliminating them and replacing them with positive ones. To identify the ones that do not work well, ask your partner for coaching or others in your life who have the opportunity to regularly observe your communication patterns.

One aspect of communication that may be a challenge in your interactions is a tendency for one or both of you to use methods that are, consciously or unconsciously, an attempt to control the other or to get something you want in an under-handed fashion. Assess whether you try to get your own way through practicing any of the unwise behaviors below. Strive to be honest with yourself in your assessment, and then work diligently to eliminate these from your communication patterns with your partner and others.

Poor Communication Habits

- Pout
- Tease
- Strategize
- Get dramatic
- Fake-cry
- Over-compliment
- Have a hidden agenda
- Distract
- Use other people to communicate for you
- Get angry
- Criticize
- Dominate
- Manipulate
- Act like a victim or "martyr"

"Before we begin, let us take a moment to reflect upon our hidden agenda."

Tips for Handling Issues Peacefully

Note: These may be difficult to do, and they will require practice and introspection, but they are vital for optimum communication.

Do:
- Sit and face each other
- Pause to pray
- Maintain an openness to learn
- Share perceptions and be willing to be influenced in your opinions
- Keep focused on the present issue
- Strive to agree, not figure out who is "right"
- Recognize when emotions are escalating and back off the discussion; reschedule for a better time
- Be courageous
- Take time to breathe deeply
- Say "ouch" if something said is hurtful
- Call a timeout
- Use active/reflective listening
- Use "I" statements, not "you" statements
- Share feelings
- Be empathetic and understanding; try to understand the other's frame of reference
- Hug at the end

Don't:
- Interrupt
- Force your viewpoint on the other
- Deliberately bring up the other's hurtful "hot button" issues
- Imply that *you* are right or that he/she is wrong
- Have a win-lose attitude
- Insult him/her
- Be sarcastic
- Conceal key information
- Be forceful or dominating
- Walk away (unless there is danger of violence)
- Answer the telephone during a heated discussion
- Threaten anyone, verbally, physically, or sexually

Repeated use of these bad habits is probably an indication of emotional immaturity or insecurity. They may also indicate a pattern of abusive communication that emotionally or mentally harms the person it is directed toward…something that will be destructive in a marriage and other relationships.

Courtship is a good time to practice positive communication habits. One of these is the ability to **be lovingly direct** with each other, either about a concern or with a request for assistance. You can watch for internal signals indicating you need to raise an issue or make a request. These signals might include feelings of resentment, tension, annoyance, frustration, or sadness. If you notice that you are feeling tense, for instance, you may wish to initiate direct communication. An example might be: "I'm unhappy because _____ didn't get done. Would it be possible for you to handle it by _____ (date and time)?" When you want to make a request of your partner, you can say, "It would support me in doing _____ if you would do _____." If you are feeling emotionally low, you could consider asking your partner to bring you flowers. You can also make direct offers of assistance to him/her by saying, "How can I support you?" Offering support and giving your partner an opportunity to clarify what support he/she needs is a very loving act in a relationship. As you learn to be clear in your communications, you will minimize conflicts and misunderstandings and better maintain family unity.

The goal is to resolve issues peacefully, not to avoid them. By raising issues promptly, any feelings of being upset are handled as they occur rather than suppressed to come out later (and usually more explosively). Obviously, in spite of your commitment to maintaining harmony, **disagreements can and will happen**. When they do, they are usually excellent opportunities to practice the principles of consultation and learn more about each other. When you are disagreeing with each other about something, often your worst qualities will come out. If you can shift into a mature, spiritual attitude and **use positive qualities in the face of difficult communication**, you will be learning skills that will help preserve your relationship. These qualities include patience, gentleness, or truthfulness. (See Chapters 3, 20, 21, and 22.)

A positive practice is to **assess your communication** and/or consultation some time after it has occurred. Look for specific examples that showed you were able to support each other, and evaluate any missteps that occurred.

Through these "debriefs", you will learn where you listened well, and where you didn't, where you respected your partner's thoughts and emotions, and where you didn't. For example, did you throw something from the past into the discussion that made the other upset or angry? Did you mean to make him/her angry? Did you raise your voice in a threatening manner or shout? It is especially helpful (and potentially surprising to your partner) if, during a difficult discussion, you stop to apologize and note that you have just fallen into a pattern or response you want to change. Your wisdom will grow if, both in the middle and following an incident, you take the time to reflect and identify lessons learned and ways to do things better next time.

You may have had **differences of expression in your respective families and background,** which carry over into your relationship with your partner. For instance, one of you may fear that your relationship will fall apart if you get angry or seriously disagree, while the other might feel the relationship isn't healthy or interesting if there isn't an occasional disagreement. Work together to identify your different patterns and whether any of them can be adjusted to achieve compatibility. Be aware of the frequency and intensity of disagreements (you may call them fights)—if they are happening often, you may not be using spiritual principles, and frequent battles may be an indication of future marital disharmony.

You have a choice to be constructive or destructive in your communications. If you focus on the **positive spirit and intent** of your communication and maintaining it, then when you are off-track, you can pause and adjust what you are saying and how you are saying it. Each couple will have their own styles and needs, and you will develop guidelines for communication that work best for you. Remember that communication between you is not about power, control, being right, or winning, but rather a sharing of mind and heart that builds understanding and agreement.

> You may believe that if someone loves you, he/she should be able to figure out what you need without you asking. An accompanying unproductive mindset is that you decide you don't really want something if you have to *ask* for it. This thinking will trap you in a cycle of unhappiness, because it is not possible to read another's mind or to discern his/her needs effectively and reliably

As in life, marriage is happiest when you **avoid speaking with contempt, faultfinding, sarcasm, insults, or criticism** to or about each other or anyone else. This may provoke a defensive and unproductive response, such as lashing out in anger or withdrawing from the person who did the criticizing. A particularly negative and related communication pattern is backbiting and complaining about others. This is highly destructive to relationships and lays a burden on the heart of the hearer. Instead, search for opportunities to praise, support, and encourage each other regularly. *Sincere encouragement is one of the most powerful, sustaining, nurturing factors in happy marriages and child rearing.* Watch your facial expressions and tone of voice—can your partner feel your encouragement, or does he or she hear a criticism behind it? Does your face look happy, or are you frowning? Are you sincere, or are you *wishing* you meant what you are saying? Encouragement, encouragement, encouragement…it bears repeating!

Maintaining a peaceful atmosphere between a couple and in a marriage includes **being quick to forgive, asking for forgiveness, sincerely apologizing, making amends, and turning the issue over to God and detaching from it**. These prevent resentments and issues from building up and festering. *Daily practice of your communication skills while preparing for marriage is important.* Effective communication skills in marriage are essential: Share what needs to be said, and consult frequently.

As a way to incorporate the spiritual principle of **bringing joy to people's hearts**, you may use **humor, teasing, and joking** in your conversations. The challenge is that what one person considers humorous, another may not. When used constructively, humor can be fun and lighten up difficult situations. However, humor can also be destructive, especially if it is sarcastic or contains a derogatory or insulting comment or insinuation. Humor can work well with some people and situations and not with others. Do the two of you find the same things funny? Are you able to use humor to add levity to difficult situations? Do you understand each other's jokes? Do you appreciate each other's sense of humor? Are there times when you don't and times when you do? What distinguishes those? Communication that works well between you will bring great happiness into your lives. It is worth the time to learn to do it well and to gain tools that build unity and harmony between you.

Note: If there are any signs of mental illness arising in your communications, you will be wise to seek professional counseling individually and/or together. Signs might include these communication patterns: excessive and unreasonable anger, paranoia, very high levels of anxiety, suicide threats, or repeated abusive and damaging comments.

Coaching

⇒ Communicating honestly, directly, and as promptly as possible helps to keep misunderstandings minimized.

⇒ When one of you withdraws or has difficulty sharing thoughts or feelings—possibly due to upbringing, culture, or circumstances, the other can be supportive by asking gentle, open-ended questions and coaxing sharing, while being cautious not to nag or pressure. Often problems seem much larger when you suppress your feelings and keep them inside rather than express them.

⇒ Find something to sincerely praise or encourage in each other every day. If you have difficulty finding something to encourage or praise, or you feel uncomfortable, start with something small that you like. You will also find tremendous joy in regularly expressing your love to each other.

Questions for Reflection and Discussion

Communications with Each Other

1. Which issues/subjects are easy for you to communicate about? Which ones cause you difficulty? What makes it easier?
2. How do you joke, tease, etc.? How does the other react or feel about it?
3. Do you find the same things funny?
4. How do you communicate when someone does something to you that you don't appreciate (Examples: tickling, interrupting, teasing)?
5. What is your reaction when someone lies to you? Has your partner lied to you? How often? How is it affecting the level of trust between you?
6. Give an example of a time when you sincerely praised your partner. What happened? How did it feel? Do you find it easy to praise each other? Why or why not?
7. What are some specific examples of you encouraging each other?
8. Give an example of when you felt criticized by the other. What happened? How did it feel? Is this a regular pattern? How would you feel about this pattern happening in your marriage?
9. Are you able to offer emotional support to each other?
10. Are you able to make requests of each other in ways that are helpful and acceptable for both of you? What are some examples?
11. Do you interrupt each other or try to finish each other's sentences, jokes, or stories? How do you feel and react when this happens?
12. What is a risk for you in communicating? What communication risks is each of you willing to take?
13. In what areas have you had disagreements, and how have you resolved them? Was it effective?

14. How will you resolve disputes or decide on a course of action when you cannot agree?
15. Do you have a tendency to want to "win" discussions, always be right about the topic, and rarely give someone else's opinion more importance than your own? Does your partner? How does this affect the quality of your communication?
16. How do you "make up" after a disagreement? How are you at apologizing? Forgiving?
17. What might be a signal to you that the communication patterns of one of you are dysfunctional or destructive?

Communications with Others

1. If it will be an interracial marriage, how would you handle communications from others who are prejudiced against you or your partner? Have you considered challenges that may arise with neighbors, friends, co-workers, and family? Do you care what others think/say about it?
2. Do you avoid gossiping and backbiting about each other? Other people? Is this an issue? Do you support one another in avoiding backbiting?
3. Would you be comfortable talking to a psychologist or spiritual counselor if needed? Under what circumstances would you be willing or unwilling?

Activities

1. Pray, meditate, reflect, and write in your journal about the positive communication skills you have both individually and as a couple and the ones that need development.

2. Try this active listening exercise:
   - Using a selection from the topics below, one of you *briefly* will share an experience. Set a timer for 3 to 5 minutes to assist you to keep it short.
   - The other person will listen carefully, not speaking until the speaker is *completely* finished.
   - The listener then will verbally summarize back to the speaker the key points he/she made. **This summary should not include *any* judgments or opinions, but should simply be a re-statement of what the listener heard.**
   - Next, switch roles so that the other person is in the role of "listener."

   Use the following (or another of your own) meaningful subject areas:
   a. A difficult experience from childhood
   b. The importance of a hobby or activity
   c. Your reasons for choosing a career or job
   d. Your favorite spiritual quote or prayer and why it is special
   e. A difficult recent encounter with your partner and how you felt (**Remember**: The listener is not to judge, interrupt, or defend his/her position, but simply to listen and summarize.)

   _____
   _____
   _____
   _____

3. Complete Worksheet 21A to understand your communication patterns

4. Complete Worksheet 21B to record your agreed guidelines for communications in your relationship.

2. I feel happy about these things that happen in our communications:

   a. _____
   b. _____
   c. _____

3. I feel frustrated about these things that happen in our communications:

   a. _____
   b. _____
   c. _____

4. When I am speaking to you, I need you to do the following so I am clear you are listening to me: (Examples: stop doing what you are doing; look at me; reflect back to me what you have heard me say)
   _____

5. When someone interrupts me, I feel: _____

6. These phrases are encouraging to me:

   a. _____
   b. _____
   c. _____

7. These phrases are discouraging to me:

   a. _____
   b. _____
   c. _____

8. It seems as if there is a power struggle or domination going on when this happens or is said:
   _____

9. When I'm having difficulty talking about something, it supports me if you:
   _____

Marriage Can Be Forever—Preparation Counts!

Chapter 21 – Doing It Better: Communication S...

10. When we appear to be starting to have a disagreement or fight, I'd like us to take ... prevent it from becoming destructive:

    a. _____
    b. _____
    c. _____

11. It upsets me when you speak to me in this tone of voice: _____

    This is when it usually seems to happen: _____

12. When someone speaks to me or yells at me in anger, I feel _____
    respond this way: _____

13. When teased, I feel _____ and I'm likely to respond this way:
    _____

14. When criticized, I feel _____ and I'm likely to respond this way:
    _____

15. When encouraged, I feel _____ and I'm likely to respond this way:
    _____

16. When I don't feel like I'm being listened to, I feel _____ and I'm likely to respond this way: _____

17. When I'm telling a story or joke, and you fill in part of it and tell it along with me, I feel:
    _____

18. When I'm telling a story or joke and you try to hurry the ending or share the punch line before I get to it, I feel:
    _____

19. When I think you expect me to know what you're thinking, I feel: _____
    and I'm likely to respond in this way: _____

20. When you don't know what I'm thinking, I feel: _____ and I'm likely to respond in this way: _____

21. When I feel our discussion has become more like a debate in a courtroom, I feel: _____
    and I'm likely to respond in this way: _____

22. When I feel like you can "out-argue" me intellectually, I feel: _____ and I'm likely to respond in this way: _____

Marriage Can Be Forever—Preparation Counts!

23. When you remind me to do something, I feel _____ and I'm likely to respond this way: _____

When you remind me more than once, I'm likely to respond this way:
_____

24. When you don't do what you promised, I feel _____ and I'm likely to respond this way: _____

25. When I feel the need to remind you of a promise, I feel _____ and I'm likely to respond this way: _____

26. When it seems that one of us is more interested in being right than solving a problem, I feel _____ and I'm likely to respond this way:
_____

27. When we talk about serious subjects, I feel:
_____

28. When there is a need for serious consultation and there are decisions to be made, I prefer to be in the following settings:
_____

29. It does not work for me to try to have serious discussions if I am in the middle of:
_____

30. It would help me to feel unified in our communications if we resolve to take the following constructive actions:

   a. _____
   b. _____
   c. _____

Reflection:

1. What are your findings about your communication with each other? What have you observed?
_____
_____

2. What would you like to reassess about your communication after a period of time?
_____
_____

3. When will you do the reassessment? _____ (Mark it in your calendar.)

Date: _____

Worksheet 21B: Communication Guidelines

DIRECTIONS: The purpose of this worksheet is to create guidelines for effective communication.
- After discussing your answers to Worksheet 21A, spend some time praying and reflecting about the practices that would support you to have excellent and peaceful communication patterns in your home.
- Then, consult together and agree on the guidelines that will support you.
- Complete the worksheet below with the ones you commit to using. (Examples: I will let you finish talking without interrupting; I will honor and accept your feelings)

Note: If you marry, you may want to create an attractive copy and post it visibly in your home as a reminder.

Worksheets may be printed from www.claricomm.com/publishing

OUR AGREED GUIDELINES FOR COMMUNICATION
1.
2.
3.
4.
5.
6.
7.
8.
9.
10.
11.
12.
13.
14.
15.

Marriage Can Be Forever—Preparation Counts!

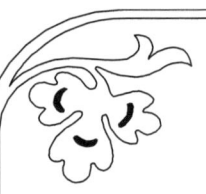

You were sure that if one tried to hurt her (Bahíyyih Khánum, Bahá'u'lláh's daughter) she would wish to console him for his own cruelty. For her love was unconditioned, could penetrate disguise and see hunger behind the mask of fury, and she knew that the most brutal self is secretly hoping to find gentleness in another....

Something greater than forgiveness she had shown in meeting the cruelties and strictures in her own life. To be hurt and to forgive is saintly but far beyond this is the power to comprehend and not be hurt.... She was never known to complain or lament. It was not that she made the best of things, but that she found in everything, even in calamity itself, the germs of enduring wisdom. She did not resist the shocks and upheavals of life and she did not run counter to obstacles. She was never impatient. She was an incapable of impatience as she was of revolt. But this was not so much long-sufferance as it was quiet awareness of the forces that operate in the hours of waiting and inactivity.
~ Marjory Morten, *Bahá'í World, Vol. 5*, pp. 182-185

In exasperating situations, we must find the time to pause and reflect if we are not afterwards to regret our words and actions. The Golden Rule, "Do unto others what you would have them do unto you" or "Do not do to others that which you do not wish done to yourself" is a useful guideline for action. By putting ourselves in our partner's shoes now and again, by trying to discover what he or she feels, we can come to realize many things about our partner, we learn to respect him more fully and we open our hearts to new levels of understanding, compassion, tenderness and intimacy. In many circumstances where tension is great and emotions are running high, knowing how to say "I'm sorry" can reduce tension and make the other person more inclined to recognize his or her own mistakes.

~ Mehri Sefidvash, *Coral and Pearls*, pp. 27-28

CHAPTER 22 – An Abundance of Feelings: Expressing the Emotions

Focus Points
- Responsible for emotional response
- Compatibility of emotions
- Emotional compatibility
- Handling hurt and upset feelings
- Forgiveness

A Couple's Story

Lindsay and James are sitting on the steps of one of the college buildings. Lindsay's brother, Jason, just called on her cell phone. The police arrested him earlier in the week for possession of marijuana.

"Why can't he get his life straightened out?!" says Lindsay, with tears running down her face. "All that time and money in rehab, and he is still messing up."

"Uh, um, uh, you want me to try to talk to him or something?" asks James.

"Nooooooooooo....I just need you to hold me."

Quotes for Guidance

✺ We have created you from one tree and have caused you to be as the leaves and fruit of the same tree, that haply ye may become a source of comfort to one another.
(The Báb: *Selections from the Writings of the Báb*, p. 129)

✺ Then, with radiance and joy, celebrate therein the praise of your Lord, the Most Compassionate. Verily, by His remembrance the eye is cheered and the heart is filled with light.
(Bahá'u'lláh: *Kitáb-i-Aqdas*, pp. 29-30)

✺ Conflict and contention are categorically forbidden in His Book. This is a decree of God in this Most Great Revelation.
(Bahá'u'lláh: *Tablets of Bahá'u'lláh*, p. 221)

✺ Jealousy consumeth the body and anger doth burn the liver: avoid these two as you would a lion.
(Bahá'u'lláh: *Compilation of Compilations*, Vol. I, p. 460)

✺ Joy gives us wings! In times of joy our strength is more vital, our intellect keener, and our understanding less clouded. We seem better able to cope with the world and to find our sphere of usefulness. But when sadness visits us we become weak, our strength leaves us, our comprehension is dim and our intelligence veiled. The actualities of life seem to elude our grasp, the eyes of our spirits fail to discover the sacred mysteries, and we become even as dead beings.

There is no human being untouched by these two influences; but all the sorrow and the grief that exist come from the world of matter—the spiritual world bestows only the joy!
('Abdu'l-Bahá: *Paris Talks*, pp. 109-110)

✶ When you notice that a stage has been reached when enmity and threats are about to occur, you should immediately postpone discussion of the subject, until wranglings, disputations, and loud talk vanish, and a propitious time is at hand.
('Abdu'l-Bahá: *Consultation*, pp. 97-99)

Perspectives to Consider

Your **emotions are an integral part of you**. Reflect on the range of emotions you feel throughout your day, your week, your month: happy, sad, excited, angry, and many more. Feelings, regardless of type, are good in themselves—they are part of what it means to be human. Think about how boring life would be without them. Expressing appropriate feelings at the right times is a healthy, balanced, and self-respecting action. When you first see your partner, you are likely to show how happy you feel; if you cannot be together for a while, it would be natural to express some sadness.

It may be easy to feel that emotions just "happen" to you. However, it is vital to understand that when an incident happens and you respond to it emotionally, you have a **choice about dwelling on the emotion or letting it go**. If you hang onto it, your behavior may not be as effective as it could be if you seek resolution through action and behavior change instead. For instance, if you feel bored, you can choose to sit around and do nothing, or you can identify the source of the emotion, re-focus your attention, and choose to generate a different emotion (such as enthusiasm) or simply choose to act, finding something to do. Very frequently, behaviors can lead to changed emotions. The next time you're really irritated, try smiling for two continuous minutes. It's unlikely you'll be able to stay irritated.

Although there are certainly external things that trigger emotions, you are **responsible for your response** and your actions related to these triggers. Being reflective and conscious of your emotions usually gives you **self-control** over how, where, and when you express them to others. Think about this in terms of marriage. You are living in close and intimate circumstances with someone else. If you feel an emotion and don't take responsibility for how, where, and when you express it with your partner, the result is likely to be significant disharmony in your home.

Recognizing and understanding your emotions can be a complex process, however. Sometimes when you are handling a very difficult situation, your emotional response may have several complex layers. You may need spiritual or psychological counseling, or support from a very understanding partner, to understand and express your emotions. Without prayer and reflection on the emotions and addressing them directly, you may easily go for weeks with an emotion simmering under the surface until it becomes clear to you what you are actually feeling.

Once you have identified that you are feeling a particular emotion, you then have a **choice about expressing it** and handling it in a conscious and constructive way. Prayer and meditation may assist you to let go of the emotion and regain a sense of peace. Sometimes you will fully express your emotions to others as well as yourself—hopefully in a constructive manner. And at other times, it will be important to control them, because they could cause irreparable harm to yourself and others if expressed destructively and without prior reflection.

Feeling and expressing jealousy, for instance, is generally destructive to relationships. Of course, if one of you is being physically or emotionally unfaithful, the destruction is already in progress. Choosing to dwell on the jealous emotion, however, rather than addressing it is *your* issue, regardless of external situations. What might be more constructive is to examine the underlying emotion that generates the jealousy. For example, do you feel hurt, concerned about being abandoned, or is your general self-esteem low? Identifying the deeper cause of jealousy offers you a better likelihood of solving the problem—hopefully in conjunction with your partner.

> **Can You Relax?**
>
> A key indicator of compatibility is whether you can relax with each other. If you are constantly tense, cautious about every word you say, and wary of your partner's emotional reactions to situations, you might ask yourself: "Do I want to spend the rest of my life feeling like this?"
>
> One of the greatest joys of a compatible relationship is feeling relaxed and comfortable in your partner's presence—physically, mentally, and emotionally.

The alternative to expressing your emotions is **suppressing** them. This is similar to denying that the emotion even exists. Before you barely recognize that you are feeling something, you may "clamp down on it" and refuse to let it surface. The problem with this is that suppressed emotions tend to pile up and are likely to affect you later, for example, being expressed explosively, creating depression, or leading to poor physical health.

Determining **emotional compatibility** between the two of you is vital; however, in all likelihood, it will not be easy. The examination of your compatibility may begin with looking at the intensity and frequency of both of your emotional expressions and the results of those expressions or suppressions. Where do you balance out each other's emotions, leading to calm and/or creativity? And where do you intensify each other's feelings so they spiral out of control? You will express your emotions at different levels of intensity depending on your personalities, histories, and the specific circumstances. If one of you is very withdrawn emotionally, this might be a test to the other. If one of you functions at high intensity, expressing yourself all the time, this could tire out someone who is different...*or* you might be a balance for each other. If either of you find that your emotions seem out of control on a regular basis, however, you may need to seek competent medical advice or professional counseling to resolve the underlying issues triggering them.

When you express your emotions to your partner, it is likely to affect him/her, sometimes positively, sometimes negatively. Think carefully about the **potential impact** on him/her before you express something. Do you want to express it or find some other healthy way to handle the emotion alone (Examples: taking time to pray, exercising, going for a walk, reflecting on the situation)?

You will each **express emotions differently**—another area to check for compatibility. If you decide to express yourself, which is very often the best possible route, sensitivity to how you convey your feelings will be important. (See Chapters 20 and 21 on communication.)

Recognize, too, that you each will also **go through cycles** affected by hormones, the weather, work patterns, or other things that influence your emotions and moods. Be aware of how different your partner is at these times, what he/she is doing to maintain balance, and whether you can live with the way he/she behaves and talks when these shifts happen.

Over time, you will find that each of you is likely **challenged by different issues** that occur—triggering different emotions for each of you. Observing and understanding each other's responses to challenges will be an important means of assessing your compatibility. Do you respond to difficulties and handle emotions maturely? How do you respond when your partner has had a difficult day? Can you express your feelings—and feel safe and trusting in the process? Can you act respectfully at the same time? Are you tempted to rescue your partner inappropriately? Can you expose your weaknesses and insecurities and still feel accepted, understood, supported, and loved in spite of *and even because of* not being perfect?

Compatibility includes being able to **emotionally support each other**. When there is a major change in your lives, or you are facing a challenge, are you able to do be supportive of the other? Support may look different to each of you. You might feel abandoned if your partner leaves you alone when you're upset, *or* you might feel grateful. When you need to talk, you might appreciate advice or prefer only a listening ear. You might want coaching, or you might not be open to it at that moment. The key is gaining a perspective regarding your own and each other's emotional needs and patterns under a variety of circumstances—and then learning to respond respectfully and appropriately to those needs.

It may be particularly difficult for one or both of you if the other **tells you what you're feeling**. Strive to respond about what you *think* the other is feeling and what leads you to believe that, but understand that only a person experiencing an emotion in the final analysis can, in the final analysis, determine whether the emotion exists within them. (See Chapter 15 for a discussion about the emotion of love.)

Obviously, at times you may feel hurt by something your partner does or says. **When your feelings are hurt**, it's important to acknowledge it to yourself and then to try to understand why you're feeling hurt. Usually the other person didn't mean to hurt you, and simple communication about your feelings will resolve the issue. This is especially true if you convey your needs and emotions without accusing, and if your partner responds to whatever you share with empathy and compassion. Remember that using "I" statements (Example: *I* feel sad.) rather than "you" statements (Example: *You* hurt my feelings.) will often assist your partner to be better able to help you and to feel less defensive. In reverse, you will frequently be able to soothe your upset partner by listening and offering a comforting shoulder to cry on.

Handling and Resolving Upset Emotions

The ability to resolve situations when you feel upset is a key skill for maintaining peaceful courting and marriage relationships. These actions can assist you to move beyond being upset.

- Start with recognizing when you *are* upset.
- Accept that the feeling of being anxious, upset, angry, or frustrated is inside of you, and don't immediately point blame at someone else.
- Think through whether your current feelings are stemming from the past; often emotions from previous incidents, relationships, childhood, or teen years can linger, and can be re-triggered in close adult relationships.
- Identify whether you committed to doing something, but you didn't follow through with action to complete it.
- Assess whether either of you has expectations that were not fulfilled.
- Understand if you did not communicate as needed and that has resulted in your partner being upset.
- Pray to forgive yourself and your partner.
- Communicate as needed to resolve any of the above.

Learning how to resolve hurt feelings promptly will support you in creating and maintaining a peaceful relationship. Below are some tips that may help.

Other things can sabotage the process of **moving beyond an argument or feeling hurt**. One is an insistence on figuring out who did what wrong and blaming them. The attachment to being right, "winning" the argument, and/or pointing a finger at someone else, seriously disrupts the feelings of love and affinity between you and does not contribute to the long-term harmony of a relationship. Instead, it sets up more hurt feelings and does not allow your relationship to move forward. You might ask friends and family whether this is a tactic they have seen you use.

Another harmful factor is the inability *to forgive*. If you don't forgive the other person, the hurt or anger stays inside and builds up in layers of pain. This pain is likely to erupt eventually, seriously disturbing your relationship, and causing much larger problems than existed in the first place. Often when you hold in pain for a long period, you may end up with stress-related health problems. Rather than suppressing, it is more helpful to release the pain through a full, frank, and loving discussion about the issue. Then, it is important to forgive, set goals for behavioral or attitude change, agree the matter is closed, and move on. If there are goals set, remember to assess your progress after an appropriate length of time. Also, recognize that is can take a long time to change emotional responses, and you may need to revisit the issue on numerous occasions — always working toward a closer and more unified outcome and understanding.

Note: This chapter primarily addresses how you process emotions between you as a couple. It will support your exploration of compatibility, however, when you observe each other's emotional expressions in a full range of circumstances with a variety of people, not just each other.

Coaching

⇒ At times, when you are upset, it may be wisest to wait a while before communicating with your partner, because with some reflection, prayer, and/or additional facts, you may realize you jumped to erroneous conclusions. Prayer and meditation can assist you to see a broader picture and the truth of a situation. You may also be able to communicate more clearly after you let some initial anger or frustration pass. Without such strong emotions, it will be easier to speak clearly and directly, without accusation. Reflection can also help you to see whether you are mixing some experience from the past or the emotions from a previous event into the present. As you get to know yourself and one another better, negotiating these circumstance will likely become easier and easier.

⇒ When someone is upset, the other person may try to solve or fix the problem for him/her. Often the upset person simply needs to know that their concern is heard, understood, and accepted. When you are dealing with something difficult and feeling the need to talk to someone, it is helpful if you indicate at the start of the conversation what level of support you are looking for. And for the person listening, it is helpful for you to use terms like "I hear you…" or "What it sounds like you're saying is…" as well as, of course, "I love you."

Questions for Reflection and Discussion

1. How do you handle emotions? Are they expressed in a mature way? Are they suppressed? How do your close family and friends answer this question about you?
2. How would someone know what you are feeling?
3. Do you handle anger differently/compatibly (compared to your partner)? Does anger ever escalate into threats or violence on the part of your partner? What is your response? Does anger ever escalate into threats or violence on your part? What can you do to remedy this appropriately and quickly?
4. Are you able to forgive each other when your feelings are hurt? What helps you do this? What interferes?
5. How quickly do you get over being upset with someone? What is the process by which you do that (e.g. solitude or communication)? How do you handle it when someone is upset with *you*?

Marriage Can Be Forever—Preparation Counts!

6. What helps you to move forward in harmony instead of holding on to past hurts?
7. Are you able to forgive *yourself* when you have hurt someone else? Why or why not? Are there other instances in which you have trouble forgiving yourself? What can you do to address this?
8. Are you able to listen patiently to each other's emotional expressions? Examples?
9. How do you handle making mistakes? What emotions do you feel when you do? How do you react to each other's mistakes?
10. How do you react to disappointment? Embarrassment? Frustration?
11. What embarrasses you the most in public? In private?
12. What emotional expressions are you comfortable or not comfortable with in public? (Examples: at family reunions, birthday parties, business events (yours or your partner's), picnics, speaking on stage?)
13. How do you respond to surprises? (Examples: a surprise party, an unexpected present, an unplanned guest) Do you feel happy, angry, upset, or anxious? Can you accept the other liking or not liking surprises?
14. How would you feel if one of you mistakenly called the other by the name of someone from a former relationship?
15. How would you handle feelings of love/desire if they developed with someone other than your spouse?
16. If either of you have to travel for work with someone of the opposite sex, are there any concerns or trust issues?
17. How do you respond to and resolve feelings of stress? How can you tell when you are relaxed rather than stressed? What can you do to assist yourself to relax in any given situation?
18. When one of you is anxious, can you help set the other at ease?
19. Change can cause a variety of emotional responses in people. How do you respond to change? What emotions do you feel? How does your partner respond to change? How do you *feel about* how your partner handles change? Is he/she ever uncomfortable with how *you* handle change?
20. What are your "pet peeves," the things that consistently irritate you? How do you express them?
21. What do you do that frequently annoys other people? Does it bother your partner?
22. How do you react when you are working on something and someone interrupts you?
23. How do you react or respond when your partner cries? When a child cries? Your mother/father?
24. What do you consider your emotional and physical boundaries? When does it feel like someone is deliberately trying to trigger an emotion in you? How do you communicate to someone to back off? How do you react when you perceive a boundary is violated?
25. What are the changes in your emotions when you are tired? Tired and hungry?
26. How do you use humor in dealing with emotions?
27. Some people believe and practice the philosophy that you should never go to bed angry with each other. What do you think about this? Are there "rules" like this you would want to set in your marriage?
28. What triggers changes in your mood? (Examples: hormones, weather, the moon) What warning signs might your partner notice? What changes or challenges in your relationship have you observed from these factors?
29. Are you on or have you been on any medications, supplements, or dietary products that affect or are designed to modify your moods? How do they work for you? How does your partner feel about these?
30. How will you know if you need professional help in handling your emotions? Will you be willing to seek it?

Activities

1. Pray, meditate, reflect, and write in your journal about the emotions that are most difficult for you to express constructively.

2. Use Worksheet 22A to help you gauge the frequency with which you feel and express different emotions. Then note how you expressed the feelings.

3. Use Worksheet 22B to understand what triggers your emotions, how your partner might know you are feeling the emotion, and how your partner can support you in expressing or resolving it.

4. After completing both worksheets, note below where you have concerns about your own expressions of emotions:
   _____
   _____

   What do you have concerns about regarding your partner's emotional expressions?
   _____
   _____

5. Pick a time when you are struggling to understand your emotions. Sometimes you can help them to surface and identify them if you set up a non-routine situation for yourself. The activity below is one example. (Another might be leaving your usual environment and activities and going somewhere new.) You may wish to try it once with silence and once with music to see if it makes a difference.

   - For this activity, set yourself up in a quiet area with a very large sheet of paper and a few markers or crayons.
   - Hold one of the markers or crayons in your non-dominant hand—your left hand if you are right-handed, your right hand if you are left-handed.
   - Start to randomly draw or scribble about what you are feeling and thinking.
   - Use a number of sheets of paper if necessary.

   Did this exercise assist you to release the emotions? What came up as you were doing it?
   _____
   _____
   _____

6. Plan and carry out an activity with your partner that you each agree will help you relax, to reduce any level of stress you are feeling. How did it go? How do you know when you are relaxed? What supports you in being relaxed generally? Are you able to relax with your partner? What supports this? What is the effect of stress on you and on your relationship? What effect does stress have on your other relationships?
   _____
   _____
   _____

Date: _____

Worksheet 22A: Expressing Your Emotions

DIRECTIONS: This worksheet is to help you recognize what emotions you are feeling, determine whether you are able to express emotions in a healthy way, and what usually triggers them. Take your time and be honest and self-reflective—this is *not* likely to be an easy exercise. Complete this worksheet separately from your partner.

- Thinking back over the last month or so *(NOT just the past few days)*, use the scales from 1-5 below to rate the **frequency with which you experience** each emotion listed.
- Then rate **how often you express** each of these emotions.
- Finally, indicate in the space provided what your expression of the emotion looks like.
- Share your worksheet with your partner and identify any areas of concern. Remind one another to be sensitive and respectful in this discussion. It may help to say prayers together before discussing the worksheets.

Additional Use of Worksheet
If it is an emotionally safe and comfortable activity, you can also re-do this exercise, but this time identifying *your* perceptions of *your partner's* emotions. **Note**: This will only represent your *perceptions*, not the *truth* of his/her emotions.

Note: You may need a trusted other, spiritual advisor or psychological counselor to support you if it is particularly difficult for you to complete this worksheet. Consider counseling, too, if you seem to experience many emotions but rarely express them, if you feel you express them poorly, or if you experience emotions in a manner that you or others think may be unhealthy.

Worksheets may be printed from www.claricomm.com/publishing

Rarely	1	2	3	4	5	Usually

Emotion	Frequency of Experiencing	Frequency of Expressing	What Did the Expression Look Like?
Afraid	1 2 3 4 5	1 2 3 4 5	_____
Amazed	1 2 3 4 5	1 2 3 4 5	_____
Amused	1 2 3 4 5	1 2 3 4 5	_____
Angry	1 2 3 4 5	1 2 3 4 5	_____
Anxious	1 2 3 4 5	1 2 3 4 5	_____
Appreciative	1 2 3 4 5	1 2 3 4 5	_____
Bored	1 2 3 4 5	1 2 3 4 5	_____
Contented	1 2 3 4 5	1 2 3 4 5	_____
Delighted	1 2 3 4 5	1 2 3 4 5	_____
Depressed	1 2 3 4 5	1 2 3 4 5	_____
Disappointed	1 2 3 4 5	1 2 3 4 5	_____
Discouraged	1 2 3 4 5	1 2 3 4 5	_____
Embarrassed	1 2 3 4 5	1 2 3 4 5	_____
Encouraged	1 2 3 4 5	1 2 3 4 5	_____
Enthusiastic	1 2 3 4 5	1 2 3 4 5	_____
Excited	1 2 3 4 5	1 2 3 4 5	_____
Frustrated	1 2 3 4 5	1 2 3 4 5	_____
Happy	1 2 3 4 5	1 2 3 4 5	_____

Rarely	1	2	3	4	5	Usually
	←――――――――――――――――→					

Emotion	Frequency of Experiencing	Frequency of Expressing	What Did the Expression Look Like?
Inspired	1 2 3 4 5	1 2 3 4 5	_____
Irritated	1 2 3 4 5	1 2 3 4 5	_____
Jealous	1 2 3 4 5	1 2 3 4 5	_____
Keyed-up	1 2 3 4 5	1 2 3 4 5	_____
Lonely	1 2 3 4 5	1 2 3 4 5	_____
Melancholy	1 2 3 4 5	1 2 3 4 5	_____
Nervous	1 2 3 4 5	1 2 3 4 5	_____
Puzzled	1 2 3 4 5	1 2 3 4 5	_____
Relieved	1 2 3 4 5	1 2 3 4 5	_____
Sad	1 2 3 4 5	1 2 3 4 5	_____
Scared	1 2 3 4 5	1 2 3 4 5	_____
Sensitive	1 2 3 4 5	1 2 3 4 5	_____
Sour	1 2 3 4 5	1 2 3 4 5	_____
Thankful	1 2 3 4 5	1 2 3 4 5	_____
Trustful	1 2 3 4 5	1 2 3 4 5	_____
Upset	1 2 3 4 5	1 2 3 4 5	_____
Warm	1 2 3 4 5	1 2 3 4 5	_____
Wide-awake	1 2 3 4 5	1 2 3 4 5	_____
Zestful	1 2 3 4 5	1 2 3 4 5	_____
_____	1 2 3 4 5	1 2 3 4 5	_____
_____	1 2 3 4 5	1 2 3 4 5	_____
_____	1 2 3 4 5	1 2 3 4 5	_____

1. As you will have noted above, feeling emotions and expressing them are two different things. Which emotions do you frequently feel but do not express outwardly?
   _____

2. Why do you suppress these emotions?
   _____

3. Which of your emotions make you feel uncomfortable?
   _____

4. What reactions do you have to others' emotional expressions?
   _____

5. How did your discussion with each other go? Were you able to learn from one another? Was it heated or difficult? What made sense? What didn't?
   _____
   _____

Marriage Can Be Forever—Preparation Counts!

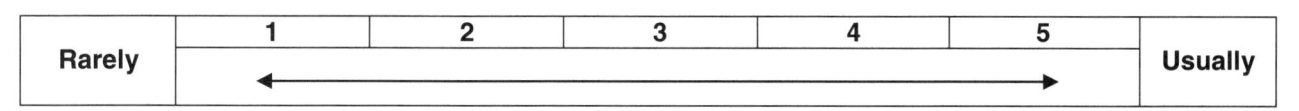

Chapter 22 – An Abundance of Feelings: Expressing the Emotions

Date: _____

Worksheet 22B: Your Partner's Emotions

DIRECTIONS: The purpose of this worksheet is to help you better understand what triggers a number of common emotions in you, how your partner might know you are feeling this way, and how he/she can support you. Each emotion expressed has an impact on the people around you. As partners, you will often assist each other in identifying the emotions you are feeling and then support one other in expressing and resolving them in constructive ways. Complete this worksheet separately and then, afterward, discuss your answers together.

Worksheets may be printed from www.claricomm.com/publishing

Emotion	Triggered By This Type of Incident	Indicators I'm Feeling This	Support Appreciated to Express or Resolve
Example: Anger	When we are running late to be somewhere	I don't talk; I don't make eye contact	Pick me up on time or early
Example: Frustration	When we are trying to consult and I can't finish a sentence without interruption	Frowning; giving annoyed looks	Let me finish before you speak

If/When I think you expect me to know what you're feeling, I feel: _____ and

I'm likely to respond in this way: _____

If/When you tell me how I'm feeling, I feel: _____ and I'm likely to respond in

this way: _____

Marriage Can Be Forever—Preparation Counts!

Spiritual Nuggets for Reflection and Discussion

> *Even as the clouds let us shed down tears, and as the lightning flashes let us laugh at our coursings through east and west. By day, by night, let us think but of spreading the sweet savors of God. Let us not keep on forever with our fancies and illusions, with our analyzing and interpreting and circulating of complex dubieties. Let us put aside all thoughts of self; let us close our eyes to all on earth, let us neither make known our sufferings nor complain of our wrongs. Rather let us become oblivious of our own selves, and drinking down the wine of heavenly grace, let us cry out our joy, and lose ourselves in the beauty of the All-Glorious.*

~ 'Abdu'l-Bahá: *Selections from the Writings of 'Abdu'l-Bahá*, p. 236

The Mirror

Man possesses two kinds of susceptibilities: the natural emotions, which are like dust upon the mirror, and spiritual susceptibilities, which are merciful and heavenly characteristics. There is a power which purifies the mirror from dust and transforms its reflection into intense brilliancy and radiance so that spiritual susceptibilities may chasten the hearts and heavenly bestowals sanctify them. What is the dust which obscures the mirror? It is attachment to the world, avarice, envy, love of luxury and comfort, haughtiness and self-desire; this is the dust which prevents reflection of the rays of the Sun of Reality in the mirror. The natural emotions are blameworthy and are like rust which deprives the heart of the bounties of God. But sincerity, justice, humility, severance, and love for the believers of God will purify the mirror and make it radiant with reflected rays from the Sun of Truth.

It is my hope that you may consider this matter, that you may search out your own imperfections and not think of the imperfections of anybody else. Strive with all your power to be free from imperfections. Heedless souls are always seeking faults in others. What can the hypocrite know of others' faults when he is blind to his own? This is the meaning of the words in the Seven Valleys. It is a guide for human conduct. As long as a man does not find his own faults, he can never become perfect. Nothing is more fruitful for man than the knowledge of his own shortcomings. The Blessed Perfection says, "I wonder at the man who does not find his own imperfections."

~ 'Abdu'l-Bahá: *Promulgation of Universal Peace*, p. 244

Chastity and Sex

Chastity—one of the rarest of all moral gems in the world to-day—means to conserve your personal sex powers, so intimate in nature, capable of conferring so much beauty on your life, for their proper expression which is with your life partner, your mate, the one who with you will share home, children, and all the glad and sad burdens of living. The decency, the spiritual cleanliness of marriage, the essential humanness of it, are enhanced a thousandfold by chastity on the part of both men and women, previous to their unions. Their chances of successful marriage are also far greater, for they will then share with each other, in every way, the new life they have embarked upon. Comparisons will not be drawn, over-emphasized appetites on the part of one or the other will not have been cultivated which might mar it, and above all, they will have put sex into its proper place, where instead of stampeding the emotional nature of the individual (as it does at present to so marked a degree), it will fulfill its natural function in rounding out life and contributing to its normality and healthfulness.

~ Rúhíyyih Rabbani, *Prescription for Living*, p. 70

MUSICAL LOVE

The beauty of creating music
is the blending of the single
notes from random places,
gathering, choosing, combining
until the song entire
bursts forth, rising
from the heart and soul.

The rhythm shifts,
grows, builds. . .
First the beat is jazz,
then a shift to rock,
finally the symphony
crescendo builds
and peaks. . .
then lingers to a sigh.

The single, clear note of a
bell sounds. A piano chord
responds in turn. The violins
begin to hum. The trombones
join the score. And underneath,
the excited heartbeat drums,
'til every instrument joins in and
every cell vibrates with joy. Gentle
rippling harp dances over all the
senses. Saxophones melt every
part, blending into one. But,
after all of this, the final sound
belongs to the cymbals. And then
the sacred air fills
with a profound hush.

~ Susanne Mariella Alexander

CHAPTER 23 – A Personal Discussion: Chastity, Intimacy, and Sex

> **Focus Points**
> - Intimacy
> - Chastity/abstinence and pre-marital sex; sex within marriage
> - Talking about sex and expectations
> - Past experiences; boundaries; abuse
> - Trial marriage; living together without marriage
> - Spiritual qualities relating to sex and intimacy
> - Having children

A Couple's Story

Lindsay and James have each on their own completed the worksheet in the marriage preparation book about intimacy and sex and sit down to go through their answers together.

"So, which ones were the toughest for you to answer?" James asks Lindsay. He wants to get her talking first.

"A few of them," Lindsay replies. "Sex was not something we talked about much in my house. When my Mom remarried, it was really weird watching them together and thinking about them having sex. It made me feel uncomfortable with the whole thing for awhile."

"What about now?" asks James. He smiles at her, but adds seriously, "Sex is important to me in marriage. Do you think you'll be okay with it?"

"You know I've been seeing a counselor this past year over at the college, and we've talked about all that stuff," says Lindsay. "She's helping me understand some of the things I've been confused about. I think that as long as I trust you and care about you, which I do, sex can be a good part of our marriage."

Quotes for Guidance

✸ The Lord, peerless is He, hath made woman and man to abide with each other in the closest companionship, and to be even as a single soul. They are two helpmates, two intimate friends, who should be concerned about the welfare of each other. If they live thus, they will pass through this world with perfect contentment, bliss, and peace of heart, and become the object of divine grace and favor in the Kingdom of heaven.
   ('Abdu'l-Bahá: *Selections from the Writings of 'Abdu'l-Bahá*, p. 122)

✸ …the Bahá'í conception of sex is based on the belief that chastity should be strictly practiced by both sexes, not only because it is in itself highly commendable ethically, but also due to its being the only way to a happy and successful marital life. Sex relationships of any form, outside marriage, are not permissible therefore, and whoso violates this rule will not only be responsible to God, but will incur the necessary punishment from society.

The Bahá'í Faith recognizes the value of the sex impulse, but condemns its illegitimate and improper expression such as free love, companionate marriage and others, all of which it considers positively harmful to man and to the society in which he lives. The proper use of the sex instinct is the natural right of every individual, and it is precisely for this very purpose that the institution of marriage has been established. The Bahá'ís do not believe in the suppression of the sex impulse but in its regulation and control.
(Shoghi Effendi: *Lights of Guidance*, p. 345)

* It must be remembered, however, that the maintenance of such a high standard of moral conduct is not to be associated or confused with any form of asceticism, or of excessive and bigoted puritanism. The standard inculcated by Bahá'u'lláh seeks, under no circumstances, to deny anyone the legitimate right and privilege to derive the fullest advantage and benefit from the manifold joys, beauties, and pleasures with which the world has been so plentifully enriched by an All-Loving Creator.
(Shoghi Effendi: *The Advent of Divine Justice*, p.33)

* Outside of marital life there can be no lawful or healthy use of the sex impulse. The Bahá'í youth should, on the one hand, be taught the lesson of self-control which, when exercised, undoubtedly has a salutary effect on the development of character and of personality in general, and on the other should be advised, nay even encouraged, to contract marriage while still young and in full possession of their physical vigor. Economic factors, no doubt, are often a serious hindrance to early marriage, but in most cases are only an excuse, and as such should not be overstressed.
(Shoghi Effendi: *A Chaste and Holy Life*, p. 56)

* Amongst the many other evils afflicting society in this spiritual low water mark in history is the question of immorality, and over-emphasis of sex…the whole matter of sex and the problems related to it have assumed far too great an importance in the thinking of present-day society. Masturbation is clearly not a proper use of the sex instinct, as this is understood in the Faith. Moreover it involves, as you have pointed out, mental fantasies, while Bahá'u'lláh, in the *Kitáb-i-Aqdas*, has exhorted us not to indulge our passions and in one of His well-known Tablets 'Abdu'l-Bahá encourages us to keep our "secret thoughts pure". Of course many wayward thoughts come involuntarily to the mind and these are merely a result of weakness and are not blameworthy unless they become fixed or even worse, are expressed in improper acts.
(On behalf of Shoghi Effendi: *Lights of Guidance*, pp. 363-364)

* "Sensuality" covers a wide range of meanings, all related to the pleasures to be obtained from the physical senses or sensations. Again, it is the extremes of this quality that are reprehensible. To renounce all sensual pleasures, or even to go beyond this and to inflict pain upon oneself falls in the region of asceticism, which the *Kitáb-i-Aqdas* prohibits. On the other hand, to be self-indulgent in regard to food, drink, and sexual enjoyment, giving oneself up to the gratification of one's appetites, becomes the licentiousness which is, likewise, forbidden in the Faith. As in the case of passion, individuals vary in the sensuality of their natures; some may need to restrain this quality, others may need to foster a greater warmth of feeling.

…How are a young couple, brought up to behave in the strictly moral ways explained in the Bahá'í teachings, to overcome the reticence which will exist between them, even though they will be free of the old attitude that sex is despicable?

Undoubtedly each couple will approach the matter differently, in accordance with the characters of the two people involved, but it is certainly here that passion and sensuality can play an important role, if accepted as normal qualities of a human being and if properly controlled and balanced by the reason and will.
(On behalf of the Universal House of Justice, *Sexuality, Relationships and Spiritual Growth*, p. 137)

Perspectives to Consider

At this point, many of you are thinking, at last, you're finally going to hear about sex! **Sex, or making love, is an important part of marriage**, but stop and think about it for a moment. How many hours in a week of marriage are you likely to be engaged in sex, and how many hours involved in all kinds of other things? You will be living together as companions and doing many other activities together. So, while sex deserves some focus, the level of preoccupation with it some of you may be experiencing might be out of balance and be influenced by the strong emphasis it receives in the media and among your peers, as well as by the effort to maintain abstinence.

When the physical attraction is very strong between you, it can be **tempting to rush into sex**, something that can create an illusion of emotional intimacy. Unfortunately, *rushing into physical intimacy can interfere with the process of getting to know each other in every other way*—it's best to first develop emotional, intellectual, and spiritual friendship and intimacy, the compatibility components that provide a foundation for a lasting relationship. This deeper intimacy and strong love between you will also make sex a more mutually pleasurable, gratifying, and unifying experience within marriage. *The goal, the self-respecting and spiritual standard, is abstinence until marriage.* **Note:** The term "abstinence" has been twisted at times in our culture to mean that it's not sex if it's oral, or it's not sex if it's intimate touching with hands, or it doesn't count if you use a condom. This is false thinking.

You might think that you need to try sex before marriage to ensure that there will not be **sexual incompatibility** after marriage, but there is no guarantee that it will turn out this way. A committed couple is more likely to pray, consult, and resolve any sexual issues that arise—issues that might have stopped a non-marriage relationship from developing, because the couple would choose to split up rather than work through problems. The best place for physical intimacy to be established is within the protection of marriage after the couple is committed; otherwise, there is danger in mistaking sexual gratification for lasting love.

Since **sex before and outside of marriage is not allowed** for Bahá'ís or many other religious groups, you will need to figure out ways to explore this topic without being physically aroused and intimate with each other. Can you openly and honestly discuss sex and sexual feelings without undue embarrassment, withdrawal, or being pulled into too much physical touching? Can you discuss your expectations about sexual experiences with each other? Do you foresee that you can continue to have an open dialogue about sex and sexual feelings after marriage? How will you move from saying "no" to sex before marriage to saying "yes" to it after marriage?

Chastity requires that you do your very best to keep your **thoughts and actions pure** (avoiding sexual fantasies is part of this). Some couples may find it helpful to read a sex manual together to support the discussion of sex; others will not be comfortable with this choice. Sex manuals tend to be very explicit and may arouse passions, and reading them may be best left until after marriage, if you need them then to coach you through any challenges. It will be wise for you to discuss your expectations about sex and any known aversions (Examples: touching certain areas of your body, kissing, etc.) with your partner, as well as the birth control method you intend to use, if any. Worksheet 23A will assist you with your discussions.

Marriage at its heart is a very **intimate experience**. Intimacy builds from sharing a life together, a life that includes helpfulness, caring, cooperation, consideration, and respect. It requires a level of maturity in all these areas:

- Emotional
- Mental
- Physical
- Spiritual

Marriage Can Be Forever—Preparation Counts!

Marriage will be spiritually intimate as your souls draw closer in worshiping God and as you serve each other. It will be mentally and emotionally intimate as you share your thoughts, wishes, goals, and dreams with each other—and develop shared visions and goals. It will be physically intimate as you explore each other's bodies to develop the sensitivity to touch each other the way you want and need to be touched. Over time, you will end up knowing each other better than you know any other human being.

This intimacy requires **trust and trustworthiness** in abundance, as well as high integrity and the balance of equality. Trust is an integral part of being friends, something that is important to have firmly established before considering marriage. For trust to last in an intimate friendship you must be honest with each other. You must be able to speak what is in your heart and soul and have the sharing respected. Whatever intimacy develops must not be abused spiritually, mentally, emotionally, or physically.

Part of your premarital discussion is likely to include some of your **past experiences**. However, be cautious about sharing unnecessary details that will simply burden your partner or that may be backbiting about someone else. Sharing your experiences is not "confession;" it is simply communicating information about your life that will affect the quality and course of your physical and sexual relationship with each other. This is vital. You also need to be clear about your reaction and response to hearing about the other person's experiences, both their positive and negative ones. How do you feel about what you have heard? Can you express it to the other? Do you need counseling to assist you with understanding and resolving the feelings and/or issues? Here are some things to consider:

- Can you discuss difficult emotional issues such as childhood abuse or times in the past when you had difficult sexual experiences?
- What about times when you did not act morally, appropriately, or engaged in risky behavior—are any of these predictors of your ability to remain faithful to your partner?
- Might you have been exposed to a disease that you could transmit to your spouse or that might affect your ability to conceive a child?
- What if you had a previous marriage partner—are there experiences that have given you expectations, positive or negative, about sex in marriage?
- Are there any indications of addiction to sexual experiences, a tendency to read or view pornography, or have excessive sexual fantasies?

A large percentage of couples in our current society choose to **live together outside of marriage** to "try it out," something that does not guarantee future marital happiness and success. As discussed in Chapter 12, the Bahá'í Teachings and those of many other faiths do not allow for this kind of arrangement. Living together prevents you from making a complete commitment to each other, to blending your lives, to creating a family with children, and to developing strong and supportive relationships with each other's families. Living together without this full commitment is likely to bring many unwanted tests and frustrations.

Once you are married, you will **consummate your relationship** by making love. Although due to life circumstances a couple might live apart for periods of time during a marriage, generally you will be sharing a household after the wedding. The frequency and quality of your sex life will then be part of the many things you sort out together. Sex between the two of you will hopefully be part of the incredible bonding experience that comes with marriage. It is one of many opportunities to be "as one" with each other in body and soul and express your love for each other with full passion. It can create a sacred bond that helps you feel a healthy exclusivity—a sense of sharing something with one other person in the world that no one else shares.

Being in a **committed and permanent relationship** with someone throughout marriage creates structure and boundaries that might be a test for you and cause resistance to marriage and the loyalties that accompany it. This is especially true if you have not matured in your judgment at that particular point in time, or if your marriage is going through a period of strain. Great happiness can come from being in harmony with your partner and your relationship. Unhappiness results if you are not spiritually, emotionally, mentally, and physically loyal and faithful to your partner before and after marriage.

It will also be important to realize that the **qualities of character** you value in each other play a role in sex. The intimacy and richness of making love with another human being are enhanced by applying these:

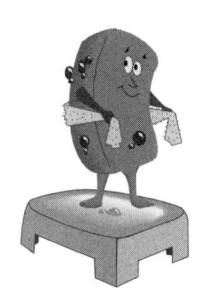

- Gentleness
- Creativity
- Generosity
- Cleanliness
- Enthusiasm
- Courtesy
- Self-discipline
- Helpfulness

- Courage
- Responsibility
- Moderation
- Confidence
- Flexibility
- Patience
- Honesty
- Respect

In your premarital discussions, talk about your level of commitment to applying these virtues and the ones that are most important to you. (See Appendix A for definitions of some of the virtues.)

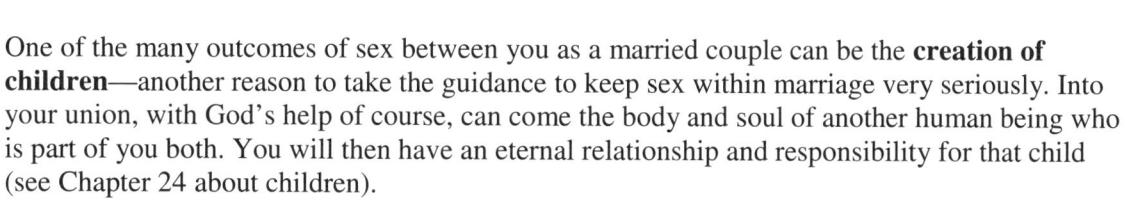

One of the many outcomes of sex between you as a married couple can be the **creation of children**—another reason to take the guidance to keep sex within marriage very seriously. Into your union, with God's help of course, can come the body and soul of another human being who is part of you both. You will then have an eternal relationship and responsibility for that child (see Chapter 24 about children).

Coaching

⇒ Our world often uses movies and novels as the models for romance and sex, and sets expectations of "fireworks" and spectacular performance standards, leaving you with often-unrealistic views of behavior in a marriage. It takes patience and time to learn the intricacies of each other's body, moods, emotions, thoughts, and cycles. It takes patience to build a level of reverence and joyfulness that can truly make being a couple full of spiritually and emotionally satisfying experiences for you both. The goal will be to concentrate on connecting and have a fun and joyful experience rather than meeting some media ideal.

⇒ As a couple, you will be happiest when you recognize that your relationship will always be changing and developing. Both of you, your relationship, and your life circumstances will change. You will be unhappy very quickly if you expect each other or your relationship to be the same as it was the day you are married.

⇒ Discussions about intimacy and sex trigger many emotions. Be as sensitive and supportive as you can with the personal issues you each raise.

Questions for Reflection and Discussion

Note: Remember to set up your discussions in a way that reduces the chances of touch and arousal. Beginning with prayer may set an atmosphere that allows you intimacy with appropriate boundaries. Be aware that some questions may be embarrassing and/or difficult to answer. Be as forthright as possible…and be sensitive with each other. There may be some emotional and vulnerable moments. You may choose to skip questions as a result, but try not to skip anything that is vital.

1. What do you know about sex? What is the source of your information?
2. What are your perspectives about intimacy? How intimate do you feel with your partner?
3. How can you develop intimacy while respecting spiritual principles? What principles apply?
4. How are you handling chastity and abstinence?
5. What aspects of your history of sex and intimacy with others (if applicable) are important to share with your partner? Can you share them? What might stop you?
6. How do you feel about either of you having been sexually intimate with someone or many people before marriage with you? Are there any issues of trusting the other to be faithful as a marriage partner?
7. If either or both of you are virgins, how do you view the transition from chastity to being married and making love?
8. Are there any things about your previous sexual experiences that would be important for your partner to know?
9. What is the role of sex in a marriage?
10. What would be the effect on your marriage if you had some serious sexual incompatibility or dysfunction? How big an issue do you think this would be, and how hard would it be to overcome?
11. If you are not sexually compatible, will you be able to talk about it and be willing to seek professional assistance if needed?
12. What expectations do you have about the frequency and/or quality of sex?
13. What are your opinions or expectations about verbal communication during sex? What kind?
14. Do either of you have a lot of sexual fantasies? Is this something you have sought or need counseling to address? Do you expect to carry out particular fantasies after marriage? Is your partner likely to be willing? Do your partner's sexual fantasies bother you? Does it make a difference if they are about you or someone else?
15. What indication, if any, are there of addiction to sexual experiences?
16. Is there any indication of a tendency to read or view pornography?
17. What bathroom or cleanliness habits do you have that might be a problem for the other?
18. Do you have any discomfort with the woman initiating sexual activity instead of the man? The man initiating?
19. Do either of you have any physical conditions or diseases that would affect the quality of your sexual experiences? In what way?
20. If you have been sexually active, have you been recently tested for sexually transmitted diseases? Are there any conditions that are being treated or need treatment? If not, why?
21. Have either of you ever had abusive or unsatisfactory sexual experiences? How did you handle it? How is this affecting you now?
22. Have you ever been pregnant or fathered a child inside or outside a marriage? What was the outcome?
23. What are your birth control choices, experiences, and expectations?
24. Under what conditions do you consider it all right to spend time with an adult of the opposite sex other than your partner?

Activities

1. Pray, meditate, reflect, and write in your journal about your emotions related to intimacy and sex.

2. Together, use popular magazines to find and cut out pictures of people projecting love, sex, or intimacy or words that reflect these themes. Create a collage by gluing them onto a large sheet of paper or cardboard. Discuss the various images in the collage and the expectations and feelings that arise for each of you in

looking at them. How are your perceptions of sex and intimacy shaped by popular media? By your family? By other sources? Are these appropriate influences?
_____
_____

3. Individually and with reflection, list all the words that you honestly associate with intimacy and then those you associate with sex. Then, discuss together your thoughts about them. What concerns, hopes, expectations, or joys did you discover? It is probably best to create the lists separately first, so you don't influence each other. Be as forthright as possible…and be sensitive with each other. There may be some emotional and vulnerable moments in this activity.

Words Related to Intimacy

His List	**Her List**

Words Related to Sex

His List	**Her List**

4. Use Worksheet 23A to explore some aspects of intimacy and sexual relations.

Chapter 23 – A Personal Discussion: Chastity, Intimacy, and Sex

Date: _____

Worksheet 23A: Discussing Intimate Feelings and Sex

DIRECTIONS: This worksheet addresses intimate feelings, touching, sex, and sex-related issues. Discussing sex and intimacy is important as part of the exploration of compatibility between you, but for some people it can lead to feelings of sexual attraction.
- Set your discussion up in a place and in circumstances to minimize the chances that this discussion will lead to inappropriate sexual activity.
- Beginning with prayer may set an atmosphere that allows you to have privacy and emotional intimacy with appropriate boundaries.
- Circle the appropriate letter(s) or word(s) or complete the following first-person statements.
- Then discuss your answers with your partner. *There are not right or wrong answers.*

Worksheets may be printed from www.claricomm.com/publishing

1. In expressing affection/love, I think you are:
    a. Very expressive
    b. Somewhat expressive
    c. Somewhat unexpressive
    d. Repressed and withdrawn
    e. Other _____

2. In expressing affection/love, I think I am:
    a. Very expressive
    b. Somewhat expressive
    c. Somewhat unexpressive
    d. Repressed and withdrawn
    e. Other _____

3. My understanding of intimacy is:
   _____
   _____

4. As we interact with each other during courtship (and marriage), I would appreciate it if you would be (**mark all that apply**):
    a. More gentle
    b. Stronger
    c. More emotionally expressive
    d. Less emotionally expressive
    e. More independent
    f. More caring
    g. More open with your thoughts
    h. Less hesitant to make decisions
    i. More attentive to my needs
    j. Less demanding
    k. More willing to be flexible and negotiate
    l. Others: _____
       _____

5. I think your most attractive physical features are:
   _____

6. I think my most attractive physical features are:
   _____

7. My understanding of chastity before and after marriage is:

   Before:_____

   After:_____

8. My understanding of abstinence is:
   _____

Marriage Can Be Forever—Preparation Counts!

9. In my family growing up, the subject of sex was (**mark all that apply**):
   a. Never discussed
   b. Delegated to siblings
   c. Regarded as private and special
   d. Joked about
   e. Openly talked about
   f. Considered "dirty" and "shameful"
   g. Other: _____

10. This is what I know about sex:

    Physical:_____

    Mental:_____

    Emotional:_____

    Spiritual:_____

11. The sources of my knowledge about sex are: _____

12. Some people think certain races are different sexually than other races. I think that because of your race, when it comes to sex you might be:
    _____

13. My feelings about sex are:
    _____
    _____

14. My fears about sex are:
    _____
    _____

15. My concerns about sex after having children are:
    _____

16. Sex in marriage **will/will not** be very important to me. Why?
    _____

17. My comfort level in discussing sex with you is:
    a. Very uncomfortable
    b. Somewhat uncomfortable
    c. Somewhat comfortable
    d. Very comfortable

18. As far as not having sex before marriage is concerned, I feel (**mark all that apply**):
    a. Accepting
    b. Frustrated
    c. Resentful
    d. Happy
    e. Resistant
    f. Other: _____

19. Modesty and privacy in our marriage looks like (consider changing clothes, bathroom use, etc.):
    _____

20. A healthy and satisfying sex life to me would include the following:
    _____

21. I think that a satisfying sex life after marriage would include intercourse _____ times per **week/month**. The time(s) of day that I think I would most enjoy intercourse include:
    _____

22. I think that physical cleanliness before intimate/sexual contact is:
    a. Not important or necessary at all
    b. Somewhat important
    c. Very important
    d. Strictly required

23. My definition of cleanliness is: _____

24. I think that birth control **is/is not** acceptable under these circumstances:
    _____

25. The birth control method I would prefer is:_____

26. My opinion about sexual fidelity within marriage is that it is (**mark all that apply**):
    a. Important
    b. Unnecessary
    c. Essential
    d. Ridiculous and boring
    e. Other: _____

27. If there were ever issues of emotional or physical unfaithfulness in our marriage, my response would likely be:
    _____

28. Once we are married, I **will/will not** take the lead at times and initiate sexual activity. Why?
    _____

29. The right to say "no" is important in relation to sex. I believe this boundary applies in marriage in this way:
    _____
    _____

30. I **will/will not** be able to say "no" if I don't feel like participating in sexual activity with you after we are married for this reason:
    _____

31. As far as I know, the following sexual acts would *not* be acceptable for either of us or between us:
    _____

32. My feelings about giving or receiving oral sex are:
    _____

33. If we experienced dysfunction or incompatibility in our sex life after marriage, I would be likely to handle it in the following way(s) (**mark all that apply**):
    a. Get counseling
    b. Visit a sex therapist
    c. Read self-help books
    d. Get coaching from you
    e. Pray
    f. Ignore it
    g. Stop having sex
    h. Talk to friends
    i. Get a divorce
    j. Other: _____

Marriage Can Be Forever—Preparation Counts!

34. I **have/have not** been improperly sexually touched by someone, sexually abused, or raped. I **have/have not** shared the information with you and have **sought/not sought** counseling. It affected me in this way:

_____
_____
_____
_____

35. I **have/do not have** a family member or friend who was sexually abused or raped. It affected me in this way:

_____
_____
_____

36. There **are/are not** issues from past sexual relationships that might affect our marriage that we have not yet discussed (Are you willing to share them?). My concerns about raising them are:

_____

37. I **have/have not** engaged in behavior that might have exposed me to HIV or other sexually transmitted diseases. I **have/have not** been tested and cleared of them. Why or why not?

_____

38. These are the other issues about intimacy and sex that I think are important for us to discuss:

_____
_____
_____
_____
_____

Notes:

_____
_____
_____
_____
_____
_____
_____
_____
_____
_____
_____

Note: You may find it helpful to re-visit this worksheet after you have been married a few months (if you choose to marry).

Your father and mother were playing love games.
They came together, and you appeared!

~ Rumi, All Rivers At Once, *The Essential Rumi*, p. 92

The purpose of marriage is children, and yet in our modern world, especially in the busy life of big cities, this fact is rapidly being lost sight of. We have drifted so far away from the good clean earth that begot us, so lost in the maze of our material civilization, that the most primitive joys and blessings which every beast possesses we are ever increasingly denying ourselves.

It is our nature to have children. It is not only good for us physically to have children and necessary for society that we do so, but it is a spiritual blessing for us as well. To have created a new life, a life like yourself, springing from you, dependent on you, calls forth a whole gamut of new emotions from the human heart. Dead indeed the heart of the man that does not beat faster at the touch of the hand of his baby! It tears away some of the selfishness with which we are always overburdened. It brings a new, keen interest into life, a new sense of responsibility. It makes a man think more of himself and more of his honor. It calls forth a new kind of love, a love that perforce must give and be patient and self-denying. In fact to have a child can and should be a self-purification for the parents. It adds a zest to life; here is a very demanding task, this new human must be provided for, helped, trained, educated. It binds the mother and father closer, renews the springs of their love, puts out green leaves on the marriage tree.

...Matter is so—one might almost say—recklessly abundant. There is so much of everything, so many suns and universes, so many teeming, multiplying forms of life, such a power of development and growth, such a careless lavishness in nature; the millions of eggs in the roe of the fish, the thousands of seeds in a single pod; for man, soul-bearing, king of creation that he is, to shut himself out from this fecundity, this lavish expression of life, is rather pitiful. He is denying himself his own fruit, depriving his life of one of its most beautiful ingredients.

There is another final, far deeper reason, for having children. We might liken life to a flight; inanimate matter has risen into animate matter, life has evolved man, man alone returns to God. The flight mounts up to an apogee we cannot as yet perceive while in this world; after death the individual goes on living, progressing, developing; we should not—unless there is some very good reason for doing so—willfully break the chain or prevent other lives from coming into being and winging their way on and up too.

~ Rúhíyyih Rabbani, *Prescription for Living*, pp. 71-72

Marriage Can Be Forever—Preparation Counts!

CHAPTER 24 – Family Time: Children and Marriage

Focus Points

- Children as an essential purpose of marriage
- Parental roles
- Patterns learned from your parents
- Spiritual education for children
- Discipline
- Children from previous relationships
- Family counseling

A Couple's Story

Lindsay is spending the day with James' mother, Sondra, helping her with spring cleaning and reorganizing at her home.

"Here, Lindsay, take a look at this photo album," Sondra says. "It's James' baby pictures. He was a cute baby. What a handful by the time he was three though…into everything."

"I agree…very cute!" Lindsay responds. "How did you handle it when he was getting into things he shouldn't have?"

"It was hard," says Sondra. "I didn't have my Mom around to ask how to do it, and I kept reading about how to discipline him, but it really came down to trial and error. I tried scolding him, taking away toys, and making him sit in the corner. Sometimes sending him to his room worked, because he preferred being out where we were. Once I finally realized how much he loved to paint and draw though, it worked best to reward him with art time when he was good."

"So, do you think he'll be a good father?" Lindsay asked.

"Yes," said Sondra. "The best."

Quotes for Guidance

✸ …He that bringeth up his son or the son of another, it is as though he hath brought up a son of Mine; upon him rest My Glory, My loving-kindness, My Mercy, that have compassed the world.
   (Bahá'u'lláh: *Kitáb-i-Aqdas*, K. 48, p. 37)

✸ That which is of paramount importance for the children, that which must precede all else, is to teach them the oneness of God and the laws of God. For lacking this, the fear of God cannot be inculcated, and lacking the fear of God an infinity of odious and abominable actions will spring up, and sentiments will be uttered that transgress all bounds…. The parents must exert every effort to rear their offspring to be religious, for should

the children not attain this greatest of adornments, they will not obey their parents, which in a certain sense means that they will not obey God. Indeed, such children will show no consideration to anyone, and will do exactly as they please.
(Bahá'u'lláh: *Bahá'í Education*, p. 248)

✸ Unto every father hath been enjoined the instruction of his son and daughter in the art of reading and writing.... He that bringeth up his son or the son of another, it is as though he hath brought up a son of Mine; upon him rest My glory, My loving-kindness, My mercy, that have compassed the world.
(Bahá'u'lláh: *Kitáb-i-Aqdas*, p. 37)

✸ ...the husband and wife are brought into affinity, are united and harmonized, even as though they were one person. Through their mutual union, companionship and love great results are produced in the world, both material and spiritual. The spiritual result is the appearance of divine bounties. The material result is the children who are born in the cradle of the love of God, who are nurtured by the breast of the knowledge of God, who are brought up in the bosom of the gift of God, and who are fostered in the lap of the training of God....

Whensoever a mother seeth that her child hath done well, let her praise and applaud him and cheer his heart; and if the slightest undesirable trait should manifest itself, let her counsel the child and punish him, and use means based on reason, even a slight verbal chastisement should this be necessary. It is not, however, permissible to strike a child, or vilify him, for the child's character will be totally perverted if he be subjected to blows or verbal abuse.
('Abdu'l-Bahá: *Selections from the Writings of 'Abdu'l-Bahá*, p. 125)

✸ Mothers are the first educators of children, who establish virtues in the child's inner nature. They encourage the child to acquire perfections and goodly manners, warn him against unbecoming qualities, and encourage him to show forth resolve, firmness, and endurance under hardship, and to advance on the high road to progress. Due regard for the education of girls is, therefore, necessary.
('Abdu'l-Bahá: *Women*, p. 374)

✸ While the children are yet in their infancy feed them from the breast of heavenly grace, foster them in the cradle of all excellence, rear them in the embrace of bounty. Give them the advantage of every useful kind of knowledge. Let them share in every new and rare and wondrous craft and art. Bring them up to work and strive, and accustom them to hardship.
('Abdu'l-Bahá: *Selections from the Writings of 'Abdu'l-Bahá*, p. 129)

✸ The basic principle of the Cause is independent investigation of truth. This applies to us as much as to our children. They should be free to choose for themselves any religion they wish. To promise that they will belong to a certain Faith and not to another is therefore not only contrary to our precepts, but is also a futile promise to give. How can we make the future generation think as we do or follow our dictates. God has made them free. All that we can do is to open their eyes and tell them of what we think to be the truth.
(Shoghi Effendi: *Lights of Guidance*, p. 156)

✸ The task of bringing up a Bahá'í child, as emphasized time and again in Bahá'í writings, is the chief responsibility of the mother, whose unique privilege is indeed to create in her home such conditions as would be most conducive to both his material and spiritual welfare and advancement. The training which a child first receives through his mother constitutes the strongest foundation for his future development, and it should therefore be the paramount concern of your wife...to endeavor from now imparting to her new-born son such spiritual training as would enable him later on to fully assume and adequately discharge all the responsibilities and duties of Bahá'í life.
(Shoghi Effendi: *Bahá'í Education*, pp. 303-304)

✸ They should realize, moreover, that the primary purpose of marriage is the procreation of children. A couple who are physically incapable of having children may, of course, marry, since the procreation of children is not the only purpose of marriage. However, it would be contrary to the spirit of the Teachings for a couple to decide voluntarily never to have any children.
(On behalf of the Universal House of Justice: *Lights of Guidance*, p. 379)

Marriage Can Be Forever—Preparation Counts!

Perspectives to Consider

Having and raising children will be a primary purpose of your marriage. Ideally and most appropriately according to the Bahá'í teachings, marriage is where children are born and grow to their fullest potential—it is the "fortress" of safety and nurturing for the next generation. Whether entering marriage with or without children, thoroughly discuss your attitudes toward children, your experiences with them, your expectations for having (more) children and how many, child rearing and discipline, and the roles and responsibilities you both have or will have as a mother and father. There can be serious disunity in a marriage where there are different expectations and experiences concerning these issues. There can also be a serious increase in joy, love, and laughter when you add children to a home!

Guidance from the Bahá'í Writings about your **roles as parents** address the high level of respect and responsibility toward mothers. The details of how you carry out your responsibilities as parents will be guided by your spiritual principles. Many details, however, will only be resolved in joint consultation and trying out different options to determine what is best for each of you and your family.

Many issues around the subject of children arise out of your past with **your parents and siblings**. Someone raised as an only child will often want to have multiple children. People from large families want to duplicate this sometimes, but others may want to have very small families instead. It can break a marriage down rapidly if one person wants to have children and the other doesn't. Many couples also experience infertility or have difficulty conceiving, so it will be wise to talk about and agree on the importance of bearing your own children or the willingness to adopt or have foster children.

The subject of the **religious/spiritual training** of the children is a critical one, especially if you are different faiths or if different faiths exist in your extended families. Whatever your beliefs, explore how you will handle spiritual issues, including:

- Teaching your children about God
- Praying as a family
- Teaching them your faith/beliefs
- Training them to develop their virtues
- Teaching them your values
- Taking them to devotional meetings/worship services and study classes

Religion must not be a source of conflict within your marriage, but rather a support to strengthen and unify it. How it affects the children and also your wider extended family will be important to explore.

It will help you to understand each other's strengths as a parent through understanding each other's philosophy about **discipline**. This will usually be very connected to how you were disciplined as a child—will you discipline your children the same way? Would you rather avoid repeating history? What worked well in how you were disciplined? What would you like to do differently?

CAUTION — WATCH YOUR STEP

Sometimes in spite of wanting to discipline differently from your own parents, in the stress of anger or upset, what you learned as a child can come out. People who were abused as children often repeat this behavior with their own children. Abuse can be physical, verbal, emotional, or sexual, so your family histories must be understood and discussed. Explore the extent to which each of you may have received help and recovered from childhood trauma. It will be wise to spend time together around children to observe and understand the dynamics of how you react to children, especially when they misbehave. These observations will probably be strongest if you do childcare/baby-sit together, but ensure you have the necessary knowledge and maturity before doing this responsibility.

Marriage Can Be Forever—Preparation Counts!

CAUTION WATCH YOUR STEP *If you would be entering marriage with children from previous relationships, you must discuss and agree who would discipline them and how, the methods that have been used to discipline them in the past, and how any other parent or caretaking adult in their lives is likely to be disciplining them.* Some couples decide that only the original parent(s) will have the right to discipline and not the stepparent. Unless he/she is always around, however, this can become unmanageable and unrealistic. When the new stepparent does not have the right and responsibility to set limits and respond to poor behavior, he/she could end up feeling resentful, powerless, and disrespected. How would the children be affected?

Blended families are common these days, with new spouses, stepchildren, half-brothers, and half-sisters. Forming a strong marriage, and then family, are very challenging endeavors in these cases. It becomes even more difficult when you add into the mixture former spouses, custody, visitation, financial support, household space, moving, school changes, jealousy about sharing a parent, and so on. Family counseling and support groups may be highly advisable. While your children cannot be the ones to make your decision about marrying, you will nevertheless want to listen to their concerns and attitudes about the blending of your families, and within reason, consider them. Unhappy children will stress your new relationship. Children's judgment is of course immature, and they will grow and go out on their own, while your partnership will continue together. The decision to marry, therefore, is your own to make as a couple. If you are happy and unified together, the children will likely adjust and be happy over time. What will you do to ensure you make time to nurture your relationship without the children present? What will you do to ensure you nurture the children within the relationship? What will you do to nurture family unity?

When children are older, as often happens with a second marriage, the new spouse will need to sort through whether to approach the children either as a friend or parent. The children may be uncertain about having someone new in their lives and uncomfortable with the prospect of you as a step-grandparent to their children now or in the future. It will be helpful to turn to your potential future spouse, their parent, for coaching and guidance about how to be successful in building a relationship with them, as well as consulting with the children as appropriate for their ages. The virtues of love, courtesy, respect, and patience all apply.

Multiracial families are also becoming more common, and they are certainly encouraged in the Bahá'í Writings. If you marry and have children with someone of a different race than you are, or you adopt children who are from a different culture or skin color than yours, you will want to understand the ways that you are part of a changing culture. You and your children may experience prejudice from family members, friends, or others. Are you prepared to handle this? How would you handle it in a spiritual way that assists others to grow in their acceptance and understanding? How would you help the children deal with being on the receiving end of prejudice?

Whether there are children present at the time of your marriage or after marrying, you must understand that **your relationship as a couple** will change because of them. They take time, attention, and energy that you may have reserved for each other. You may find it useful to agree to obtain childcare and have time alone to nurture your relationship. The spiritual and emotional strength of your marriage will be vital for the well-being of your children.

Grandparents and extended family also have relationships with any children you have or will have. Consult together and decide how much contact your current children will have with prospective future family. Are these relationships you want to nurture now or not until marriage between you is a certainty? Explore together what you see as the role of other family members with any of your children. Do you value these relationships, even if it means traveling distances to nurture them? Or, will there be limited contact with family?

Marriage Can Be Forever—Preparation Counts!

Often households can feel very stressful when parents and children are going many different directions, priorities are constantly shifting, and the **responsibilities** feel overwhelming. Before marriage, it may be helpful make a commitment to prevent situations like this from blowing up into a crisis. You might talk about ways that you can support each other to reduce stress. Perhaps you will agree to schedule regular family prayer and/or meeting times. Perhaps it will be by offering a cup of herbal tea or suggesting taking a walk, playing music, or having quiet meditation time.

Equality is also a principle that often applies when people in a household are juggling many responsibilities—will you *mutually* handle what needs to be done and offer support? Does equality look like both of you alternating responsibilities involving the children and household? What if this means you would rarely be with your children together? Would you be able to hire a cleaning service or live-in nanny? Or ask for help from relatives, neighbors, or friends?

Support from professional services may also be necessary in some situations. **Marriage and family counselors** can often help a family through periods of difficulty or adjustment. You may want to consider doing this before marriage occurs if you already have children and be willing to do it in the future if needed. At times, your family may also find spiritual assistance through a Bahá'í Spiritual Assembly, your clergyperson, or by attending training courses or workshops. Seeking support and assistance would maximize your ability to maintain your marriage and family. You may feel some resistance to talking about your problems with a professional, and some people are adamantly opposed to it. In your pre-marriage discussions, therefore, consult on and agree what actions you would be willing to take if you run into difficulties.

Coaching

⇒ It may be wise to consider giving yourself time to establish your marriage firmly before having children.

⇒ It can be a serious point of marital disharmony when a couple cannot agree on the timing and number of children. You may *mutually* change your mind after marriage, but having an agreement before marriage can protect you from a painful struggle later on. As always, don't assume the other person is going to change his/her mind, particularly in a direction you would prefer!

⇒ Parents and stepparents often think they should be able to raise their children perfectly. Give yourself permission to make mistakes, the grace to acknowledge them and apologize, and the wisdom to learn from them and not repeat them.

⇒ Ask others for help and assistance when needed. Form a parent's support group if there isn't one. Read religious and self-help books. Find a family counselor. There are many resources available when you need help.

⇒ Hug your children, love them, and give them space to grow and learn from their mistakes.

⇒ 'Abdu'l-Bahá counsels parents to "Bring them [children] up to work and strive, and accustom them to hardship." As parents, you will often wish to shield your children from difficulties and soften their paths. But working hard and handling hardships helps children develop the qualities and skills they will need to be successful in their lives.

Marriage Can Be Forever—Preparation Counts!

Questions for Reflection and Discussion

Note: *Strongly* consider consulting expert books (including religious ones) and professionals for information on raising children. Many questions below ask for your opinion, but it's wise to balance opinion with expertise.

Having Children

1. Do you want to have children/more children? Why or why not? Are you physically capable of having children?
2. How many children do you want? What if you change your mind later?
3. Do you have a gender preference? Why? What if the child that is born is the other gender?
4. What are your fears about being a parent? How can you resolve these?
5. If it will be an interracial marriage, or if you already have or will be adopting children of various races, how will you handle raising multiracial children? What challenges might arise? How will you handle prejudice toward you and them? What are your expectations of teaching them about their original cultures?
6. How much time do you want to wait after marriage before having children?
7. What is important for you to accomplish in your relationship and in your lives before having children?1
8. How many years apart do you want your children to be?
9. What do you plan to do about birth control?
10. How would you cope with infertility if one or the other of you is infertile? Would you consider adoption then? Why or why not?
11. What are your feelings about adoption in general? Would you ever be willing to be a foster parent?
12. Would you consider adoption, or even prefer it, if you are both able to have children? Why or why not? How many? What gender? Is there a specific race that you would prefer or not consider? Would you adopt a special needs child? A younger or older child? Would any members of your extended family have prejudices that would affect adoption? How would you deal with that?
13. Have you ever had an abortion? What are your beliefs about abortion?
14. Are you pregnant? Is the other parent the one you are dating/courting? How will this affect your preparation process and your marriage plans?

Roles and Responsibilities

1. What spiritual principles will guide you in deciding on your roles and responsibilities as parents?
2. Have you considered or discussed the possibility of reversing typical male and female roles in parenting where it's not against your spiritual principles?
3. Which parent will support the family, and which will be a homemaker/stay-at-home parent when the children are young? Can you give priority to the mother? Will you both work? Will one of you work from home?
4. Will the woman have a job? A career? How does this interact with having children; for example, how long would she put her career on hold during the raising of the children? Would the man put his career on hold and take care of the children for awhile, instead of the woman? If so, for how long? Under what circumstances?
5. What about childcare? Family member as caretaker? Non-family member? A childcare center? How will you deal with the finances of any of these?
6. What differences might the two of you have in training and disciplining the children? What similarities?
7. How will you handle the situation if/when your child asks to do something and you and your spouse disagree on the response?
8. When would you apologize to your child? When would you expect your spouse to?
9. How will you teach your children the principle of the equality of women and men?
10. Do you need parent education and training? If so, how will you get this?

Discipline

1. How were you and your siblings disciplined or punished as a child? How did you react? How do you feel about it now?
2. What are your expectations of children's behavior?
3. What are your expectations of children's training/education?
4. What are your expectations of parental behavior?
5. At what point, if ever, is spanking a child appropriate?
6. How would you discipline a child who is frequently disrespectful to others? (Note: You might find it helpful to think of specific circumstances and talk them through together. For instance, how would you discipline a 3-year-old child when he or she yells at you or hits you in the face when you are verbally correcting his or her behavior, will not sit still in time-out (gets off of chair), and when you send him or her to a room for time out, screams and breaks things there?)
7. How do you react toward children when you become angry? Has your partner observed this? Any concerns?
8. At what point, if any, is yelling at a child appropriate? How would you feel if it is a regular occurrence?
9. Would you ever give the child a say in or the choice of what his/her discipline should be?
10. What if you disagree with how the other parent is handling discipline?

Training and Education

1. How will you educate your children? Public schools? Private schools? Bahá'í or other religious schools? Tutors? Home schooling?
2. If you have older children from previous relationships, how will you handle higher education expenses early on in the marriage? How would you like to handle these expenses for children born later on during the marriage?
3. At what age do you think that a child has a sense of what you are saying about him or her and has feelings about what you say about him or her? What do you think is appropriate to say in front of them and about them at different ages?
4. What is your opinion about correcting a child in public or private? When might one be appropriate and when might the other be preferred?
5. What is the appropriate role of television in a child's development, if any? What will be "off limits"? What about the Internet? What about movies?
6. How firmly would you insist on your children receiving Bahá'í or other religious education? How would you handle their attendance at Bahá'í or other religious activities, if they don't want to attend? Bahá'u'lláh designates age 15 as the point someone can make spiritually mature decisions—would this affect how you handle attendance?
7. What do children do at the Bahá'í 19-Day Feast or a religious service when they are 1-year-old? When they are 3-years-old? When they are 8-years-old? When they are 14-years-old? What is your role as his/her parent at those ages?
8. What years in a child's life do you think are the most critical for developing his/her core character and personality, self-esteem, and emotional security? What do you need to do during this period to foster positive development in these areas?
9. At what ages do you think children are ready to make their own decisions about:
    a. Bedtime
    b. Getting food for themselves from the refrigerator
    c. Going outside by themselves
    d. The distance they can go from home on their own
    e. The cut, length, or coloring of their own hair
    f. Piercing body parts or getting tattoos
10. Would you permit your children to date? If so, with or without chaperones? At what ages? Does this differ for sons and daughters? If so, why?

11. If your children would be multiracial, what issues are there to consider? How would you teach them to handle any prejudice they may encounter from others?
12. At what age would you give a child an allowance or spending money? Why?
13. How would you handle the child being responsible for household chores? At what ages? Would you ever pay them money for doing these?
14. How might you handle behavior in your child such as:
    a. Lying
    b. Drinking alcohol
    c. Using drugs
    d. Being sexually promiscuous (either heterosexually or homosexually)
    e. Cheating at school
    f. Cutting classes at school
    g. Stealing
    h. Backbiting
    i. Being disrespectful to a family member
15. Have any of the issues above arisen in children you already have? How were they handled?
16. How might you respond to having a child with a serious illness or impairment?

Activities

1. Pray, meditate, reflect, and write in your journal about what kind of parent you think you are or will be. Write also about what kind of parent you most want to be, and how you can grow into that type of parent. Be as specific as possible.

2. Spend a day together taking care of a young child or children. You may choose to do this more than once with children of different ages, genders, and abilities. You may try it with children who are related to you and ones who are not and see if there are differences and similarities. You might also benefit from interacting with children from another culture or ethnic group to see the effect of children raised with different values than you. How did it go? What was the experience like? What emotions did you experience? What did you observe? What concerns do you have?

3. Design and present a class or series of children's classes for your community.

4. Pick up a child development and child-rearing book at the library and go through it a chapter at a time together. Discuss any issues that come up. **Note:** See what answers the book has to questions posed in this chapter.

5. Go through photo albums, videos, or other media that has pictures of each of you when you were growing up. Use this time to explore family interactions, incidents that happened, favorite activities, and so on. What are the memories that make you happy? Sad? Explore with each other what your future family after marriage might look like. What are the similarities and differences it might have compared to your own growing up experiences? What new information did you learn about each other?

6. Discuss the implications of this comic for your family life:

"I'm going to be late again tonight, dear. Have the kids grown much?"

What kind of parent do you want to be?

What are the qualities of a great parent?

Do you observe these qualities in each other?

FATHER/MOTHER MAY I?

May my life be a sacrifice
May my service be with love
May my growth be toward You
May my dreams show Your Will
May I let You water every seed
May I help You tend the plants
May I care enough to cry
May I love enough to laugh
May I be patient enough to try
May I be strong enough to detach
May I see wisdom in the pain
May my life be a sacrifice to Thee

~ Susanne Mariella Alexander

CHAPTER 25 – On the Move: Service and Time Choices

> **Focus Points**
> - The importance of service
> - Maintaining balance and moderation in time choices
> - Spending time separately and together
> - Making choices and sacrificing for family time

A Couple's Story

James is working a lot of overtime lately and he and Lindsay are seeing each other less often as a result. All in the same week, the Mayor of the town asks James to serve on a youth advisory council, his friend Tony asks him to help work on his car, and Lindsay asks him to get more involved in volunteering at the Literacy Center. Feeling overwhelmed, he and Lindsay talk over dinner at a restaurant about what to do.

"I know one thing for sure…I miss you," says Lindsay. "Maybe we could make a list of everything you are doing right now. Then we can consult together about what makes sense for you to say 'yes' and 'no' to."

"That is a good idea," says James. They create the list and talk about the reasons and spiritual principles for doing each thing. He has concerns about how he can say "no" to people without feeling guilty about it. They consult about how he can do that effectively.

"Since you hate working on cars, does Tony have someone else who could help him?" asks Lindsay. "And I wonder if your manager would be willing to cut back some of the overtime. Could you approach him about hiring a part-time assistant?"

James is saving the overtime money in case they get married, and he is reluctant to give it up totally. Lindsay agrees. Together they go through the list and consult about the choices James could make. At the end of the discussion, he has a plan he's going to follow.

Quotes for Guidance

✸ …all effort and exertion put forth by man from the fullness of his heart is worship, if it is prompted by the highest motives and the will to do service to humanity. This is worship: to serve mankind and to minister to the needs of the people. Service is prayer. A physician ministering to the sick, gently, tenderly, free from prejudice and believing in the solidarity of the human race, he is giving praise'.
('Abdu'l-Bahá: *Paris Talks*, pp. 176-177)

✸ Thou canst take unto thyself a husband and at the same time serve the Cause of God; the one doth not preclude the other. Know thou the value of these days; let not this chance escape thee. Beg thou God to make thee a lighted candle, so that thou mayest guide a great multitude through this darksome world.
('Abdu'l-Bahá, *Selections from the Writings of Abdu'l-Bahá*, p. 100)

Marriage Can Be Forever—Preparation Counts!

❋ Therefore, order your lives in accordance with the first principle of the divine teaching, which is love. Service to humanity is service to God. Let the love and light of the Kingdom radiate through you until all who look upon you shall be illumined by its reflection. Be as stars, brilliant and sparkling in the loftiness of their heavenly station. Do you appreciate the Day in which you live?
('Abdu'l-Bahá: *Promulgation of Universal Peace*, p. 8)

❋ …you should not neglect your health, but consider it the means which enables you to serve. It—the body—is like a horse which carries the personality and spirit, and as such should be well cared for so it can do its work! You should certainly safeguard your nerves, and force yourself to take time, and not only for prayer and meditation, but for real rest and relaxation. We don't have to pray and meditate for hours in order to be spiritual.
(Shoghi Effendi: *Compilation of Compilations, Vol. II*, p. 242)

❋ A healthy social life and Bahá'í work can go hand in hand, but not always in times of crisis, such as these days…when great sacrifice can alone meet the demands of the situation.
(Shoghi Effendi, *The Unfolding Destiny of the British Bahá'í Community*, p. 456)

❋ The words, the deeds, the attitudes, the lack of prejudice, the nobility of character, the high sense of service to others—in a word, those qualities and actions which distinguish a Bahá'í—must unfailingly characterize their inner life and outer behavior, and their interactions….
(Universal House of Justice: *Lights of Guidance*, p. 638)

❋ …the unity of your family should take priority over any other consideration. Bahá'u'lláh came to bring unity to the world, and a fundamental unity is that of the family. Therefore, we must believe that the Faith is intended to strengthen the family not weaken it. For example, service to the [Bahá'í] Cause should not produce neglect of the family. It is important for you to arrange your time so that your family life is harmonious and your household receives the attention it requires.
(On behalf of the Universal House of Justice: *Preserving Bahá'í Marriages*, p. 26)

Perspectives to Consider

Your values will drive choices of how you spend your time. If something is important to you, you will direct your time to accomplish it. If you value nature and you enjoy doing things outdoors, you will likely spend time there and perhaps live close to a natural environment. If spiritual activities are important, you will choose those. If entertainment is a high priority, you may choose to spend your time watching TV, going to the movies, attending concerts, and so on. If family is important, you will spend time with them regularly. If living a prayerful life is valued, how often will you spend time in prayer? Working to earn a living is an important value. How much time will you spend on it during your marriage? Will you stay out of work for a Holy Day? (See Chapter 26 about work.)

Your personality will also affect how you spend time (See Chapter 19). If you love to be in social situations, you are unlikely to spend all your time curled up in a corner of your house with a book. When humor is important to you, a comedy club might be inviting. If you are serious, a lecture might appeal instead. Risk-taking individuals might spend the day parachuting from an airplane. The questions later in the chapter will assist you with exploring the many facets of how you spend your time.

Compatibility with time choices will directly affect the amount of time you spend together. If you like to spend most of your time doing very different things, how would this affect your ability to sustain a marriage based on friendship? This does not mean you will have to spend every minute together to be happy as a married couple—you will have some different interests. However, it will not be a good idea to attempt to sustain a marriage when your values are very different and/or you rarely see each other.

Being of service to others is one key value you will consider when making choices for how to spend your time. This value is woven into the very fabric of being a Bahá'í, and it is a strong value in many other faiths as well, so it is relevant to consider what part it will play in your marriage relationship. Part of marriage is being of service to each other. What does this look like to you going into marriage? What do you think you would do for each other within marriage? The choices are endless:

- Handling the dishes
- A massage at the end of a difficult day
- Answering the telephone while the other is resting
- Serving tea or coffee to the other
- Doing the household filing
- Cooking or baking
- Tidying the house
- Fixing a squeaky doorknob
- Bringing chocolate

> Don't worry about keeping track of what you do for each other and competing to keep it equal. Simply take *delight* in being of service to each other.

Part of service is what you do for others outside your immediate family—with your Bahá'í or other religious community, with the greater community near you, and with the global community—all of which need many things from people with willingness and skills. This kind of service will likely be an integral part of your married life. Do you have similar interests so this will bring you together? Consider such activities as traveling for your faith or attending training or study courses that prepare you to serve well. Or alternatively, in order to serve, will you frequently be apart from each other? What does balance between family and service outside of the family look like to each of you?

Everyone has an **abundance of items on their "to do" lists**. Without clergy, Bahá'ís seem to be especially challenged in handling community service responsibilities. There are committee meetings and Spiritual Assembly meetings and community service and, and, and…. All these things can bring great joy and often do. But they can also separate family members and disrupt family unity if they aren't managed well. So, it's about balancing, prioritizing, and consulting through your choices and making joint decisions about how you use your time.

Throw school, work, and parenting all into the mix of time choices, and you might be excused for feeling spread a little thin. Or, perhaps your time choices are more toward relaxing, having fun, and avoiding anything serious? Is there anything wrong with this? Perhaps not, unless you are significantly neglecting school, family, work, service or developing your spiritual life. But can you marry someone who thinks that you and he/she have to be busy working all the time either?! **Balance is the key**.

Coaching

⇒ As a couple, being of service to others is one of the best ways for you to learn about each other's character.

⇒ Stretch out of your comfort zones and spend time doing something one or both of you have never done.

⇒ Be clear that you can accept and live with each other's choices of how you spend leisure time.

Marriage Can Be Forever—Preparation Counts!

Chapter 25 – On the Move: Service and Time Choices

> **❓ Questions for Reflection and Discussion**

Note: Observe your partner while involved in as many service and time choice activities as possible. Identify which ones seem compatible with your own choices and which ones cause you concern.

Service

1. Have you been of service to others? What kinds of service have you been involved with and what were the circumstances?
2. What would constitute a proper balance in the amount of time you or your spouse spends at work? What about in community service?
3. What are your favorite types of community service?
4. What are the service needs of your Bahá'í or other religious community? What do you see as your responsibility to meet them?
5. What are the service needs of the area, neighborhood, town, or city you live in? Are you involved in meeting them? Why or why not?
6. What social or economic development projects are already underway near you that you could participate in?
7. What are the joys and challenges you have experienced in serving on administrative committees or task forces?
8. What have you learned from doing service? Skills? Attitudes? Character development?

Time Choices

1. How do you relate to punctuality? How often are you early or late for events or commitments? How do you feel about being early or late? How does your partner feel?
2. For what reasons do you take time off work? What about for Holy Days?
3. What is your approach/regularity of attending religious or Bahá'í events such as 19-Day Feasts? Schools? Conferences? Study circles? Worship/devotional meetings? Others?
4. What are your views about spending time on education for yourselves? What about for your children?
5. What do you do with your spare time?
6. How much solitude per day do you need to be in balance? Is there a particular time of day that you need this? What do you do with that solitude? How will you feel if your spouse needs solitude away from you? At what point would that seem excessive?
7. How much time do you need with friends? Others of your own gender? Doing what kinds of activities? Do you expect this to change or be the same after marriage?
8. How much do you watch TV? How many hours per day or week? Are there any types of TV that would be hard for you to give up or to begin to watch? Do you disagree about what to watch?
9. What is the role of entertainment in your life? Do you like regular periods of play and entertainment?
10. What kinds of entertainment do you enjoy? Do you prefer passive entertainment (such as TV or video games), or do you prefer active entertainment (such as participation in sports or outdoor activities)? Which kinds of entertainment do you find annoying or repulsive? What types of movies or TV programming would you avoid or ask not be presented in your home? What would you want your spouse to give up?
11. What kinds of books do you read? How much time do you spend reading?
12. When you read or watch TV, are you totally engrossed and unaware of the people and happenings around you? Are there other things that totally engage your attention? Will this be upsetting for your partner?
13. If your partner enjoys a particular leisure activity that you do not share, such as sports, coin collecting, shopping, etc., at what point would you feel neglected or lonely?
14. How much do you care about the news? How do you get your news (local, national, international or Bahá'í/religious)? What would you like your partner's approach to be?

Marriage Can Be Forever—Preparation Counts!

15. What hobbies, sports, or leisure activities do you prefer?
16. Do you like the same kind of music? Can you stand each other's music? For how long? How will you deal with this on car trips?
17. Do you exercise or spend time in physical activity to support your health?
18. How much time do you spend daily on the computer doing e-mail or on the Internet? At what point would this be excessive for your partner?
19. What kinds of vacations do you like to take? Do you like to be a full-time tourist? Sit quietly on the beach? A combination? How often? How long? What would you think about combining it with religious service?
20. Are either of you involved in politics? Fond of political discussions? How does this affect the other? [**Note:** The Bahá'í Teachings state to avoid partisan politics and divisive political discussions.]
21. Are there any rituals in your life—things that you do the same way or same time every day? What is your description/explanation of them? Would they affect your spouse?
22. Are your time or service choices causing you stress? Why? From doing too much or not enough? How are you dealing with this?

Activities

1. Pray, meditate, reflect, and write in your journal about how you spend your time now, how you would prefer to spend your time, and what parts do service, prayer, and spiritual self-development play in your time choices.

2. Spend a day running errands for each other. How did you feel about doing this?

3. Find an unexpected service to perform for one of your parents and carry it out together. What did you observe?

4. Serve on a spiritually focused service committee together. What do you notice about your own participation and that of your partner?

5. Join a community service or community development project together for a day or for a few weeks (or longer). What do you notice about your own participation and that of your partner?

6. Do an activity of the other's choice that you would not normally do. What did you do? How did you feel about the experience?

7. Discuss the following and its implications for marriage:

**What is the highest and best use of your time?
Are you making wise or unwise choices?**

Marriage Can Be Forever—Preparation Counts!

WORK

This marvelous capacity we have to *do*, to *produce*, is at once the spring of our health, and, to a great extent, our happiness in life. Nothing can convey so solid a feeling of satisfaction in this world as something we have accomplished. A job well done, be it making a pie or writing a book or building a bridge, can produce a degree of contentment, a sense of buoyancy and fulfillment, that practically nothing else can.... Because work is necessary for us, it sets the very essence of our being in circulation, and just as the blood performs so many services in our body essential to health, such as carrying away impurities, re-oxygenizing itself in the lungs, bringing food to the tissues, so work seems to give tone to our whole machine, exhilarates us, and calls forth a new flow of energy.

~ Rúhíyyih Rabbani, *Prescription for Living*, p. 86

CHAPTER 26 – Money In, Money Out: Earning, Budgeting, and Spending

Focus Points

- Defining work; requirement to work
- Spiritual principles and qualities that apply to managing money and working
- Money challenges in marriage
- Family histories with money
- Career and education issues related to money
- Religious and charitable donations
- Budgeting and other skills
- Understanding assets and liabilities; net worth
- Handling debts

A Couple's Story

James and Lindsay decide to set up a joint checking account to save toward a set of nice lawn furniture as a present for his parents. They think this will give them some practice at seeing how they handle finances together. Lindsay is upset because James has withdrawn the money and bought the furniture without telling her ahead of time.

"Why didn't you wait until I could go with you to the store?" asks Lindsay.

"I saw a sales flyer and decided to go check it out," says James. "It was such a good deal, I couldn't resist, so I bought it."

"But we agreed that we would pick it out together, since the present was from both of us," says Lindsay, with some frustration and hurt in her voice. "All you had to do was call me on my cellphone, and we could have decided if it made sense for you to go ahead or wait for me. Why didn't you think of me?"

"Oh, jeez, I didn't mean to upset you. I messed up, huh?" asks James.

"Yes, I really feel left out," says Lindsay."

"I'm sorry," says James. "I didn't think it would be a big deal. What can I do differently so something like this doesn't happen again?"

"Can we agree to consult before making big purchases?" suggests Lindsay.

"Yeah, for sure," says James. "Would you like to go back and pick out something different with me? Or if you like this set, would you still be willing to go with me to give it to Mom and Dad?"

Marriage Can Be Forever—Preparation Counts!

> **Quotes for Guidance**

* It is incumbent upon each one of you to engage in some occupation—such as a craft, a trade or the like. We have exalted your engagement in such work to the rank of worship of the one true God....Waste not your hours in idleness and sloth, but occupy yourselves with what will profit you and others.
    (Bahá'u'lláh: *Kitáb-i-Aqdas*, p. 30)

* They must show forth such trustworthiness, such truthfulness and perseverance, such deeds and character that all mankind may profit by their example.
    (Bahá'u'lláh: *The Advent of Divine Justice*, p. 23)

* Should a man wish to adorn himself with the ornaments of the earth, to wear its apparels, or partake of the benefits it can bestow, no harm can befall him, if he alloweth nothing whatever to intervene between him and God, for God hath ordained every good thing, whether created in the heavens or in the earth, for such of His servants as truly believe in Him. Eat ye, O people, of the good things which God hath allowed you, and deprive not yourselves from His wondrous bounties. Render thanks and praise unto Him, and be of them that are truly thankful.
    (Bahá'u'lláh: *Gleanings from the Writings of Bahá'u'lláh*, p. 276)

* They have not properly understood that man's supreme honor and real happiness lie in self-respect, in high resolves and noble purposes, in integrity and moral quality, in immaculacy of mind. They have, rather, imagined that their greatness consists in the accumulation, by whatever means may offer, of worldly goods.
    ('Abdu'l-Bahá: *Secret of Divine Civilization*, p. 19)

* All the friends of God...should contribute to the extent possible, however modest their offering may be. God doth not burden a soul beyond its capacity. Such contributions must come from all centers and all believers.... O Friends of God! Be ye assured that in place of these contributions, your agriculture, your industry, and your commerce will be blessed by manifold increases, with goodly gifts and bestowals. He who cometh with one goodly deed will receive a tenfold reward. There is no doubt that the living Lord will abundantly confirm those who expend their wealth in His path.
    ('Abdu'l-Bahá: *Bahá'í Prayers* (US 2002), p. 84)

* We cannot possibly say that because a person also has many virtues, faults as grave as lying and dishonorable conduct regarding money, can be overlooked!
    (Shoghi Effendi: *Arohanui: Letters to New Zealand*, p. 52)

* You ask about the admonition that everyone must work, and want to know if this means that you, a wife and mother, must work for a livelihood as your husband does.... Homemaking is a highly honorable and responsible work of fundamental importance for mankind.
    (Universal House of Justice: *Lights of Guidance*, pp. 626-627)

* With regard to your question whether mothers should work outside the home, it is helpful to consider the matter from the perspective of the concept of a Bahá'í family. This concept is based on the principle that the man has primary responsibility for the financial support of the family, and the woman is the chief and primary educator of the children. This by no means implies that these functions are inflexibly fixed and cannot be changed and adjusted to suit particular family situations, nor does it mean that the place of the woman is confined to the home. Rather, while primary responsibility is assigned, it is anticipated that fathers would play a significant role in the education of the children and women could also be breadwinners. As you rightly indicated, "'Abdu'l-Bahá encouraged women to 'participate fully and equally in the affairs of the world.'"
    (Universal House of Justice: *Lights of Guidance*, pp. 626-627)

> **Perspectives to Consider**

One of the most challenging and often divisive areas for married couples is money—who earns it and how, who handles it, how does it get spent and by whom, what is wasteful, what is generous, what is stingy, and so on. *Before* marriage, it is wise to understand:

- Your financial resources and debts
- Discuss who will pay the bills (on time!)
- How you will structure the bank accounts
- What savings and investing patterns you want to have (including any for children's education)
- Whether someone else will help manage your money
- Whether you will develop and follow a budget
- How you will handle faith-related and charitable donations
- How you might handle a layoff, job loss, or other reduction in income
- Your expectations and preferences for the number of hours you each spend working each week
- How you might handle a job transfer
- Balancing and prioritizing education and career plans
- Balancing work and family life
- Your retirement plans
- Your commitment to having a will/trusts

How you view and handle money often has many layers to it that connect to your pasts, so it will assist you in discussing how you handle money in the present and in a marriage if you explore your **financial histories**. Does money mean security? Love? Freedom? Control? Power? Or were there instances that taught you lessons, or where you drew conclusions that affect how you view money today? Where a wife and husband have different conclusions about what money means based on past experiences, there could be disagreements between them over money. Some questions to start you thinking about this subject are below.

Your History With Money

- Were you taught to save or spend? Both?
- Have you had training in making wise investments?
- Did you ever steal money or anything else as a child? How was it handled?
- Did your parents trust or distrust banks?
- Did your grandmother (or other older relative) hide her money under the bed or in the freezer?
- Did a bully extort your lunch money from you? How was this handled?
- Were you taught to live and spend in the moment and not plan for the future?
- Were you taught to save everything for the future and not enjoy spending any money as you earn it?
- Were you taught that children should work for the family out of love and not be paid for it?
- Did you get an allowance? If so, how much? Did your friends get more or less? How did you feel about that?
- Do you think parents should pay all college expenses and not require their children to work during college?
- Do you think people over 18 should pay their expenses for everything and not count on parents for financial help?
- Did either of you have relatives who gave you large sums of money that affected your attitudes and spending habits?
- Were you required to work or did you choose to work once you were old enough? At what age? How did you manage your earnings?

Marriage Can Be Forever—Preparation Counts!

All of these things and more could cause you to look at money in different ways. Understanding the influence of the past on your attitudes and behavior involving money can help you with what you want to do going forward, which patterns you want to learn from your partner, and which new things you want to try together.

There are **many ways for you to earn your money**. You may be in high school or college and at the beginning of exploring the kind of work you want to do or the kind you want to be trained to do. You might be in your first job and have job changes ahead of you. You could be in an established career. The main point is that you need to have a livelihood. This can be in the arts, construction, teaching, homemaking, or medicine—almost anything you choose as a way to work and serve.

There may be issues for you to explore related to the **types of work you each do** or will do. This will include understanding whether you have any prejudice against your partner's profession or any concerns about what he or she does or is likely do in the future. Here are some examples:

- If he or she does manual labor, what do you think about him or her coming home dirty?
- A firefighter or police officer? What about his or her life being at risk?
- A TV broadcaster? What about the work hours? The public exposure?
- A medical worker? How would the shift work affect your home life?
- If one or both of you is in the armed forces, how would you handle relocating frequently and the possibility of your partner being involved in fighting? Are there religious beliefs either of you have that relate to this occupation?
- What if a job involves a lot of traveling? Shift work?
- Work that has moral or ethical issues for you?

Any of these job-related issues could strain a marriage and are best talked about ahead of time.

You will want to observe and understand the **work ethic** you each have. Is working important to you? How hard do you work at it? Do you work excessively (workaholic)? People have many reasons for working. These include income, power, financing vacations, self-esteem, status, the ability to be generous, the ability to buy symbols of wealth (large house, fancy car, etc.), to support children's education, and so on. It is best to understand what *motivates* you and your partner to work and earn a certain income and then to determine whether the *values* that underlie the motivations are ones that you would appreciate in a spouse.

Once someone has an income, they then **manage the money** in a variety of ways. You may set up a savings account, invest it, pay bills, give gifts, pay off debts, donate to charity, and much more. It takes skills to handle the money effectively, such as balancing a bank account, choosing wise investments, paying bills in a timely manner and in amounts that don't result in high interest payments, knowing what you can afford to spend, and so on. Handling money responsibly will contribute to peacefulness in your household. Are you confident in your ability to do this? Do you need to seek training? Would someone else need to assist you?

It is wise to understand your patterns **for spending** (or overspending) and how you think you would handle your collective income. For instance, you might each have your own discretionary funds to spend as you wish, or you might put all money in a joint account. In marriage, there are a multitude of issues that come up around property, insurance, wills, financial obligations, expenditures, and debts, all of which need to be handled responsibly and in unity. What are your thoughts at this stage?

You may also want to consider the values that influence how you spend your money. Some people are happy or accept having very little. Others start to show competitive behavior, buying what they see others buying. This might include the latest clothes, videogame, vehicle, home, and much more. What if trying to keep up with this standard required you to go into debt? What are your views about accumulating material things? How attached are you to them? What are your spiritual beliefs about buying material possessions?

Once you are working and you have enough money to handle basic expenses, Bahá'ís and people of other faiths are encouraged or required to **give donations to their faith and/or to charity**. Your life, family, and work are blessed by sharing part of your wealth. One of you, however, might be a random and spontaneous giver and the other a planned one. One of you may want to give large amounts and the other modest. You may be of different faiths and have different guidelines for giving. Or you could be on the same page. You will need to sort out whether consultation is required before either of you give money away or whether you are comfortable trusting each other's judgment. Does the amount make a difference? Does it matter where the donation goes?

Money brings up the qualities of **trust and trustworthiness** in every aspect. You may be treasurer of an organization, responsible for paying the family bills on time, have bank deposits or withdrawals to make, or a business payroll to meet. In all these cases, there are people counting on you to manage the money carefully, to not lose or steal it, and to be responsible for accurately accounting for it. If this trust is ever broken, it will be difficult to regain it. Consultation is a valuable skill that can assist you with maintaining trust (see Chapter 3). If you have any decisions to make or complex issues to handle when managing money, talking them through with someone else can help you in making wise and spiritually-based choices.

Coaching

⇒ Budgets are primarily a useful tool when they start as mutual agreements. Disaster can happen when one person in a family sets up a budget as a means of trying to force someone else to control his or her spending.

⇒ If you don't have financial skills, turn to experts or skilled others, perhaps in your families, for assistance. Think through whether you might get training yourselves so you have the necessary skills.

⇒ If one of you is not generating an income and/or is working at your home, you will need to be vigilant in ensuring that respect and equality are still present in your relationship. It will be wise to not assume this person will do all the housework or run the errands during the day.

⇒ Practicing generosity, creating abundance, and living in a spirit of confidence are much more empowering than living in a spirit of scarcity and loss. Prayer and meditation on these concepts will support you in making wise financial decisions.

Questions for Reflection and Discussion

Education/Training Plans

1. What are your plans for earning a living? For further education? How attached are you to these plans?
2. If you have further education planned, how will you finance it or pay off student loans?
3. Is one person going to have to delay or change his/her education/career plans for the spouse's career or for the family? How do you feel about doing this?
4. Are you both willing to relocate for a job/career? What are your feelings about it?
5. How might the equality of women and men be practiced and supported in making each of your education plans?

Earning Money/Income

1. What are your career goals?
2. If the man were to make a lot more money than the woman, would there be any sense that the man had priority in deciding how the money was spent—that to some degree more of the money was really "his?" Each of you should say how you think it would really feel for you as well as how you think it "ought" to be.
3. If the woman was to make more money than the man, how would you each feel?
4. Is either or both of you self-employed or business owners? Are there any concerns about how much time is involved in the business? How steady is the income? What would be the risks to the family finances if the business were to fail or go bankrupt?
5. If one or both of you worked at home, how would the home responsibilities be handled? How do you feel about this? Does the one who is at home all day do more or does it make no difference in dividing up responsibilities?
6. Would you take time off work for a Holy Day? What might prevent you from doing this?
7. Who would provide financial support for the family, both before and after there are children? How? Would it vary with circumstances? Such as?
8. Would you keep your money separate or combine it? Why? What are your issues about this? Are they realistic? Valid?
9. What guidelines are important for you about how to spend your money? Do you try to keep up with other people? Why? What if the two of you have different perspectives on this?
10. What is your understanding of the concept of "detachment" from material things? When is it a challenge for you to feel detached from them?
11. What hours do you work? Are there any concerns about schedules?
12. What do you like most about your work? What do you like least?
13. What is your work history? Have you had a lot of jobs? Been fired? Had to relocate for a new job?
14. How often do you work longer than an 8-hour day? More than a 5-day workweek? Overtime? How often do you work excessively to the exclusion of anyone and anything else (symptom of being a workaholic)? Does the amount you work ever bother other people?
15. What other sources of income do you have? Interest from savings? Investments? Property rents? Trust fund?
16. How would you handle a "windfall" such as an inheritance or winning a contest?

Money/Debts Brought to the Marriage

1. What is your financial status? What financial assets and debts would you bring to the marriage?
2. What do you want your financial condition to be before you enter into marriage?
3. What outstanding debts do you have? What are your patterns of going into debt? Are you now or have you ever been bankrupt?
4. Do you have good or bad credit?
5. How many credit cards do you have? What are the spending limits? What are the balances?
6. Are there traditions or laws about dowry in your culture, country, or faith? Will you follow them?
7. Laws vary about whether money a person has before marriage is still held by the person or is shared or transferred to the new spouse. What laws would apply to you?
8. How would you handle any debt incurred before the marriage?
9. What do you think about borrowing money? What about borrowing from family members? Do you have a written agreement with people you lend money to? What if they don't pay you back?
10. What do you think about lending money? What about lending it to family members?
11. Do you have a history of regularly overspending or spending money on unnecessary things? Are you an impulse spender?

Handling Finances

1. What is your history of handling finances? Doing budgeting? Saving? How would someone know that you were handling money responsibly?
2. Were there any issues involving handling money in previous relationships? If so, what were the problems? What have you learned/changed from it?
3. What is your approach to gift-giving to each other? To others?
4. How do you feel about your partner's integrity and trustworthiness?
5. What are your shopping patterns? How often? What do you buy? Do you comparison-shop?
6. Are you familiar with paying income and property taxes? Have you ever deliberately misreported items to change the amount of tax you owe? How do you expect to behave with these in the future?
7. Do you balance your checkbook? How do you use ATM machines?
8. What do you believe about carrying life insurance or property insurance? Do you carry them?
9. How would you describe yourself in relation to spending money on yourself and on others? Miserly, frugal, generous, impulsive, wasteful, and so on?
10. What if you were to become disabled? Die prematurely? What would happen to your income?
11. Would you pool all of your income, expenses, assets, and debts, or are there some of these that you would keep separate and account for separately? Would you both have access to bank accounts? Whose name(s) would be on the accounts? What if one spouse controls access to the money and is very stingy with it?
12. If you share accounts, would you have separate funds for entertainment/personal purchases, or would all money be pooled?
13. Who would manage the household and/or family income? What are individual and what are joint decisions?
14. How would you handle it if you suspected or realized that your spouse was irresponsible with money? What if he/she doesn't change in this matter?
15. What is the appropriate balance between generosity and frugality and between planning and spontaneity in spending money?
16. What is your desired standard of living? House? Car? Vacation? Gifts? Clothes?
17. How would you deal with having too little money to maintain your desired standard of living? When would you borrow, and when would you reduce your standard of living below comfort level, and how?
18. How much time is best for you take in deciding on financial commitments of various sizes, such as a house, a car, a stereo, a camera, clothing, CDs, or a book? Which of these would you need to consult with your spouse about first, and which ones wouldn't require mutual agreement? How would you decide about expenditures and budgeting?
19. How would you use credit? What is an excessive debt? What are the requirements for avoiding excessive debt? Would each of you have credit/debit cards in your own names?
20. Do you pay off your credit card bills each month or carry a balance? What affects your choices to do one or the other?
21. If you have a mortgage, how did you decide the terms for interest and length?
22. Do you have payments to make to ex-spouses or children, and are you honoring the obligations? Why or why not?
23. How do you handle investments? How would you handle them after marriage? What is your comfort level with investments that carry a risk of loss in capital? Do you have a long-term or short-term investment approach? Are you conservative or a risk-taker?
24. Do you have any history of gambling? If so, how has that affected your life? What steps have you taken to deal with it? [**Note:** Gambling can include excessive stock market speculation.]
25. Is there currently drug and/or alcohol abuse? How might that affect your finances?
26. Have you held positions, perhaps as the treasurer of an organization, where you were required to demonstrate your trustworthiness with other's money? What was the outcome?
27. Have you ever had an ethical disagreement with someone (for example, an employer or business partner) about how he/she handled money? About how you handled it? What was the outcome?

Marriage Can Be Forever—Preparation Counts!

28. What would you do if your parents or another family member became dependent on financial assistance from you? What if they wanted/needed to live with you? If others live with you, how do you then handle any financial assistance to them?
29. How would you feel about living on government assistance payments if it became necessary to do so?

Donations

1. What funds or charities would you donate to, who would make the donations, and how would the decisions be made?
2. Are you in agreement about how to determine regular and sacrificial donations to your faith?
3. How would you handle donations if only someone of that faith is allowed to contribute and you are interfaith and have a joint bank account? [**Note:** Only Bahá'ís can give to the Bahá'í Funds.]
4. Bahá'ís pay Huqúqu'lláh, something that brings blessings to the life of the donor. It involves giving a percentage of income after some expenses and assets are deducted. How and when will you consult on calculating it? Will you pay as individuals or as a couple? What categories of assets and expenses will you want to exclude when calculating it? (Activity 3 will assist with this.)

Activities

1. Pray, meditate, reflect, and write in your journal about the attitudes and beliefs you have about money and you perceive your partner has about it.

2. Use Worksheet 26A to do a preliminary budget as if you were married.

3. Use Worksheet 26B to calculate your current assets, liabilities, and net worth.

4. Use Worksheet 26C to explore your views of necessities and luxuries.

5. What have you observed about your ability or inability to discuss financial issues with your partner?
   _____
   _____

6. Plan and carry out a shopping trip with a specific purpose (one you have a genuine interest in) and a set amount of money. Determine together who contributes what amounts of money to the activity. Were you tempted to spend more? Could you shop effectively and peacefully together? Is this important to you or not? What other observations did you have?
   _____
   _____
   _____
   _____

Chapter 26 – Money In, Money Out: Earning, Budgeting, and Spending   225

Date: _____

Worksheet 26A: Preparing a Budget

DIRECTIONS: Create a preliminary budget as if you were married.

Worksheets may be printed from www.claricomm.com/publishing

What is your monthly income?
- His _____
- Hers _____
- Other _____
- Total _____ =**A**

What are your monthly payments on your debts?

	His	Hers
Car loan	_____	/ _____
Credit card	_____	/ _____
Mortgage	_____	/ _____
Student loan	_____	/ _____
Other	_____	/ _____
Total	_____	/ _____ =**B**

Combined total (B) = _____
(Use this below)

Budget: What would you expect your monthly expenses to be?
- Donations _____
- Savings[1] _____
- Debt payments _____ (B – from above)
- Housing _____
- Groceries _____
- Utilities _____
- Car expenses _____
- Insurance _____ (life, car, home, etc.)
- Phone(s) _____
- Medical _____
- Children _____
- Clothing _____
- Entertainment _____
- Gifts _____
- Hair _____
- Fitness Clubs _____
- Vacations _____
- Other _____
- Total _____ =**C**

━━━ Balance Your Budget ━━━

What will it take for A to be more than C?
_____
_____

What concerns, if any, do you have in looking at the numbers? How will you handle these?
_____
_____

---

[1] Consider long-term retirement; medium term, such as down payment on a house; and short term for building up a safety margin.

Marriage Can Be Forever—Preparation Counts!

Date: _____

Worksheet 26B: Calculating Net Worth

DIRECTIONS: Calculate your current assets, liabilities, and net worth by adding what you each have together.

Worksheets may be printed from www.claricomm.com/publishing

Assets

- Current vehicle(s) value _____
- House/Property value _____
- Business asset value _____
- Retirement funds _____
- Investments _____
- Bank/Savings accounts _____
- Jewelry/artwork _____
- Furniture _____
- Books _____
- Other: _____ _____
- Other: _____ _____
- Other: _____ _____
- Other: _____ _____
- Other: _____ _____

Liabilities

- Student loan _____
- Credit card balance _____
- Mortgage balance _____
- Other: _____ _____
- Other: _____ _____
- Other: _____ _____
- Other: _____ _____

Assets - Liabilities = Net Worth _____

What concerns, if any, do you have in looking at the numbers? How would you handle these?

_____
_____
_____

Marriage Can Be Forever—Preparation Counts!

Date: _____

Worksheet 26C: Distinguishing Necessities and Luxuries

DIRECTIONS: Many couples have different views about spending money and what counts as a necessity or a luxury. For Bahá'ís, this is a necessary distinction to make for figuring Huqúqu'lláh, a payment made that brings blessings to the life of the giver. It involves giving a percentage of income after some expenses and assets are deducted. Additionally, if one of you spends money on what the other considers a luxury, there could be disharmony between you, particularly when money is tight. Complete this worksheet to help you understand your views of each. (You may require additional paper.)

Worksheets may be printed from www.claricomm.com/publishing

1. Brainstorm a list of all the things you spend/could spend money on.
   _____
   _____
   _____
   _____
   _____
   _____
   _____

2. Then divide the list into necessities and luxuries below. Complete this list together:

Necessities	**Luxuries**
_____	_____
_____	_____
_____	_____
_____	_____
_____	_____
_____	_____
_____	_____
_____	_____
_____	_____
_____	_____

   Are there any areas of significant disagreement?
   _____
   _____

   How will you resolve them?
   _____
   _____

3. How did you each feel about discussing this topic? Did any concerns or anxieties arise?
   _____
   _____

Marriage Can Be Forever—Preparation Counts!

Home?

My things in scattered disarray
befuddle me in searching
for the one thing that I knew
I'd packed so carefully

And boxes filled and piled
daunting in their cardboard
holding treasures and
the junk that time too short
prevented leaving well behind

I'm lost a bit—what place
is this? His or mine or ours?
Is the challenge integrating
or is it really now creating
something very new?

It's not quite home as yet—
a place where heart feels
peaceful and serene
although it's getting close
when his waiting arms
enfold me.

~ Susanne Mariella Alexander

CHAPTER 27 – Who Will Cook Tonight?: Your Future Home

Focus Points

- Blending personal possessions in one home
- Household habits
- Quality of housekeeping
- Cleaning
- Division of labor
- Food: Shopping, cooking, serving, mealtimes, and cleaning up
- Hospitality

A Couple's Story

James and Lindsay decide to cook dinner for his parents one evening, using his parents' kitchen. They decide on the menu and shop together for the groceries. Sondra and Marvin agree to stay out of the kitchen while the couple cooks.

"Wait, don't put that spice in yet," says James to Lindsay. "It'll be too weak by the time it all cooks."

"Okay, that's the third time you've said something about how I'm doing the soup," says Lindsay. "I think this would work better if we each took charge of part of the meal instead of both of us trying to do all of it."

"Hmmm…sounds good," says James. "What about if you do the meat and vegetables and I'll finish the soup and do the salad?"

"Okay, that works better for me," says Lindsay.

Quotes for Guidance

❋ My home is the home of peace. My home is the home of joy and delight. My home is the home of laughter and exultation. Whosoever enters through the portals of this home, must go out with gladsome heart. This is the home of light; whosoever enters here must become illumined….
   ('Abdu'l-Bahá: *Compilation of Compilations, Vol. I*, p. 397)

❋ The home should be orderly and well-organized.
   ('Abdu'l-Bahá: *Lights of Guidance*, p. 219)

❋ …the young Bahá'ís in every city should make a point of keeping in touch with local youth activities and clubs…. Above all they should set a high example to them; chastity, politeness, friendliness, hospitality, joyous optimism about the ultimate future happiness and well-being of mankind….
   (On behalf of Shoghi Effendi: *Lights of Guidance*, p. 629)

Marriage Can Be Forever—Preparation Counts!

Perspectives to Consider

Part of setting up a household would involve the **blending of each of your personal possessions**, incorporating wedding gifts, and purchasing new things. It means figuring out what possessions you keep, what you get rid of, what is for your use only, and what can be shared. If you were going into a place where only one of you lived before, how could the new person feel as if it is his or her home, too? There might be artwork or pictures on the walls of both of your previous homes. How would you now blend them together? You could be moving from a college dorm with posters on the wall and be facing bare walls in your new home. How would you decide on decorations?

Different household habits can be a constant irritant. How are you when it comes to neatness or sloppiness? What is your clutter style—do you accumulate, collect, toss, or organize? What is important to keep and what could you live without? Once all your possessions were in one place and some disposed of, who would feel surrounded by clutter? Who would feel deprived of needed possessions? If one of you would perpetually pick up after the other, then there would likely be resentment simmering under the surface. If one of you can't stand a speck of dust on a table at any time, compulsive dusting might become an irritant to your partner. You might find it helpful to visit your parents' homes together and then talk about how their housekeeping patterns have affected yours. Be clear about where you can compromise and adjust your standards of housekeeping and where you can't. If one or both of you doesn't know how to do particular cleaning tasks, you might teach the other, or both of you would learn how to do them together. You may have to ask someone for help who does know how if you can't figure it out.

Cleaning is a regular household task—you may already be good at this, or you may have to learn how to do it well. It will be good for you to agree on the general goal of how clean you would want to keep your house and who would do what. At times, you might have to shift these responsibilities and share them because of a social gathering at your house or because of your partner's work or responsibility load. One might dust and the other vacuum; one could do the bathroom and one the kitchen.

Old and perhaps unconscious habits and patterns of traditional **division of labor** based on inequality between women and men may come up as an issue in household management, and both of you may inadvertently perpetuate them. While you would probably sort out who does what based on who is best at it or who wants to learn to become better at it, there may be times when you make traditional assumptions that are not in the best interest of your marriage or example for your children. Recognize too, that if you have been trained to do tasks along traditional lines, that it may be good for the husband to learn to clean toilets and for the wife to learn to fix the lawnmower, for instance. How would you come to the awareness that you need to make a shift to reflect equality? How would you address it?

Household management will include **food**—how you shop, prepare, and serve it. And who cleans up the kitchen afterward. All of this will be affected by any particular diet you are following, food allergies, your exercise level, your commitment to your health, and so on. Grocery shopping can be time consuming, and some find it fun while some don't. Even if one of you agrees to do the shopping, the other might assist from time to time. If either or both of you are inexperienced cooks, you might want to take cooking lessons or buy a good cookbook. If you can afford it, you may eat out or hire a cook (or go to a lot of potlucks!). Would you both cook, or just one of you? Who would cook on what night? What is shared and what is separate?

Issues will come up regarding food preparation—do you wash vegetables first, do you chop or grate the carrots, or do you tear or cut the lettuce. What is thrown away, and what is kept? Does one or both of you prefer composting? If one of you is vegetarian and one is not, how would you manage the meals? Would the vegetarian object to meat in the house? If either of you have special food needs, how will you manage this and how will the other feel about accommodating it?

Talk about your mealtime expectations. Some couples and families are committed to having most meals together around a table. Others are happy with everyone fixing meals on their own when they get hungry. Some start the meal with a prayer, and some don't. For some, family meal time is for sharing the day's activities and interesting happenings. For others, it is a quiet time to simply re-nourish their bodies. How do you feel about answering the phone during mealtimes (for personal or business reasons)? Is the TV on during meals? Are you comfortable with others being invited to join meals, or are meals just for family members? Do invitations need to be planned, or can they be spontaneous and last-minute?

One of the most fun or most stressful activities you will do as a married couple is **hosting others in your home**. Hospitality is encouraged in Bahá'í homes and spiritually-based marriages, and there are many opportunities to open your home to friends, family, and people you would like to get to know better. How comfortable you each feel with others in your home will affect how comfortable the guests feel. Your ability to be welcoming can touch the hearts of those who visit you.

Setting up a mutual household can be fun and stressful both. You won't really know all the challenges until you do it. When they arise, remember to pray and consult about them, determine where you can compromise, and where you can make adjustments. It takes time for all household details to feel harmonious.

Coaching

⇒ Sometimes a good motto to follow is, "He who has the need, does the deed." But don't do this to excess!

⇒ Setting up and maintaining a household will require flexibility, compromise, and consultation. Some things you will decide are very important, and other things you will decide are minor. You may not agree on these things completely—consultation, patience, and respect will help you understand on e another better and learn manageable compromises. Consider the spiritual qualities and principles of cleanliness and orderliness as you discuss how you would handle what needs to be done.

⇒ Be aware when something another person does or is likely to do constantly irritates you. If you decide it's something that really bothers you, it will be best to have frank and loving consultation about it in a way that doesn't make him/her feel defensive.

⇒ You might find it wise to agree how you will react to and handle experiments in food preparation that don't turn out very well. An inexperienced cook may need gentle feedback and a minimum of criticism while he or she builds confidence. Ridicule may result in the food being deposited on your head ☺.

> **? Questions for Reflection and Discussion**

Household Use and Management

1. Where would you want to live? Where could you not stand to live? What part of the country? What part of the world? City, suburb, town, village, country, farm, or wilderness?
2. How would you divide responsibilities in the home?
3. How would you organize your lives, while meshing your schedules and individual needs?
4. Are you compatible regarding your needs for personal space in a house? Do you need your own offices? Will you need a place for your own things that is off-limits to the other? Do you need a guestroom so guests aren't in your living area? How flexible can you be about not having enough space and for how long?
5. When you are done eating, what do you usually do with your dishes? Do you leave them where you ate or leave them on the kitchen counter? How long before they get washed or put in the dishwasher and by whom? Who puts them away when they are clean? How do you feel about having a dirty/messy kitchen? How do you define dirty/messy?
6. Do you typically leave things lying where you were done with them or put them away promptly? How does the other feel about this?
7. What do you do with your dirty clothes when you take them off? How is your laundry usually done? By whom?
8. What is your clutter tolerance level?
9. What temperatures are comfortable for you in the house during the different seasons?
10. Do you like the sheets and blankets tucked or untucked around your feet?
11. How do you feel about the toilet seat being left up or down?
12. How will you react if your partner regularly leaves the cap off the toothpaste? Or squeezes the tube in a different place than you? Would you prefer having your own tubes?
13. How do you feel about sharing or not sharing bathroom items, such as toothbrushes, toothpaste, towels, and washcloths?
14. How do you feel about bathroom privacy? Do you always close the door? Can you be in the bathroom together? Will you need to be alone no matter what you are doing?
15. How long do you shower and spend in the bathroom? Would this inconvenience your partner?
16. Do you know how to clean well? How do you define "clean"? Who would do the cleaning? How thoroughly do you clean?
17. How would household repairs be handled?
18. How are you at taking and conveying telephone messages for other people?
19. What "pet peeves" do you have about living with someone? What have family/roommates told you that you do that would be pet peeves/annoyances for others?
20. What strong needs do you have when living with someone?

Food

1. How do you feel about grocery shopping? Who is likely to do this task?
2. How do you decide what to buy at the grocery? When you shop, do you follow a list? Are there problems that arise if you don't?
3. How good a cook are you? Do you enjoy similar foods? Are you conservative or adventuresome with food? Do you like to cook? How are you at following recipes?
4. How do you want dinners to be prepared? Who will cook them? How fancy; how many courses?
5. What times of day do you like to eat your meals, and when are the major meals of the day?

6. What kinds of food do you like?
7. Are you vegan or vegetarian? If so, why (moral grounds, health, etc.)? Are either of you considering a change in this? How strongly do you feel about this? Do you differ on this? How will you reconcile this, if you differ?
8. What limits or concerns do you have when you choose food? How strict are you about these? How does this fit in a marriage?
9. Do either of you have food allergies or sensitivities? How do you handle them? Do you have any severe reactions?
10. What do you think about the use of vitamins or other supplements?
11. What family histories of specific foods or types of food preparations might affect your meals?
12. Do you have any eating disorders or are there any in your families? How might this be an issue? How would it affect food purchases, storage, and preparation?
13. Do either of you participate in a religious Fast? How would this affect the other?
14. How often would you eat out? Are there any concerns about money, time, or health related to eating out?
15. Do either of you have health concerns with junk food? How much of it can you tolerate/accept in the house?
16. How do you feel about eating leftover food from previous meals?
17. How would you organize your lives to accommodate your preferences for being together or not at mealtimes?
18. Do you watch TV during meals? Answer the phone? Would you expect to still do these things after marrying?
19. Would your children eat with you or before you?
20. Would everyone eat the same thing, or would the preparer have different foods for different tastes? Are you a picky eater? How would that affect the other?

Hospitality

1. What do you think about hosting individuals in your home? Does it differ if they are family or non-family?
2. How do you feel about overnight guests? Any limits on how long they could stay? Are there any who would not be welcome? Is it different if it is family or not?
3. What about hosting events in your home? What size crowd would you be comfortable with?
4. How often would you prefer to entertain? On what occasions? How often?
5. Who would prepare the home for company, and what preparations would be needed?
6. Are you introverts or extroverts? Would you be socially compatible in having people in your home?
7. Do you need to have every inch of the house clean and tidy before anyone comes over, or are you relaxed about how the house looks? Can you easily handle drop-in guests?
8. Do you like to decorate for guests?
9. How do you show people they are welcome? (Examples: greeting them at the door; not do anything else around the house while the guests are present, etc.)
10. Could you balance each other in getting things ready for guests with each of you doing part of the work?
11. Is being an attentive host important to you? Do you prefer to let people fend for themselves? How would you host as a couple?
12. What atmosphere do you like to create for guests?
13. What family occasions might they expect you to host? Are there any issues with this? What would you want to host?
14. How do you handle hosting/entertaining? Is it fun? Stressful? Difficult? Easy? Wonderful? All of the above? What do you find the most challenging?
15. Are you compatible in offering hospitality to others?

Marriage Can Be Forever—Preparation Counts!

Activities

1. Pray, meditate, reflect, and write in your journal about what a spiritually-based household looks and feels like?

2. In Worksheet 27A, identify your experiences and lessons learned in sharing living space with someone else.

3. Volunteer to clean and organize someone's apartment or home together. It may be one of your own homes or that of a friend or relative. What did you observe about how you work together and how you approached the various tasks?
   _____
   _____

4. Share photographs of each other's living areas on a typical day (especially if you are geographically separate). What do you notice?
   _____
   _____

5. Plan and cook a meal together for friends. Try it at each other's place and at someplace neutral and see if it is different in different locations. What did you observe about how you worked together?
   _____
   _____

6. Design your dream home together using the computer or art supplies. Do you appreciate similar features?
   _____
   _____
   _____

7. Discuss the following:

WHO WILL DO THE "DIRTY WORK?" HOW WILL EVERYTHING ELSE GET DONE EQUITABLY AND PEACEFULLY?

Marriage Can Be Forever—Preparation Counts!

Date: _____

Worksheet 27A: Experiences in Sharing Living Space

DIRECTIONS: Identify your experiences and lessons learned in sharing living space with someone else. This could be a sibling, parent, other relative, college roommate, or anyone else. The experience does not need to be recent to be applicable.

1. With whom have you shared a living space or home?

   _____
   _____
   _____

2. What has been difficult about living with someone else?

   _____
   _____
   _____

3. What worked well about living with someone else?

   _____
   _____
   _____

4. What would the person you lived with say about living with you, both positively and negatively? What about regarding your housekeeping and cleaning habits?

   _____
   _____

5. What skills do you think are important in living with someone else peacefully and successfully?

   _____
   _____
   _____

6. What might be difficult for you in living with a husband/wife?

   _____
   _____
   _____

7. What do you look forward to in living with a husband/wife?

   _____
   _____
   _____

To My Love

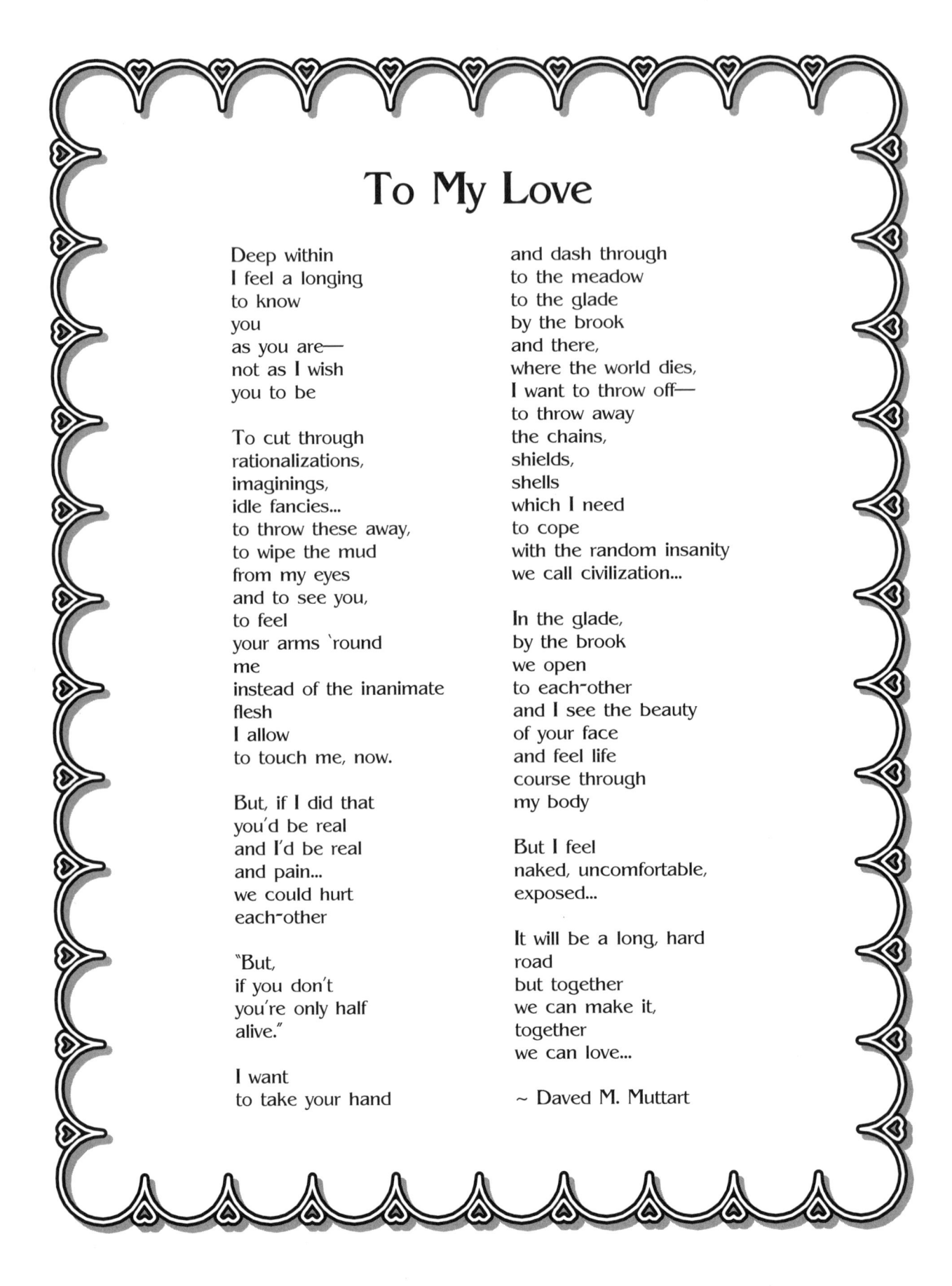

Deep within
I feel a longing
to know
you
as you are—
not as I wish
you to be

To cut through
rationalizations,
imaginings,
idle fancies...
to throw these away,
to wipe the mud
from my eyes
and to see you,
to feel
your arms 'round
me
instead of the inanimate
flesh
I allow
to touch me, now.

But, if I did that
you'd be real
and I'd be real
and pain...
we could hurt
each-other

"But,
if you don't
you're only half
alive."

I want
to take your hand
and dash through
to the meadow
to the glade
by the brook
and there,
where the world dies,
I want to throw off—
to throw away
the chains,
shields,
shells
which I need
to cope
with the random insanity
we call civilization...

In the glade,
by the brook
we open
to each-other
and I see the beauty
of your face
and feel life
course through
my body

But I feel
naked, uncomfortable,
exposed...

It will be a long, hard
road
but together
we can make it,
together
we can love...

~ Daved M. Muttart

CHAPTER 28 – Rocks on the Path: Handling the Tough Stuff

NOTE: This chapter only briefly touches on many serious issues. You may wish to seek further information and assistance to ensure proper handling of them.

Focus Points

- Tests, difficulties, illness, and stress in close relationships and marriage
- The denial factor
- The importance of knowing your partner's history and present issues
- Spiritually handling problems and illnesses
- Professional and spiritual counseling, medical care, and other assistance
- How tests can strengthen character

A Couple's Story

Lindsay rushes to the hospital to meet James. His father has been admitted with another heart attack. She reaches out and hugs him and Sondra in the waiting room.

"How is he doing?" she asks.

"He's still alive—it was a mild one. They are doing a procedure to see if they can open up one of his clogged arteries," says James. "I'm glad you're here…and I appreciate your support. So does Mom."

"Just tell me what you need me to do," says Lindsay, reaching out to give him a hug.

Quotes for Guidance

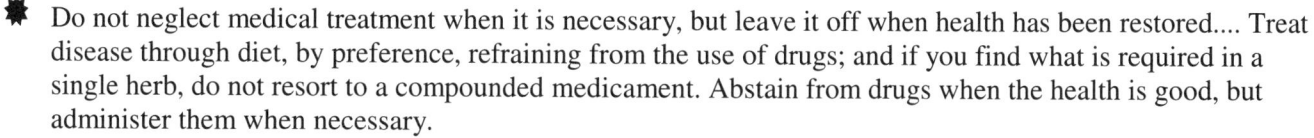

✻ Do not neglect medical treatment when it is necessary, but leave it off when health has been restored.... Treat disease through diet, by preference, refraining from the use of drugs; and if you find what is required in a single herb, do not resort to a compounded medicament. Abstain from drugs when the health is good, but administer them when necessary.
(Bahá'u'lláh: *Compilation of Compilations—Health and Healing*, Vol. I, p. 460)

✻ The friends of God must be adorned with the ornament of justice, equality, kindness and love. As they do not allow themselves to be the object of cruelty and transgression, in like manner they should not allow such tyranny to visit the handmaidens of God.... No Bahá'í husband should ever beat his wife, or subject her to any form of cruel treatment; to do so would be an unacceptable abuse of the marriage relationship and contrary to the Teachings of Bahá'u'lláh.
(Bahá'u'lláh, quoted by the Universal House of Justice: An unpublished letter January 24, 1993, to an individual)

Marriage Can Be Forever—Preparation Counts!

❋ Be thou not sad, neither be thou unhappy; although the divine tests are violent, yet are they conducive to the life of the soul and the heart. The more often the pure gold is thrown into the furnace of test, the greater will become its purity and brilliancy and it will acquire a new splendor and brightness.
   ('Abdu'l-Bahá: *Tablets of 'Abdu'l-Bahá Vol. 2*, pp. 302-303)

❋ ...prayer and fasting is the cause of awakening and mindfulness and conducive to protection and preservation from tests.
   ('Abdu'l-Bahá: *Tablets of 'Abdu'l-Bahá Vol. 3*, pp. 683-684)

❋ There are two ways of healing sickness, material means and spiritual means. The first is by the use of remedies, of medicines; the second consists in praying to God and in turning to Him. Both means should be used and practiced.
   Illness caused by physical accident should be treated with medical remedies; those which are due to spiritual causes disappear through spiritual means. Thus an illness caused by affliction, fear, nervous impressions, will be healed by spiritual rather than by physical treatment. Hence, both kinds of remedies should be considered. Moreover, they are not contradictory, and thou shouldst accept the physical remedies as coming from the mercy and favor of God, who hath revealed and made manifest medical science so that His servants may profit from this kind of treatment also. Thou shouldst give equal attention to spiritual treatments, for they produce marvelous effects.
   ('Abdu'l-Bahá: *Bahá'í World Faith*, pp. 375-376)

❋ If a Bahá'í woman suffers abuse or is subjected to rape by her husband, she has the right to turn to the Spiritual Assembly for assistance and counsel, or to seek legal protection. Such abuse would gravely jeopardize the continuation of the marriage, and could well lead to a condition of irreconcilable antipathy.
   (Universal House of Justice: An unpublished letter January 24, 1993, to an individual believer)

❋ It is difficult to imagine a more reprehensible perversion of human conduct than the sexual abuse of children, which finds its most debased form in incest.... A parent who is aware that the marriage partner is subjecting a child to such sexual abuse should not remain silent, but must take all necessary measures, with the assistance of the Spiritual Assembly or civil authorities if necessary, to bring about an immediate cessation of such grossly immoral behavior, and to promote healing and therapy.
   (Universal House of Justice: *Developing Distinctive Bahá'í Communities*, 15.27)

❋ Neither you nor your husband should hesitate to continue consulting professional marriage counselors, individually and together if possible, and also to take advantage of the supportive counseling which can come from wise and mature friends. Non-Bahá'í counseling can be useful but it is usually necessary to temper it with Bahá'í insight.
   (On behalf of the Universal House of Justice: *Preserving Bahá'í Marriages*, p. 28)

Perspectives to Consider

In the flush of romance, it might be easy to believe that you will never experience trials and tribulations. This rosy belief can blind you to already existing problems in your partner or ones that are highly likely to arise later. And *it does not work to believe that the problems will just go away with marriage*. They don't. In fact, they often become worse, because the person was hiding issues during the courtship (or the issue wasn't triggered and didn't surface).

There are many tests, difficulties, illnesses, and stresses that come up in life, and this book can neither address them all, nor solve them. When the need arises, turn to the Bahá'í Writings or the scripture of your faith for guidance on the subject. You may need to seek professional or spiritual counseling or get medical help. Also identify respected others such as family or friends to consult with about the issues. Whether you are experiencing/observing issues now or not, **you do need to be aware of some of the tests, difficulties, and stresses that can particularly affect a marriage relationship**, talking through or seeking guidance about whether the issue currently exists in your relationship or is likely to occur in the future. If so, how will you handle it? Or...are there issues present that you know now you don't want to handle, and you want to stop considering marrying this person?

You won't really know your strengths and weaknesses until the moment a test comes and you evaluate your response to it. However, it is possible to get a sense of each other's attitudes, beliefs, and past behaviors. Explore the role of prayer, community, the Spiritual Assembly, religious or secular counselors (for Bahá'ís, this may include Auxiliary Board members or their assistants), support groups, and help from each other in handling whatever challenge comes up.

Many religious books address the purpose of, the source of, and the solutions to tests, and they include guidance that address illness, healing, and obtaining help for relationships that are breaking down. There are spiritual qualities and actions that can support you during tests; such as, faith, confidence, strength, resolution, prayer, studying, accepting the Will of God, steadfastness, detachment, obedience, patience, perseverance, spiritual transformation, apology, forgiveness, teaching others about God, meditation, and consultation.

Unfortunately, you may automatically **resist or deny** that there is a problem going on, either in yourself or in someone you are close to. It can be a protective but potentially counterproductive measure to guard against the pain of dealing with something difficult. Overcoming that denial is critical both for you and your partner, because it makes it possible for you to seek out and accept help. Overcoming denial will also allow you to determine if it wise and best for you to be married in the circumstances.

Some people struggle with **depression, are bi-polar, have anxiety attacks, or have some other condition**, and may or may not be taking the appropriate medication. **Mental illness** comes in a variety of forms and severities. Do you understand the problems? (Talking to a doctor might help you understand your own or your partners condition.) Can you live with them in a marriage? What if one of you becomes suicidal or has been previously? How have you or might you handle this? What if there is a threat of suicide when the idea of breaking off the relationship comes up? Will you/do you have enough strength to go for help, whether the problem is yours or your partner's? It can be easy for the partner of someone who is depressed to also lose his or her joyfulness in living. It is best to be clear about any symptoms or diagnosis of mental illness and their implications before considering marrying. You may choose to go ahead, but it will be with an understanding of the ramifications of doing so.

One set of problems that can test a relationship is the range of **addictions, substance abuse, and disorders** people can have related to alcohol, illegal and prescription drugs, food, sex, gambling, and so on. These all tend to pull people away from God, even though they are tests that need to be handled with prayer, consultation, and confidence in God's assistance and healing. Look at your family histories regarding these conditions, whether they currently exist and how they are being handled. Is the addiction or problem being acknowledged or denied? Have either of you participated in support groups to assist with the issue? For how long? Successfully? Have you or are either or both of you getting counseling? You will want to understand the prognosis, the risk of relapse, and the emotional, financial, and household issues that arise with these issues. For the person who has the condition/illness, there may be ongoing struggles with relapse, hospitalization, counseling, and so on. For both of you, you may need to dispose of leftover prescriptions so they aren't taken inappropriately, not buy certain binge foods, avoid certain people or places, or take other actions that support managing addictive tendencies. Talk through how you might handle a relapse and what your boundaries are, especially if any activity is against civil or Bahá'í law.

Beyond addictions, there can be many **illnesses or accidents** that arise and cause restricted physical activity for a while or temporary or permanent physical or mental disability. These are very difficult tests for the person directly affected, and you will need to take advantage of whatever medical and spiritual support is available.

Marriage Can Be Forever—Preparation Counts!

There is also an effect on the spouse in these circumstances. Even when you know that the affected person's soul is still the same, living daily with someone in this condition can be very stressful and can cause marriages to fail. Your marriage vow and the level of your commitment become key sustaining factors at this point. What is your tolerance level to illness? Your own? Family members'? Talk through what you might do to handle these situations, what adjustments you might be willing to make, and how they might affect your relationship.

One of you may have an **illness or disability** that restricts you in some way. If you are in a wheelchair or partially paralyzed, how might this affect everything from household chores to sex? What about children? How well are you as the disabled partner managing your disability physically, emotionally, and spiritually? How is it affecting your relationships? Is either of you severely allergic to pets? How might this affect animals one of you already owns?

Smoking is another health issue and potential test to a relationship. Smoking is discouraged in the Bahá'í Faith due to a commitment to cleanliness and health, but it is not forbidden. Society is beginning to understand the many harmful health effects of smoking, and new laws are starting to restrict where smoking is allowed. If one of you smokes, do you understand the negative effect on your body and on the people around you? Talk through the implications of exposure to second-hand smoke, whether smoking would happen in your shared home, and whether it would be okay with you if guests smoke in or around your home. If there are family members who are not able or willing to be around smoke, how might smoking in your home affect relationships and hospitality?

Tests can also arise from your own **personal choices and actions**. These can include infidelity, emotional dependence, money mismanagement, and abusive behavior of all kinds. Talk through your personal histories, how to prevent unwise actions, and how to handle issues that arise. You need to know what your boundaries are, what you will and will not live with, what you can forgive and put behind you, and what you can't. Whether you have children or not should be a factor in the discussion, both in protecting them and in providing them with positive examples.

Issues arise in intimate relationships when one or both partners have experienced past **sexual abuse**. If you were abused or raped as a child or teen, or if you have experienced abuse or rape as an adult, it will likely affect how you interact with each other throughout your marriage and child rearing, as well as including how you respond to intimacy of all kinds. Explore what you can do to support healing, your counseling needs, and whether there has been enough healing for you to be in a marital relationship. The other partner must explore and understand how the abuse has affected him/her and if you can live with his/her reactions/behavior, because the effects of sexual abuse and issues can be long-lasting. If either of you has raped, sexually coerced, or abused the other (or anyone else), it is highly questionable whether you can trust each other enough to establish a healthy marriage.

A sexual issue that is prevalent in society is that of **homosexuality**. Perhaps there have been homosexual encounters or relationships in your past…how is this affecting you now? How would this affect your ability to be in a heterosexual marriage? [The Bahá'í Teachings prohibit sexual activity outside of marriage, whether the activity is homosexual or heterosexual.]

Then there are the tests that arise from **uncontrollable external sources**. Your parents may need full-time care, a storm might destroy your home, a thief might steal your car, floods might threaten your town or village, you might be sued, or a neighbor's behavior might be consistently loud or annoying. You might talk through a variety of scenarios, how you might handle them, and what you might put into place to assist you in coping with them. This could include appropriate insurance or joining a neighborhood association.

Although you cannot plan for every possible eventuality in your lives, you can get a sense of each other's character in difficult circumstances and how you might **respond to challenges** that come up. Some people handle tests by turning to God and prayer, some brood, some swear, some retreat into substance abuse, some strike out, some turn to friends, some run away, some become assertive advocates, some cry, some become immobile, some look for solutions, some resist and try to change things back the way they were. Gaining an understanding of probable reactions will help you to better understand each other's character, and whether you are compatible as life partners.

It is also important to recognize that a negative background is not necessarily a barrier if you have risen above it, and you have effectively learned and grown from it. Everyone encounters difficulties and has frailties. **Human beings are always capable of transformation—they can and do change.** Regaining wholeness, reclaiming chastity, finding a healthy balance, and more are all possibilities. Mistakes can be sacred learning experiences. However, a dreadful background or great mistakes from **the past must be given due weight**, and you must both recognize that threads of the past will likely affect your marriage to some degree. It's important to avoid wishful thinking that someone will change and instead use a rational thought process to determine if, in fact, someone has changed enough and is ready and able to create a healthy marriage.

> When you have a tough break, ask yourself, "What can I learn from this? How can I be better prepared to handle a situation like this in the future?" Will the "fortress" of your marriage be strong enough to handle tests of all kinds?

Coaching

⇒ Know you and your families' complete medical histories and the implications of the histories (include any history of psychological problems). You may be wise to talk directly with your partner's family members.

⇒ Listen to your intuition giving you warning signs and avoid thinking, "It will all be better after we get married." Marriage doesn't make problems go away. Sometimes, living in close personal space with someone actually accentuates or exacerbates problems. What are you observing that concerns you?

⇒ If friends or family are aware of your partner's problems, and they don't want to share the information out of desire to avoid backbiting or gossip, it is best for them to share the information directly with a Spiritual Assembly, clergy member, or spiritual counselor (such as an Auxiliary Board member or assistant, for Bahá'ís) and allow them to discuss the matter with you.

⇒ Find support groups, counselors, books, and literature that can give you facts about the situation. Don't use information from your partner as the only source of information.

⇒ Know that marriage is neither a cure-all nor a rescue mission.

⇒ Bonding happens through a variety of shared experiences. It may be unwise, however, to rely on bonding that has happened primarily during a test or tragedy—a resulting marriage may be based on a feeling of gratitude toward someone because he or she helped and supported you during a crisis, something unlikely to sustain a long-term relationship.

? Questions for Reflection and Discussion

Physical Health and Disease

1. Have you had a recent, complete physical examination? What were the results?
2. Do you have similar commitments to maintaining health/exercise?
3. How frequently do you use alcohol? Illegal drugs? Have there been or are there incidents related to drugs or alcohol use in the past or present? If so, what steps are you taking to address the issues?
4. Are there any other issues of addiction or substance/food/other abuse in the past or present?
5. Have you been tested for sexually transmitted diseases (STDs) and HIV/AIDS? Are you clear of disease? If not, how will you handle this?
6. Do you have physical or mental disabilities? How do these affect your life and activities?
7. Are there allergies to pets or food that could be a challenge?
8. What makes you anxious? What are your symptoms?
9. What causes you to feel highly stressed? How do you act? How do others describe you when you are stressed?
10. Have you ever been assessed, diagnosed, or treated for a psychological condition or mental illness? What was the outcome?
11. Do you smoke? If so, will you:
    - Smoke in the house?
    - Smoke in front of the children?
    - Smoke in the car?
    - Smoke when guests or family are present?
    - Allow others to smoke in your house?
    - Expect to smoke in other people's houses

Past History

1. What is your history of illnesses or hospitalizations?
2. What was the frequency of violence in your home growing up? Toward a parent? A sibling? Yourself?
3. Have you ever been abused? Verbally? Emotionally? Physically? Sexually? What were the circumstances and frequency? What have you done to handle/address this?
4. Have you ever been abusive? Verbally? Emotionally? Physically? Sexually? What were the circumstances and frequency? What have you done to handle/address this?
5. What is the family history of diseases such as breast cancer, heart disease, diabetes, alcoholism, genetic abnormalities, etc.? Have you had or do you have them? How has the family handled them?
6. What is your history of criminal activity? Your family's?
7. What is your history of suicide attempts? Your family's?
8. What is your history of depression or other mental illnesses? Your family's?
9. Has anyone close to you ever died? How did you handle it?

Handling Tests and Difficulties

1. What are you observing in your partner and/or your partner's family that is of concern to you?
2. What would you do if your spouse became verbally, emotionally, physically, or sexually abusive to you? To others?
3. How would you handle taking care of aging parents? Infirm siblings?
4. How would you handle it if children or stepchildren are/become disabled or ill?
5. How might you handle infidelity in your relationship?
6. How have you handled past crisis experiences, individually and together?
7. Are you open to marital or other kinds of counseling, group therapy, or support groups if needed? What would indicate that help is needed? Can you agree on this?

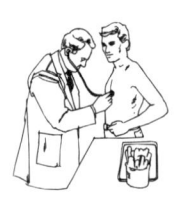

8. For what matters would you seek spiritual counseling? Are there matters that you would consider off limits for seeking this kind of guidance?
9. When do you apologize? Are you able to apologize? What is an example of when you couldn't apologize?
10. What does forgiveness look like to you? What behavior and attitudes accompany true forgiveness?
11. Under what circumstances have you practiced forgiveness? Are there circumstances where you have been unable to forgive? How has this affected you?
12. Do you turn to prayer and spiritual guidance when you are faced with tests and difficulties? Sometimes, often, or always? What other spiritual resources do you turn to?
13. What other actions do you take or methods do you use when you are faced with tests?
14. How do you behave when you are sick? Do you want to be pampered? Want to be left alone? Get cranky and whiny? Act like it's a catastrophe? Call Mom? Has your partner been around you when you were sick? How did he/she respond to you?
15. How do you or are you likely to handle long-term illness in yourself? In your spouse?

Activities

1. Pray, meditate, reflect, and write in your journal about the major challenges you have experienced in your life and the ones you have concerns about in marriage.

2. Put yourselves in situations where you will be exposed to people going through tests and difficulties. This might include visiting a nursing home, hospital, orphanage, 12-Step meeting, homeless shelter, or helping a housebound friend. [**Note:** Guests are welcome at 12-Step meetings if they are there to learn about the topic of the meeting.] What were your feelings, reactions, and concerns about the situations you encountered?

3. Meet with a married couple that you know has gone through severe problems and successfully addressed their issues. Consult with them about the situation and how they handled it. Do they have any advice for you?

4. Meet with a counselor and/or your Spiritual Assembly (or clergy member) for assistance with any situation you are facing…or for insights, advice, and skill building on how to handle difficult things in the future. What did you learn from them?

5. A ceremony of forgiveness and detachment might be a visible means of assisting you to forgive something or someone from the past and move forward. You could do it by yourself, with your partner, or with an appropriate and trusted group. You can be very creative with this, as this is not a ritual of any faith. However, this also may not be an activity that suits everyone. You might write the old issues, actions, and problems on pieces of paper or take old letters from the person and burn them in a campfire or fireplace. You could plan a devotional service of prayers and music for yourself or with a group. If the person has died, you could take flowers and pictures of their favorite things and place them on the grave. You might participate in an indigenous tribal ceremony, such as a Native American sweat lodge. You could stand or sit under a waterfall and pray to be cleansed from the pain of the past. What did the ceremony look like? How did you feel at the end of it? What, if anything, do you need to do further to let go of pain from the past?

A Spiritual Nugget for Reflection and Discussion

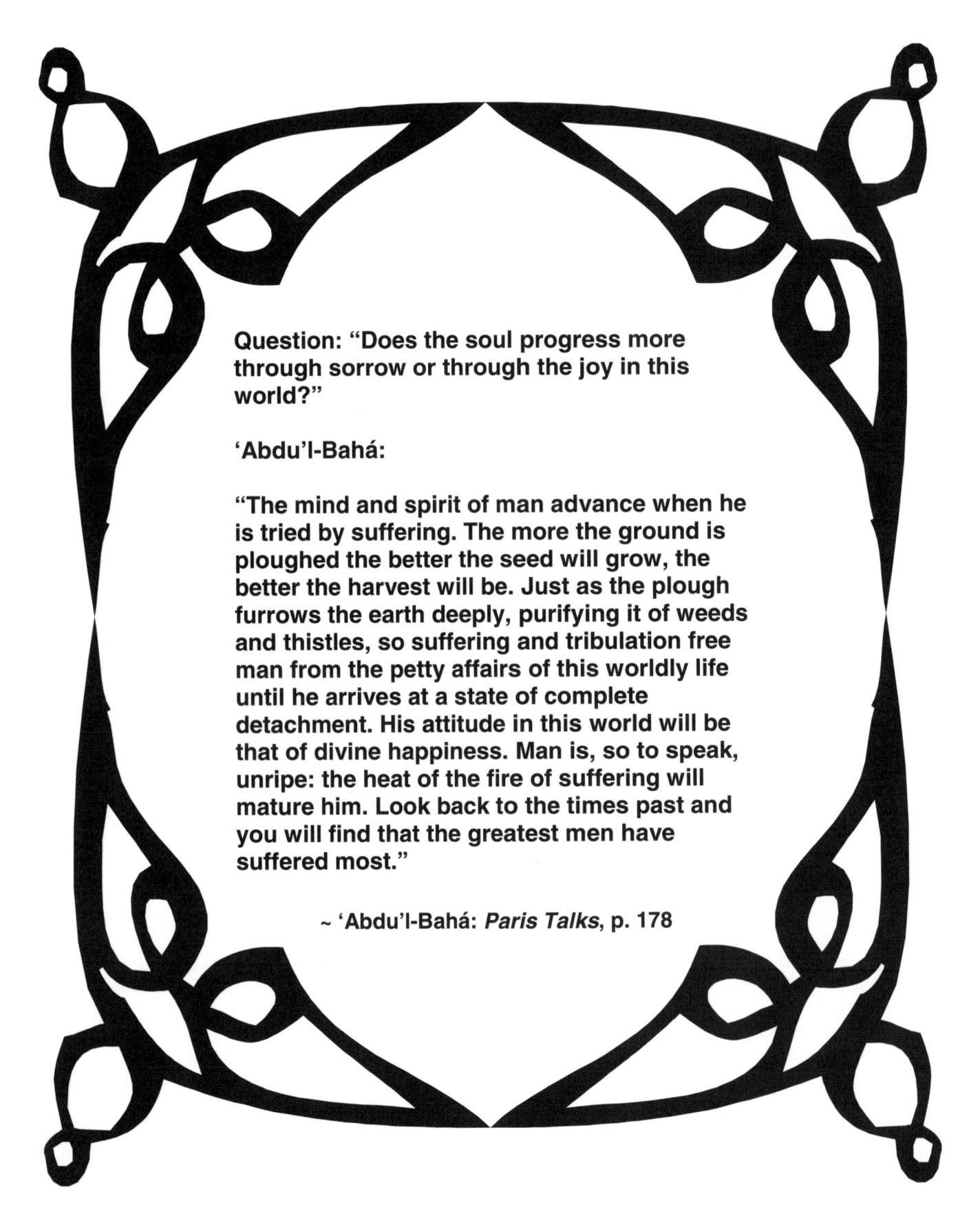

Question: "Does the soul progress more through sorrow or through the joy in this world?"

'Abdu'l-Bahá:

"The mind and spirit of man advance when he is tried by suffering. The more the ground is ploughed the better the seed will grow, the better the harvest will be. Just as the plough furrows the earth deeply, purifying it of weeds and thistles, so suffering and tribulation free man from the petty affairs of this worldly life until he arrives at a state of complete detachment. His attitude in this world will be that of divine happiness. Man is, so to speak, unripe: the heat of the fire of suffering will mature him. Look back to the times past and you will find that the greatest men have suffered most."

~ 'Abdu'l-Bahá: *Paris Talks*, p. 178

Step 5

Come to Commitment: You and Your Parents

Marriage Can Be Forever—Preparation Counts!

The Bride of ʻAbduʼl-Bahá

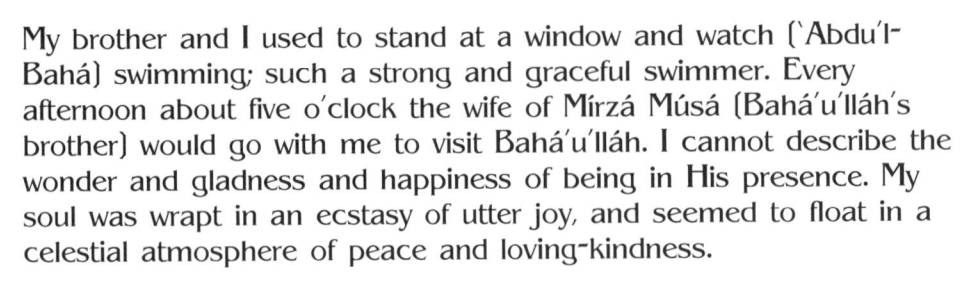

My brother and I used to stand at a window and watch (ʻAbduʼl-Bahá) swimming; such a strong and graceful swimmer. Every afternoon about five o'clock the wife of Mírzá Músá (Baháʼuʼlláh's brother) would go with me to visit Baháʼuʼlláh. I cannot describe the wonder and gladness and happiness of being in His presence. My soul was wrapt in an ecstasy of utter joy, and seemed to float in a celestial atmosphere of peace and loving-kindness.

Many beautiful daughters were offered from time to time by parents anxious that their child should have the honor of becoming the wife of (ʻAbduʼl-Bahá). He refused to consider any of them, until I arrived; we met each other once, and our marriage was arranged....

Baháʼuʼlláh spoke wonderful words to me:

"Oh Muníríh! Oh my Leaf! I have destined you for the wife of (ʻAbduʼl-Bahá). This is the bounty of God to you. In earth or in heaven there is no greater gift. Many have come, but We have rejected them and chosen you. Oh Muníríh! Be worthy of Him, and of Our generosity to you."

Baháʼuʼlláh chanted the prayers (at the wedding).

Oh the spiritual happiness which enfolded us! It cannot be described in earthly words.

The chanting ended, the guests left us. I was the wife of my Beloved. How wonderful and noble He was in His beauty. I adored Him. I recognized His greatness, and thanked God for bringing me to Him.

It is impossible to put into words the delight of being with (ʻAbduʼl-Bahá); I seemed to be in a glorious realm of sacred happiness whilst in His company.

...then, in the youth of His beauty and manly vigor, with His unfailing love, His kindness, His cheerfulness, His sense of humor, His untiring consideration for everybody, He was marvelous, without equal, surely in all the earth!

For fifty years my beloved and I were together...years (that) fled by in an atmosphere of love and joy and the perfection of that Peace which passeth all understanding, in the radiant light of which I await the day when I shall be called to join Him, in the celestial garden of transfiguration.

~ Muníríh Khánum, *The Chosen Highway*, pp. 87-90

Marriage Can Be Forever—Preparation Counts!

CHAPTER 29 – What Do We Want?: A Vision of Marriage

Focus Points

- Envisioning your marriage relationship
- The use of creativity
- The power of words, commitments, and promises
- The role of love in creation
- Parental input about creating a marriage

A Couple's Story

"So, IF we decide to get married," says James, "what do you think we could do so we have a good marriage?"

"I think we've gotten off to a good start by praying together regularly," says Lindsay, after some reflection. "I think we need to talk a bit more about what kind of relationships we want to have with our families though."

"Yeah, and where we would live after the wedding," says James.

"The biggest thing though is that we are figuring out how to consult with each other. I think that will get us through almost anything," says Lindsay.

Quotes for Guidance

✸ Utterance must needs possess penetrating power. For if bereft of this quality it would fail to exert influence. And this penetrating influence dependeth on the spirit being pure and the heart stainless. Likewise it needeth moderation, without which the hearer would be unable to bear it, rather he would manifest opposition from the very outset. And moderation will be obtained by blending utterance with the tokens of divine wisdom which are recorded in the sacred Books and Tablets. Thus when the essence of one's utterance is endowed with these two requisites it will prove highly effective and will be the prime factor in transforming the souls of men.
(Bahá'u'lláh: *Tablets of Bahá'u'lláh*, pp. 198-199)

✸ May spiritual brotherhood cause rebirth and regeneration, for its creative quickening emanates from the breaths of the Holy Spirit and is founded by the power of God. Surely that which is founded through the divine power of the Holy Spirit is permanent in its potency and lasting in its effect.
('Abdu'l-Bahá: *Promulgation of Universal Peace*, p. 130)

✸ Every created thing in the contingent world is made up of many and varied atoms, and its existence is dependent on the composition of these. In other words, through the divine creative power a conjunction of simple elements taketh place so that from this composition a distinct organism is produced. The existence of all things is based upon this principle.
('Abdu'l-Bahá: *Selections from the Writings of 'Abdu'l-Bahá*, p. 289)

Marriage Can Be Forever—Preparation Counts!

✸ Strive, therefore, to create love in the hearts in order that they may become glowing and radiant. When that love is shining, it will permeate other hearts even as this electric light illumines its surroundings. When the love of God is established, everything else will be realized.
   ('Abdu'l-Bahá: *Promulgation of Universal Peace*, p. 239)

✸ The words of Bahá'u'lláh and the Master, however, have a creative power and are sure to awaken in the reader the undying fire of the love of God.
   (Shoghi Effendi: *The Importance of Deepening*, p.17)

✸ You should at all times fix your gaze on the promise of Bahá'u'lláh, put your whole trust in His creative Word, recall the past and manifold evidences of His all-encompassing and resistless power and arise to become worthy and exemplary recipients of His all-sustaining grace and blessings.
   (Shoghi Effendi: *Dawn of a New Day*, p. 90)

Perspectives to Consider

Marriage exists as God's broad creation, but it will be up to you, drawing on inspiration and guidance from God, to **create your own unique marriage**. You have tremendous power and latitude in doing this. As you move toward the decision to marry (unless by now you have realized there are serious incompatibilities), it will start to become clear you are choosing to create something new in the world that has never existed before. It is something far greater than simply the sum of you as individuals.

There is tremendous **power in words**, for instance. Declaring to each other, your parents, and the broader world that you are going to be creating a marriage and a family begins to bring it into being [but should only occur after you have parental consent, of course; see Chapters 32 and 33]. As challenges come up throughout your lives together, it will empower you to re-declare and re-create your commitment both to each other and to the institution of marriage. This will help you to affirm that your marriage is a strong and viable entity. When you are tired, and the car has a flat tire, the bills are due, you disagree about who is going to clean the bathroom, the kids are picking on each other, and it all just seems too much, re-declaring your commitment to your marriage will be part of restoring balance.

At your current stage in determining whether to marry or not, marriage exists only as a possibility in your minds. If you were to marry, what might that marriage look like? What do you want to create? What are you both committed to creating together as partners? The creative process comes from your clarity, energy, and joy about all these things.

Clearly, a key element in creating marriage is **love**. Bringing the love of God into your relationship and building love between the two of you is vital for your family's health and happiness. Each time you declare or express love to each other, positive energy releases into your relationship. This empowers the relationship to progress and each of you to grow and achieve your best in your family, at work, and in your community.

Coaching

⇒ Find creative ways to express your feelings for each other, like a surprise note inside a book one of you is reading or a plant delivered to the other's home or workplace.

Marriage Can Be Forever—Preparation Counts!

⇒ Experiment with saying, writing, or singing words that reflect what you want to have in your relationship and marriage (which helps you to then create these things).

⇒ Honor and acknowledge your partner by sharing with him/her the things you love about him/her.

❓ Questions for Reflection and Discussion

1. What does it mean to you to use creativity to determine what you want your marriage to look like?
2. Have you ever experienced the power that comes from declaring a goal and achieving it?
3. What might cause you to lose your commitment to the ongoing process of creating and maintaining your marriage (after you are married)?
4. What might divorce, the opposite of creation, look and feel like?
5. What could you do in your marriage to prevent divorce?

When considering marriage, you might find it valuable to ask your parents/a married couple the following:

1. What loving and encouraging practices have helped you be successful in your marriage?
2. What have you tried in your marriage that was not successful?
3. What coaching can you give us about communication?
4. What coaching can you give us about maintaining a spiritual relationship?
5. Do you have insights for us on intimacy and making love?
6. What coaching do you have about children and/or stepchildren?

Activities

1. Pray, meditate, reflect, and write in your journal about the loving and encouraging practices you feel are vital to have in your marriage. (Examples: looking for ways to be of service to each other, praising each other's accomplishments, praying together daily)

2. Role-play various marriage scenarios with each other to help you generate ideas of what is important to you in marriage.

3. Complete Worksheet 29A using the sample Marriage Intentions Statement that follows to also give you ideas.

4. Discuss together what you will have to do to fulfill the intentions you develop.

_____

_____

5. How often will you review these intentions during your marriage? **Note:** It will be wise to review them more often in the early months and years while you are setting the patterns for your marriage. Since change will be part of your marriage, however, you may also benefit from re-visiting them on a long-term basis. Your wedding anniversary is a good time to consider doing this review.

_____

Sample Marriage Intentions Statement

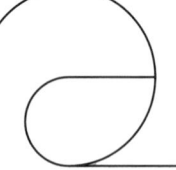

United in mind, heart, and soul, we affirm that the intent of our relationship is to create an extraordinary family. Our commitment is to:

- Treat others, and especially each other, family, and friends with love, honor, respect, courtesy, and integrity.
- Support and encourage each other's personal growth and transformation and the transformation of others.
- Honor and respect our own and each other's physical, mental, emotional, and spiritual needs and assist each other in meeting those needs wherever possible.
- Fully express and share all aspects of our selves and our lives.
- Nurture a spirit of community with others.
- Deal with issues that arise as soon as possible.
- Be fully conscious, fully present.
- Maintain some time alone as individuals.
- Cherish, honor, and respect our children by nurturing bonds of communication and love.
- Build and maintain loving and open relationships with all family members.
- Enrich our lives with separate and mutual friendships.
- Pray and read Bahá'í Writings separately and together daily.
- Be examples of service to ourselves, each other, our families, friends, and communities.
- Be playful, have fun, and incorporate humor into daily life.
- Act with integrity in all things, particularly in our finances, our work, and our service commitments.
- Enrich our lives with the arts.
- Be patient, accepting, and nurturing, maintaining the constancy of our relationship through times of adversity and when we are not being our best selves.

Date: _____

Worksheet 29A: State the Intentions of Your Marriage

DIRECTIONS: Begin developing a Marriage Intentions Statement (the romantic version of a corporate Mission Statement!).
- First, pray together for inspiration.
- On a separate piece of paper, brainstorm all the possible things that you might want to have as spiritual, mental, emotional, and physical practices in your marriage. Include what you would do both separately and as a couple.
  - For example, do you want to commit to praying together daily? Do you want to encourage musical talent in each other? Do you want to pursue further education?
- See the Sample Marriage Intentions Statement preceding this worksheet for more ideas.
- When you have generated the list(s), then go back through it together, consult, and choose the ones that are most meaningful for you as a couple. As you agree on each practice, enter it in the worksheet below.

Your level of agreement on these practices will be an indication of your compatibility and an assurance that you are moving in the right direction.

Worksheets may be printed from www.claricomm.com/publishing

We are committed to establishing the following behaviors and practices in our marriage:

Marriage Can Be Forever—Preparation Counts!

Dynamics of Prayer
For Solving Problems or Obtaining Assistance

First Step — Pray and meditate about it. Use the prayers of the Manifestations (Prophets and Messengers of God) as they have the greatest power. Then remain in the silence of contemplation for a few minutes.

Second Step — Arrive at a decision and hold this. This decision is usually born during the contemplation. It may seem almost impossible of accomplishment but if it seems to be as answer to a prayer or a way of solving the problem, then immediately take the next step.

Third Step — Have determination to carry the decision through. Many fail here. The decision, budding into determination, is blighted and instead becomes a wish or a vague longing. When determination is born, immediately take the next step.

Fourth Step — Have faith and confidence that the power will flow through you, the right way will appear, the door will open, the right thought, the right message, the right principle or the right book will be given you. Have confidence, and the right thing will come to your need. Then, as you rise from prayer, take at once the fifth step.

Fifth Step — Then, he said, lastly, ACT; Act as though it had all been answered. Then act with tireless, ceaseless energy. And as you act, you, yourself, will become a magnet, which will attract more power to your being, until you become an unobstructed channel for the Divine power to flow through you. Many pray but do not remain for the last half of the first step. Some who meditate arrive at a decision, but fail to hold it. Few have the determination to carry the decision through, still fewer have the confidence that the right thing will come to their need. But how many remember to act as though it had all been answered? How true are those words — "Greater than the prayer is the spirit in which it is uttered" and greater than the way it is uttered is the spirit in which it is carried out.

~ Attributed to Shoghi Effendi: *Principles of Bahá'í Administration*, p. 90

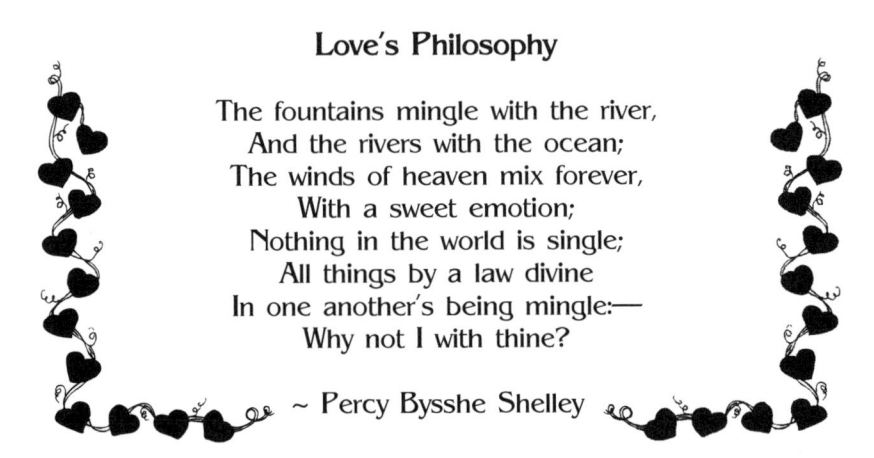

Love's Philosophy

The fountains mingle with the river,
And the rivers with the ocean;
The winds of heaven mix forever,
With a sweet emotion;
Nothing in the world is single;
All things by a law divine
In one another's being mingle:—
Why not I with thine?

~ Percy Bysshe Shelley

CHAPTER 30 – We Do or We Don't: To Marry or Not

Focus Points

- Rituals and equality in proposing marriage
- Reassessing readiness and emotions
- Role of consultation
- Reaching a decision to marry

A Couple's Story

It's a beautiful day, and James and Lindsay are walking in the park and feeling deeply connected and at peace with one another. Each of them is feeling like it's time for them to make the decision about marrying, but aren't sure about beginning the conversation.

"So, I've been thinking about that list we made of all the things we'd like to see in a marriage," says James.

"So have I," says Lindsay. "It made me feel pretty positive. How about you?"

"Yeah, me too," says James. "So, what do you think we should do next?"

Lindsay stops walking and turns to face James. "I think we both know what we want to do next." She grins at him. "Let's get married!"

Quotes for Guidance

✸ As for the question regarding marriage under the Law of God: first thou must choose one who is pleasing to thee, and then the matter is subject to the consent of father and mother. Before thou makest thy choice, they have no right to interfere.
   ('Abdu'l-Bahá: *Selections from the Writings of 'Abdu'l-Bahá*, p. 118)

✸ This principle [of the equality of the sexes] is far more than the enunciation of admirable ideals; it has profound implications in all aspects of human relations and must be an integral element of Bahá'í domestic and community life. The application of this principle gives rise to changes in habits and practices which have prevailed for many centuries. An example of this is found in the response provided on behalf of Shoghi Effendi to a question whether the traditional practice whereby the man proposes marriage to the woman is altered by the Bahá'í Teachings to permit the woman to issue a marriage proposal to the man; the response is, "The Guardian wishes to state that there is absolute equality between the two, and that no distinction of preference is permitted...."
   (Universal House of Justice: An unpublished letter January 24, 1993, to an individual)

Chapter 31 – To Mom and Dad: Seeking Consent

👓 Perspectives to Consider

This is a **time for reflecting and assessing** whether you have carefully prepared and are ready for a successful marriage. You might review the previous chapters of this workbook to determine whether you have gone through a full range of experiences together and have a clear understanding of each other's character, personality, behavior, and so on.

- Re-examine the questions and the worksheets. Are there any changes in your responses?
- Are there any lingering areas of compatibility that you need to explore further?
- Are there any lingering doubts, concerns, or issues?
- How might all of your discoveries about each other affect you when living together?
- Have you discovered things that make you realize living together in unity and harmony would be very difficult or impossible?
- Have you, alternatively, strengthened your friendship in the marriage preparation process and become more certain than ever that you can be together happily and successfully in marriage?

Even though you will still have time between your engagement and your wedding to change your minds, it is far easier to do it now before getting involved in the consent process with your parents. And definitely before planning your wedding and inviting your guests!

By now, you have completed a significant amount of preparation for marriage, and it's time to make a decision: **Will you choose to marry each other or not?** Are you sure:

- There is a powerful connection of love and soul between you
- You understand the core qualities of each other's characters
- You have fully explored the histories, experiences, and nuances of each other's lives
- You have considered any issues related to current and future children
- You will likely be compatible in living together
- You are committed to creating a spiritually-based marriage
- You are prepared to build a unified family

Then, it's up to the two of you to **mutually decide to marry**. Either the man or the woman can initiate a discussion or proposal of marriage. As part of the principle of the equality of women and men, there is no requirement in the Bahá'í Faith for the man to propose marriage to the woman. In fact, you may mutually decide in consultation to marry. Those of other faiths may choose mutual consultation as their decision method as well, or you may simply use whatever proposal style works for you.

Coaching

⇒ Bahá'u'lláh has indicated that for Bahá'ís, the rituals of the past no longer have to be followed. This means you don't have to do any of the traditional rituals associated with proposals in your culture. There is no requirement to have an engagement ring, for instance. So be creative!

⇒ Certainty and clarity are vital at this stage. Honestly assess your motives and carefully reflect on the quality of your relationship up to this point. Be very certain of the compatibility points you have discovered, and how you will deal with any incompatibilities.

Marriage Can Be Forever—Preparation Counts!

❓ Questions for Reflection and Discussion

1. Have you known each other long enough and had enough experiences together to thoroughly know one another? What reservations do you have, if any? Have you consulted in depth about these?
2. Have you spent time together in the same geographic region and interacted on a regular and frequent basis? How long or how many times have you been in the same place at the same time? Are you certain you have been together enough to be certain marrying is a good choice?
3. If one of you moved to be close to the other, is this now pressuring you to marry even though you aren't sure you want to? How will you handle this?
4. Do you love each other? Why?
5. Why do you want to be married? Why to each other?
6. Are you friends? Do you like each other? What is the nature of the friendship? Comfortable? Forced? Open and sharing? Closed from others?
7. How do you get along with each other's family? Are any of them expressing strong reservations about your relationship? What points are they raising? Do they have validity?
8. How do you get along with each other's friends? Are any of them expressing strong reservations about your relationship? What points are they raising? Do they have validity?
9. Have you seen each other at your worst (or at least pretty close), physically, emotionally, mentally, and spiritually? How was this experience?
10. Are there any signs of distrust or jealousy between you? What are the reasons?
11. How do you express your love for each other? Are you comfortable with this?
12. How are you fostering positive personal and spiritual growth in each other (coaching each other)? If so, how? If not, what are the implications for the well-being of your marriage? If you are fostering growth, are you able to do it in a loving, courteous way? How is it accepted by the other?
13. Do you attentively listen to each other? Are there times when this is difficult? Easy?
14. Are you able to keep conflicts, disagreements, and disharmony at a minimum?
15. Do you have supportive people in your lives besides each other?
16. For what reasons would you seek spiritual counseling or guidance from a Spiritual Assembly, Auxiliary Board member/assistant, or clergyperson? Are there matters about your married life that you would consider off limits for seeking this kind of guidance? Why?
17. For what reasons might you seek assistance from a professional counselor after marriage?
18. Have you identified a need for and sought professional premarital/family counseling? How has that been?
19. For what reasons might you seek assistance from a professional counselor? After marriage?
20. Have you effectively addressed any "tough stuff" issues? If not, why haven't you? If so, are there any issues still outstanding? (See Chapter 28.)
21. Are you hesitant about compatibility, but scared to break off the relationship? Are you forcing yourself to go forward? Why? What can you do to be more honest with yourself, your partner, and your family?
22. Are you confident and comfortable with a decision to go forward?

Activities

1. Pray, meditate, reflect, and write in your journal about whether you and your partner are ready for marriage or not.

2. Use Worksheet 30A to help you review the content and the completed worksheets from previous chapters.

3. It is now time to lovingly and honestly consult with each other and reach a decision about whether you want to marry each other or not. Are you happy together, connected with love, and confident in your ability to have

a strong, lasting marriage? If either of you are Bahá'ís, are you ready to ask your parents for consent to marry? Make a list below of any lingering concerns or issues that are strongly on your mind.

   a. _____
   b. _____
   c. _____
   d. _____
   e. _____
   f. _____

4. List below anything you are convinced will change with marriage (How realistic is your expectation?).

   a. _____
   b. _____
   c. _____
   d. _____
   e. _____
   f. _____

5. If you decide ***not to get married***, what do you need to do to bring closure to your relationship or to maintain a non-romantic friendship? **Note:** You might need to have time apart first before you can work this out effectively.

   _____
   _____
   _____

6. Pray together for your future marriage and for the consent process. Some possible prayers are in Appendix B.

7. If you consult and decide you want to be married and request consent, celebrate the occasion by doing something special!

Date: _____

Worksheet 30A: Trends in Your Relationship

DIRECTIONS: Much of the work that you have done in this book captures your skills, thoughts, or emotions at a given point in time. Relationships, however, are *dynamic and ever changing*, with habits and behavior patterns developing and changing almost imperceptibly. These can range from picking up after the other to how you react to the other's emotional expressions. This worksheet will assist you to *begin* assessing trends in your relationship, but it cannot cover all aspects of it. Use this as a starting point, and consult together about other trends you observe. This practice of ongoing relationship assessment will serve you well in courtship and in marriage, if you choose to move forward. Refer to work you did in previous chapters as the starting point. **Take your time** and understand that there is a lot of information to review. Simply completing this worksheet quickly will not give you the insights that are vital for you to examine the dynamic changes and needs of your relationship.

- First complete this worksheet individually; **refer back to the relevant chapters to refresh your memory.**
- Then together compare and consult on your worksheet results.
  - Think about how you understand yourself and each other differently now than you did in the beginning, how you are managing issues, any shifts in attitudes or behavior, where have you advanced or regressed, any problems that have arisen, how unified and compatible you are, and how well you are encouraging and supporting each other.

Use the scale below to rate your previous level (early in your relationship) and your current level.

Worksheets may be printed from www.claricomm.com

Poor or Unhealthy Understanding, Skills, Behavior, or Interactions	1	2	3	4	5	Excellent and Healthy Understanding, Skills, or Interactions
	←				→	

Refer to Chapter	Topic/ Focus Area	Previous Level	Current Level	Notes Any Successes? Concerns?
2	Fulfilling Purpose of Life			
3	Consultation Skills			
6	Understanding Each Other's Character			
8	Solid Friendship at Base of Relationship			
10	Large Range of Courting Activities			
11	Willingness to Make and Keep a Commitment			
14	Compatibility			
15	Experiencing a Deep and Lasting Love			
16	Faith Issues Explored and Addressed			
17	Building Unity in Family Relationships			
18	Behavior and Attitudes Reflecting Equality of Women ad Men			
19	Personality Assessment Complete and Certain of Compatibility			
20	Communication Skills and Harmony			
22	Expressing Emotions			
23	Ability to Maintain Chastity; Emotional Intimacy Progressed; Ability to Discuss Sex			
24	Increased Knowledge of Children			
25	Service and Time Choices			
26	Handling Money			
28	Handling Tough Stuff			

Marriage Can Be Forever—Preparation Counts!

The Promise of Tomorrow

Oh there was a time not long ago when your face I could not see
The memories of that time are dim and seem so far away.
But now I have the pleasure of your time and company
And the freshness of these feelings will not fade or go away.

I'm looking at my future now—no memory of the past
As time ticks ever onward and gently slips away
The fears and failures of before are things that could not last
But the promise of tomorrow is in your eyes today.

Yesterday's sorrow, the trials of today
The promise of tomorrow makes sorrow go away
The promise of tomorrow makes everything okay.

Oh if I never was to live to see another day
Or if tomorrow found me in some cold forgotten land
His journey had just started, you might hear someone say
But my traveling days were ended with the warm touch of your hand.

Yesterday's sorrow, the trials of today
The promise of tomorrow makes sorrow go away
The promise of tomorrow makes everything okay.

So to the heavens raise your vision see the stars shine bright
These walls we've raised around us with a touch come crashing down
The gift of love the giver gives is a tender heart's delight
And true bounty only springs from seeds in fertile soil sown.

Yesterday's sorrow, the trials of today
The promise of tomorrow makes sorrow go away
The promise of tomorrow makes everything okay
And the freshness of these feelings will not fade or go away.

~ Steve Traina

CHAPTER 31 – To Mom and Dad: Seeking Consent

NOTE: Parental consent for marriage is required for Bahá'ís; however, people of other faiths may also wish to practice this concept to support unity in your families.

Focus Points

- Arranged marriages prohibited
- The purpose of parental consent
- The responsibilities of the couple and the parents
- Relationship with parents
- The importance of honesty
- The role of the Bahá'í Spiritual Assembly

A Couple's Story

Lindsay and James decide they want to talk to each of their parents in person about their decision. They want to be able to emphasize the importance of consent to Lindsay's parents in particular, since they aren't Bahá'ís and are not as familiar with it as James' parents are. Lindsay and James have made sure they've spent time with all their parents over the months they've been together, so they know each other fairly well. But, they still know there will be concerns, and they want to hear what those are and consult about them.

"I know you mentioned this requirement before, but you're an adult. Why do you need my consent to get married?" asks Lindsay's mother, Kerry.

"It's because we're Bahá'ís, Mom," says Lindsay. "Bahá'u'lláh says family unity is important, and that includes having you be sure I'm going to marry someone who can be a good husband and father."

"I like James…so, I guess the answer is 'yes,'" says Kerry.

"Thank you, Mom, but we really want you to take your time with this. We want to hear any concerns you might have and anything you see that we might have missed in thinking that we could have a good marriage together."

"Oh," says Kerry and pauses for a moment. "There probably are. I know I've been wondering about how James would deal with the likelihood that you will earn more as an engineer than he will as a graphic designer. And, I'd like to know what you think it will be like having multiracial kids…."

Quotes for Guidance

✹ …marriage is dependent upon the consent of both parties. Desiring to establish love, unity and harmony amidst Our servants, We have conditioned it, once the couple's wish is known, upon the permission of their

parents, lest enmity and rancor should arise amongst them. And in this We have yet other purposes. Thus hath Our commandment been ordained.
   (Bahá'u'lláh: *Kitáb-i-Aqdas*, p. 42)

✸ Beautify your tongues, O people, with truthfulness, and adorn your souls with the ornament of honesty. Beware, O people, that ye deal not treacherously with any one.
   (Bahá'u'lláh: *Gleanings from the Writings of Bahá'u'lláh*, p. 297)

✸ Bahá'u'lláh has clearly stated the consent of all living [natural] parents is required for a Bahá'í marriage. This applies whether the parents are Bahá'ís or non-Bahá'ís, divorced for years or not. This great law He has laid down to strengthen the social fabric, to knit closer the ties of the home, to place a certain gratitude and respect in the hearts of the children for those who have given them life and sent their souls out on the eternal journey towards their Creator.
   (Shoghi Effendi, *Kitáb-i-Aqdas*, Notes, p. 207)

✸ We Bahá'ís must realize that in present-day society the exact opposite process is taking place: young people care less and less for their parents' wishes, divorce is considered a natural right, and obtained on the flimsiest and most unwarrantable and shabby pretexts. People separated from each other, especially if one of them has had full custody of the children, are only too willing to belittle the importance of the partner in marriage also responsible as a parent for bringing those children into this world. The Bahá'ís must, through rigid adherence to the Bahá'í laws and teachings, combat these corrosive forces which are so rapidly destroying home life and the beauty of family relationships, and tearing down the moral structure of society.
   (Shoghi Effendi: *Lights of Guidance*, p. 370)

✸ About the consent of parents for marriage: this is required before and also after the man or woman is twenty-one years of age. It is also required in the event of a second marriage, after the dissolution of the first whether through death or through divorce. The parental consent is also a binding obligation irrespective of whether the parents are Bahá'ís or not, whether they are friendly or opposed to the [Bahá'í] Cause. In the event of the death of both parents, the consent of a guardian is not required.
   (On behalf of Shoghi Effendi: *Compilation on the Consent of Parents to Marriage* by the Research Department at the Bahá'í World Center)

✸ …entering into a marriage is a step that has tremendous implications for a whole range of people beyond the couple themselves, both in this life and in the next. The laws of the Faith are established on very sound foundations, and obedience to them is not only important for the proper development of society, but also for the attainment of true personal happiness.
   (On behalf of the Universal House of Justice to a National Spiritual Assembly: August 10, 2000)

Perspectives to Consider

In the past, parents arranged marriages for their children without the children's agreement or input. They also had the full right to interfere in the relationship between their child and the person their child wanted to marry. In some cultures, this has now shifted to the extreme that many consider **any** parental involvement unnecessary and unhelpful.

Bahá'u'lláh has created a revolutionary new system, different from both of these alternatives. You as a couple make your own **free choice as to who to marry, without parental interference**. Then, Bahá'í marriage requires parental consent, a process that is intended to draw you both closer to all your parents and contribute to the strong foundation of your marriage and a more stable society. Before you have made your choice, your parents are not to interfere; in other words, according to Bahá'í law, they are not allowed to come between the two of you or be an obstacle to your relationship. It is important to note that interference is not the same as avoidance, however, and hopefully you have provided opportunities during your courtship for your parents to get to know both of you and as a couple before you ask them for consent (see Chapters 32 and 33 for further details). Otherwise, it will make it difficult for the parents to have enough information on which to base their consent, and they may request more time together with you both and to make their decision than you might prefer now. You will find it frustrating to delay your marriage while this important activity occurs.

A marriage between you two as individuals creates a synergistic third entity—**your mutual relationship**. That relationship will affect your families, friends, and community. Love and relationships carry forward into the next world when you die…marriage has eternal implications. You also create the beginning of a **family**, where children will be part of your eternal relationships as well. Your parents can assist you in making sure this decision to marry is one that will have blessings forever and not regrets.

Bahá'u'lláh does not provide any formula for how to ask for, give, or deny consent. Parents and couples must make their own choices as to how they carry it out. This process is a culture change, and parents are learning how to do it effectively. At the very least, you can safely assume that a spirit of courtesy, respect, and love will enhance the process. At first, you may dread seeking consent, but you may find it empowering if you choose to embrace the process instead. *You might even strongly encourage your parents to be very thorough with the process and not just agree to your marriage as a formality or just dismiss it as unimportant.* This is a gift designed to ensure your future happiness and a strong marriage.

For the parents, the consent process is both a **serious responsibility** and an opportunity to establish or further **establish a strong relationship** with you as a couple. *They are in effect deciding whether to invite someone new into their family.* This consent process can become the foundation for strong family unity and support throughout your marriage. Couples that marry in disobedience of the law can create disunity that may be long lasting and disruptive to long-term family relationships, including the relationships between your parents and their grandchildren (see Chapter 33 for further information).

You might also be tempted to hide information, not to be honest with your parents, and perhaps even to lie to them out of your very strong desire to be together. You may be so focused on ending up married that you regard consent as a mere formality. All these things negatively affect your spiritual well-being and bring disunity and alienation into the family. Establishing your marriage with wholehearted obedience to the Bahá'í marriage laws and on an **honest foundation** contributes to the long life and happiness of your marriage. *Honesty with your parents builds trust with them and gives them information that they need in order to be effective at their God-given responsibility to give or deny consent.*

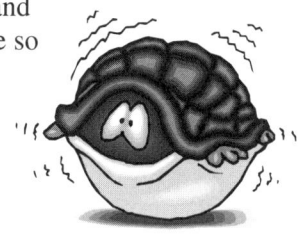

A Bahá'í Spiritual Assembly can be a support and source of guidance and information to you and your parents if you have questions or trouble during the consent process. Anyone involved can request to **meet with the Spiritual Assembly** at any juncture, whether they are a Bahá'í or not. This is especially important if there are any circumstances in your lives or your parents' lives that may affect consent. If any of the parents are not Bahá'ís, you may wish to seek guidance on explaining consent to them.

The central theme for the consent process is unity. What you build with your family during this process will provide a foundation for the rest of your lives together, and for the lives of your children and grandchildren.

Marriage Can Be Forever—Preparation Counts!

Coaching

⇒ If any of your parents indicate a discomfort, unwillingness, or disinterest in participating in the consent process, advocate on your own behalf that it be thorough, for the well-being of your future marriage.

⇒ If you have any unusual circumstances whatsoever, promptly seek guidance from your Spiritual Assembly, National Spiritual Assembly, or the Universal House of Justice about any adjustments to the consent process. These circumstances could include such things as one of you being adopted, the victim of parental abuse, unable to locate a parent, or having a parent who is somehow incapacitated.

⇒ If you don't have parents with whom to go through the consent process, you might find it helpful to invite other relatives and/or friends to play the role of parents in asking you questions. Of course, they cannot give or withhold consent to your marriage, but their guidance may be of assistance to you in evaluating compatibility and in feeling a sense of family or community support.

Questions for Reflection and Discussion

1. What is your attitude toward the requirement of parental consent for your marriage?
2. How will your attitude toward it help or harm the process of seeking consent?
3. How will you contact and approach your parents? Separately? Together?
4. Do you want to pray with your parents before talking to them about consent?
5. Do you have any specific concerns? What can you do to address them?
6. What do you think are your parents' perspectives on consent? Will you have to explain it to them?
7. What do you think are your parents' perspectives on your relationship?
8. What things can you do to have the consent process be a positive experience?
9. How might you respond if your parents refuse to give consent?
10. How will you address consent from parents you have had limited or no contact with?
11. What, if anything, will you do to involve or honor non-biological parents who are not required to be part of the consent process?

Activities

1. Pray, meditate, reflect, and write in your journal about how you feel about the consent process. Pray together and take time to carefully read and study the Bahá'í Writings about consent. Consider including your parents in this process.

2. Role-play with each other or with close friends the process of asking for consent from your parents. How did it feel? What changes will you now make?

_____

_____

3. Examine and discuss your fears, concerns, surprises, joys, and adventures with the consent process.

4. As the process of consent unfolds, discuss your feelings about how it is going. What lessons are you learning? What are you learning about each other and your family that will be helpful in the future?

5. What are some ways to expand the unity between you and your parents?

Somebody Higher Than Me

You came to me
And taught me to look towards the sky.
My wildest dreams came true.
And I will never quite know why.

Where did this love come from?
Who is the fashioner of this?
Who is the cause, and what are the circumstances?
When I hear these questions, it's then I really know it's up to:

Somebody higher than, Somebody higher than,
Somebody higher than me.

I know there's time
But how much time is time enough?
For so many riddles and rhymes
That we can't solve when things get tough.

Like:
Why is the sky so blue?
Who is the fashioner of this?
Who made the stars, and what are they doing up there?
When I hear these questions, I know that there
Is truth in that there's...

Somebody higher than, Somebody higher than,
Somebody higher than me.

~ Henry Adam and Beverly Iffland

CHAPTER 32 – Now It's Up to You: Parents Considering Consent

NOTE: This chapter is for *the parents* of the couple seeking consent, not to you as a couple, so please share it with them. (However, you will learn from reading it too!)

Focus Points
- Consent a significant and serious responsibility
- Self-assessment and preparation for parents
- Avoiding prejudice as a factor in the decision-making process
- The importance of objectivity
- Understanding the characters of both parties
- Courage in raising difficult issues and questions

A Couple's Story

Lindsay's parents talk on the phone and agree it would be best for them to meet in person to discuss whether to give consent or not. They know they have to independently decide whether to agree to the marriage or not, but they feel it's also important to try to be unified on the decision for Lindsay's sake.

"So, Sam, what do you think about all this?" asks Kerry.

"It's weird," says Sam. "They've even said they won't get married if we don't give them consent. Nobody does it like this any more. But, I'm glad my opinion matters too, you know. We didn't do very well at marriage, and I'd like her to do better."

"Yeah, I agree," says Kerry. "James seems to be good for her. He talks to her a lot and treats her well. She seems happy…I suppose that's what's most important for me. I'm a bit concerned about how people will treat them though. Mixed marriages are getting more common, but they still aren't accepted everywhere, that's for sure."

"Hmm…I'm just glad he's got a good job," says Sam. "They'll figure out how to handle the race stuff. I'm more worried she'll drop out of school and not finish her degree."

"I didn't think of that," says Kerry. "I definitely don't want that to happen."

Quotes for Guidance

Note: Many of the quotes that are in Chapter 33 also apply to this chapter, so you may wish to refer to it.

✺ …marriage is dependent upon the consent of both parties. Desiring to establish love, unity and harmony amidst Our servants, We have conditioned it, once the couple's wish is known, upon the permission of their parents, lest enmity and rancor should arise amongst them.
   (Bahá'u'lláh: *Kitáb-i-Aqdas*, para. 65)

- …The best beloved of all things in My sight is Justice; turn not therefrom if thou desirest Me, and neglect it not that I may confide in thee. By its aid thou shalt see with thine own eyes and not through the eyes of others, and shalt know of thine own knowledge and not through the knowledge of thy neighbor.
  (Bahá'u'lláh: *Hidden Words*, Arabic, No. 2)

- As to the question of marriage, according to the law of God: First you must select one, and then it depends upon the consent of the father and mother. Before your selection they have no right of interference.
  ('Abdu'l-Bahá: *Tablets of 'Abdu'l-Bahá Abbas, Vol. 3*, p. 563)

- If it be possible, gather together these two races, black and white…and put such love into their hearts that they shall not only unite but even intermarry.
  ('Abdu'l-Bahá: *Bahá'í World Faith*, p. 359)

- It is perfectly true that Bahá'u'lláh's statement that the consent of all living parents is required for marriage places a grave responsibility on each parent. When the parents are Bahá'ís they should, of course, act objectively in withholding or granting their approval. They cannot evade this responsibility by merely acquiescing in their child's wish, nor should they be swayed by prejudice; but, whether they be Bahá'í or non-Bahá'í, the parents' decision is binding, whatever the reason that may have motivated it. Children must recognize and understand that this act of consenting is the duty of a parent. They must have respect in their hearts for those who have given them life, and whose good pleasure they must at all times strive to win.
  (Shoghi Effendi: *Lights of Guidance*, pp. 370-371)

- The freedom of the parents in giving or refusing consent to the marriage of their children is unrestricted and unconditioned. The parents' responsibility in this regard is based on their conscience and they are answerable to God. This is not to say that there may not be cases when they give consent reluctantly; this is something that the parents themselves would know, in the same way that the children know that they have pressured their parents to grant permission because of certain considerations. Therefore, it is not correct to say that when parents give their consent to the marriage of their children, it is necessarily wholehearted. On the other hand, some parents may be persuaded by their children to give their wholehearted consent after their initial reluctance to do so.
  (Universal House of Justice: *Consent of Parents*, p. 37)

- There should be a spirit of mutual respect and consideration between parents and children, in which the children turn to their parents for advice and direction, and the parents train and nurture their offspring. The fruit of this relationship is that the children grow into adulthood with their powers of discrimination and judgment refined, so that they can steer the course of their lives in a manner most conducive to their welfare.

  Within the framework of this mutual respect, the parents are called upon to show wisdom and discretion when their offspring are developing friendships which might ultimately lead to marriage. They should consider carefully the circumstances under which advice should be given, and conditions under which their intervention would be construed as interference.

  For their part, the offspring should recognize that their parents are deeply interested in their welfare, and that the views of the parents warrant respect and careful consideration.
  (On behalf of the Universal House of Justice: *Consent of Parents*, p. 27)

- Bahá'í law places the responsibility for ascertaining knowledge of the character of those entering into the marriage contract on the two parties involved, and on the parents, who must give consent to the marriage.
  (On behalf of the Universal House of Justice: *Lights of Guidance*, p. 369)

Perspectives to Consider

To you, the parents:

To prepare yourselves for the consent process, it will be helpful for you to introduce or refresh yourself on the principles of consultation (see Chapter 3). Prayerful consultation with the couple, the other parents involved, and with trusted others, while respecting the dignity and privacy of your son/daughter and his/her intended, may be a helpful tool in assisting you to come to a decision.

Your son/daughter and the person he or she wishes to marry have approached you to ask for your consent to their marriage. If one or both of them are Bahá'ís, this is a requirement—without your consent, they cannot marry each other. **The consent process** is one that gives you the opportunity to get to know your child and his or her intended spouse better (or for the first time). It is designed to build unity and love between you. It is also an opportunity to assess and invite someone new to join your family (if you decide to give consent). **Note:** Be aware that if you are not a Bahá'í, giving consent in no way implies or states that you have pledged your belief in the Bahá'í Faith.

As parents, you have a vital role in **safeguarding family unity and taking consent seriously**. As one quote says, you "cannot evade this responsibility by merely acquiescing in [your] child's wish." Because the consent process is a new one for parents to learn, it will take time for families and society to understand its purpose and wisdom fully. It is clear, however, that consent and marriage are designed ideally to bring you closer together to your son/daughter and his or her future family, so your full involvement at this stage is crucial. *You must also remember that consent of all four living biological parents (both sets of parents) is required, so each of you must be free to reach your own conclusions without intimidation or coercion from your children or any other parent involved.*

Every family will approach consent differently. A good place to start is to read **the quotes in the Bahá'í Writings** on consent and marriage. As there are few specifics given about the process, you will have to use your own best judgment about how to go about it. You may find it helpful, for instance, to go through your own **self-assessment process** before beginning the consent process with your son/daughter and his or her intended spouse. You must be sure that you have the best interests of them and your families in mind and that your judgment is not clouded by prejudices of any kind: race, nationality, economic status, education, age, class, and so on. It may also be helpful for you to examine your feelings and attitudes about the law of giving consent itself, which may seem difficult or unfamiliar to you.

An important concept for you to consider in this consent process is **respect for the couple**—they (and you) may or may not want the consent process to be known to anyone beyond those of you directly involved. How will you ascertain that? Will you be able to each respect the other's wishes? What if you wish to consult with others beyond the couple and parents? If there are cross-cultural differences or inter-family differences on what can be shared, how will the parents and couple address this? The issues of privacy and confidentiality are often critical for one or all of the parties, and this may be a potential clash among you. If consent is denied, this privacy becomes even more important, as any number of people may feel hurt and may not want it shared. What if one family gives and one withholds consent? What if anyone is angry or humiliated? What if the parents have all known one another and/or will have to interact in the future? All these are reasons to try to keep this low-key and private for all. Don't take this to an extreme level, however, as consultation is a critical tool for this process.

You may think that you should simply trust the judgment of the couple, which is not in the spirit of the consent process. Or you may think that consent is only important if your son/daughter is under a certain age. Others struggle with prejudices, and these become factors in giving or withholding consent. These things are all tests for you as parents to understand and handle, because it is clear from the Bahá'í Writings that you must act fairly in the couple's best interest.

Marriage Can Be Forever—Preparation Counts!

You (and the couple) will have to exercise patience during the consent process, ensuring that you are thorough in helping them decide whether they can make a wise and strong marriage or not. Parents must be very **knowledgeable about the character of their child's intended spouse** (see Chapters 6 and 19). This will require spending time together and gaining enough experience and trust with each other to be completely honest. How will you do this? How will you know when the process is complete? How will you make it a relationship-building experience instead of the individuals feeling like they are under a microscope? How can you convey an open mind during the process? If you are critical or judgmental toward your child's choice, he or she might withdraw, and you will never truly know what he or she is like. How can this consent process help you to grow as a family in your consultation and communication skills?

Remember, too, that there are probably **two other parents** considering whether to give consent as well. Have you met them? Have they perhaps seen more of the couple than you have and might have different insights? Would a joint consultation assist in the decision-making process? None of you can coerce the decision of any of the others, but in the process of consulting together and getting to know each other, you may uncover important insights about the couple that assists you in coming to your own conclusion about whether they should marry or not. Do you want to get to know the other family? Would doing some shared activities assist you to assess the couple's compatibility? This could be tense, as any of you could feel that you as parents are now under the microscope with one another, or you may not like the fact that the other family is evaluating your son/daughter. However, done with tact, respect, and openness, this approach may assist the process. It might also be helpful to become familiar with family to assess any positive or negative family behaviors or patterns. Be vigilant in avoiding judging the other family but also in gaining information that you think would assist you.

As the consent process proceeds, you may have to be courageous in **bringing up difficult issues** with the couple. Openly and carefully speak to and listen to each other. *As a parent, you can often bring calm, dispassionate viewpoints into a consultation with a couple, especially if you perceive their judgment is clouded by romance.* Check to see whether there are previously unrecognized issues between the couple or between them and you. You can facilitate this by meeting separately and together with each of the individuals and with all of you together.

Long Distance Consent

In our global community, parents and children are often far apart during the consent process, and financial, work, health, or other considerations may prevent you from traveling to meet with the couple. If you cannot be in the same geographical location, you will have to devise other means of finding the information that you need to make an informed decision, especially if you have never met the person your son or daughter has chosen. Discuss with the couple their ideas and suggestions for how to accomplish the goal of getting to know them better and supporting them in being sure they should marry. Here are some possibilities you might consider:

- Send a number of the questions in this book to the couple and request they answer them individually (and without discussion with each other) and return the answers to you.

- Ask your prospective son- or daughter-in-law to provide you with character reference letters from people who know him/her well.

- Ask the Spiritual Assembly or administrative body in the area where the person lives to provide a character reference letter and an assessment of the couple's readiness for marriage.

- Deputize a trusted person to meet with both your child and his or her intended partner individually and with both of them together. Ask this person to share his or her thoughts and feelings with you after the meeting(s).

- Do telephone and email "interviews" and discussions.

- Schedule a conversation (perhaps with video cameras) over the Internet or through a videoconference center.

- And remember to constantly rely on prayer and the power of meditation in your efforts from afar.

Marriage Can Be Forever—Preparation Counts!

Try to share important information or ask key questions **to the couple together** instead of communicating with the couple via your own son/daughter. Otherwise, there is potential for miscommunication and misunderstanding that can cause people to get upset. Obviously, since your son's/daughter's partner is someone you may have in your family, you will likely have to work with them on sensitive issues in the future —now is the best time to see how that goes and how/whether you can become closer in that dialogue. Marriage isn't just a conversation for the couple, it's often a larger conversation for the family.

If questions or concerns arise, or if you need guidance on any part of the Bahá'í Writings, you can choose to request a **meeting with a Spiritual Assembly**. It will do its best to research an answer for you and provide the necessary guidance.

The responsibility of giving consent is a great one. It reminds your son/daughter of the bonds of shared experiences, memories, and love between you. **Consent fully and freely given** is a gift of support to the couple. **Consent withheld for valid reasons**, no matter how difficult to communicate to the couple or for them to accept, is a mature and important act in support of your son's/daughter's growth and development. Often a waiting period allows a couple to resolve problems that might have eventually harmed their marriage. In other cases, it becomes clear that it is God's Will that they do not marry.

When you as parents married each other and had to ask your parents for consent, reflect on what was helpful or harmful to you in the process. Remember, this is a culture change in progress, and there are lessons learned along the way. What do you wish your parents' or your spouse's parents had done differently? What would you like to imitate? If you were denied consent to marry, how do you feel about that now? Have you dealt with (accepted; forgiven) any emotional issues from your own consent process?

If you did not have to ask for consent to be married and have been married, how might that have assisted your marriage to be stronger? If there are any facets that you think would have assisted it, what would you like to offer now that you are being asked for consent? What might have been harmful to you? How would you like to avoid that?

It may be useful to you to talk to other parents who have given or denied consent. What processes did they use to come to their conclusions? What do they wish they'd done differently? Try to find parents who have children with successful marriages as well as parents of children who have married and divorced. What do they think their child did effectively or ineffectively in getting to know his/her future spouse? What would they recommend you advise your own child and his/her partner to do? What advice do they have for you about consent?

You might also talk to couples you know who are successfully and unsuccessfully married and who received consent. What do they suggest to assist you in the process? What do they see as pitfalls in the process of giving/denying consent? Do they have insights that will help you better imagine what the couple is feeling in this process?

Prayer and meditation will probably be particularly critical for you at this point. You might pray that you be guided, that you see with clarity, and that you act with freedom from prejudice and in the best interest of your son/daughter, the couple, and your potential grandchildren. Meditate on what you feel as you pray. What thoughts come to you after you pray and as you meditate? Refer back to the "Dynamics of Prayer For Solving Problems or Obtaining Assistance" in Chapter 30.

> Ask your son/daughter and his/her intended about what they've learned in this book. There is a section of questions in each chapter that you might want to explore with them to better understand their potential compatibility and how well they've come to know one another.

Once you have **made a decision**, you will share it with the couple. Carefully think through anything you want to convey to them. Love? Support? Concerns? Requests? Will you want to pray together with the couple for either their forthcoming wedding or their strength in handling your denial. If you are giving consent, do you want to have a family celebration? This may also be a good time to discuss how to share the news about the engagement with others. Does the couple want to do it themselves, or can you be participants.

Marriage Can Be Forever—Preparation Counts!

Chapter 32 – Now It's Up to You: Parents Considering Consent

Everyone has their roles to play in the consent process—the couple, the parents, and the Spiritual Assembly. When they do this fully, it supports strong, healthy marriages.

Note: Reading Chapter 33 about denying consent may assist you in gaining a more complete perspective on the consent process. Remember, as well, that if any concerns arise for you during the couple's engagement, you have the option to withdraw consent. This is not a law to provoke a sense of power in your ability to do so. It is, rather, to ensure the parent has full latitude for making the best decision for the future well-being of his/her son/daughter.

Coaching

⇒ The questions throughout this book and many of the worksheets will assist you with determining the character and personality of your son/daughter and his/her intended spouse as well as the couple's compatibility. You might set aside a peaceful time (or series of times) to discuss them with the couple. Your in-depth involvement is vital in helping to ensure that they have the ability to sustain a long and happy marriage and be unified and effective as parents.

⇒ The consent process can be an incredible opportunity to heal, solidify, or create a relationship between children and parents, whether or not consent is forthcoming. Be open for opportunities to accomplish this.

⇒ Some parents like to put loving messages to their children in consent letters that they write. (Check with the Spiritual Assembly about whether they require it to be in writing.) Often a Spiritual Assembly is willing to return the original consents to a couple to keep.

⇒ If you choose to deny consent, this can also obviously be done lovingly. Consider writing a letter to your child and to his/her intended (separate or shared letters) telling them kindly and lovingly why you are refusing consent. You might include things that you admire about them individually as well. If you feel that your decision could change in the future if certain conditions were different, you might convey that to each of them so that they can work toward those goals. Their effort (or lack of) toward these goals may give you clarification and a more positive regard for their potential marriage. However, this would in no way bind you to giving consent in the future.

⇒ If you choose to make your consent conditional on the completion of something, be very clear with your child and his/her intended what the requirements are and any timing involved in completing them.

Questions for Reflection and Discussion

To the Parents:

1. What are your attitudes about the law of consent?
2. How might your attitudes affect the consent process?
3. What do you need to do to prepare yourselves to participate effectively?
4. Have you given or withheld consent before? What did you learn from the experience?
5. What virtues are most important for you to practice during the consent process?
6. How well do you already know the couple?
7. What methods of information gathering do you want to use for the process?
8. What activities can you do with the couple to better assess their readiness and compatibility?

Marriage Can Be Forever—Preparation Counts!

9. How will you know when you understand the character of your child's intended spouse? (See Appendix A)
10. What do you see as your role in determining if the couple is compatible? How can you assess their compatibility?
11. Do you want to consult with any of the other parents involved in the process? How will you do this?
12. Are you able to ask the couple or each of them as individuals any difficult questions about concerns you have?
13. Are you able to challenge answers you receive that you feel lack sincerity, truthfulness, or candor?
14. How will you know you are ready to give the couple your answer?
15. What do you want to say when you give consent?
16. What do you want to say if you are denying consent? (See Chapter 33 about consent denial.)

Activities

1. Pray, meditate, and reflect about the couple and your feelings about giving consent.

2. What do you need to know from/about the couple before you can give or deny consent?

3. What will you do to find out this information (in a way that is not a problem for the couple)?

4. Plan and carry out a social activity with the couple. What did you learn?

5. Plan and carry out a social activity with the couple and the other parents. What did you learn?

6. Plan and carry out a work or service project together with the couple. (Examples: a home repair or reorganizing project, hosting an overnight youth group, doing a cleanup of a city area) What did you learn?

7. Plan and carry out one or more study sessions on marriage with the couple. You may choose to use the quotes in the chapters on aspects of compatibility (Step 4) for example. This may give you an opportunity to share your own wisdom and experiences of marriage with the couple. What has come up in these sessions?

8. If you are uncomfortable about any of the communications with the couple, role-play with each other or close friends what you want to say. You may also wish to do this exercise before you give the couple your answer about consent.

9. If you are considering denying consent, you will find it helpful to review Chapter 33 that follows.

Marriage Can Be Forever—Preparation Counts!

LONELY-NESS

The problem of together-ness
is the after birthing lonely-ness

In reaching out to empty space
where solid-ness once lay

In lifting lips for kisses
and meeting only ghostly-ness

In turning, smiling wanting sharing
and finding him imaginary-ness

Contrary-ness. It's just my stubborn-ness
that wants him here instead

And then perhaps it's scary-ness
that I will be alone each day
And find myself in solitary-ness

But right-ness creeps between the sighs
I know the blessings of together-ness
are not forgotten, banished lost
They're warmed inside my heart
to soothe some of the after lonely-ness

~ Susanne Mariella Alexander

CHAPTER 33 – When the Answer is "No": Consent Denied

NOTE: This chapter is addressed to the couple, but it may also assist parents. Consider sharing it with your parents at the beginning of the consent process.

Focus Points

- Handling the emotions
- Relationship between the couple and the parents
- Understanding the reasons for denial
- The law of consent; appealing the denial

A Couple's Story

James' parents have given James and Lindsay their consent and blessings. The couple travels to meet with Lindsay's parents to hear their response.

"We've reached a decision," says Sam to the couple. "It's sort of provisional consent. Lindsay has just a few months to go until her degree is complete, and we think it would be wise for you both to have time together when she's not a student. She graduates in May, so if you're still sure about getting married, you can get engaged then. You said you wanted to be engaged for less than 3 months, so the wedding could then happen in August."

"We've talked about that too, Dad, that it would be good to have some time together when I'm not buried in books and exams," says Lindsay. "We're anxious to be married, but we can wait that long. Thank you both so much for taking us seriously and helping us to be together."

Quotes for Guidance

Note: Many of the quotes that are in Chapter 32 also apply to this chapter, so you may wish to refer to it.

- …loving-kindness to one's parents hath been linked to recognition of the one true God!
  (Bahá'u'lláh: *Kitáb-i-Aqdas*, Questions and Answers, p. 139)

- Think not that We have revealed unto you a mere code of laws. Nay, rather, We have unsealed the choice Wine with the fingers of might and power.
  (Bahá'u'lláh: *Kitáb-i-Aqdas*, p. 21)

- It is surely a very unfortunate case when the parents and children differ on some grave issues of life such as marriage, but the best way is not to flout each other's opinion nor to discuss it in a charged atmosphere but rather try to settle it in an amicable way.
  (Shoghi Effendi: *Bahá'í Marriage and Family Life*, p. 23)

Marriage Can Be Forever—Preparation Counts!

- There is nothing in the Writings, however, which requires a couple to get married once they have consent from all parents; they are quite free to change their minds. Likewise, if a parent changes his or her mind, he or she can withdraw his or her permission at any time before the marriage takes place, in which case the couple cannot get married.
    (Universal House of Justice: *Consent of Parents*, p. 40)

- All too often nowadays such consent is withheld by non-Bahá'í parents for reasons of bigotry or racial prejudice; yet we have seen again and again the profound effect on those very parents of the firmness of the children in the Bahá'í law, to the extent that not only is the consent ultimately given in many cases, but the character of the parents can be affected and their relationship with their child greatly strengthened.
    Thus, by upholding Bahá'í law in the face of all difficulties we not only strengthen our own characters but influence those around us.
    (Universal House of Justice: *Lights of Guidance*, p. 372)

- Bahá'ís who cannot marry because of lack of consent of one or more parents could consult with their Local Spiritual Assembly, to see whether it may suggest a way to change the attitude of any of the parents involved. The believers, when faced with such problems, should put their trust in Bahá'u'lláh, devote more time to the service, the teaching and the promotion of His Faith, be absolutely faithful to His injunctions on the observance of an unsullied, chaste life, and rely upon Him to open the way and remove the obstacle, or make known His will.
    (Universal House of Justice: *Developing Distinctive Bahá'í Communities*, 16.15)

- As to whether you may continue indefinitely to seek your parents' consent, there is nothing in the law of Bahá'u'lláh to prevent this, but no engagement should be announced until consent has been obtained.
    (Universal House of Justice: *Consent of Parents*, p. 54)

- ...consent of parents must be obtained in all cases before marriage can take place. Obedience to the laws of Bahá'u'lláh will necessarily impose hardships in individual cases. No one should expect, upon becoming a Bahá'í, that his faith will not be tested, and to our finite understanding of such matters these tests may occasionally seem unbearable. But we are aware of the assurance which Bahá'u'lláh Himself has given the believers that they will never be called upon to meet a test greater than their capacity to endure. It therefore becomes a matter of demonstration of the depth of one's faith when he is faced with a divine command the wisdom and rationale of which he cannot at that time understand.
    (Universal House of Justice: *Bahá'í Marriage and Family Life*, 24.78)

- The Universal House of Justice will offer ardent prayers in the Holy Shrines that your parents' hearts may be inspired and enlightened to see and consider the best interests of their daughter. It may be helpful in this regard to ask the assistance of the Local Spiritual Assembly of the area where your parents live, or of some wise and mature Bahá'ís to meet with your parents and gradually familiarize them with the tenets of the [Bahá'í] Faith and remove the misconceptions they have… You are strongly advised by the House of Justice to continue your loving attitude towards your parents and be assured that your dutiful obedience to your parents will attract Bahá'u'lláh's blessings and will ensure your future happiness.
    (Universal House of Justice: *Consent of Parents*, p. 39)

- While the House of Justice deeply sympathizes with the difficult situation facing Mr. … and well understands your earnest and sincere desire to be of assistance to him, the free consent of parents is necessary and binding, regardless of the reason which the decision to withhold consent is based on. As you are undoubtedly aware, entering into a marriage is a step that has tremendous implications for a whole range of people beyond the couple themselves, both in this life and in the next. The laws of the Faith are established on very sound foundations, and obedience to them is not only important for the proper development of society, but also for the attainment of true personal happiness.
    (On behalf of the Universal House of Justice to a National Spiritual Assembly: August 10, 2000)

Perspectives to Consider

If one or more of your parents has denied consent for you to marry, **the emotions** for you as a couple at this time are likely very mixed. There might be anger, frustration, disappointment, hope, relief, determination, love, denial, grief, or resignation. You will find it helpful to have the loving support of friends, family, and your Spiritual Assembly at this time. Be cautious, however, of slipping into self-pity and/or involving other people in being so sympathetic toward you that you stay buried in negative emotions. Also, be cautious and avoid anyone's attempts (including your own) to criticize and attack any of the parents.

Denial of consent is both **a test for the parents communicating their decision and for the couple**. For Bahá'ís, how you handle the denial is connected to how strong your faith in Bahá'u'lláh and His laws is—it's a test of faith. At times people think of the laws as a hindrance, whereas they are meant to bring people divine freedom, joy, and order. It may be some time before you feel His sweetness and grace, but faith will help you trust that all existence comes from divine love. At times, you may have difficulty recognizing that laws are part of the order of the universe.

Every circumstance will have different factors affecting how you handle the denial. In some cases, you might separate and stop your relationship altogether, you might address the concerns your parents have, or you may seek guidance from a Spiritual Assembly in handling specific issues that parents have raised.

Are you able to discuss with your parents the **reasons they have withheld consent**? If they can clarify their reasons, how do these affect your ongoing relationship with them? Do their points have validity, and you were not able to see them before? If you perceive that the reason is prejudice-based, is there anything you can do to help them shift their perspective? How can you honor your parents and maintain a relationship with them during this test? As a couple, examine your hearts and your willingness to be obedient and not marry. It may take you a period of prayer, meditation, consultation, and the passing of time before you reach acceptance.

At this time, determine whether you **should stop seeing each other** as potential marriage partners or whether you will **stay connected**. After a while, if you are still convinced that you wish to marry each other, you may wish to re-approach your parents. Be sure you have carried out anything they suggested you do. Perhaps they asked you to finish your education, grow in an aspect of maturity, not have any contact with each other, or live in the same geographic location as your intended partner. If they didn't give you specific guidelines, consult and pray together about what you can do to grow in your compatibility—and see if your parents are willing to give suggestions at a later point.

Depending on the reasons and circumstances, when consent is denied, there is **risk of disunity** as a result—between you as a couple, between your parents, and perhaps with others who have strong feelings or opinions on the matter. Avoiding this and focusing on unity is vitally important. Remember that one of the guidelines for consultation, which is likely applicable, is that everyone must abide by the decision in order to determine the best ultimate outcome (see Chapter 3). This will require great spiritual strength and maturity.

It is also wise to understand that there are **spiritual consequences if a Bahá'í chooses to disobey Bahá'í law and proceed with marriage without consent.** If a Bahá'í marriage does not happen, and only a civil one or one of another faith occurs, the Bahá'í community and institutions do not regard the couple as married. Breaking the marriage law can also result in a Bahá'í losing his or her administrative rights, which excludes the person from voting in elections, serving on administrative bodies, attending the 19-Day Feast, and giving to the Bahá'í Fund. The individual(s) would then have to consult with the Spiritual Assemblies at the local and national level about remedying this painful situation.

Marriage Can Be Forever—Preparation Counts!

Over time, you may start to see the **wisdom behind the denial**. Perhaps it is possible there were character concerns your parents could see but you couldn't. Perhaps there were issues that needed time for the two of you to resolve before marriage. Perhaps you discover someone else who becomes a potential marriage partner for you, and you are able to obtain consent with him or her. The reality is though, that painful as it may be, you may never know why and that this is fundamentally a question of faith. Use your energy to pray for strength, to take action to serve others, and to focus your energies on your own continuing development.

Coaching

⇒ Allow yourself to feel any negative emotions that come up, but begin to move toward the positive ones as soon as possible.

⇒ Stay in communication with your parents. Don't punish them or yourselves for their decision, even if you can't understand or don't agree with their reasons.

⇒ Strengthen your relationship with God through prayer, meditation, reading, and consultation with your spiritual community.

Questions for Reflection and Discussion

Parents

1. Are you clear about your motives and reasons for denying consent?
2. Are you willing to communicate your motives and reasons to the couple?
3. How will you support the couple in accepting your decision?
4. Are you clear about what would need to be different for you to change your mind(s) and give consent in the future?
5. Have you clearly communicated this to the couple?

Couple

1. What are your thoughts and feelings at this moment?
2. Will you continue or stop seeing each other?
3. Will you wait before going on to another relationship and patiently hope your parents change their minds and give consent?
4. What would you do to help your parents change their minds?
5. Will you part and search for someone else to be married to?
6. Will you consult with a Spiritual Assembly about the situation?

Activities

1. Spend time *separately* in a spiritual retreat for prayer, meditation, self-assessment, spiritual strengthening, and renewal. You may find it helpful to understand the reasons your parents have denied consent by re-reading the quotes from this book on consent (see Chapters 31-33) and reviewing your answers on the worksheets in the chapters in Step 4 about compatibility. Write in your journal about how you are feeling and what you think the future will be for you.

2. What are your feelings and how are you behaving?

   _____
   _____
   _____

3. What are you learning from this test?

   _____
   _____
   _____

4. Find someone you trust and share your feelings with him/her. Consider together how you can grow and move forward. What are the possibilities?

   _____
   _____
   _____

5. Pray, reflect, and then list what you love and appreciate about your parents.

   _____
   _____
   _____

6. When you can do so emotionally, sincerely share the above list with your parents. What was their response?

   _____
   _____

7. Outline two to three steps or goals you can accomplish in the next month to assist you to get through this difficult time. Revisit this list daily or weekly.

   _____
   _____
   _____

Marriage Can Be Forever—Preparation Counts!

Spiritual Nuggets for Reflection and Discussion

Bend to God's Will and Pleasure

Make me ready, in all circumstances, O my Lord, to serve Thee and to set myself towards the adored sanctuary of Thy Revelation and of Thy Beauty. If it be Thy pleasure, make me to grow as a tender herb in the meadows of Thy grace, that the gentle winds of Thy will may stir me up and bend me into conformity with Thy pleasure, in such wise that my movement and my stillness may be wholly directed by Thee.

~ Bahá'u'lláh: *Prayers and Meditations*, p. 240

The source of all good is trust in God, submission unto His command, and contentment with His holy will and pleasure.

~ Bahá'u'lláh: Tablets of Bahá'u'lláh, p. 155

Step 6

Move Forward: Wedding and Marriage

Marriage Can Be Forever—Preparation Counts!

Never Take a Relationship for Granted

When we are engaged, we tend to be very active. We look after ourselves and take care of our physical appearance. We make sure we always appear before our partner in the best possible way. We watch what we say and control our actions. We try to make up quarrels before parting so that no unpleasantness remains. It is easy for us to apologize to one another and make our peace. We each court the other and think that he or she is the most important thing in our lives. We live for the moment when we can see each other, embrace, speak and just be together. Even the smallest things done or experienced together are magical, acquire special meanings and evoke particular emotions such that a simple walk becomes a magnificent adventure. Afterwards we recall all the details and secretly relive every moment...It is amazing how much attention we pay and how actively we participate in what is going on when we are in the company of the person we love!

I am not suggesting that when we marry we can continue to dedicate the same level of attention to each other as the years go by, but we can at least make an effort not to take our relationships for granted and not to fall into the dullness of habit. It is important to make this effort so that our partner can be again for us a truly special person, not "just" a husband or a wife, the father or the mother of our children, but the person with whom we wish to share our significant moments. We should consciously reaffirm the choice we made at the beginning of the relationship and not simply take it for granted or put up with it because at this point we have to make do.

Love should be renewed every day....

~ Mehri Sefidvash, *Coral and Pearls*, pp. 2-3

CHAPTER 34 – It's Almost Here: The Engagement Period

Focus Points

- Age-level for marriage
- Length of time for engagement
- Activities during the engagement period
- Meeting with the Spiritual Assembly/clergyperson
- Building family relationships
- Handling doubts

A Couple's Story

"Man, I can see why Bahá'u'lláh said short engagements were a good thing," says James. "I'm so ready to be married. Whoever said cold showers worked was crazy. At least one thing you'll know about my character though is discipline and perseverance!"

"I agree, but there are just a few weeks left," says Lindsay. "We can do it. Here's another stack of invitations to address."

Quotes for Guidance

✸ It is unlawful to become engaged to a girl [or boy] before she [he] reaches the age of maturity [15 years old].
(Bahá'u'lláh, *Kitáb-i-Aqdas*, p. 150)

✸ Bahá'í engagement is the perfect communication and the entire consent of both parties. However, they must show forth the utmost attention and become informed of one another's character and the firm covenant made between each other must become an eternal binding, and their intentions must be everlasting affinity, friendship, unity and life.
('Abdu'l-Bahá: *Tablets of 'Abdu'l-Bahá, Vol. 2*, p. 325)

✸ The pledge of marriage, the verse to be spoken individually by the bride and the bridegroom in the presence of at least two witnesses acceptable to the Spiritual Assembly is, as stipulated in *The Kitáb-i-Aqdas* (The Most Holy Book): "We will, all, verily, abide by the Will of God."
('Abdu'l-Bahá: *Bahá'í Prayers* (US 2002), p. 117)

✸ The Laws of *The Kitáb-i-Aqdas* regarding the period of engagement have not been made applicable to believers in the West, and therefore there is no requirement that the parties to a marriage obtain consent of the parents before announcing their engagement. However, there is no objection to informing the believers that it would be wise for them to do so in order to avoid later embarrassment if consents are withheld.
(Universal House of Justice: *Consent of Parents*, p. 54)

Marriage Can Be Forever—Preparation Counts!

❋ ...the law of *The Kitáb-i-Aqdas* that the lapse of time between engagement and marriage should not exceed ninety-five days, is binding on Persian believers wherever they reside, if both parties are Persian. This law is not applicable, however, if one of the parties is a Western believer.
    (On behalf of the Universal House of Justice: *Lights of Guidance*, p. 377)

Perspectives to Consider

Once all parents have given their consents, you can feel free to **share with others that you are engaged** (hopefully you didn't choose to do it beforehand since you were *not* engaged without consent being offered), and you can begin to plan the wedding. Additionally, you are encouraged to continue getting to know one another other and **each other's character**. This can often be a stressful time for couples, which will give you an opportunity to understand how you both respond to and support each other when faced with tests. The virtues of honesty, truthfulness, and self-discipline (such as with chastity) have been important throughout your relationship, but they are especially important at this stage. You are close to committing to an eternal partnership, and you must continue to be truthful with each other about your pasts, your thoughts, your feelings, in short, anything at all that might be relevant, appropriate, or might affect the success of your marriage.

Review the marriage vision/intentions you created in Chapter 29, and continue consulting about the extraordinary wonder of **creating your marriage**. What practices such as praying together, being of service to others, participating in the arts together, and so on, will help ensure your marriage will be a strong "fortress for well-being and salvation"? Looking forward to your marriage is a reminder that your focus must be more on the *marriage* you are creating than on the *wedding day* details.

Early in the engagement period, **meet with the Spiritual Assembly and/or clergyperson** that will handle the official paperwork for your wedding (see Chapter 35). For Bahá'ís, a Bahá'í ceremony is required, and the Spiritual Assembly is the administrative body that ensures all details are in order for the marriage to be carried out correctly under both Bahá'í and civil law. It will review any paperwork from previous marriages and divorces, **verify parental consents, and approve the two witnesses** you choose to observe the Bahá'í wedding vow. *Spend some time praying and thinking about who is special to you both that you would like to have witness your wedding.*

The Spiritual Assembly cannot approve or disapprove your marriage, nor does it have the right to stop or discourage you from marrying. However, you may wish to ask for its advice about preparing for marriage and the ceremony as well as about your compatibility. If you **request its input**, the Spiritual Assembly is free to give it to you. *This may be a very wise and helpful request for you to consider making as a commitment to being thorough in your preparation process. The Spiritual Assembly may have perspectives you never considered.* Here again, being truthful and candid is necessary for your future happiness. *Lying or hiding concerns, facts, or details from the Spiritual Assembly about your situation will put cracks in the foundation of your marriage "fortress."* If you are meeting with a clergyperson, he/she may also have input for you. Many religious congregations and their leaders offer formal **marriage preparation programs** and may require you to participate in them during your engagement. Many communities and organizations also offer helpful courses or counseling sessions on preparation for marriage for engaged couples. Workshops based on this book may be available to you (or you can organize one!).

You will set your desired **engagement length**, and the Bahá'í Faith encourages this stage to be short. While the Bahá'í law restricting the engagement to 95 days is only applicable for Persians [people from Iran, where the Bahá'í Faith began], it is an option for any couple to follow it, and you may wish to reflect on its wisdom and potentially abide by it. The longer the engagement, the more difficult it will likely be to abstain from sex. As well, you may be tempted to spend months or years and considerable resources planning a very elaborate wedding instead of going forward into marriage.

The engagement period (and planning the marriage ceremony) is also a good time to develop your **relationships with your parents, families, and future in-laws** even more. You may involve them in planning your wedding provided this can be done peacefully. This is a good time to discuss with them what you want your relationship to be like after the wedding, how frequently you will likely see each other, whether you wish to visit them or have them visit you or both, and what roles (there will be multiple roles probably) you will play in each other's lives. You may wish to consult about what support or assistance they might offer, and how much involvement they will wish to have with any children you currently have or may have in the future.

You may feel very sure about your relationship when you head into your engagement. As time draws closer to the marriage commitment, however, **you may have doubts.** You might simply have concerns about the responsibility that accompanies marriage, and you will be able to reassure each other. You might be feeling stress from planning the wedding or wishing to be together faster. Are you having difficulty consulting with each other? Are you clear what your doubts, fears, and concerns are? *If the doubts that are arising relate to your partner's character (or your own!) or your potential incompatibility, you must pay attention and not shove them aside because you fear the consequences of postponing or canceling the wedding. You could also be thinking that all will well once you are married. Be very careful, as this may be false and unwise thinking.*

The consequences of moving forward into marriage with serious problems are likely to be far worse than any consequences of **postponing or canceling the wedding**. When the incompatibility or issues arise *after* marriage, they may lead to a very painful divorce. You need to trust the Spiritual Assembly, your clergyperson, your parents, your partner, a counselor, or someone else enough to sort out your feelings, talk through your concerns, and then take appropriate action. *Even on your wedding day, you could choose to cancel the ceremony and turn it into a party and celebration of friendships and families rather than go through with the marriage.* Many couples who have divorced have said they knew they were making a mistake on their wedding days and wished they had turned it into a party and celebration instead. Who knows? If they had delayed, perhaps they still would have married but would have had a sustainable marriage.

Alternatively, you may start your engagement very certain that you want to be married and be just as sure as the wedding approaches and on your wedding day. This is wonderful! You can then **confidently go forward** into the ceremony that will join you eternally as companions in a spiritually-based marriage.

Note: Many couples also use this time to plan a **honeymoon trip** to take after the ceremony. This is certainly not a requirement, and not all couples may be able to afford the money or time to take one. Consider it carefully, however, as it can be a restful time to recover from any pre-wedding stress and give you an opportunity to start your marriage away from daily responsibilities.

Coaching

⇒ Decide to learn one new thing about your partner each week.

⇒ The engagement period can be an opportunity to build relationships with friends and family in new and exciting ways. Plan activities that will fill each day with fun and love.

Marriage Can Be Forever—Preparation Counts!

❓ Questions for Reflection and Discussion

1. When will you announce your engagement?
2. How will you continue to learn about each other's character?
3. What if you discover something that seriously concerns you?
4. Do you have any other doubts or concerns? How will you handle them?
5. What if you need to call off the wedding? What might stop you? Can you consult and come to an agreement on this?
6. If you do decide to call off the wedding, who will handle announcing it, returning gifts, and stopping the arrangements? Or, will you go forward with a party for friends and family instead of a wedding?
7. How will you cope with stress that may come up during this planning period?
8. Will you have an engagement party? Who will plan and pay for it? Will there be gifts?
9. How widely will you announce your engagement?
10. Who will notify people about your engagement? Shared?
11. Who will you choose as your two witnesses (if it's a Bahá'í wedding)? Has the Spiritual Assembly approved them?
12. Will you use an engagement ring or other mutual commitment symbol? (**Note:** This is optional.)
13. Will you have a honeymoon? When? For how long? Who will make the plans? Who will pay for it?

Activities

1. Pray, meditate, reflect, and write in your journal about the things that are important to you during engagement in addition to planning the wedding.

2. Plan and carry out an activity that you have never done together that will challenge you both in new ways. What did you do and how did it turn out? Did you learn anything new about each other?
   _____
   _____

3. Plan, prepare, and serve a meal for your future in-laws. How did it work out?
   _____

A Spiritual Nugget for Reflection and Discussion

> Wherefore, wed Thou in the heaven of Thy mercy these two birds of the nest of Thy love, and make them the means of attracting perpetual grace; that from the union of these two seas of love a wave of tenderness may surge and cast the pearls of pure and goodly issue on the shore of life.
>
> 'Abdu'l-Bahá: *Bahá'í Prayers* (US 2002), p. 119)

The Song of Life

From my young and tender years
Through my hopes and all my fears,
I've been nurtured by a wondrous loving song.

As I've learned to deal with life
Through my joy and through my strife,
I realized I've heard it singing all along.

And I've learned that all the times
I've ever yearned were the times
When I've been taught of right and wrong.

I've found that the longing of my heart
Has been for you right from the start.
The song is life.
The song is love.
You are the song.

Some songs are sung only by the very young,
When life was still unfettered new and free.

And when the truth is told
Some are sung when very old,
And there are some that must be sung in harmony.

The song of life sung by a husband and a wife
Is a song of union blessed by God above.

Come, sing with me and we will be a family
That sings of life,
And sings of joy,
and sings God's love.

And we will, all, verily, abide by the Will of God.
And we will, all, verily, abide by the Will of God.
And we will, all, verily, abide by the Will of God.

~ John Taylor

CHAPTER 35 – The Big Day: Creating Your Marriage Ceremony

Focus Points
- The ceremony's required elements
- Other religious wedding ceremonies
- The Spiritual Assembly's obligations
- Creating your own ceremony
- Responsibility for arrangements

A Couple's Story

James and Lindsay are deep in the middle of finalizing their wedding plans. They meet with the local hotel manager to consult about having the ceremony there, and look at options on Lindsay's campus. James starts out feeling strongly that they should rent the hotel and have a large and fancy wedding. He and Lindsay consult through all the options and the reasons for each. In the end, they agree on having the ceremony near the lake in a park they both love and a reception at the hotel.

"I'm so glad the ceremony is going to be simple, and that all our family will be with us," says James. "By the lake is the perfect place."

"And having the people who are coming to the reception bring books for the Literacy Center along with or instead of their presents is such a cool idea," says Lindsay. "It will make people happy to do it, and it's great for the kids too."

"Yeah, Mom had a great idea with that one," says James. "And who would have ever guessed Tony has such a great voice…his song will be perfect."

Quotes for Guidance

- Glory be unto Thee, O my God! Verily, this Thy servant and this Thy maidservant have gathered under the shadow of Thy mercy and they are united through Thy favor and generosity. O Lord! Assist them in this Thy world and Thy kingdom and destine for them every good through Thy bounty and grace. O Lord! Confirm them in Thy servitude and assist them in Thy service. Suffer them to become the signs of Thy Name in Thy world and protect them through Thy bestowals which are inexhaustible in this world and the world to come. O Lord! They are supplicating the kingdom of Thy mercifulness and invoking the realm of Thy singleness. Verily, they are married in obedience to Thy command. Cause them to become the signs of harmony and unity until the end of time. Verily, Thou art the Omnipotent, the Omnipresent and the Almighty!
  ('Abdu'l-Bahá: *Bahá'í Prayers* (US 2002), p. 120)

✸ The obligation of the Spiritual Assembly is to ascertain that all requirements of civil and Bahá'í law have been complied with, and, having done so, the Assembly may neither refuse to perform the marriage ceremony nor delay it.
(Universal House of Justice: *Lights of Guidance*, p. 368)

✸ Normally the size of the wedding celebration, the place in which it is to be held and who is to be invited are all left entirely to the discretion of the bride and groom.
(Universal House of Justice: *Lights of Guidance*, p. 387)

✸ When two Bahá'ís are marrying, the wedding ceremony should not be held in the place of worship of another religion, nor should the forms of the marriage of other religions be added to the simple Bahá'í ceremony. When a Bahá'í is marrying a non-Bahá'í, and the religious wedding ceremony of the non-Bahá'í partner is to be held in addition to the Bahá'í ceremony, both ceremonies may, if requested, be held in the place of worship of the other religion provided that equal respect is accorded to both ceremonies. In other words, the Bahá'í ceremony, which is basically so simple, should not be regarded as a mere formal adjunct to the ceremony of the other religion. The two ceremonies are clearly distinct. In other words, they should not be commingled into one combined ceremony.
(On behalf of the Universal House of Justice: *Lights of Guidance*, p. 389)

✸ When the consent of the parents is obtained, the only other requirement for the ceremony is the recitation by both parties in the presence of two witnesses of the specifically revealed verse: "We will, all, verily, abide by the Will of God." The following quotations from letters written by the Guardian's secretary indicate the desirability of the Bahá'í marriage ceremony being simple:

> "There is no ritual, according to the *Aqdas*, and the Guardian is very anxious that none should be introduced at present and no general form accepted. He believes the ceremony should be as simple as possible.... The only compulsory part of a Bahá'í wedding is the pledge of marriage, the phrase to be spoken separately by the Bride and Bridegroom in turn, in the presence of Assembly witnesses."
(On behalf of the Universal House of Justice: *Lights of Guidance*, pp. 387-388)

Perspectives to Consider

The Spiritual Assembly or clergyperson that is responsible for legalizing your wedding will likely want to meet personally with you both. Some may choose not to, but be sure to meet with them at any point if it's important to you. Spiritual Assemblies and the clergy are responsible for promoting, supporting, and encouraging strong marriages in their communities. If, unfortunately, an aversion develops between you later, and you separate, they would be involved in counseling you. Establishing a strong, loving bond with them, therefore, is often beneficial to you and can help *prevent* divorce.

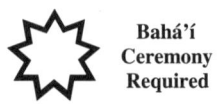

Bahá'í Ceremony Required If at least one of you being married is a Bahá'í, then a Bahá'í marriage ceremony must be one ceremony that occurs. It may be the only one, if you live in a place where it is legally recognized. You may also be having a ceremony from another faith. Remember that if a Bahá'í one will be held as well, the two ceremonies cannot be co-mingled, although they can occur at the same place.

If you are having a **Bahá'í wedding**, you marry each other during the ceremony by reciting the vow, **"We will, all, verily, abide by the Will of God"** in front of two Spiritual Assembly-approved witnesses and under the authority of a Spiritual Assembly. Essentially no one is marrying you; you are marrying each other, as there is no clergy in the Bahá'í Faith. All other aspects of the ceremony are your own choice.

The **marriage ceremony** will likely reflect your personalities and cultures. You may choose music, readings, and prayers—in any combination you wish. 'Abdu'l-Bahá and Shoghi Effendi both presented examples to Bahá'ís of holding simple spiritual ceremonies in contrast to the lavish displays that are common today.

In deciding on the form, content, and flow of your marriage ceremony, the principles of consultation are once again helpful tools to rely upon. Try to ensure that each of you is able to share your desires about what the ceremony should feel like, where you would like to have it, how many guests you will have, and so on. The manner in which you consult about the wedding will likely be a good prelude to how you will consult on other important matters in your marriage (see Chapter 3).

Your consultation might also include the involvement of your family in planning the wedding. Very often, family members have a strong attachment to how a couple's wedding "should" go. Pray and consult together about how you think different family members would like to be included and how you would like (or not) to include them. This is clearly your wedding—and it is also likely to be a special day for your family. Your approach to the inclusion of your family in planning your wedding and the wedding itself may offer you significant insights into how you expect other family dynamics to play out over the course of your marriage.

If you invest excessive time and money in the wedding and everything associated with the ceremony, this might prevent you from voicing doubts and stopping the wedding if you change your mind(s) about marrying. It could also leave you with debts that handicap you early in marriage.

When you are going confidently forward into marriage, the ceremony can be an opportunity for a community of friends and relatives to gather in love, support, and celebration of a new family. It is a transition ceremony, allowing you and others to acknowledge you as a married couple and not just two individuals. With the wedding, your relationships with your family, friends, and community become different. A marriage ceremony marks the beginning of the eternal journey of your two souls together.

Coaching

⇒ Consult with each other about what would make your guests and family happy. You may find that if you have the focus on them, you will create a wonderful occasion for yourselves as well. What atmosphere do you want? Reverent? Party? Sophisticated? Laid-back? It's up to you to design what is important to you.

⇒ Consider that you have a choice between receiving gifts and requesting that people donate to a worthy cause instead, or provide both as options. Bahá'ís could contribute to the Bahá'í funds in your honor, and people of other faiths may choose to do something similar. Your guests could perhaps bring non-perishable food that you donate to a food bank that serves hungry families.

Questions for Reflection and Discussion

Note: This book is not intended to be a wedding planner manual. You may wish to locate other resources.

1. What atmosphere and experience are you trying to create in the ceremony? (Possibly consider this prayerfully and silently first before beginning your consultation on the question.)

2. Who, if anyone besides the two of you, would you like to include to help you plan the wedding?
3. What resources/people might you draw on to assist you in carrying out the details of the wedding once you have decided upon them?
4. Who would you like to invite? Who would you miss having there if they couldn't come?
5. What do you want the total budget for your wedding to be? How will you ascertain what items will cost and what is a reasonable budget? How will you ensure you maintain the budget? Who pays for what? (This decision-making process will be another indicator for you of how you are likely to handle other financial issues in your marriage.)
6. What things, if any, will you ask your parents to pay for?
7. How will you invite people to come? Printed invitations? Handwritten notes? Traditional? Unique? E-mail? Hand delivered? On balloons? (Remember: You can be as creative as you like.)
8. Will you create a website with all the wedding details and directions for people to easily access?
9. If you decide to have a gift registry, how will you let people know about it? Will you make that available on-line?
10. Will you require people to let you know they are coming to the wedding/reception (RSVPs)? Will it be open invitation to whomever wants to come? If you do have RSVPs, who will handle the replies from guests?
11. Where will the ceremony take place? If you choose an outdoor location, what will be your backup plan if there is poor weather?
12. Will there be decorations? If so, who will do them? Will there be flowers?
13. Will you have a program or a handout? What content will you put in it? Design? Printing?
14. Are there any cultural customs or practices to include, avoid, or take into consideration?
15. Will someone explain Bahá'í weddings, the Bahá'í Faith, or any other unfamiliar ceremony elements to the guests? Who will do this, and will you review the content beforehand?
16. What will be the ceremony content (prayers, readings, music, vows, etc.)?
17. Who will participate in the ceremony? What will your parents' and families' participation be?
18. Will you have a reception? Where? On the same day as the wedding? Same location? Will there be music? Dancing? Anything else?
19. Will you offer refreshments or a meal? How much food/drink? Who will pay for this? Who will prepare the food? Who will serve the guests?
20. Will you have any particular guidelines for food and other items used during the ceremony? (Examples: everything organic and eco-friendly; no alcohol served at Bahá'í weddings)
21. Will there be music or a band? Who chooses this?
22. Will you have a still photographer? A videographer? Will you have time away from your guests to do photos? Before or after the ceremony? With or without family? How long do you want to take for this? What instructions will you give the photographers/videographers? Will you allow photography during prayers?
23. Who will coordinate all the details of the event? Have you considered all the travel and accommodation logistics? Do you have it written down to assist participants and family?
24. Will it be one event, or will there be a weekend-long or series of events surrounding the wedding?
25. What are you including in the occasion that will consolidate your relationship as a couple with the people who attend?
26. Is there an element that you would like to add that relates to service? (Examples: giving out seeds to be planted for flowers or trees, doing a service project with the guests rather than a reception, hosting a larger community event rather than a formal reception to celebrate your union, having canned foods donated at the wedding)
27. Will you have a practice/rehearsal? When? How will you ensure participants are there? Will you need anyone to assist you in coordinating the practice? (**Note:** If it's near the time of the wedding, you may be grateful not to have to gather your family and friends who are participating, but to have someone else do it.)
28. Will you use wedding rings or other commitment symbols? (**Note:** This is optional.)
29. What will your last names be after the ceremony? The same name that one of you already has, a newly created name, or a combined name? If it is the same name that one of you already has, whose previous last name will you use?
30. If one or both of you change your last name, what steps will you have to take to change names legally with the government and on various documents and financial records? Who will be responsible for this?

Marriage Can Be Forever—Preparation Counts!

Activities

1. Pray, meditate, reflect, and write in your journal about what is important for your marriage ceremony.

2. Agree on a vision and desired feel for your marriage ceremony:

   _____
   _____
   _____
   _____

3. Draw a picture or create a collage of what a creative and enjoyable ceremony for you might look like by cutting out pictures and words from magazines and gluing them on a large sheet of paper or cardboard. How do you want people to remember the day? How do *you* want to remember the day? (An alternative might be to write a poem or song.)

4. Whose needs do you want to meet as part of the wedding, including your own? Whose have a higher priority? What are their specific requirements and desires? Can you keep them simple?

   _____
   _____
   _____
   _____

5. Use Worksheet 35A to brainstorm creative ideas for your ceremony/ceremonies.

6. Continue to consult and plan the ceremony together. Set timelines, goals, and check on the details.

Chapter 35 – The Big Day: Creating Your Marriage Ceremony

Date: _____

Worksheet 35A: Planning the Marriage Ceremony

DIRECTIONS: Brainstorm creative ideas for your ceremony/ceremonies. What will make it special for everyone? For the Bahá'í ceremony, you can create whatever you wish beyond the necessary inclusion of the marriage vow and the presence of two approved witnesses; so be creative about what you want and don't want! Remember that brainstorming is a creative flow experience. There are no wrong answers—don't react negatively or give feedback on any ideas at this stage. You may find it helpful to do this as a three-step process:

- Separately from each other, write down what you would like to have as part of the ceremony and as activities around the ceremony, if any, such as a family dinner the night before or a reception afterward.
- Then come together and fill out the sheet below with all your combined ideas. Add more possibilities as they come up, *without judging them or evaluating*. Even if an idea seems ludicrous (or worse) at first, if you show respect to your partner and allow any and everything to be shared, it is likely that other more reasonable and useful ideas will be generated. Criticism or judgment at this stage will limit the value and creativity of the consultation.
- Once you have the full, creative, and potentially unfeasible list, consult about what to keep and what not to. If you don't agree, then pray, take a break, or come back to it later.

Worksheets may be printed from www.claricomm.com/publishing

Consult—Keep It?	IDEAS

Marriage Can Be Forever—Preparation Counts!

A Spiritual Nugget for Reflection and Discussion

Circle of Unity

Bahá'u'lláh has drawn the circle of unity, He has made a design for the uniting of all the peoples, and for the gathering of them all under the shelter of the tent of universal unity. This is the work of the Divine Bounty, and we must all strive with heart and soul until we have the reality of unity in our midst, and as we work, so will strength be given unto us. Leave all thought of self, and strive only to be obedient and submissive to the Will of God. In this way only shall we become citizens of the Kingdom of God, and attain unto life everlasting.

~ 'Abdu'l-Bahá: *Paris Talks*, p. 54

World-Stopped Moment

sun, wind, and sky
soaring eagle, flying hearts
entwining, connecting
linking hands, touching minds
reassuring of caring
windlift and lakebreeze
gulls holding in air
deep spring green grass
yielding its scent
driftwood and shells
covering still-wintered beach
crunching and crackling
'neath unisoned feet
fresh-air kissed skin
lakesparkled treasure
words lifted to God
enriching and precious
moments of time

~ Susanne Mariella Alexander

CHAPTER 36 – An Adventure: The First Year Together

> **Focus Points**
> - The emotional roller coaster
> - The sanctity of marriage and family
> - The importance of consultation
> - Adjusting to each other
> - Adjusting to shared living space
> - Getting to know each other's families and friends
> - The importance of love and spiritual practices
> - Mentoring and counseling
> - Consolidating your relationship with love, fun, and service

A Couple's Story

Lindsay walks through the door after spending the day at her new job. James is already home and comes to greet her with a hug. "Ah, hugs are one of the best parts of marriage," she says. "I just love being married to you."

"I never thought we'd get through those first few weeks, though," says James. "Adjusting to being together in that small apartment was rough. I'm so glad we've found something bigger."

"Yes, it's been fun setting it up and decorating it," says Lindsay. "And now we've each got some space for our desks."

"How about a walk before we cook dinner?" asks James.

Quotes for Guidance

✸ In this glorious Cause the life of a married couple should resemble the life of the angels in heaven—a life full of joy and spiritual delight, a life of unity and concord, a friendship both mental and physical. The home should be orderly and well-organized. Their ideas and thoughts should be like the rays of the sun of truth and the radiance of the brilliant stars in the heavens. Even as two birds they should warble melodies upon the branches of the tree of fellowship and harmony. They should always be elated with joy and gladness and be a source of happiness to the hearts of others. They should set an example to their fellow-men, manifest true and sincere love towards each other and educate their children in such a manner as to blazon the fame and glory of their family.
('Abdu'l-Bahá: *Lights of Guidance*, pp. 220-221)

✸ Never speak disparagingly of others, but praise without distinction.
('Abdu'l-Bahá: *Promulgation of Universal Peace*, p. 453)

Marriage Can Be Forever—Preparation Counts!

✸ According to the teachings of Bahá'u'lláh the family, being a human unit, must be educated according to the rules of sanctity. All the virtues must be taught the family. The integrity of the family bond must be constantly considered, and the rights of the individual members must not be transgressed. The rights of the son, the father, the mother—none of them must be transgressed, none of them must be arbitrary. Just as the son has certain obligations to his father, the father, likewise, has certain obligations to his son. The mother, the sister and other members of the household have their certain prerogatives. All these rights and prerogatives must be conserved, yet the unity of the family must be sustained. The injury of one shall be considered the injury of all; the comfort of each, the comfort of all; the honor of one, the honor of all.
('Abdu'l-Bahá: *Promulgation of Universal Peace*, p. 168)

✸ ...the House of Justice feels it most essential for your husband and you to understand that marriage can be a source of well-being, conveying a sense of security and spiritual happiness. However, it is not something that just happens. For marriage to become a haven of contentment it requires the cooperation of the marriage partners themselves, and the assistance of their families.
(Universal House of Justice: *Compilation of Compilations, Vol. II*, p. 384)

✸ Family consultation employing full and frank discussion, and animated by awareness of the need for moderation and balance, can be the panacea for domestic conflict. Wives should not attempt to dominate their husbands, nor husbands their wives...
(On behalf of the Universal House of Justice: Universal House of Justice: *Compilation of Compilations, Vol. II*, p. 383)

Perspectives to Consider

Adjustment *is probably the single most applicable word for the beginning of marriage.* You will have to practice the virtue of flexibility often! It's like an orchestra—the instruments have to tune up and practice a bit before they sound melodious. You will likely go back and forth between being on your best "honeymoon" behavior and wondering what on earth possessed you to marry this person. One moment, you'll wonder why he or she can't be more like you. And the next, you'll be glad he or she isn't.

Privacy, together and alone time, space, intimacy, schedules, roles, responsibilities, and the like will take months (or years!) to adjust to and sort out. Over time, you will likely feel comfortable sharing space so closely with another human being. This can be even more challenging if you are living with other people, such as your parents or children from previous relationships. And there will be the moments when you reach out to hug or pray or share something funny, and you are so very, very glad the other person is right there sharing your life with you.

There will be days when you may think you can't handle one more stress, challenge, adjustment, meeting to go to, class to take, load of laundry, newspaper to pick up, or diaper to change. Then a **flood of love** for your partner will fill you up and light your heart, and you are glad he or she is there to share the one more stress and challenge with you. And laugh with you, tease you, and sympathize with you.

Every **issue that you did and didn't spot during your courtship** is likely to surface in the first year. It's a major milestone to persevere and make it to the first anniversary for some couples. Others sail through it on a perpetual honeymoon...and don't start to lose that rosy glow until around year three. Does one of you always want to make love when the other has a term paper due? Are the dishes never done except on weekends? Does one of you have a problem with alcohol or drugs? Are hormonal cycles a difficult time?

Marriage Can Be Forever—Preparation Counts!

In addition to adjusting to each other, you probably have also both gained extended families. So, there are new relationships to build, sensitivities to watch out for, new patterns to develop. Whose house do you go to for holidays? Does your mother-in-law (and new husband) think you should cook the exact same way as she does? Does your father-in-law insist on taking you fishing, which you hate? Does your spouse's ex-wife or ex-husband insist on different child custody than you want? Do all your kids insist on having meals cooked their own special way? Does your sister-in-law disapprove of you playing in a rock music band?

The more challenging life is, the more it will help to spend time each day praying together and **keeping God and love as the foundation of your relationship**. A significant part of what can sustain couples through these challenges is a mutual spiritual life. If you are praying, studying spiritual books together, and spending time with your spiritual community it will support you through the cycles and changes of married life. Continue to develop your friendship with each other within the "fortress for well-being and salvation." Nurture your marriage through continuing to build trust, respect, the ability to praise and encourage each other's positive attributes and qualities, honesty, sharing, and giving each other the space to be yourselves.

Nurture your marriage every day. Hug each other often and long. Offer to **be of service to each other**—a massage, a bubble bath, or an invitation out for a "date" at the right moment can be a wonderful gift. Be committed to sharing your concerns and not burying them. Give each other permission to offer coaching comments lovingly when there is an area for growth. Take time to play, laugh, and have fun together. Express your love to each other often. Communicate, communicate, communicate. Love, love, love. And be blessed....

Coaching

⇒ Mentoring is a concept that has often been successful in the business world. Married couples might also find it beneficial to connect regularly with an established married couple or trusted individual for coaching and guidance.

⇒ Many cities, Bahá'í communities, Bahá'í schools, faith-based non-profits, and all types of congregations offer marriage classes that can be a resource for you.

⇒ Every few weeks, review the Intentions of Your Marriage that you developed as an activity in Chapter 29. Assess your progress in incorporating these practices in your marriage.

⇒ Set up a nightly "debriefing" of two things that were effective in the marriage that day and two things that could be improved upon. At this time, you might also each share one thing or virtue you are working on in your own personal development so you can support each other with it.

Questions for Reflection and Discussion

1. Where will you live and for how long?
2. Are you setting aside your own pleasure at times to do something that is important for your spouse? Do you feel this is a positive or negative thing? Is it in balance?
3. How do you act when you introduce your husband or wife or speak about him or her to others? Happy? Proud? Embarrassed? Loving? Critical?

4. How are you fostering positive character growth in each other?
5. How are you doing with consulting before making decisions and listening respectfully and attentively to each other's points of view?
6. Are you setting aside time each day to share your experiences and thoughts about the day with each other?
7. Are you asking each other what went well and what could be improved in your communications and in other facets of the relationship?
8. How are your finances working? What could you change to improve your situation? What would you like to keep doing and building upon?
9. What goals/intentions are you accomplishing together? How about with your individual goals? Is there anything that you want to re-commit to doing or that you need to begin doing?
10. What things are you doing regularly that show you care about each other?
11. Are you comfortable asking each other for what you need?
12. How is the division of labor in your household? Is it reasonable and fair?
13. How is the balance in your activities and service?
14. How do you greet each other when you have been apart?
15. How are you regularly reaffirming your love for God and each other?
16. Are you allowing enough time to read, pray, and meditate on your own? Are you reading and praying together?
17. How are you building family unity?
18. Is your marriage or are your shared efforts being of service to others? If so, how? If not, would you like them to be? What could you do to accomplish that as an ongoing goal?
19. Are you deepening your knowledge of the Bahá'í Faith—or your chosen religion? Are you sharing it with others?
20. Are you finding the marriage a place where you cannot only successfully grow as a couple, but where each of you can continue to learn and grow individually?

Activities

1. Pray, meditate, reflect, and write in your journal about how your marriage is going and what you would like to see happening differently. Also write what you would like to continue to have happen that is working well. Share both of these with your spouse.

2. Pick a time of day that fits your schedule to pray together. Try it for 3 weeks, and see if it becomes a spiritual practice that you want to continue.

3. Memorize a prayer or quote together once a week or every other week.

4. Study the Bahá'í Writings or other scriptures together.

5. Request a need be met you've never asked for before, figure out together how to meet it, and then reciprocate. (Examine whether you can meet your partner's desire *without* a need for reciprocation.)

6. Set aside a few hours or a weekend and "run away" to do something fun.

7. Spend time going back through this book together. Are there chapters where the questions or worksheets can assist you?

8. Use Worksheet 36A to develop your goals and plans for the future.

Date: _____

Worksheet 36A: Partnership—Your Goals for the Future

DIRECTIONS: Use this sheet to develop your goals. What is your SHARED dream for the future?

Worksheets may be printed from www.claricomm.com/publishing

1. What would you most like to accomplish with your lives together?

   _____
   _____

2. At the end of your lives here on earth, what would you like to be said about you as a couple? What will you have done to contribute to the well-being and prosperity of the world?

   _____
   _____

3. What is your 5-year or 10-year plan for working toward these shared lifelong goals?

   a. Outline your specific goal(s):

      _____
      _____
      _____
      _____
      _____

   b. Strategy(s) for achieving goal(s):   By When?

      _____   _____
      _____   _____
      _____   _____
      _____   _____

4. What can you do now to begin to achieve your life goals together?

   _____
   _____
   _____

5. What additional tools or skills do you need to gain to work toward these shared goals?

   _____
   _____
   _____

Note: Remember to write the timeframe and goals in your planner or calendar. Agree on when to evaluate and revisit them. Mark these dates in your calendar as well.

Marriage Can Be Forever—Preparation Counts!

And when He (God) desired to manifest grace and beneficence to men, and to set the world in order, He revealed observances and created laws; among them He established the law of marriage, made it as a fortress for well-being and salvation, and enjoined it upon us in that which was sent down out of the heaven of sanctity in His Most Holy Book. He saith, great is His glory: "Enter into wedlock, O people, that ye may bring forth one who will make mention of Me amid My servants. This is My bidding unto you; hold fast to it as an assistance to yourselves."

~ Bahá'u'lláh

CHAPTER 37 – It's Just the Beginning: Marriage Can Be Forever

This is the end of this book, but you are just at the beginning of your marriage, a new life that can create unimaginable synergy with everything you do and everyone whose lives you touch. This is a new life, filled with new possibilities. You are participating in God's "fortress for well-being and salvation," something you cannot create on your own. The new creation that comes from pairing two souls together is greater than if you remained apart as individuals. ***Just remember, nurturing counts—marriage can be forever!***

May God Assist Your Marriage to Be Spiritually-Based and Blessed!

**Do you have room for a bit more?
We've got a few extras here at the end...**

Appendices

Marriage Can Be Forever—Preparation Counts!

APPENDIX A – What's Your Character?: The Virtues Defined

Note: This is not a comprehensive list of every virtue. However, it is a list of most of the critical virtues for marital success. These descriptions may be helpful to you in the process of assessing both your own character and the character of a potential marriage partner. These Virtues definitions are excerpted from the Virtues Cards with permission of The Virtues Project, Inc., www.virtuesproject.com. They are based on *The Family Virtues Guide* by Linda Kavelin-Popov. The Virtues Project, Inc. holds the copyright, and no duplication is permitted without its permission.

Assertiveness: Being assertive means being positive and confident. Assertiveness begins by being aware that you are a worthy person. You have your very own special gifts. When you are assertive, you think for yourself, and express your own ideas, opinions and talents. When you do this, you make a difference in the world in your own special way. You have the self-confidence to tell the truth about what is just.

Caring: Caring is giving love and attention to people and things that matter to you. When you care about people you say and do things that help them. When you do a careful job, you give it your best effort. Caring comes from within. It is a sign of love. When you care for someone, you notice how they feel and what they need. Caring is a special way of paying attention.

Cleanliness: Cleanliness means washing often, and keeping your body clean. Cleanliness can be in your mind as well as your body. A clean mind means that you can concentrate your thoughts on things that are good for you. You can "clean up your act" by deciding to change when you have done something you aren't proud of or when you have made a mistake.

Commitment: Commitment is caring deeply about something or someone. It is the willingness to give your all to a friendship, a task, or something you believe in. It is the ability to make decisions and follow through on them. It is keeping your promises.

Compassion: Compassion is understanding and caring for someone who is in trouble, is hurt, or has made a mistake. It is being kind and forgiving when others are sorry for what they have done. It is caring deeply and wanting to help even if all you can do is listen or say kind words. It is important to show compassion to others and also to yourself.

Confidence: Confidence is having faith in something or someone. It is a kind of trust. When you have self-confidence, you trust that you have what it takes to handle whatever happens. When you are confident in others, you count on them. Confidence in God is a sense of trust that your Creator loves you and watches over you as you go through life. Confidence brings the strength to try new things.

Consideration: Consideration is having regard for other people and their feelings. It is thinking about how your actions will affect them and caring about how they will feel. Consideration is thoughtfulness. It is paying attention to what other people like and don't like, then doing things that give them happiness.

Courage: Courage is personal bravery in the face of fear. It is doing what needs to be done even when it is really hard or scary. Courage is going ahead even when you feel like giving up or quitting. Courage is needed in trying new things, in facing the truth and in picking yourself up after a mistake, ready to try again. It comes from knowing down deep what is right for you and believing in yourself to do it. Courage can come from prayer, and the trust that God will help.

Courtesy: Courtesy is to be polite and to have good manners. It is to be considerate of others. It is a way of speaking and acting with people which gives them a feeling of being valued and respected. "Please," "Thank you," "Excuse me," and "You're welcome" are courteous expressions which let people know you appreciate them and care about their feelings. Courtesy brightens people's lives. It helps to make life graceful.

Creativity: Creativity is the power of imagination. With creativity, people can discover new ideas, new thoughts that might never have been thought of before. Creativity is a way to use what the Creator has given you, to bring something new into the world. It is seeing something in a new way, finding a different way to solve a problem or get something done.

Detachment: Detachment is experiencing your feelings without allowing your feelings to control you. It is choosing how you will act in a situation rather than just reacting. With detachment, you are free to do what you really want and choose to do. Detachment is a way to use thinking and feeling together, so that you don't let your feelings run away with you.

Determination: Determination is focusing your energy and efforts on a particular task and then sticking with it until it is finished. Determination is using your will power to do something even when it isn't easy. It means you care about something so much that even when it is really hard, or you are being tested, you still keep going.

Enthusiasm: Enthusiasm means "God within." It is being filled with spirit. Enthusiasm is being cheerful and happy. It is doing something wholeheartedly, with zeal and eagerness, giving 100% to what you do, holding nothing back. Being enthusiastic is being excited about something, looking forward to it. It comes from having a positive attitude. When you are enthusiastic, you enjoy yourself. With enthusiasm, even the dullest job can be fun.

Excellence: Excellence is giving your best to any task you do or any relationship you have. No matter what you are doing, excellence means you are giving it the best that you have to give. Excellence is effort guided by a noble purpose. It is a desire for perfection. The perfection of a seed is the fruit which grows from it. Excellence in your life is bringing your gifts to fruition.

Faithfulness: Faithfulness is being true to someone or something. It is holding to what you believe is important no matter what happens. Faithfulness is commitment. When you are faithful to your beliefs, such as a belief in God, honesty or friendship, others can see your values in the way you act. You "walk your talk." When you are faithful, you make your ideals real.

Flexibility: Flexibility is being open to the need for change. It means not always having to have your own way—you are open to the opinions and feelings of others. With flexibility, you are willing to change your mind. If something doesn't work, you try a new way. Flexibility means getting rid of bad habits and learning new ones. Making changes doesn't mean you are losing yourself, only that you are becoming better.

Forgiveness: Being forgiving is overlooking the mistakes others make and loving them just as much as before. You can even forgive yourself when you do things you are sorry for. Forgiving yourself means to stop punishing yourself or feeling hopeless because of something you did. It is moving ahead, ready to do things differently, with compassion for yourself and faith that you can change.

Friendliness: Friendliness is taking an interest in other people, being warm and courteous. When you are friendly, you happily share the things you have. You share your time, your ideas, your feelings and yourself. When you are a friend, you share the good times and the bad times together. Friendliness can be shown in a warm smile, a gentle touch, or a kind word. Friendliness is caring without being asked to care. It is the best cure for loneliness.

Generosity: Generosity is giving and sharing. It is giving freely because you want to, not with the idea of receiving a reward or a gift in return. Generosity is a quality of the spirit. It is an awareness that there is plenty for everyone. It is seeing an opportunity to share what you have and then giving just for the joy of giving. Generosity is one of the best ways to show love.

Gentleness: Gentleness is acting and speaking in a way which is considerate and kind to others. It is using self-control, in order not to hurt or offend anyone. You can be gentle with people and animals in the way you touch them and the way you speak to them. Being gentle with things means to be careful so that they will not break or be hurt in any way. Gentleness is moving wisely, touching softly, holding carefully, speaking quietly, and thinking kindly.

Helpfulness: Helpfulness is being of service to someone. When you are being helpful you do useful things that make a difference. Helpfulness can be doing something that others cannot do for themselves, things they don't have time to do, or just little things that make life easier. There are times when you feel helpless. That is a good time to ask God for help and to let others be helpful to you. There is plenty of help if you're willing to ask.

Honesty: Being honest is being sincere, open, trustworthy and truthful. When people are honest, they can be relied on not to cheat, steal, or lie. Honesty is telling the truth no matter what. It is admitting mistakes even when you know someone might be angry or disappointed. Being honest means that you don't make false promises you do what you said you would do. Your actions match your words.

Honor: Honor is living with a sense of respect for what you believe is right. It is living by the virtues, living up to the gifts which the Creator placed within you. When you are honorable, you don't have to feel ashamed of who you are or what you are doing. You are worthy of the respect of others. You set a good example. People of honor distinguish themselves by doing what is just, regardless of what others are doing. It is a path of integrity.

Humility: When you are humble, you don't consider yourself more important than other people. You are happy to serve others and think other people's needs are important. When you are humble, you don't criticize others. You don't criticize or shame yourself. You admit mistakes and learn from them. You don't need to boast. You feel thankful for your gifts.

Idealism: A person with "high ideals" is a person who really cares about what is right and meaningful in life. When you practice idealism, you have beliefs that mean something to you and you follow them. You don't just accept things the way they are. Idealists dare to have big dreams and then act as if they are possible.

Integrity is standing up for what you believe is right, living by your highest values. It is being honest and sincere with others and yourself. You are integrous when your words and actions match. You don't fool yourself into doing what you know is wrong. You fill your life and your mind with things that help you to live a good, clean life.

Joyfulness: Joyfulness is being filled with happiness, peace, love and a sense of well-being. Joy is inside us all. It comes from a sense of being loved. It comes from an appreciation for the gift of life. Joy comes when we are doing what we know is right. Joy is the inner sense that can carry us through the hard times, even when we are feeling very sad.

Justice: Practicing justice is being fair in everything that you do. It is seeing with your own eyes and not judging something or someone by what other people tell you. Being just is standing up for your own rights and the rights of other people. If someone is hurting you, it is just to stop them. It is never just for strong people to hurt weaker people. Justice means that every person's rights are protected.

Kindness: Kindness is being concerned about the welfare of others. Kindness is showing you care about anyone or anything that crosses your path, knowing that everything is a part of God's creation. Kindness means to care for others and the earth as much or more than you care about yourself. Kindness is showing love to someone who is sad or needs your help.

Love: Love is caring for someone, wanting to be near them, and wanting to share with them. Love is the power of attraction. It is a special feeling that fills your heart. Loving people is treating them with special care and kindness because they mean so much to you. You can show love in a smile, a pleasant way of speaking, a thoughtful act, or a hug. Love is treating other people just as you would like them to treat you with care and respect.

Loyalty: Loyalty is standing up for something you believe in, having unwavering faith. It is being faithful to your family, your country, your friends or your ideals when the going gets tough as well as when things are good. When you are a loyal friend, even if someone disappoints or hurts you, you still hang in there with them. Loyalty is based on commitments you make and plan to keep forever.

Mercy: Justice is giving people what they deserve mercy is giving people more than they deserve. Mercy is a quality of the heart. When you are being merciful, you are willing to forgive when you have been hurt. God is very merciful to us by giving us lots of blessings and lots of chances to keep learning from our mistakes. A mercy is a blessing. When you practice mercy you are giving others the gift of your tenderness.

Moderation: Moderation is creating balance in your life. It is having enough not too much or not too little. Moderation is stopping before going overboard. It is using self-discipline to keep from overdoing. Moderation is what keeps us from being blown about in the winds of our desires.

Modesty: Modesty is having a sense of self-respect. People who practice modesty are not showy or boastful. Modesty comes when you have a sense of self-acceptance and quiet pride. Modesty means to accept praise without getting conceited or puffed up with a feeling of superiority. You are grateful for your gifts and you know that others have gifts too.

Obedience: Obedience is following what is right and playing by the rules. It is listening to what your parents and others in authority have to say and doing it as faithfully as you can. As you grow and mature, obedience means listening to yourself the place of truth within you that knows what is truly right. The purpose of obedience is to guide you and protect you. When you are obedient, you obey the law even when no one is watching. To be obedient is to be trustworthy.

Orderliness: Orderliness is being neat, and living with a sense of harmony. It is having a place for things you use and keeping them there so that you can use them whenever you need to. It means planning something so that it works, doing something step by step, staying on track instead of going in circles. Being orderly makes it easier to accomplish things. When you appreciate the order of creation, you can see the beauty and harmony of all living things.

Patience: Patience is quiet hope and expectation based on trust that, in the end, everything will be all right. Patience means waiting. It is enduring a delay or troublesome situation without complaining. It means having self-control because you can't control the way someone else is acting or when things don't go as you'd like. Patience is being calm and tolerant when difficult things happen. Patience is seeing the end in the beginning.

Peacefulness: Peacefulness is an inner sense of calm that can come in moments of silent gratitude or prayer. It is a way of getting very quiet and looking at things so you can understand them. It is facing your fears and then letting them go. It is trusting that things will be all right. Peacefulness is giving up the love of power for the power of love. Peace in the world begins with peace in your heart.

Prayerfulness: Prayerfulness can be practiced in many ways. Prayer is talking with God. You can pray in silence or out loud in any language. You can sing or dance your prayer. God always hears your thoughts and understands your heart. Prayerfulness is living in a way which shows that you are in the presence of your Creator. Prayerfulness is quiet reflection. It is allowing the Great Spirit to speak to you. It is listening and receiving God's guidance.

Purposefulness: Purposefulness is having a clear focus. Instead of being fuzzy or unsure what you're doing or why you're doing it. When you have a goal you are working toward, you are acting on purpose. You concentrate your mind and your efforts so that you can keep your goal before you and something good will happen as a result. With God's help, when you are purposeful, you can achieve just about anything.

Reliability: Reliability means that others can depend on you. It is doing something that you have agreed to do in a predictable way, without forgetting or having to be reminded. You really care about doing what you said you would do. When you are practicing reliability, others can count on you to do your very best to keep your commitments.

Respect: Respect is an attitude of honoring oneself and others and caring about their rights. Being respectful is reflected in the courtesy with which we speak and act and treat one another. Acting respectfully gives people the dignity they deserve. Respect is behaving in a way which makes life more peaceful and orderly for everyone.

Responsibility: Being responsible means that others can depend on you. It is doing something well and to the best of your ability. Being responsible is being willing to be accountable for what you do or do not do. It means accepting credit when things go right (humbly of course), and accepting correction when things go wrong. When you are responsible, you keep your agreements. Being responsible is the ability to respond ably.

Reverence: Reverence is behaving with an awareness that you are always in the presence of the Creator and that all life is precious. Reverence can be experienced in moments of prayer or reflection. It is treating Holy Books and other sacred things as very, very special. Whether you are in a place of worship or spending time in a place of beauty, reverence is being still and allowing the wonder you feel to shine through.

Self-Discipline: Discipline means control. Self-discipline is self-control. It means getting yourself to do what is important to do, rather than being a leaf in the wind of your thoughts or feelings. With self-discipline, you can be moderate. You don't lose control of yourself when you feel hurt or angry, but decide how you are going to talk and what you are going to do. With self-discipline, you take charge of yourself.

Service: Service is giving to others and wanting to make a difference in their lives. Helping other people is one of the very best ways to serve God. Having an attitude of service means looking for ways to be of help rather than waiting to be asked. The needs of others are as important to you as your own. When you work with a spirit of service, you give any job your very best effort. You make a real contribution. People who want to be of service can change the world.

Steadfastness: Steadfastness is being steady and dependable, sticking with something no matter what. Steadfastness is being faithful and purposeful. It is remaining true to someone or something in spite of any tests or obstacles that appear to stop you. When you are steadfast, you commit yourself to something for however long it may take. You are like a strong ship in a storm. You don't let yourself become battered or blown off course. You just ride the waves.

Tact: Tact is thinking before you speak. It is telling the truth in a way that does not disturb or offend others. It is knowing what to say and what is better left unsaid. Tactfulness is sharing your view with others in a way that makes it easier for them to hear it. This is especially important when you feel angry or upset. Tact also means knowing when to stay silent. It is telling the truth with kindness. You are as careful about others' feelings as you would like them to be of yours.

Thankfulness: Thankfulness is to be grateful for what you have. It is an attitude of gratitude for learning, loving, and being. It is also being grateful for the little things which happen around you and within you every day. It is an openness and willingness to receive each of God's bounties. To be thankful is to have a sense of wonder about the beauty of this world and to welcome all of life as a gift. Thankfulness is a path to contentment.

Tolerance: Tolerance is being able to accept things that you wish were different. When you practice tolerance, you have flexibility. You don't expect others to be just like you. You accept differences. When you are practicing tolerance, you are able to sort out what is important from what is not. You show patience and forgiveness when people make mistakes. You accept what you cannot change with good grace.

Trust: Trust is having faith. It is relying and believing in someone or something. It is having confidence that the right thing will come about without trying to control it or make it happen. Sometimes it is hard to trust when life brings painful experiences. Trust is being sure, down deep, that there is some gift or learning in everything life brings.

Trustworthiness: Trustworthiness is being worthy of trust. You can be counted on. When you are trustworthy, if you make a promise or vow, you keep your word no matter how hard it becomes. Others can rely on you. They can trust that if it is at all possible, you will do what you said you would do, even if it becomes really hard. You keep your word.

Truthfulness: Truthfulness means your words and actions are full of truth. Telling the truth means you don't lie, to protect yourself or anyone else. Being true to yourself means you show people who and what you are without exaggerating to impress them or trying to be something you are not. You live by your own true nature. You investigate the truth for yourself. You see with your own eyes. Look into your heart and speak of what is true for you.

Unity: Unity is a very powerful virtue and brings with it great strength. It is a way of seeing the universe as one, designed by the One Who created us all. Unity brings harmony, like the sound of music made by the different instruments in an orchestra. When you practice unity, you value what each part brings to the whole. With unity, you can strive for harmony with your family at home and your human family around the world.

APPENDIX B – The Spiritual Connection: Prayers for Marriage

✸ He is the Bestower, the Bounteous!

Praise be to God, the Ancient, the Ever-Abiding, the Changeless, the Eternal! He Who hath testified in His Own Being that verily He is the One, the Single, the Untrammelled, the Exalted. We bear witness that verily there is no God but Him, acknowledging His oneness, confessing His singleness. He hath ever dwelt in unapproachable heights, in the summits of His loftiness, sanctified from the mention of aught save Himself, free from the description of aught but Him.

And when He desired to manifest grace and beneficence to men, and to set the world in order, He revealed observances and created laws; among them He established the law of marriage, made it as a fortress for well-being and salvation, and enjoined it upon us in that which was sent down out of the heaven of sanctity in His Most Holy Book. He saith, great is His glory: "Enter into wedlock, O people, that ye may bring forth one who will make mention of Me amid My servants. This is My bidding unto you; hold fast to it as an assistance to yourselves."

(Bahá'u'lláh: *Bahá'í Prayers* (US 2002), pp. 117-118)

✸ O my God! O my God! Unite the hearts of Thy servants, and reveal to them Thy great purpose. May they follow Thy commandments and abide in Thy law. Help them, O God, in their endeavor, and grant them strength to serve Thee. O God! Leave them not to themselves, but guide their steps by the light of Thy knowledge, and cheer their hearts by Thy love. Verily, Thou art their Helper and their Lord.

(Bahá'u'lláh: *Bahá'í Prayers* (US 2002), p. 238)

✸ He is God!

O peerless Lord! In Thine almighty wisdom Thou hast enjoined marriage upon the peoples, that the generations of men may succeed one another in this contingent world, and that ever, so long as the world shall last, they may busy themselves at the Threshold of Thy oneness with servitude and worship, with salutation, adoration and praise. "I have not created spirits and men, but that they should worship me."[1] Wherefore, wed Thou in the heaven of Thy mercy these two birds of the nest of Thy love, and make them the means of attracting perpetual grace; that from the union of these two seas of love a wave of tenderness may surge and cast the pearls of pure and goodly issue on the shore of life. "He hath let loose the two seas, that they meet each other: Between them is a barrier which they overpass not. Which then of the bounties of your Lord will ye deny? From each He bringeth up greater and lesser pearls."[2]

O Thou kind Lord! Make Thou this marriage to bring forth coral and pearls. Thou art verily the All-Powerful, the Most Great, the Ever-Forgiving.

('Abdu'l-Bahá: *Bahá'í Prayers* (US 2002), pp. 118-1119)
[1] Qur'án 3:67; [2] Qur'án 56:62

✸ Glory be unto Thee, O my God! Verily, this Thy servant and this Thy maidservant have gathered under the shadow of Thy mercy and they are united through Thy favor and generosity. O Lord! Assist them in this Thy world and Thy kingdom and destine for them every good through Thy bounty and grace. O Lord! Confirm them in Thy servitude and assist them in Thy service. Suffer them to become the signs of Thy Name in Thy world and protect them through Thy bestowals which are inexhaustible in this world and the world to come. O Lord! They are supplicating the kingdom of Thy mercifulness and invoking the realm of Thy singleness. Verily, they are married in obedience to Thy command. Cause them to become the signs of harmony and unity until the end of time. Verily, Thou art the Omnipotent, the Omnipresent and the Almighty!

('Abdu'l-Bahá: *Bahá'í Prayers* (US 2002), p. 120)

✸ O my Lord, O my Lord! These two bright orbs are wedded in Thy love, conjoined in servitude to Thy Holy Threshold, united in ministering to Thy Cause. Make Thou this marriage to be as threading lights of Thine abounding grace, O my Lord, the All-Merciful, and luminous rays of Thy bestowals, O Thou the Beneficent, the Ever-Giving, that there may branch out from this great tree boughs that will grow green and flourishing through the gifts that rain down from Thy clouds of grace. Verily Thou art the Generous, verily Thou art the Almighty, verily Thou art the Compassionate, the All-Merciful.

('Abdu'l-Bahá: *Bahá'í Prayers* (US 2002), p. 121)

APPENDIX C – *A Foundation for Well-Being's Fortress, An Essay on Marriage Preparation*

by David Bowers

Our culture virtually brainwashes us young folk into being obsessed with sex and relationships. Certainly finding a spouse is a worthy pursuit, yet we are so overtaken with this desire that we forget to ask *how* to find the right partner in the first place the thought that we should have to learn such a thing is itself a novelty. We get into relationships only to get out of them again. Everyone knows that relationships hardly ever last for life, and many have given up hope that they ever can. Fortunately, I have found the teachings of the Bahá'í Faith to be invaluable in formulating a response to this crisis of love especially in terms of helping young people like me acquire a refined character as a solid foundation for marriage, as well as an understanding about the family's role in the world, both of which will help ensure the happy relationships we so strongly desire.

People today often speak about love as if it "just happens," as if we must "find the right person" and discover "a match made in heaven." We often tend to look for romance as a passion-filled festival of the heart without considering the logic of our search at all. We end up failing to take full responsibility for the health of our married life by acting as if there is nothing we can actively do to prepare for marriage. We usually just wait for magic to happen all on its own.

This creates a predicament for those people who recognize that God will probably not deliver to them a wonderful marriage without effort on their part. Since so few people are trying to learn how to be married, effective guidance on the matter is scarce at best. "What 'oppression' is more grievous," wrote Bahá'u'lláh, the Founder of the Bahá'í Faith (*The Kitáb-i-Íqán*, p. 31), "than that a soul seeking the truth, and wishing to attain unto the knowledge of God, should know not where to go for it and from whom to seek it? For opinions have sorely differed, and the ways unto the attainment of God have multiplied." We see a torrent of "advice" about relationships constantly raining down on us, but true understanding is as rare as fresh water in the ocean.

In reversing this trend, we must radically change our perspective. The Bahá'í Teachings indicate that successful marriage has a lot more to do with our conscious efforts to acquire the attributes of God than it does with fate. God does not make the "right one" magically appear for us without action on our part. Rather, God guides us through the efforts we make in His path. Bahá'u'lláh said that marriage is "a fortress for well-being." God's greatest gift is in making us work at building this fortress brick by brick He will never do it for us. A friend of mine once told me, "God can't steer a parked car."

Rather than ask ourselves, "How will I *find* the right person?" we might find it much more fruitful to ponder, "How shall I *become* the right person?" Clearly, the foundation of the fortress of marriage, a praiseworthy character, is laid in the two partners' hearts long before they get engaged, and usually before they even meet each other. If we understand this, we have a precious opportunity to demonstrate the process of self-discovery through prayer, meditation, and self-refinement that one must undertake before being ready for marriage.

Only after a number of the necessary qualities for marriage have been acquired in this process can we recognize other potential partners who have acquired them also. Then the question of finding will be much simpler. For me, this process has meant getting a clear idea of what qualities are most useful in a marriage and then setting out to acquire them, long before looking for marriage myself. One must examine the various difficulties people have in marriage, try to understand what usually brings them about, and prepare oneself for overcoming them. A healthy sense of humility will encourage us on our way, too: we can never know everything about this, and frankly, we don't have to. God knows everything we have to become as connected to Him as possible, and then seek out that knowledge through our relationship with Him.

My general rule of thumb is this: my future wife (whoever she is) and I will be more or less the same together as we are apart. If each of us maintains a happy disposition individually, we will probably be happy together. If each of us looks for the best in each person we meet, and succeeds in loving all humanity on a daily basis, then we should be able to love each other very well. If the two of us naturally take the initiative in service to humanity, if we are each different enough to complement one another in this service, and if we both handle great difficulties with maturity and composure, then we will probably be of great benefit to the world together. We should each have our own passionate love for God; we should each have similar goals in this earthly life, as well as harmonious lifestyles, world-views, dispositions and habits; we should both be socially adept enough to know how to emotionally gratify the other person, to set them at ease, to make them laugh, and to let them know our deep, sincere love for them on an daily basis [note that we should already be doing this for our other friends and family; if we are not, then we will probably not do it for each other]; and finally, we should both be attracted to each others' bodies, and feel very comfortable in each other's arms for hours on end.

On this last point, I find that physical attraction in a mature person has as much to do with the mental and spiritual qualities of the loved one as it does with their physical appearance. Furthermore, as we refuse to let society tell us what beauty should look like, we will find that great varieties of features make most people very attractive.

Attaining all this requires a lot of individual work outside of romantic relationships. We must learn these qualities based in everyday life before we even think about using them in marriage or romance. It is unfortunate that our society never systematically teaches us these qualities, and encourages us to "practice" with romantic relationships instead. Such practice tends to confuse the issue more often than it helps, because it focuses us so much on specific relationships instead of on the broader skills of living that we need to make them work. We get involved as lovers before we can even make ourselves happy. We try to fill a void in our lives with a new person instead of a new attitude.

Relationships cannot "make us happy" so much as they can add to a happiness that we already have. Romance without readiness will bring misery, just as romance with readiness will almost never end.

Consider for a moment, if I may slightly digress, that we could teach these qualities in kids very early. It is a lot harder for a 23-year old such as myself to develop them in himself than it is for a 10 or 11 year old. If we "grown-ups" had been encouraged to greedily acquire happiness and maturity as children, it would be a lot easier for us to marry wisely, even at a young age. If we, in our turn, look to the future of the children we educate, we may see them thanking us profusely for actively teaching them how to have healthy relationships before the big questions about "love" even arise. As their peers will begin to blunder terribly with the opposite sex, they will already be equipped to protect themselves and to use their knowledge in assisting others.

Another radical change the Bahá'í Teachings call for is in our perspective on the nature and purpose of marriage. We often think of marriage as a "fortress for (*our own*) well-being." This view, definitely the predominant one in our society, is a self-centered approach. The Bahá'í Writings imply that God created marriage for the betterment of the whole human race. If we do not recognize this, our efforts to make ourselves happy will only lead to our misery.

In general, a fortress is not a place of peace and tranquility. A fortress is often a stronghold in a battlefield, a particularly strategic spot on the landscape that requires protection from enemy forces. As I understand Bahá'u'lláh's vision for a spiritual World Order, there is no school more important than the family, no teachers more necessary than the mother and the father, and no pupils more worthwhile and critical than the children. That strategic spot on the landscape is none other than the future of these kids.

It is the family's responsibility to secure their children against the manifold forces of evil in the world by imbuing them with the love of God and the knowledge of His teachings for this Day. These children will, in their turn, grow up to be the redeemers of humanity, the dawn-breakers of a peaceful world civilization, the bricklayers of a great peace beyond our wildest dreams. As the challenges and difficulties of the world they inherit from us must increase, so we need to empower them to surmount heights we could never dream of, and surpass us in all the paths of service to God and humanity. That is the primary goal of this "fortress" for the "well-being" of the whole human race.

This fortress, if it understands its role properly, should constantly devote itself to the good of all people. Each member of the family needs to be aware of his mission as a servant of God and humanity, and work unitedly with the others to expand the borders of the country of God's Love. A spiritual family will naturally collectively arise to promote spiritual thought and action. Children can be progressively encouraged to share their spirituality with their fellow human beings from the time they are first able to speak and reason. The parents can first lead their children by example, and then systematically instruct them as to how to do what they are doing. Action is the primary text in this school, and words but supplements to it.

In short, we need not seek at first to "find someone," but rather to "become someone." By steadily adopting a spiritual perspective, and acquiring those skills of love that enable us to be happy, selfless, and mature, we will become most able to discern a good partner from a bad one, and will firmly establish a "fortress for well-being." We will ensure our own happiness in the quest to serve humanity and nurture the future of our children. As we understand our role in history as parents and educators to be sacred and inestimably important, we will extend through our actions a priceless gift to all the thousands of human generations yet to come.

APPENDIX D – Spiritual Revelation: A Glimpse of the Bahá'í Faith

1. **The Báb**, a title meaning "The Gate" (Siyyid 'Alí-Muhammad), 1819-1850 – A descendent of Muhammad and founder of the Bábí Faith in 1844 in Iran. He prepared the people for the coming of Bahá'u'lláh.

2. **Bahá'u'lláh**, a title meaning the "Glory of God" (Mírzá Husayn-'Alí), 1817-1892 – A descendent of Abraham, born in Iran, and Founder of the Bahá'í Faith in 1863.

3. **'Abdu'l-Bahá**, 1844-1921, Bahá'u'lláh's eldest son and the person He designated for His followers to turn to for guidance after His death.

4. **Shoghi Effendi**, 1897-1957, 'Abdu'l-Bahá's eldest grandson, appointed to be the Guardian of the Bahá'í Faith after 'Abdu'l-Bahá's death in 1921.

5. **The Universal House of Justice**, 1963 to present. Elected every 5 years, Bahá'u'lláh promises that its decisions are divinely guided, ensuring ongoing infallible guidance.

6. **The Continental Board of Counsellors and Auxiliary Board members and assistants**, are appointed to assist the Bahá'í community with maintaining strength, unity, and growth.

The Bahá'í Faith and Its Teachings

The Bahá'í Faith is widespread throughout the world, established in 235 countries and territories. Its members come from over 2,100 ethnic, racial, and tribal groups and number some 5 million worldwide. Bahá'í communities around the globe have been working to break down barriers of prejudice between peoples and have collaborated with other like-minded groups to promote the model of a global society. At the heart of Bahá'í belief is the conviction that humanity is a single people with a common destiny. In the words of Bahá'u'lláh, "The earth is but one country, and mankind its citizens."

Bahá'u'lláh taught that there is one God Who progressively reveals His Will to humanity. Each of the great religions brought by the Messengers of God Moses, Krishna, Buddha, Zoroaster, Jesus, and Muhammad represents a successive stage in the spiritual development of civilization. Bahá'u'lláh, the most recent Messenger in this line, has brought teachings that address the moral and spiritual challenges of the modern world. Their common purpose has been to bring the human race to spiritual and moral maturity. Humanity is now coming of age. It is this that makes possible the unification of the human family and the building of a peaceful, global society. Among the principles which the Bahá'í Faith promotes as vital to the achievement of this goal are:

- The abandonment of all forms of prejudice,
- Assurance to women of full equality of opportunity with men,
- Recognition of the unity and relativity of religious truth,
- The elimination of extremes of poverty and wealth,
- The realization of universal education,
- The responsibility of each person to independently search for truth,
- The establishment of a global commonwealth of nations, and
- Recognition that true religion is in harmony with reason and the pursuit of scientific knowledge

For more information: www.bahai.org; www.bahaiworldnews.org

APPENDIX E – Our Gratitude for Use: Permissions

We extend respect and gratitude to Linda Kavelin-Popov for her generosity in allowing us to use materials from The Virtues Project, Inc. Virtues definitions in Appendix A are excerpted from the *Virtues Cards* ©1997, The Virtues Project, Inc., www.virtuesproject.com, with permission. The cards are based on *The Family Virtues Guide*, by Linda Kavelin-Popov, et al, Penguin/Putnam, New York, 1997, ISBN 0-452-27810-4.

David Bowers wrote a wonderful essay, "A Foundation For Well-Being's Fortress," and we are grateful to him for his permission to publish and share it, © 2003 David Bowers.

Thanks to Daved Muttart, Susanne's brother, and friends Blair Maxwell, Judy Parsley, and Steve Traina for their willingness to share their poetry. © 2003 Daved M. Muttart, © 2003 Blair Maxwell, © 2003 Judy Parsley, and © 2003 Steve Traina.

We appreciate the song Henry Adam and Beverly Iffland wrote for our wedding, "Somebody Higher Than Me", and we thank them for allowing us to publish the lyrics. ©1999 Henry Adam and Beverly Iffland. We also appreciate Mindy Malone giving permission to publish John Taylor's song lyrics for "The Song of Life."

The cover design is © 2003 Justice St Rain, exclusively licensed to ClariComm Publishing.

Our thanks to:

George Ronald, publisher, for permission to quote from *Prescription for Living* and *Coral and Pearls*.

Bahá'í Publishing Trust of the United Kingdom, for permission to quote from *The Chosen Highway*.

Special Ideas (Justice St Rain), for permission to quote from *Falling Into Grace*.

Sandra Gray Bender, for permission to quote from *Recreating Marriage with the Same Old Spouse*

APPENDIX F – Behind the Scenes: About the Authors

Susanne M. Alexander and Craig A. Farnsworth

Susanne M. Alexander and Craig A. Farnsworth have been married since August 1999, a second marriage for both of them. They have four adult children and one son-in-law. Susanne has a daughter, Jennifer, and Craig has three children Michelle, David, and Leah. Michelle is married to Hooman Tashakor.

Susanne is a full-time journalist and writer and holds a BA in Communications from Baldwin-Wallace College in Berea, Ohio. Her articles have been published in *Newsweek Japan*, *The (Cleveland) Plain Dealer*, *Crain's Cleveland Business*, *Writer's Digest*, and *Massage Magazine* among others. She has written about business, people, education, sports, music, religion, the arts, events, and social issues. She is president of ClariComm Group, which offers a writing, editing, and communications coaching service. Susanne is a member of the American Society of Journalists and Authors and the Society of Professional Journalists. She is part of an author team that has written a college textbook, *College and Career Success Simplified*, to be published in 2003.

Craig is a full-time market manager for Radix Wire Company and holds a BA in Physics and a BA in Elementary Education from Hiram College in Hiram, Ohio. He has had technical articles published in a variety of industry publications. He is business operations manager for ClariComm Group and serves on its advisory board. He is a member of the American Society of Gas Engineers and serves on the steering committee for the International Appliance Technical Conference. Craig is a musician, playing many types of flutes and the guitar. He sings bass in the Northeast Ohio Bahá'í Choir and has sung nationally in the United States with the Voices of Bahá choir, including in Carnegie Hall.

Johanna Merritt Wu, Ph.D.

Johanna Merritt Wu is a psychologist with a specialization in training, leadership development and assessment, organizational development, systematic planning, and coaching people in how to be effective and successful. She leads a variety of workshops, among them marriage preparation for individuals and couples and marriage preparation facilitator training. *Marriage Can Be Forever—Preparation Counts!* includes many worksheets that she developed. Johanna's dissertation topic was on leadership development for manufacturing high-tech team leaders and identifying characteristics that made them effective. In the business world, Johanna was most recently a Cultural Integration Leader at GE Capital, working on mergers and acquisitions. In her five years at General Electric, she was involved in organizational development, human resources, and Six Sigma/Quality. Johanna has served at the Bahá'í World Center in the Personnel Office and is a member of the leadership governing board of Bahá'í Business Forum for the Americas. She has also served in a number of other Bahá'í capacities locally, nationally and internationally. Johanna and her husband, Steven Wu, currently live in Columbus, Ohio, where he is a professor of agricultural economics at Ohio State University. They have been married for three years.

Please contact us as follows:

It will be a gift to us and other readers of this book to hear back from you about your experiences with this book, and anything that would improve its usefulness.

ClariComm Publishing
P.O. Box 23085, Cleveland, OH 44123
E-mail: Susanne@ClariComm.com; Craig@ClariComm.com
Website: www.ClariComm.com/publishing

Note: The website has a PDF downloadable version of the worksheets for individual or workshop use.

APPENDIX G – Where Can I Get Copies?: Ordering Information

Australia:	**Bahá'í Distribution Services** bds@bahai.org.au
Canada:	**Unity Arts Inc.** Phone: 416-609-9900; Order Desk: 1-800-465-3287 Fax: 416-609-9600 orders@bahaibooksonline.com www.bahaibooksonline.com and www.unityarts.com
Europe:	**Bahá'í Publishing Trust** Phone: 44 (0) 1572 722780 Fax: 44 (0) 1572 724280 bpt.sales@bahai.org.uk www.bahai-publishing-trust.co.uk
United States and International:	**Bahá'í Distribution Service** Phone: 1-800-999-9019 Fax: 404-472-0119 bds@usbnc.org **Bahá'í Gear** www.bahaigear.com **Barnes and Noble, Inc.** www.barnesandnoble.com **Images International** Phone: 423-870-4525 Fax: 423-870-4774 images@chattanooga.net www.images-international.com **Special Ideas** 1-800-326-1197 orders@special-ideas.com www.special-ideas.com

Note: This book may also be available through other sources; check with your local bookstore or distributor.

"The earth is but one country, and mankind its citizens."
(Bahá'u'lláh: *Gleanings from the Writings of Bahá'u'lláh*, p. 250)

NOTES

NOTES

NOTES

NOTES

NOTES